GREAT WESTERN COACHES from 1890

Previous page Flat-ended 60ft corridor third No 5776, built 1933, and with 9ft wheelbase, pressed-steel bogies. (Lot 1489—Diagram C.65).
(above) A 3031 4-2-2 at the head of a Truro–Paddington express, made up of a Dean clerestory corridor set, a much older clerestory vehicle and a Siphon.
(below) Castle class 4-6-0 No 5013 *Abergavenny Castle* approaching Stapleton Road, Bristol, in 1938 with a West to North express. Note the variety of rolling stock, including a recently-built corridor composite (second vehicle), Diagram H.38 dining car and 'Sunshine' stock corridor (second from end).

GREAT WESTERN COACHES from 1890

Michael Harris

With 154 photographs and 25 line drawings

DAVID & CHARLES
Newton Abbot London North Pomfret (Vt)

British Library Cataloguing in Publication Data

Harris, Michael, 1945–
Great Western coaches from 1890.—3rd rev.
updated & enl. ed.
1. Great Western Railway—History
2. Railways—England—Passenger—coaches—History
I. Title
625.2′3′0942 TF64.G7

ISBN 0–7153–8050–8

Phototypeset by Typesetters (Birmingham) Limited
Smethwick, Warley, West Midlands
and printed in Great Britain
by Butler & Tanner Limited, Frome
for David & Charles (Publishers) Limited
Brunel House Newton Abbot Devon

Published in the United States of America
by David & Charles Inc
North Pomfret Vermont 05053 USA

CONTENTS

PREFACE TO THE THIRD EDITION

Twenty years have elapsed since the first edition of this book was being prepared, and the passing of time has made a new Preface necessary. But the statement in the original Preface that 'Beeching's rationalisation . . . destroyed the line of history of the old "Big Four" companies of 1923–47 more surely than the 1948 nationalisation ever did' also holds good as a verdict to be made in hindsight. Really that had been the reason for writing the book, for the Preface had gone on to say, 'the evidence of the development of GWR coaches (has) disappeared in little over a decade . . . something of a permanent record was indicated to record these changes'. Since then, attitudes have strengthened and the growth of railway preservation is testimony to a widespread interest in recording the past. If the number of coaches acquired for preservation is anything to go by, then what seemed to be a blind spot in recording the history of British railways has been rectified. But in the mid-1960s preservation was largely in its infancy, and although artefacts were being collected their restoration had yet to come.

What would have seemed remarkable in 1963/64 is that twenty years later it is possible to recapture the spectacle of GWR coaches in service – the atmosphere, sounds and even the smells. A senior BR manager was with me when we stepped out of an excursion train which had brought us to Bewdley from Waterloo. Alongside was the stock of the Severn Valley Limited with its fine rake of GWR-design vehicles. 'That's what preservation is all about', was his verdict. How true! Sadly, one great achievement in preservation appears to belong to the past, and that is the Great Western Society's Vintage Train of GWR coaches which made its last run on the main line early in 1980. To travel in this train was a nostalgic experience par excellence, particularly on a winter evening with the steam heating in operation. The sight of the Vintage Train with its Super Saloons winding along the route of the Central Wales line was certainly memorable. Other developments which underline the recent growth in interest in historic passenger vehicles include the establishment of the Royalty and Empire Exhibition at Windsor & Eton Central station, for which two 1897 Royal Train coaches have been 'recreated', and the appearance of several excellent 4mm gauge proprietary models of GWR coaching stock vehicles. All told, one cannot help remarking that many distinctive and attractive coaches were produced by Swindon Works and it is good that interest in them has been fostered in so many ways. But this book is not about preservation, although for many people interest in restored GWR vehicles may be an inspiration to further study of their features. Also, in passing, it must be said that it is a pity that several interesting types of preserved GWR coaches – clerestories, the sole surviving 'Dreadnought' and bow-ended stock – have not yet been restored. The finances and skills for their restoration are regrettably in short supply.

The original Preface talked of the early/mid-1960s as something of a watershed in the history of GWR coaches, and of the role of Swindon Works as a centre for carriage construction. Yet the manuscript for the First Edition travelled down with the author to the publisher in a 1940-built GWR composite. Today, another turning-point has been reached. Except for the narrow gauge Vale of Rheidol stock, and a diminishing list of vehicles in engineering use, GWR-design coaching stock has now disappeared from BR's own inventory; the last 'Siphons' in capital stock were withdrawn as newspaper vans during 1983. Service vehicles provided an opportunity to study once-familiar types and outlines long after these had disappeared from passenger use. During the resignalling of Paddington in the late 1960s, it was something of a shock late one night to come upon a rake of 'Toplights' and bow-enders serving the S & T engineers, drawn up in Platform 10 at the terminus. Now old age and present-day Health & Safety requirements are seeing to the demise of many of the remaining GWR vehicles in service use, with the exception of the evergreen 'Whitewash Coach'! Even in 1984 a 'Toplight' coach stands in Exeter still serving the S & T engineers carrying out resignalling there.

Yet the Swindon tradition lives on, in the shape of the Swindon-designed BR-bogies on which are mounted the Mk 2 coaches, again the work of the Swindon design team of the 1960s. Swindon Works has once again handled the repair of passenger stock, in addition to the BR-design diesel multiple-units which continued to be overhauled there after the closure of the carriage and wagon works. During the late 1970s and early 1980s, Swindon was the centre for the refurbishing of the Southern Region's gangwayed electric multiple-units, although such activity may not continue. Speaking of the diesel units it is interesting that from the late 1970s Swindon fitted a number of vehicles with an adaptation of the familiar GWR suspended gangway. It seems only fitting to offer this book as some sort of tribute to the efforts of the men and women who, over the years, built and administered the building and overhaul of coaches at Swindon, as well as a general compliment to the Great Western Railway.

And so to the Third Edition itself. This has been thoroughly revised and use has been made of some records now held at the National Railway Museum, York, and of other sources. Although nearly all the photographs used in the First Edition have reappeared, the tally is augmented by a wider selection of material, as well as some new drawings. All this has been made possible by the assistance of several friends and correspondents whose interest and work are greatly appreciated. Of them, I should like to single out two really notable 'friends' of GWR coaches. Bob Timmins has become something of a legend in his time as a result of his painstaking and excellent work in the restoration of a number of historic coaches, most notably on the Severn Valley Railway, but also Pullman cars. He is one of the very few professionals in this field, as a result of a career involved – and continuing to be involved – with the painting and finishing of passenger coaches. I am very grateful for his interest over the years, and in particular for his revision and expansion of the section dealing with liveries. David Rouse is another legend, deservedly so in view of his long-term involvement with the acquisition of GWR coaches for preservation. His wisdom in marking down worthwhile and sound vehicles perhaps has been undervalued – would that he had been listened to in certain other instances, too! His friendship and help in the course of revising this work is similarly recorded with grateful thanks.

As previously, this work begins with activities in the year 1890, a somewhat arbitrary date, it is true, but for a variety of reasons it has been thought best not to extend coverage to earlier days. But one or two other omissions in the First Edition have been rectified, by means of inclusion of the Vale of Rheidol stock, engineers' saloons and bullion vans, and of one or two other aspects dealt with in the appendices, while the section dealing with Travelling Post Office vehicles has been extensively revised. Still excluded are the 'brown' (painted) vehicles such as Siphons and also the GWR's diesel railcars, although the latter appear in the Lot Lists, but without amplification. The railcars, as an inspection of the preserved No 4 will reveal, represented a radical departure in British rolling stock practice, and I believe that they deserve a special study of their own. At any rate, they are not covered in this work.

Mention of the 'brown' vehicles provides an opportunity to return a compliment. Jim Russell's excellent *A Pictorial Record of Great Western Coaches, Parts One and Two* included a generous reference to the First Edition of this work. This Preface enables me to recommend readers to regard Jim Russell's books as complements to this volume, and to point out that he does the 'brown' vehicles proud in coverage. As for the title of this edition, there is a minor change from the original editions carrying the dates 1890–1954, for while it is true that the last GW designed coach was delivered in 1954 the story goes on beyond that date, and even now 30 years on continues in preserved form.

As regards compilation of *Great Western Coaches from 1890*, I remain indebted to the British Railways Board, in particular the Mechanical Engineer (Design) at Swindon Works during the early 1960s, and of his then staff, Mr H. J. Ridout, for permitting me access to material held by his department, and to Rowland Jones who helped me unfailingly in my enquiries and requests. At the time, Ken Loughland of the Public Relations and Publicity Officer's staff, WR Paddington, tirelessly and courteously dealt with my requirements, and although we now have dealings with current BR developments in another sphere, this gives me an opportunity to recall his help twenty or more years ago. Last and not least, I shall always remain grateful to Jack Slinn for his continual advice and suggestions in the preparation of the First Edition and for drawing up the content of the Lot List Appendix. To members of my family and friends, I would like to express my deep gratitude and hope that I have recorded something of my appreciation in the list of Acknowledgements.

But the person who, beyond all, was the encouragement in producing the book in the first place, and who ever since has given me help, inspiration and shown a very special concern, is my Mother, Doreen Harris. To her, as ever, I owe the most personal indebtedness.

MICHAEL HARRIS

Ottershaw,
Surrey

May 1984

1
SIXTY YEARS IN OUTLINE

In the mid-1880s, the GWR was in one of the most depressed periods of its history. In many respects this reflected the turgid economic conditions of the time but more than that the GWR was, on one side, weakened by the cost and trouble of the Severn Tunnel completion and, on the other, expending much of its energy and resources in the abolition of the broad gauge. It was also scarcely dynamic: Grierson, the general manager, had been in office since the 1860s, and G. N. Tyrrell, the superintendent of the line, was opposed to change. Criticism of the GWR's condition is best expressed in Foxwell and Farrer's well-known work, *Express Trains, British and Foreign*.

In virtually ten years, from 1885–95, the administration changed: H. Lambert became general manager, Burlinson succeeded the reactionary Tyrrell, and Viscount Emlyn became chairman of the GWR. Under their sponsorship, the train service was re-cast, and corridor trains with steam heating, restaurant car services, and new 'crack' corridor expresses with accommodation for all three classes became the general policy. The carriage department under Dean reacted by producing some of the finest standard coaches built and it is a little surprising to realise that the output of coaches over the 1895–1905 period was greater than in the more highly organized, systematic Churchward era. It was a period of regeneration for the GWR. To quote MacDermott, one of 'rapid progress in bringing the whole system up to date and recovering the leeway of the last twenty-five years'. However, although the new passenger coaches incorporated numerous general improvements, it was done within the classical clerestory outline and to the old 'coachbuilders' ' standards of Dean.

As is so often the case, a dual attitude existed towards the GWR's regeneration. The progressives were often critical. The GWR was extremely cautious in its introduction of restaurant cars – due reference being made to this in Chapter 4 – and *The Engineer* greeted their introduction as follows: 'Although the East and West Coast companies have found it advisable to run third-class as well as first-class cars for some time, the GWR is only just starting and the cars are first-class only, at that'. In actual fact, it was not until the more striking changes occurred that progress was appreciated by the progressives and deprecated by the reactionaries. The most notable instance can be found following the appearance of the elliptical-roof 'Dreadnought' coaches in 1905. *The Railway Magazine*'s 'Pertinent Paragraphs' section sometime during that year remarked, under the heading 'Is the clerestory to disappear?:

> Well, since engine design on the Great Western Railway has completely changed of recent years, we suppose we must expect alterations in the contour of passenger coaches. The clerestory was certainly an institution, and a distinguishing one, on the Great Western Railway, and for the Great Western Railway to cease to use it, seems like needlessly throwing away a valuable trade mark.

The appeal of the Churchward revolution, and appreciation of its range and impact, could best be noticed by the engineer. By the time Churchward standardisation has become revered in the 1930s, it was already passing out of date.

Churchward's standardisation was achieved by a certain amount of experimentation, as much with carriages as locomotives. Some of it was revolutionary but unpopular – with particular reference to the 'Dreadnought' corridor stock. Every feature of the design and production of coaches was ruthlessly examined. The resultant standard 57ft and 70ft 'Toplight' corridor coaches built from 1907 onwards were thoroughly practical, handsome and comfortable vehicles. They were solidly and splendidly Edwardian. With modification, much of the design survived in corridor stock built up to 1935. The five years or so before the outbreak of the First World War epitomised consolidation of the Churchward revolution: production proceeded steadily and new improvements made to the 'Toplights' kept them well abreast of contemporary practice. It was possibly a little monotonous for those who hankered after the 'old' GWR, the more so now since the coaches, painted chocolate lake, were in a livery which, although practical, lacked a sense of the historic.

After the end of the First World War, much of the GWR's energy at general manager's level was spent in wrangling with the Government over compensation for use of the railway's resources in the war. On the carriage department side, large-scale renovation of 'Toplight' coaches, sold to the Government during the war and now on hand at Swindon, was the sole feature. The contrast between recovery from the First World War and that following 1945 is rather striking.

Following Churchward's retirement, comparatively little action ensued, apart from the reintroduction of chocolate and cream livery. Most of the attention was focussed on locomotives with the introduction of the 'Castles' and 'Kings'. The only prodigies of the carriage department were the buckeye couplers and the articulated sets, both developments which never really made good. Matters improved, ironically, in the 1929–31 period, when the very creditable 60ft-plus corridor stock appeared and, at the same time, inauguration of a striking restaurant car outline. The crowning achievement in 1931 was the appearance of the superlative 'Super Saloons'.

About the time of the adoption of the 'GWR' monogram in 1934, more imaginative and modern designs began to appear: the 'Quick-Lunch Bar Cars' and the 1935 Excursion stock. The GWR visibly stirred during its centenary year and produced, without doubt, one of the finest designs ever – the 'Centenary' stock for the 'Cornish Riviera'. The new standard coaches built from 1936 were good, although some of the interior details were a little skimpy. During the 'golden years' of British railways between 1935 and 1939, the GWR lost ground to the LNER for premier place in express passenger services.

The late 1930s marked the start of the replacement of the corridor stock built at the beginning of the century during the years of expansion. Most curiously, carriage production at Swindon in the 1935–39 period was full of variety, and even the standard corridor coaches were built to varying lengths. But it was 1938 before vehicles appeared capable of general operation over other 'Big Four' companies. The famous and very original diesel railcars formed an important step in the history of British railcars, while a restaurant car pair of 1935 was the first fully air-conditioned stock in this country. At the other end of the scale, such varying lines as the Burry Port and Gwendraeth Valley and the narrow-gauge Vale of Rheidol received modern steel-panelled stock. Much credit has been accorded to the GWR for maintaining its dividend through the depression years, while several of the GWR's ideas were relevant for recent years. From 1936 onwards, the majority of pre-1914 restaurant cars were given 'face-lifts' with flush steel-panelling and more modern windows in a very practical way. Renovation of interiors, another sensible policy, belongs more to the post-war period.

End of the old order on the GWR: a broad gauge Rover 4-2-2 passes Flax Bourton with a train made up mostly of broad gauge convertible stock, but with at least one original article.

Near the end of the war, the GWR carriage department was the subject of a major change in coach building and design technique under the aegis of F. W. Hawksworth, Chief Mechahical Engineer from 1941. Not only was a modern direct-building scheme for standard stock drawn up – replacement of the 1890–1900 era stock was now very urgent – but vision was extended to contemplation of light alloy construction, fluorescent lighting, plastic finishes and automatic buffet cars. In the event, prevailing shortages of everything saw a less ambitious programme and curtailment of the more interesting ideas. Without expressing a political opinion, it is a good example of the disappointments and lack of initiative of nationalisation in the interests of standardisation that, apparently, all the forward-looking ideas

The GWR of the new century: a 3031 4-2-2 on the 10.30am Paddington–Falmouth express, east of Bath Spa. Modern Dean clerestory corridor stock and a restaurant car (third vehicle from end).

Top:
3031 4-2-2 No 3067 *Duchess of Teck* on a down local to Birmingham near Bentley Heath in 1913/14. Note the two slip coaches at the front of the train, otherwise consisting of a local set. The leading slip would appear to be a Diagram F.12 vehicle; note the vacuum reservoir on this and the other slip-coach.

Above:
An up Reading fast near West Drayton behind 36xx 2-4-2T No 3601. Clerestory stock with two Toplight non-corridors amidships.

evolved by the GWR were discarded in favour of a moderate and conservative policy for rolling stock. The lack of research on new systems of lighting and construction, in particular, resulted in British Railways building technically obsolete coaches long after the majority of Continental railways.

Nationalisation, however, changed the old GWR system very little for many years. Coaching stock, of types unique to the GWR, continued to be produced, and among the final batches of non-standard coaches built at Swindon were some auto-trailers, which coincided with the introduction of diesel railcars.

Although this history technically finishes at 1954, some of the most interesting developments in rolling-stock by the Swindon engineering design team were yet to come. These, however, deserve consideration from a more technical angle in Chapter 2.

'We are building carriages over fifty feet in length, with eight wheels. It is only when the train comes to a standstill that you realise how splendidly they are balanced. We attach great importance to our stock. . . .' This fine example of self-congratulation came from H. Lambert, general manager, during an interview given to *The GWR Magazine* late in 1894. It was certainly true that the GWR took great care with the running characteristics of its stock, Dean's cleverly-designed suspension bogies being the prime example. This was probably because the broad-gauge trains had been characterised by steadier riding than was experienced on most standard-gauge lines. In the 1890s, despite the fact that the GWR was turning out some very creditable stock, it certainly could display no real advantages over comparable coaches built by the Midland or North Eastern Railways. In comparison with these railways, it was also slow to develop amenities such as dining-cars.

It is interesting that while Dean seemingly authorised the release of a considerable amount of technical information for the use of the railway press, Churchward's period was characterised by a lessening of this effort. In fact, interest in publicity was not regained until after Grouping. The vigorous publicity department of the GWR in the inter-war period deserves a study in itself. There is no doubt that it greatly fostered public esteem of the railway by means of the various well-known publications and, particularly, in the medium of *The GWR Magazine*, which reached its heights during this period. Both as a means of staff communication and as public relations material, this journal did an effective job in presenting the GWR as a friendly holiday line, while emphasising new commercial and technical developments. In the feature, 'From People We Have Pleased', which printed letters of public appreciation, the impression of a courteous and helpful staff operating smooth-running, reliable trains was as much an inspiration to railwaymen, as evidence of a well-liked concern.

Much publicity was aimed at holiday-travellers or excursionists, in contrast to more recent disenchantment shown by British Rail towards these categories of passengers. The GWR was *the* 'holiday line' whose chocolate and cream coaches were as much a part of the holidays as the seashore. On the other hand, the more pompous aspects of the GWR – such as particularly unctious treatment of first-class passengers – were often apparent. Much of the publicity surrounding new coaches during the 1920s plays up the 'holiday line' characteristic. The best example was with the 60ft plus stock built for the 'Cornish Riviera' in 1929 which though creditable was unremarkable except for the unique feature – so it was claimed – of 'Vita-glass'. Of this, *The Engineer* rather cuttingly commented: 'Whether this remarkable glass is suitable for the purpose remains to be proved – on a blazing day it may pass too much of the sun's rays for the comfort of those who are near the windows'.

Finally, of course, the publications written for the GWR by W. G. Chapman, such as *The Cheltenham Flyer*, were a chatty everyman's guide to the railway and astutely aimed at fostering the interest of railway-minded youngsters. The approach is conspicuously dated today, yet appealed to the public of the 1930s, and sold in amazing quantities. The GWR was very conscious of its lack of 'streamliners' in the late 1930s and could only rely on its appeal as the 'old firm', apart from the lamentable disfiguring of No 5005 *Manorbier Castle* and No 6014 *King Henry VII*.

After the Second World War, attention was turned to publicising the new standard of rolling stock that was soon to appear. A very real sense of a quick return to better things came through, even if it was not achieved, for the programme of rolling-stock renewals was 18 months–2 years in arrears.

Although the GWR was anything but a cultivator of third-class travel in its earlier days, its attitude had greatly changed by the 1890s when the new 'Cornishman' sets were among the first corridor trains to have accommodation for all three classes. The 1892 prototype corridor train had, indeed, inaugurated this feature. Although the original dining-cars were first-class only, it seems more likely that second- and third-class passengers were considered less ready to make use of the facilities, rather than an insistence on exclusiveness. In 1905, an important step was made towards the abolition of second-class, as the new 'Dreadnought' sets for the 'Cornish Riviera' were first- and third-class only, despite an original intention to accommodate all three classes. It was also significant that both the new services of the 1905–7 period, the Fishguard boat trains and the Wolverhampton–Penzance expresses, were introduced with two-class stock only. As regards restaurant cars, the GWR quickly changed to building unclassed vehicles. With the 'Dreadnought' sets for the 1905 'Cornish Riviera', two interesting innovations came about. On one of the few occasions on British railways, men and women train attendants were provided and, because of the limited formation, seats could be reserved on payment of a shilling.

During this period, a start was made with the provision of some form of light refreshments, notably in the 1900 Milford Boat sets but, also, by the conversion of two compartments of various brake thirds to a small pantry-cum-kitchen serving tea, coffee and snacks.

A refinement in seat reservation arrangements for the 'Cornish Riviera' came during 1906, when passengers were issued with differently-coloured reservation tickets to indicate the portion of the train in which they would be travelling.

Right into the 1920s, few changes occurred in the provision of facilities for passengers. From October 1921, simplified two-course lunches were available in a number of restaurant cars on major expresses; this has only become a general feature in more recent times. The seat reservation arrangements were extended to many expresses,

Top:
The up Cheltenham Flyer in the Thames Valley, west of Reading, behind the partially 'streamlined' Castle 4-6-0 No 5005 *Manorbier Castle,* c1935/36. Bow-end corridor stock makes up the formation.

Above:
The up Cornish Riviera Limited on the Westbury cut-off in 1936 behind King 4-6-0 No 6015 *King Richard III*. Centenary stock in the train is in original condition with Beclawat windows.

including holiday reliefs, in the summer of 1922. In many cases, all seats in the train were reservable during the peak period.

Much of the coaching-stock policy during the 1920s followed Edwardian practice too closely. The first 1925 articulated sets, although only eight-coach sets, had separate first- and third-class restaurant cars. Later sets had the more sensible arrangement of unclassed accommodation. In 1929, three day-sleeper third-class coaches were tried cautiously, but it was not long before the generally 'first-class only' facility of sleeping-car travel was decisively altered.

From the mid-1930s, a number of changes took place. After experiments with converted clerestory restaurant cars, new vehicles providing buffet service were built, two full-length cars, and two following the idea of a 'miniature buffet-car'. It is worth noting that the 'Bristolian' was

Top:
The archetypal GWR branch line train. 4575 2-6-2T No 5535 on a Witham–Yatton train near Cheddar 1936 and featuring a 61ft 2in body non-corridor B set.

Above:
A Western Region Royal Train of the 1950s. HRH Princess Margaret was travelling to Solihull in March 1954 when Castle class 4-6-0 No 7026 *Tenby Castle* was photographed near Bearley. The formation comprises the two 'Royal' Hawksworth brake composites at each end, one of the two Diagram G.59 saloons (second), a Hawksworth sleeping car next and, then, Royal Saloon No 9006 or 9007.

Below:
Castle class 4-6-0 No 5010 *Restormel Castle* with a down Fishguard Harbour express near Cholsey in 1949. At a rough count, there are eight different designs of GWR corridor coach in the formation.

allocated a buffet car from its inception. A surprising number of short-distance services at that time offered full meal facilities. The excursion trains built from 1935–39 were in part-answer to the challenge of motor-coaches for works' excursions and football traffic, and offered all-in meals-at-every-seat facilities. The introduction, from 1936 onwards, of coaches with entry by means of end-doors only on the compartment-side did much to break the practice of locking doors between first- and third-class accommodation on all corridor trains, excepting those with restaurant-car facilities. The generously proportioned windows of this so-called 'Sunshine' stock greatly improved passengers' view of the passing scene.

It has already been mentioned that the pre-eminence of the 'Cornish Riviera' among British trains in the 1920s was supplanted by the LNER 'streamliner' services during the late 1930s. However, the 'Centenary' stock of the 'Cornish Riviera', which appeared a few months before the 'Silver Jubilee', constituted one of the finest trains available to passengers without a supplementary fee. It was also noticeable that much was done to reduce the disparity between first- and third-class. Curtains and mats were provided in the compartments of the latter and the upholstery was little different from that in the first-class. The other crack trains – the 'Bristolian', 'Torbay Express' and the 'Cheltenham Flyer' – were undistinguished in the matter of stock and it has always seemed curious that they did not receive coaches similar to the 'Centenary' sets. But the GWR made satisfactory progress with the renewal of its passenger stock fleet during the 1930s. By late 1936, only 335 four-wheeled, and 50 six-wheeled coaches were still in traffic.

Despite the encouraging prospectus offered by the GWR for post-war passenger comforts, impending nationalisation and prevailing shortages prevented their implementation and we can only guess at what might have been.

2

COACH PRODUCTION: DESIGN AND CONSTRUCTION

Examination of the development in design of a railway's passenger coaches is a very different task from a similar study of locomotive development. Much has been written concerning the chief mechanical engineer's personal attention to a particular locomotive design, but it is not very meaningful to talk of a 'Churchward'- or 'Collett'-designed coach because the chief mechanical engineer generally had less interest – and did not need to have – in the more detailed aspects of coach design. Providing certain requirements for the traffic department were met, he would do little more than sign the drawings. The real decisions concerned control and administration of production by means of standardisation, and adoption of new materials or design features. Churchward's great significance lay in his ready acceptance of developments in both these fields.

So far as standard, general service stock was concerned, changes in design generally occurred only when the current type was seen to be obsolescent in relation to other railways – this would be a traffic department decision in any case – or when the other two guiding principles

A Dean non-corridor composite of the late 1880s, typifying the standard construction of the period.

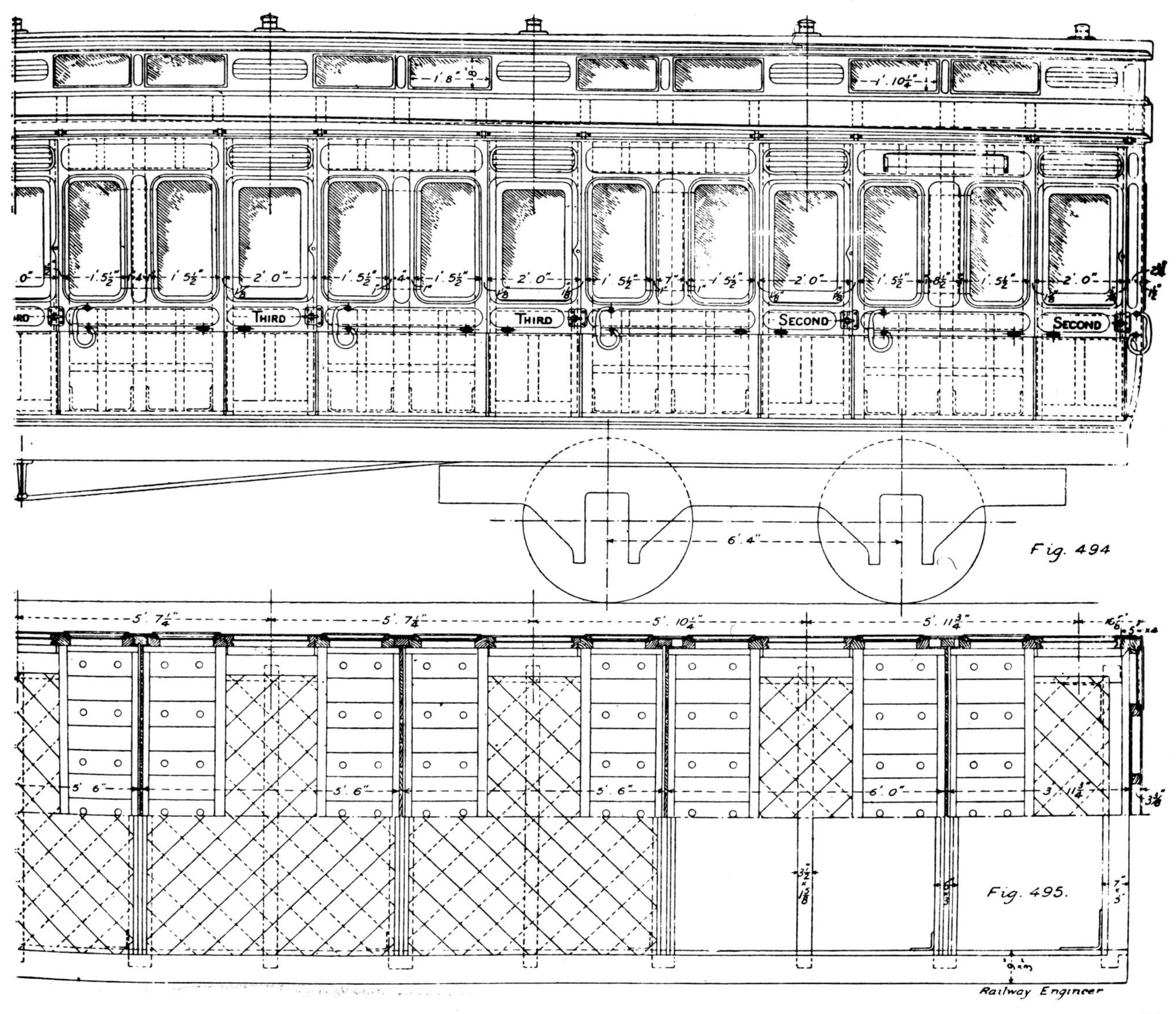

A fair variety of rolling stock to be seen on the 2.45pm Birmingham Snow Hill–Paddington behind Star 4-6-0 No 4023 *King George* on 19 April 1912, near Bentley Heath. Two non-corridor clerestories lead the train, then a clerestory slip coach, and a real mixture follows, including a Dreadnought restaurant car.

mentioned above were altered by the chief mechanical engineer. Specialised vehicles were, of course, different, but, even then, responsibility for particular features could hardly be attributed to one person. Another point is that the design of coaches was much more subject to the control of the traffic department. Particular enthusiasms of the chief mechanical engineer, which could be indulged in locomotive design with the justification of improved efficiency, were less likely to be incorporated in passenger coach design, although there are examples. Finally, of course, it was well demonstrated in several cases – the 'Dreadnought' and Milford Boat sets in particular – that innovation in the layout and design of coaches, particularly for general service, was likely to be baulked by the innate conservatism of passengers. Experiments with coaching stock design were liable to meet with unpredicted reactions by users, and risked the chance of expensive failures. Again, there was nothing in the manner of a design panel to analyse trends in demand for different types of accommodation and service; the science was not really introduced until the 1960s. Choice of furnishing materials was also similarly unprofessional, although from the 1930s onwards, much greater awareness was shown in the adoption of new styles – the art deco fittings of the 1935–39 excursion stock are a good example – and it seems to have been well developed on the GWR after the Second World War. In spite of all these considerations, the policy adopted by the GWR for passenger coach design and construction was remarkably vigorous, except for a 'dead' period in the 1920s and early 1930s.

William Dean, who had become Locomotive & Carriage Superintendent in 1877, was, by training, primarily a coaching-stock man. By the 1890s, a number of interesting designs had been produced under his administration, including the well-known batch of 'bay-window' convertible sleeping-cars of 1890. Dean had assembled a good staff at Swindon and two of his department later moved on to important posts: James Holden became locomotive engineer of the GER in 1885, and Surrey Warner was in charge of the LSWR's carriage department during the Edwardian period. The facilities for coach production at Swindon in the 1890s enjoyed a high reputation and they were certainly tested by the process of converting broad-gauge stock to standard-gauge use. An example of the high pitch of operations at Swindon was demonstrated to the L & YR directors early in 1890, when they were taken down to the Works in a broad-gauge saloon and, during the hour in which they were inspecting the works, it was remounted on standard-gauge bogies to take them down the Gloucester line.

Dean's control of his department slackened during the last years of his tenure of office and Churchward necessarily had to be very much a 'new broom' on taking over the post of chief mechanical engineer in 1902. Churchward had, of course, been assistant carriage works manager from 1882 and chief assistant to Dean since 1897, and had been the driving force on the carriage side for some time before he gained supereme control. There was certainly little at fault with the actual capacity for coach construction at Swindon in the 1890s; the total of 737 coaches built between 1894 and 1899 was not surpassed by the efforts during the 1905–14 period. For the most common types of corridor and non-corridor stock there was remarkable standardisation, often more so than in much later years.

Although new ideas were not lacking at Swindon during Dean's tenure, the feeling appears to have emerged that the GWR was too set in a rut of the old chocolate and cream tradition and everlasting clerestory designs. At any rate, Churchward made a complete sweep of all this. Another interesting angle appears in a report on the cleaning of passenger carriages, dated 11 November 1902, after Churchward had taken charge. This highlighted the inadequate control of the cleaning and overhaul of stock and drew attention to the insufficient stock of 'float' coaches to cover others gone for repair. The report advised construction of 400 new coaches, giving a cost of £400,000 for these, which would then allow every coach on the line to be systematically taken out of traffic for cleaning. Concluding that it would be reasonable to expect a substantial saving in maintenance if modern methods of cleaning and shelter were adopted, it was interesting to observe that someone in the general manager's department had pencilled in the margin: 'exact money saving cannot be given – Mr Dean has always said there would not be any'.

Churchward has received many eulogies for his work on the locomotive side. His influence in the carriage department was no less striking. He was very impressed by American practice and the resultant effect on locomotive design has already been noted. On the carriage side, he seems to have studied the construction of American stock very carefully. In a paper given to the Swindon Junior Engineering Society in January 1896 he emphasised that the framing of British coaches was weaker and more disjointed than American stock because of the practice of providing exterior doors to all compartments.

The steam rail-motors of 1903 were his first new design and their slab-sided saloon bodies with large windows bore traces of American influence. The 'Dreadnoughts' of 1904–5 were the first main-line stock without exterior doors to every compartment, although they had the normal droplight and two quarterlights arrangement. The public disfavour of their layout must have forced Churchward to revert to the traditional pattern. Other American influences were to be found in under-frame construction and, most markedly, with bogie design.

Another observation of American practice can be seen in Churchward's keenness to improve the passenger/weight ratio of coaches by building 70ft stock. Dean's clerestories, with their separate men's and women's lavatories and wasteful, half side-corridor/half centre-corridor arrangement, could only offer economic seating capacity in slightly cramped compartments. But safety considerations resulting in the use of fireproof flooring and steel-panelling meant that later 70-footers showed up less favourably with the Dean coaches. By comparison, the BR standard Mark 1 corridor second comes off badly.

PASSENGERS PER TON
(second/third-class corridor coaches)

54ft Dean clerestory	(1902)	2.67
70ft 'Toplight'	(1909)	2.38
70ft steel-panelled 'Toplight'	(1914)	2.25
63ft BR standard Mark 1	(1961)	1.73
75ft BR standard Mark 3	(1975)	2.25

Churchward's improvements in Swindon Works generally will be mentioned later. Not least, he was keen to build up an enthusiastic design staff, and competition to get into the design departments during this period was very fierce. He was always ready to send his staff to America to study railway practice and, as well as being an astute locomotive engineer and good manager of staff, he was also an efficient administrator. One of his characteristic comments on coaches was an alleged remark that he didn't care if their outside were tarred over so long as the insides were comfortable – which was the antithesis of the supposed Swindon veneration of the chocolate and cream livery and presumably referred to its abolition in the late 1900s!

Earlier reference has been made to the relative stagnation during the 1920s and 1930s so far as the carriage department was concerned. The decline in the pre-eminence of the engineering function – or, rather, Paddington's domination over Swindon – has been attributed to Sir Felix Pole's tightening of the general manager's control. There is no doubt that much of the energy at Swindon before 1914 was at Churchward's own

The lengthy body-members of this 1907 restaurant car under construction at Swindon Works prove Churchward's point about the superior features of American design which he followed.

Pacific No 111 *The Great Bear*, picking up water from Goring water-troughs at the head of a down Bristol express with Toplight stock to the fore, 1923.

initiative but, in later years, other circumstances had control. The Depression of the 1930s inevitably meant that capital for investment was limited and the 'Big Four' generally justifiably sought to obtain the quickest return on new capital by means of operating improvements: electrification on the Southern, resignalling of large stations and new locomotives. Investment in new workshop equipment was comparatively small. As a result, coach-building techniques continued very much as before on all railways.

The exception was the LMS, which decided to improve the output of new coaches by standardised mass-production building and reduction of weight by means of lightweight construction. The GWR, SR and LNER showed little inclination to move away from previous patterns of construction. The SR continued building coaches with wood and canvas roofs – in fact, up until 1951 – and the LNER clung to its faith in teak-bodied stock until the early 1940s. The GWR had tried all-steel construction for one or two experimental vehicles but was not sufficiently impressed to discard wood-framed, metal-panelled coaches.

J. W. Innes gave an interesting paper in 1939 to the Swindon Junior Engineering Society in which he outlined several of the reasons for not adopting all-steel coaches. It was, he said, generally considered that automatic train control provided a better insurance against the possibility of fatal accidents than heavy, collision-proof coaches. The weight factor was also important and it is interesting that in post-war days Swindon turned its attention to experiments with light-alloy framing and panelling, rather than steel construction. Additionally, all-steel coaches required thirty per cent more heating surface; they were liable to corrosion and were said to be noisier.

After the war, the policy adopted towards coach-building gave promise of being very progressive. The direct-building system, adopted for production of the Hawksworth corridor and non-corridor stock, not only permitted speedier output but made better use of existing workshop facilities. The experiments with light-alloy construction were certainly in the right direction and, as mentioned earlier, it seems unfortunate that the work could not have been applied to the design of the BR standard stock. Using rough estimates, an all-light-alloy Hawksworth coach might well have tared about twenty-six tons only and, with the refinements of fluorescent lighting and plastic panelling, could have been an important milestone in British passenger coach development.

Nationalisation, although depriving Swindon of complete initiative for locomotive-hauled stock design, nevertheless saw some of the most interesting developments produced by the works. These will be outlined as, although lying outside the strict limits of the title, they have some bearing on work instigated during GWR days, as well as terminating the story of Swindon as a design centre. The works was entrusted with bogie design as its particular contribution to the evolution of the BR standard corridor coach, and the BR1 bogie was based largely on the 1933 GWR double-bolster type.

The most important task of the design department at Swindon during the 1950s was, however, the development of the 'Inter-City' diesel railcars. The specification for these was that the coaches should be able to withstand the same 200-ton end compression load as the BR standard coach but, of necessity, be considerably lighter. The solution adopted was to produce an integrally-constructed, all-steel body – which would also permit adequate space underneath for power equipment – all parts of which would be stress-bearing. After vigorous testing at the SNCF installation at Vitry, in France, it was decided to develop a new, integral-construction, standard, locomotive-hauled corridor-coach. Work on this began in the late 1950s and early 1960s, when the bulk of new BR standard stock being built was of heavy 'battleship' design principles, in which the frame alone was sufficient to take the target end-loading. It was not until mid-1963 that the prototype integral-construction coach appeared: first-class corridor No. W13252. Its design was adopted for the large-scale construction of the BR Mark 2 standard coaches from 1964–75.

The other significant product from Swindon was the B4-type bogie. There was early evidence of the quick deterioration in riding qualities of the original Swindon-developed BR1 bogie. Primary suspension in the B4 bogie was by coil-springs and great attention was paid to the control of lateral movements by longer swing-links. The B4 bogie became standard for new construction by BR and was also adopted by the CIE. The standard BR coach of the 1960s/1970s was, therefore, almost entirely a Swindon-inspired creation, and Swindonians are keen that this should be acknowledged, in view of the transfer of design responsibility to Derby in 1967. Another notable production was the dynamometer car for diesel locomotive testing, which appeared in 1961.

Despite Swindon's obvious prowess in the design field during the 1950s and 1960s, it was apparent that its usefulness as a carriage-building works was nearly ended. The BR workshops plan drawn up by Sir Steuart Mitchell in 1962 proposed that the carriage works would close, except for the repair of diesel multiple-units and non-passenger-carrying coaching stock, by 1965, the bulk of redundancies occurring in 1964. The last new production vehicles of Swindon design were the Class 123 'Inter-City' B4-bogied diesel units produced early in 1963. The very last coach to be built at Swindon was a BR standard corridor brake first No. M14027 to BR Lot No. 30718 outshopped in November 1963. Major overhauls of passenger-carrying stock continued until July 1964, when the responsibility for the remaining GWR-design passenger coaches passed to Wolverton Works. In October 1964, the last few coaches received attention at Swindon.

The extension of coverage from 1954 up to 1964 enables history to be completed. Even if the promises of 1945–48 died a sudden death, it is possible to trace the lineage of present-day integral construction stock into the era of chocolate and cream-painted coaches.

Coach Production

One of the more remarkable features of coach production in the 1890s was its comparative standardisation. In spite of a wide range of types of both corridor and non-corridor coaches, body outline, underframe construction and bogie types were changed surprisingly little over a period of twenty years. It would be wrong to infer that this could be termed mass production: despite the outstanding boom in new construction in the late 1890s, Dean's workmen were essentially craftsmen coachbuilders. However, the building of 1,300 coaches in ten years, an average of over two completed each week, was a fair achievement. Output, even allowing for more advanced techniques and appreciable investment in new machinery, did not increase above this level during the 1905–14 period. As to the costs of coaches built in the middle and late 1890s, four-wheelers cost about £380–£450, while the clerestory corridor stock was in the £1,000–£1,200 range. Of the specialist stock, the first restaurant cars costing £2,130 were obviously an expensive proposition at the time; the 1903 vehicles were, on average, £1,770 apiece. Churchward, with his interest in American practice, was aware that, good as Dean's designs were, they belonged to a tradition that was now conservative and obsolescent.

Production facilities in Swindon Works at the time were good in relation to other railways. An interesting series of articles on British passenger coaching stock practice appeared in *The Railway Engineer* between 1892 and 1895. The 'good facilities' for machining and putting together rolled iron underframes at Swindon were specifically mentioned; the rivetting work involved in their construction was carried out with portable hydraulic machines.

Much of the Churchward 'revolution' was occupied in improving production facilities by the refurbishing of the works with modern equipment and a number of new machines were electrically driven. Since the construction of larger stock up to 70ft in length was to be general practice, the works had to be geared to handling a completely new standard of vehicles. In addition, towards the end of the period, a number of other innovations had to be accommodated – the increasing use of galvanised steel for body panelling, and fireproof materials for flooring. In 1911, a fire in the paint shop destroyed a number of coaches, and

Carriage construction at Swindon: 60ft bow-ended stock is being built, *c*1929.

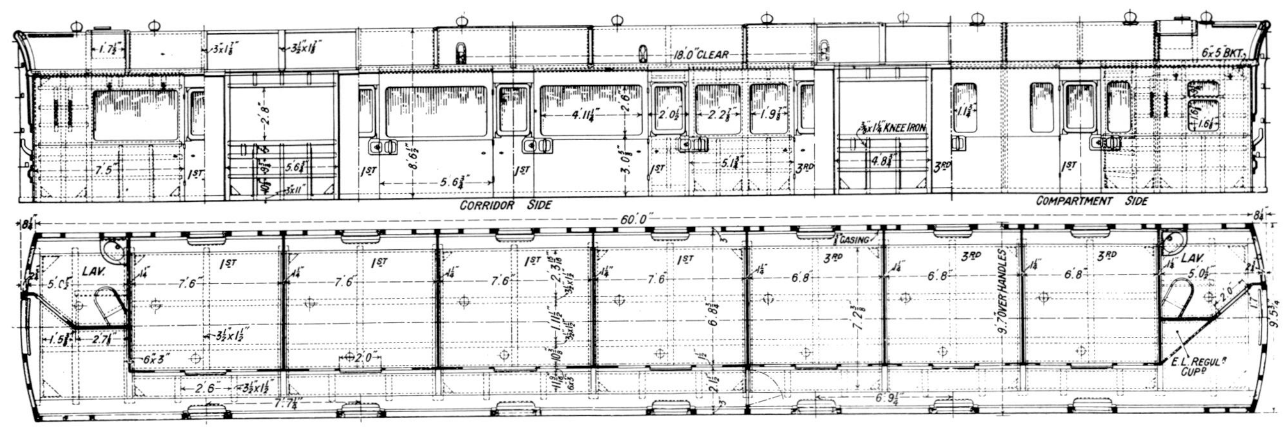

Elevation and plan of a 1929 61ft 4in body bow-end corridor coach.

sprinklers were thereafter fitted throughout the carriage works. As mentioned earlier, greater attention was now being paid to coach overhaul procedure and better facilities were established during the period. Churchward was backed up by a fine team of officers in the carriage department. F. W. Marillier, carriage manager from 1902–20, can not only claim credit for day-to-day work successfully carried out but also contributed in other ways. He was instrumental in organising the fitting-out and supply of ambulance trains by the British railways during the First World War, as well as patenting such useful features as the heating system for water tanks in passenger stock.

The standard 57ft 'Toplight' coaches cost about £1,200 each for the first wooden-panelled batches, while the final lots with steel-panelling were in the £1,500 range. The restaurant cars were costing between £2,000 and £2,300 each, while auto-trailers were valued at £1,200 each. Between 1905 and 1914, 1,200 new coaches were built at Swindon. Some indication of the capital expended on coaching stock can be given by the following figures:

COACHING STOCK (PASSENGER-CARRYING) AUTHORISED

Year	No. of coaches	Value
1909	150	£208,970
1910	101	£139,170
1911	63	£ 87,966 (year of paintshop fire)
1912	77	£112,216
1913	183	£237,525

In the inter-war period, there was little change in carriage-building techniques, as previously mentioned. In 1925, a special shearing machine for steel roof-panels was installed, the GWR being the first of the 'Big Four' to standardise steel roofs for coaches. An automatic rivetting machine for roof panels was a further development, introduced in 1933. In this year a standard corridor third cost £3,600 and took eight weeks to build. Some speeding up of construction time was made possible by the installation of a 190ft carriage-making machine in the Old Saw Mill at Swindon in 1936.

GWR Swindon Works in the 1924–54 period. The area to the east of the Cheltenham line has now been cleared completely; south of the main line the former shops are mostly demolished and used for car-parking space. From GWR plan dated 1924 but with alterations to 1954.

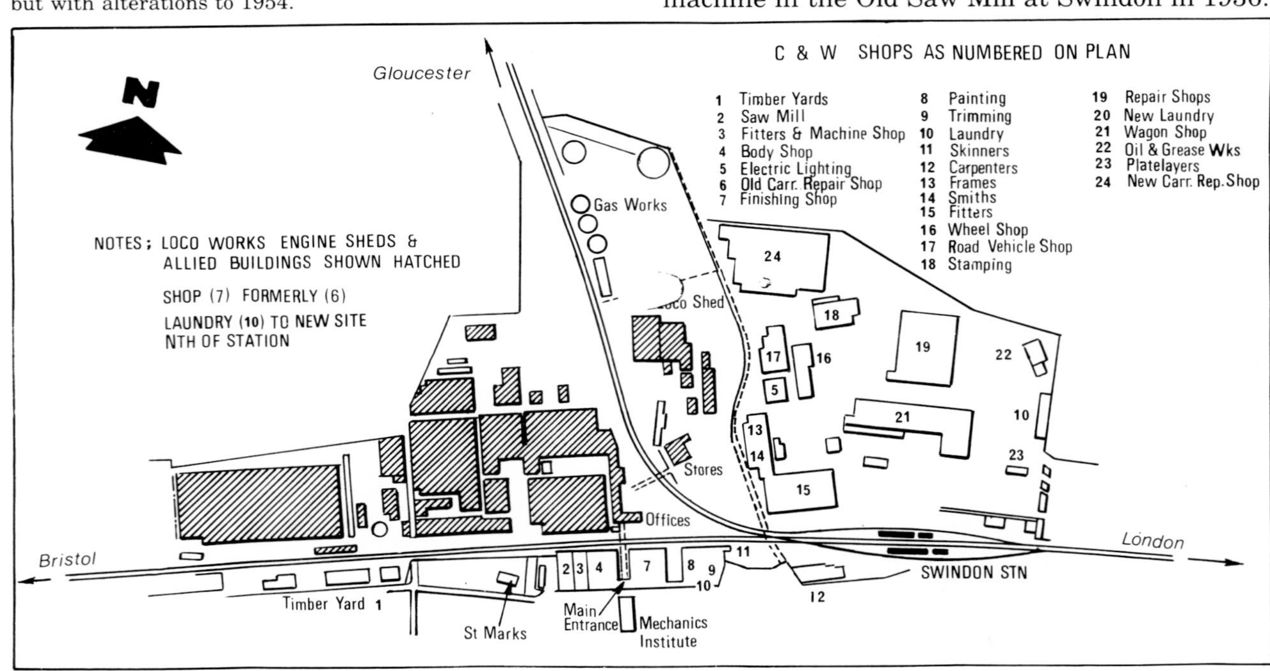

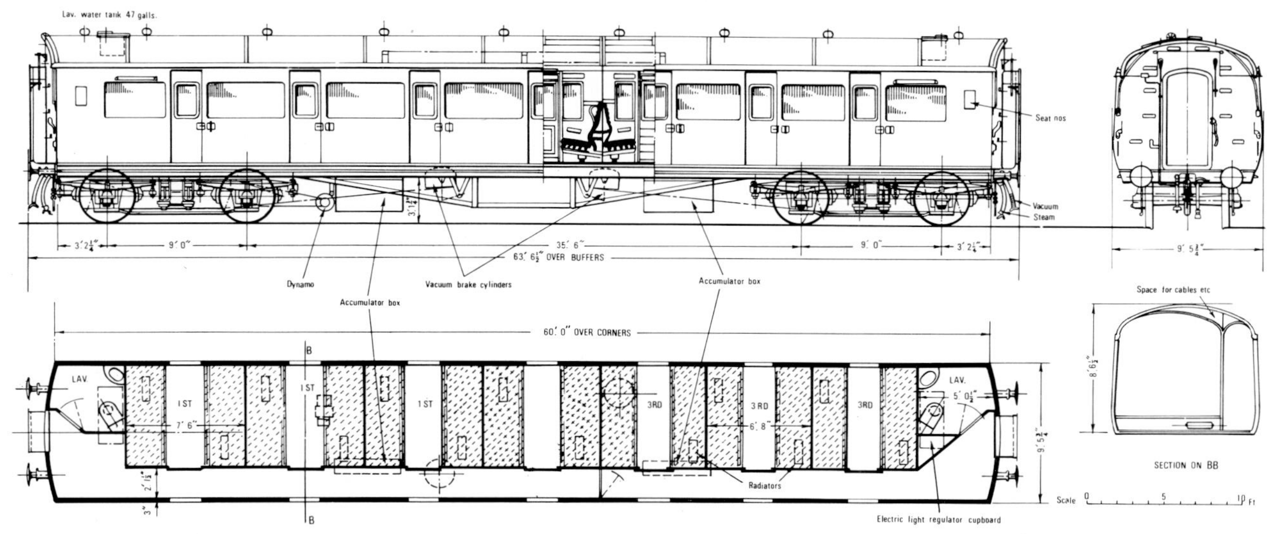

Drawing showing a variety of detail on a 1929 61ft 4in body bow-end corridor composite coach on Lots 1424/33 – Diagram E.137. This shows typical underframe layout, and the difference between first-class and third-class seating. The communication gear was fitted at one end only.

This facilitated the construction of coaches by being able to accommodate the long bottom sides of vehicles for morticing. During the late 1930s, the usual output of new stock for each year was in the 250–400 range while, simultaneously, a considerable amount of renovation work was being carried out on many of the pre-1923 restaurant cars. A carriage storage shed was built in 1939 at Swindon for storing coaches built during the winter months and not released to traffic until the summer. It seems unlikely that its capacity of 265 coaches was ever fully utilised.

Restrictions on the use of materials seriously hampered post-war construction which, during 1946–8, ran only at a total of 100–130 coaches per year. This was supplemented by the completion of lots by outside contractors, and the final series of GWR non-corridor coaches in the early 1950s were built by private workshops. The target for the construction of Hawksworth corridor stock had been to turn out five coaches a week by the use of sectionalised construction and direct assembly of the bodies on to the frames, although this was not achieved. Simultaneously, much energy had to be expended in restoring the coach fleet from the heavy wear of wartime work, and in renovating the majority of post-1923 restaurant cars and sleeping-cars.

The Carriage Works

With the appearance of Alan S. Peck's excellent *The Great Western at Swindon Works* (Oxford Publishing Co), it seems sensible to refer readers to this source for the overall development of the works. As a broad gauge railway, the GWR had at first ordered stock from outside suppliers and did not have a carriage works. In mid-1865 it was announced that a new carriage and wagon works for the whole system would be built at Oxford. The academics were outraged, and in view of their objections other towns, including New Swindon, offered to accommodate the new Works. When Sir Daniel Gooch was elected Chairman of the GWR, he disentangled the Company from the Oxford plans and in March 1868 proposed to the Board that a carriage works should be built at Swindon.

By the end of 1868, the first building in the new works was ready to be equipped, and by the following May the GWR was able to concentrate new orders at Swindon. During the early 1870s the carriage workshops facilities were expanded, and by the end of that decade the works was virtually in its final form. In 1930 the final major addition came in the shape of No 24 carriage shop, including a paint mill, the last rolling stock repair shop to be built at Swindon; this was to the north of the station.

The accompanying plan of Swindon Works covers the period 1924–54, and effectively illustrates the carriage workshop facilities throughout that period.

In the mid-1950s the Carriage and Wagon Works employed 4,500 staff, and its capacity was given as including the construction of 250 new coaches annually and the repair of 5,000 coaches each year. Its rundown, as a result of the BR workshops rationalisation plan, has already been mentioned. The remaining carriage repairs were accommodated after 1964 in the locomotive works and were largely concerned with the maintenance of diesel multiple-units. The former carriage and wagon sites were cleared. Then, in 1967, the Swindon design, research and development staffs were moved to the newly opened Railway Technical Centre, Derby. In June of the same year, the area of the carriage and wagon workshops north of the main line was handed over to Swindon Corporation for redevelopment. This saw the end of the former C & W management offices. The area south of the line still partly remains in BR ownership and now includes the works car parks.

The carriage works was divided in two parts. The main shops for new construction, finishing and trimming, as well as the sawmill, were on the down side of the London to Bristol lines. The carriage and wagon forging, stamping and 'iron-

A real connoisseur's photograph! Old Oak Common carriage sidings, June 1939. Note the new Diagram C.77 thirds nearest the camera, restaurant car pair (to the right) and an enticing variety of GWR corridor stock from Dean clerestories to Excursion open stock.

work' departments, together with the repair shops, were to the north of Swindon station on the up side. As shown on the plan, the locomotive workshops were distinguished by an alphabetical series, the carriage and wagon departments by numerical designations. The offices of the chief mechanical engineer were located to the west of the fork formed by the Gloucester and Bristol lines.

Down side Carriage Shops

No. 2 Sawmill. Preparation of wooden components.

No. 3 Fitting. Interior and constructional fittings. Steel components for bodywork.

No. 4 Coach-body. Construction of coach-bodies from components produced in shops Nos. 2 and 3. Completion of body-fittings, including doors, seat-frames and partitions Body mounted on underframe constructed by No. 15 shop. Coach then run into No. 8 paint shop for undercoat.

No. 5 Repairs. Later concentrated on Nos. 19 and 24 shops. No. 5 shop then dealt with electric train lighting.

No. 7 Finishing. Preparation of interior woodwork for coaches, interior fittings. Glazing work. Veneer presses.

No. 8 Paint shop. Preparation of steel panels, application of undercoat, main colours and coats of varnish. Accommodation for about forty coaches.

No. 9 Trimming. Upholstery, blinds, floor coverings, gangway hoods and leatherwork.

North side Carriage (and Wagon) Shops

No. 13 Frame shop. Underframes for coaches and wagons.

No. 14 Smiths. Forging of ironwork such as springs.

No. 15 Fittings. Miscellaneous metal work.

No. 16 Wheel shop.

No. 18 Stamping.

No. 19 Carriage and wagon lifting and repair shops, including balancing machines, etc.

No. 24 Carriage repairs. The new shop dated from 1930.

3

UNDERFRAMES TO UPHOLSTERY – THE GWR COACH IN DETAIL

The underframes for the Dean clerestory stock had bulb-section angle solebars, the middle longitudinals consisting of two similar girders. The headstocks were of channel sections backed with timber, cross-bearers and diagonals were 8in by 3½in angle-irons. The vacuum brake apparatus for stock built largely to Dean-period designs had the arrangement in which the brake cylinder moved while the piston was rigidly attached to the underframe. The gas reservoirs were held to the frame by bands bolted to the cross-bearers, with bolts at the end to prevent sideways movements. The frame-trusses were circular rods with queen posts at 2ft intervals. With the introduction of 50ft-plus stock in the mid-1890s, the original underframe pattern for 40ft stock had been little altered beyond stiffening by means of an extra cross-bearer and strengthening the middle longitudinal with a tie-rod.

In the Churchward standard stock designs, diagonal members were dispensed with, while there were fewer sections all of which were I-section channel girders connected by angle-brackets. The drawbar pulled directly on to the end cross-bearers. Underframe trussing differed between various series of 57ft and 70ft 'Toplight' coaches as described on page 72, the later batches having rigid non-adjustable L-section angle-irons.

An experimental, all-steel, 57ft 'Toplight' was built in 1921 which had the underframe constructed on the Livesey-Gould principle of rolled-steel sections, in which channel beams forming the central girder were trussed with transverse cantilevers. Diagonals attached at one end to the headstock behind the buffers and, at the other end, to the centre girder, transmitted the shocks received by the buffers.

The 'Dreadnought' sleepers of 1907 were unusual in having wooden headstocks and solebars, together with mainly wood-framed bogies, all aimed at reducing noise for the sleeping passengers.

Inter-war underframe designs varied little, being constructed from rolled-steel sections rivetted together and developed from the Churchward standard pattern, with the same 'box-girder' channel sections at the ends taking the brunt of buffing and drawgear stresses.

Late in 1944, the GWR ordered the first batches of Hawksworth stock which were to be constructed by the direct-method, that is, with the bodies 'built-off' the frames. Included in the original series of lots was a prototype with an underframe including aluminium sections. The work done by Swindon in BR days in producing diesel railcars and integral construction locomotive-hauled passenger stock has already been noted. The application of welding techniques for underframe fabrication was not taken up by the GWR beyond an experimental stage; but it is believed that at least one completely welded underframe was produced.

Bogie designs on the GWR were extremely interesting; at least until the almost uniform adoption of a standard pressed-steel double-bolster design from 1932/3 onwards. Dean's bogies were a fascinating study in themselves. The

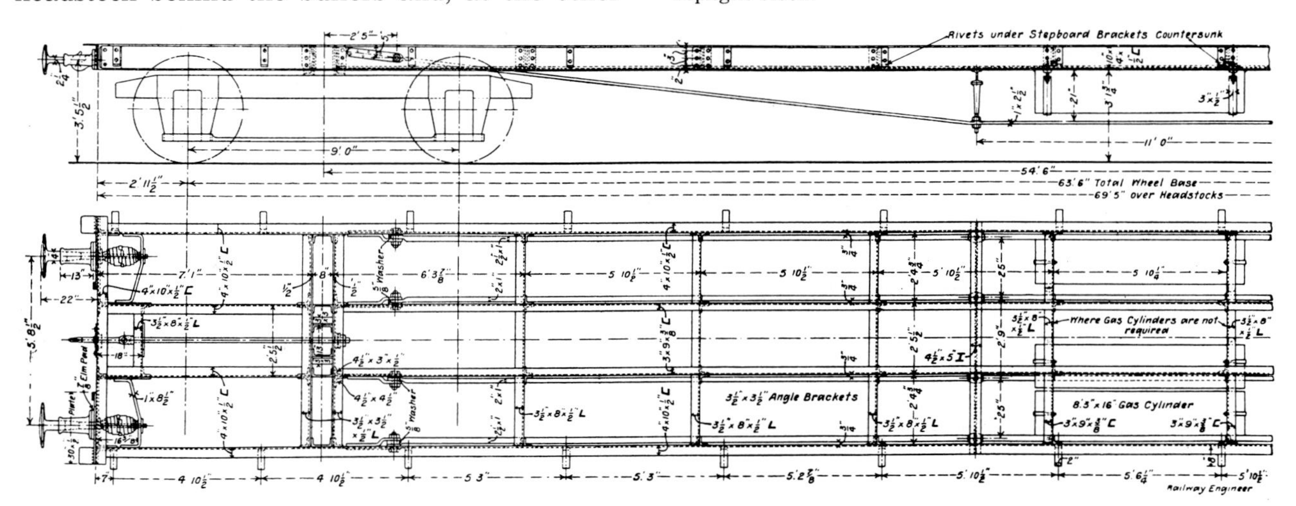

General arrangement of 69ft 5in underframe used for 70ft Toplight stock.

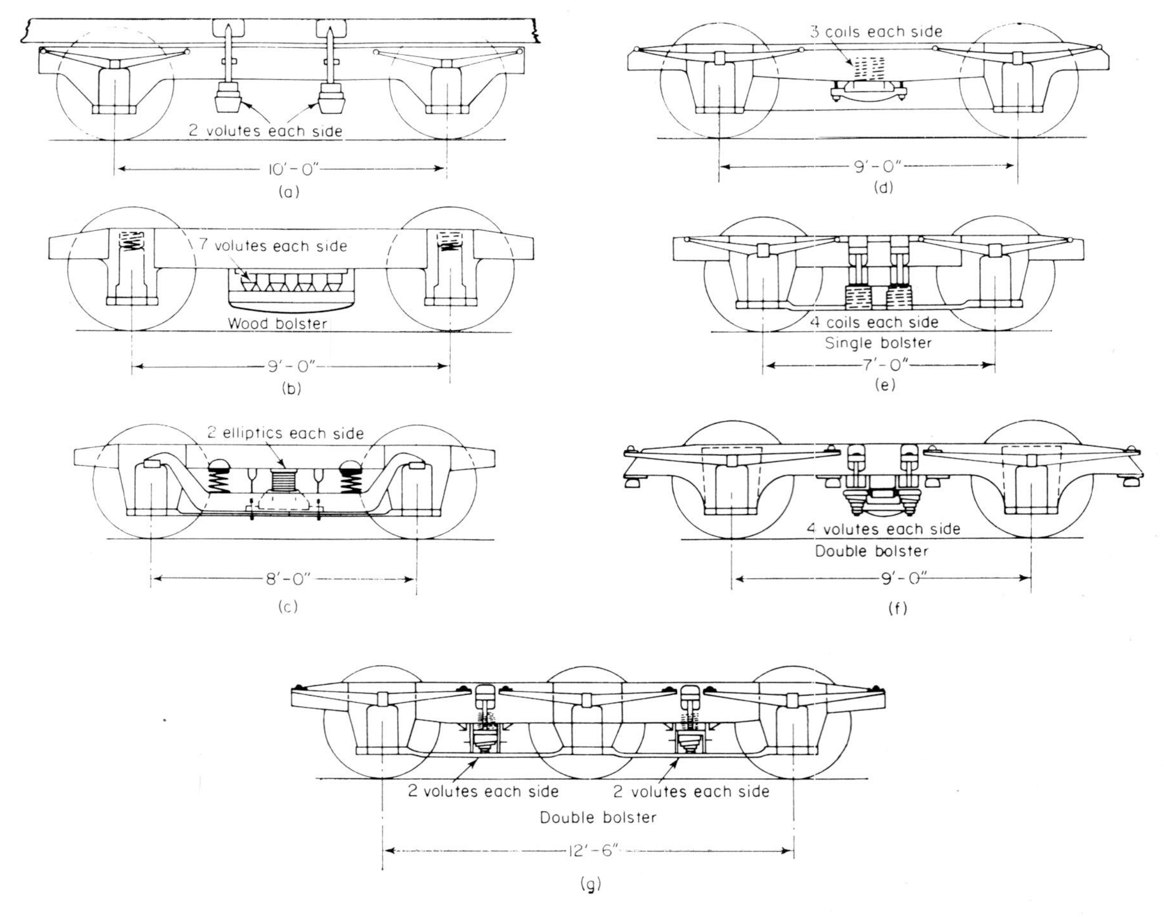

A selection of GWR bogie designs 1890–1950: (a) 10ft wheelbase standard Dean suspension bogie, 1895–1904; (b) 9ft wb 'plate frame' bolster bogie, 1903; (c) 8ft American equalised beam bolster bogie, c1907–11; (d) 9ft light bolster bogie, c1910–25; (e) 7ft single bolster bogie, 1925–33; (f) 9ft standard double bolster, pressed steel design, 1932–54; (g) six-wheel standard bogie, used 1929 onwards.

earliest Dean suspension bogies mounted under vehicles covered in this book were of 6ft 4in wheelbase. With these bogies the spring hangers were attached to scroll-irons which, in turn, were fixed to the underframe.

Much better known, however, were the 8ft 6in and 10ft wheelbase suspension bogies generally introduced from 1892 and 1895 respectively. After the introduction of the 10ft type, the 8ft 6in bogies seem only to have been put under vehicles with a body length of less than 50ft. The centre-pin of the bogie floated in a casting positioned in the vee of the converging longitudinal members. The bogie scroll-irons, attached by brackets to the bogie frames, were also bolted to the coach solebars. The bases of each pair of scroll-irons were connected by a cross-stay which contained four circular pockets resting upon volute springs. A suspension bolt passed upwards through each spring and fitted into a spherical cup in the bracket, which was fixed to the bogie frame. The two main features of this design of bogie were, first, that contrary to general practice, the whole weight of the coach was not supported merely on the centre-pins of the bogies and therefore directly on bolsters; instead, it was distributed through the eight vertical scroll-irons.

The second factor was that bogie movement, both vertical and lateral, was permitted by the suspension bolts, the spherical bearings of which could move freely out of the vertical position in the cups. However, any such movement was controlled, firstly, by the volute springs, and generally by the centre-pin and its casting. This type of bogie avoided the problem of bolster bogies where the centre of support, that is the bogie centre-pin, transmits a rolling action to the coach body since there is little lateral control. This was achieved at some cost in maintenance but the bogies lasted some fifty years or so.

It has been suggested that Churchward may have been responsible for the principle of the suspension bogie design but it is noticeable that suspension bogies were discontinued with the last batches of clerestory stock. Some non-standard, elliptical-roofed, non-corridor thirds turned out in 1904 had an adaptation of the 10ft suspension bogies to a bolster design.

However, a more sophisticated type of bolster bogie was designed to take the place of the Dean suspension bogies. For the non-powered bogies of the earlier steam-railmotors, an 8ft type was produced in which a centre-casing rested upon, and was bolted to, wooden bolsters under which there were fourteen volute springs – seven each side – bearing on two 'vees'. Triple volute springs, placed on top of the axleboxes, fitted into the cast-steel horn-blocks. By this arrangement, the weight was transmitted from the bogie side-plates to the centres of the journals, so avoiding the twisting movement common to ordinary bolster bogies. The plate frames of this design were most striking: a similar pattern, with coil springs, was produced in limited numbers for corridor passenger stock and a few 'Dreadnoughts' were mounted on them.

Although some of the 'Dreadnoughts' and other elliptical-roof stock of the 1904–6 period were mounted on ordinary heavy bolster bogies of 9ft wheelbase, from about 1906 Swindon adopted equalised bogies of American design, with beams supported by coil springs, for the majority of standard coaches, railmotors, trailers and passenger brake vans. Both 8ft and 9ft wheelbase types were produced until just before the First World War. A newer, orthodox type of 9ft wheelbase was given the epithet 'fishbelly', as the bottom edge of the bogie frame was bowed. These were standard for new 57ft stock until 1924 and a number of earlier vehicles appeared to have been remounted on them.

Only a few six-wheel bogies were produced during this period. Two or three restaurant cars and the 1907 sleeping-cars were mounted on an American-pattern equalised type, but one or two of the later restaurant cars had a more ordinary British variety. In the majority of cases four-wheel 9ft wheelbase bogies were considered most suitable for the 70ft stock and the GWR vehicles were probably the longest at the time to run on four-wheel bogies.

For the 1922 'South Wales' stock, a new heavy-type 9ft bogie was produced which was used until 1932 for coaches over 60ft in length, restaurant cars, sleeping-cars, and, in addition, the 'Cornish Riviera' 60ft stock of 1929. However, from 1925 onwards, standard 57ft stock was mounted on a bogie of no more than 7ft wheelbase which had apparently been the outcome of many coach-riding trials, but its design seems to have been prompted by an official interest in reducing flange wear. No more 70ft stock was produced after 1925 because the flange-wear was thought excessive and the amount of lateral movement of the buffers on sharp curves brought the 70ft length into further disfavour. The 7ft bogie, however, reversed the generally held dictum that the longer the wheelbase the steadier the riding. Even at the end of their lives, the 7ft bogies gave quite a pleasant ride with a noticeably abrupt 'clicketty-click' over the rail-joints. Nearly all standard stock built between 1925 and 1932 was mounted on these bogies, although the majority of special duty vehicles, including the 1929 'Cornish Riviera' stock, were given the heavy-type 9ft wheelbase bogies. Little seems to have been done in the way of fitting roller-bearing axle boxes to GWR coaches, beyond a set of Timken bearings on a 1931 non-corridor suburban coach with 7ft bogies.

After 1932/3, a 9ft wheelbase, double bolster, pressed-steel bogie was standardised for virtually all new construction and, with slight variations,

The 8ft 6in wheelbase articulation bogie, joining coaches Nos 10006/07 of the 1925 articulated corridor stock. (Lots 1361/60 – Diagrams C.51/D.92) 'HW' painted on the body ends denoted that the lavatories had a hot water supply.

was used for all GWR-design stock up until 1954. From about 1938, however, new restaurant cars and older vehicles of this type currently being renovated were mounted on an 11ft 6in wheelbase six-wheel design, which was also applied to the Hawksworth sleeping-cars of 1951. Swindon was responsible, after nationalisation, for the production of a new standard bogie, and the pre-war pressed-steel design formed the basis of the new BR bogie, but with the addition of coil springs to its previously springless inner bolster and a reduction in wheelbase to 8ft 6in.

Until about 1906, round-shank, 2ft-long buffers with oblong heads were used for passenger stock, the length over buffers of a 56ft 0¾in body coach being 59ft 5in. After 1906, a 1ft 10in buffer with a square shank was standardised and, as a number of earlier coaches were fitted with this type, they consequently became four inches shorter in length over the buffers. The gangways of the early corridor coaches were side-positioned, which necessitated their being kept in permanent sets until they were later rebuilt. The majority of brake composites and saloons, as built in the 1890s and 1900s, were dual-fitted with vacuum and Westinghouse brakes.

One of the trademarks of the GWR was its perseverance with slip coaches and the fact that it perfected the system to a fine art. In 1909, the system of slipping coaches was considerably improved. In the old method, although the guard could apply the vacuum brake after operating the slip-lever, he had no means of releasing the brakes again and had to use his judgment to make the stop properly in the station (it should be remarked that horses were used to haul slip coaches into one or two stations until about the 1920s!). With the 1909 improvement of the apparatus, the vacuum pipes were fitted with adaptors to allow them to seal themselves automatically, thus preventing brakes being applied on the main section of the train.

Simultaneously, on pulling the slip-lever which

The guard's end of Toplight single slip No 7101. (Lot 1150 – Diagram F.14) Note the arrangement of couplings.

drew the bolt from the slip-hook, the guard's action also opened a valve applying air to the brake cylinder. Now, however, it was possible, once speed had dropped to between fifteen and twenty miles per hour, to put back the slip-lever into middle position, which restored vacuum to the brake cylinder by opening a valve connected to the six vacuum-reservoir tanks and exhausting the air in the cylinder. This permitted slips to be made further in advance of the stations and made the system obviously safer. As a result of the 1909 modification, the older clerestory slip coaches were fitted with vacuum reservoirs in the form of cylindrical tanks running most of the length of the roof alongside the clerestory. Two points worth mentioning about slip coaches are that the coaches were fitted with foot-operated warning horns and that the maximum permissible number of eight-wheel coaches which could be slipped was four – although in no circumstances could they be 70-footers.

Although the GWR did not contemplate Pullman gangways in the 1910s, the Continental ambulance trains formed during the First World War were required to be fitted with these throughout.

The necessity to keep a stock of dual-fitted vehicles was a problem which died out soon after 1925. In 1920, for instance, there were some 170 Westinghouse-equipped passenger coaches held at some eighteen stations, and, as late as 1923, a batch of new brake composites was built with dual fittings.

In 1922, two 'Toplight' composites and a restaurant car were fitted with buckeye couplers and formed as a set to obtain experience for future application. The original 'South Wales' sets of 1922–23 not only appeared with buckeye couplers of the Laycock pattern, but also Pullman gangways. Instead of applying these two features to the whole coach fleet, the GWR discarded neither screw couplings nor 'British Standard' gangways for its stock. By the late 1930s, the problem of coupling the two different types of gangways was found to be more acute, as the 'yellow disc' standard stock could now work on to LMS and LNER territory on a wider scale. From about 1938 onwards, therefore, gangway adaptors were fitted to several new coaches and gradually older vehicles were equipped. By the late 1950s, most of the stock likely to be marshalled with Pullman gangway coaches had received gangway adaptors. All corridor stock built from 1925 onwards had the 'suspended' gangway in place of the 'scissors' type, the new design having the gangway suspended from two steel rods hanging down from overhead brackets.

In 1929, the oblong-headed buffer was replaced as the standard type by a large circular variety with a convex bearing-face. No major alterations were made to the braking systems during this period. By way of record, Churchward gave the interesting snippet of information in 1921 that a train of fourteen 70ft coaches would stop on the level in about 700 yards from a speed of 70 m.p.h.

Bodywork

It sometimes seems surprising that the clerestory roof was so widely adopted by the British railways in view of its expense, the problem of condensation and the fact that its presence caused a weak roof assembly. With GWR stock the decklights and ventilators corresponded with the bodyside windows and ventilators, the vents in the clerestory being worked by projecting levers. The body framing of the Dean clerestories was built up from Stettin (Polish) oak, which was easily steamed, and teak. The standing and door pillars were morticed into the bottom sides and fixed by wrought-iron knees. The practice was to make the bodies to a plain 54, 56 or 58ft length and generally of 8ft 6in width, while the panelling and moulding accounted for the extra ¾in on each dimension. The partitions and floor were double-boarded. All external panelling was of Honduras mahogany.

Some of the earlier corridor coaches had blank, that is, non-opening, 'doors' to the centre compartment of the smoking-saloon. Except for very few, all side-corridor clerestory coaches had the awkward arrangement of hinged doors in the corridor partitions, although Dean's assistant, L. R. Thomas, patented sliding doors running on roller bearings in the 1890s. The second 1901 set of Milford boat stock had the unusual feature of wide sliding doors to the luggage compartment of the brake thirds. As mentioned on page 41, a number of non-corridor coaches built from the mid-1890s

onwards had 'pseudo-corridor' ends to take corridor connections, if required, at a later date, as did some slip coaches and non-corridor stock to 'Toplight' designs. After 1905, iron holders were fitted to the main part of the roofs of clerestory stock to take destination boards.

Churchward had pointed out, as previously mentioned, that British coaches were weaker than American stock because of the need to have a disjointed bodyside framing to accommodate the exterior compartment doors. The 'Dreadnoughts', therefore, demonstrated his point, since their lack of outside doors to every compartment permitted bodyside horizontal members of 30ft lengths; there being only three entrance doors to each side. Unfortunately, as described elsewhere, the public wanted compartments with individual outside access. Stock such as the 70ft 'Toplights', the body construction of which is illustrated on the following two pages, had the traditional layout.

The 'Toplight' stock, typifying GWR Edwardian practice, had bodies and roofs largely of oak framing, with double floors packed with sawdust. The bolection mouldings round the windows indicated that the glazing, set in window panes, was fitted into the bodyside from the outside. However, it was with the 'Toplight' stock that the greatest changes occurred in the use of materials. This was largely due to the rising cost of wood and, more directly, to a greater concern for fireproof coaches after two disastrous fires had broken out in derailed Midland Railway trains during the period. At the same time, gas lighting was superseded by electricity.

From 1910 the use of mahogany for body panelling was gradually discontinued, and in 1911 a 57ft 'Toplight' was completed with galvanised

A slip has been made at Didcot West Curve Junction on 7 June 1960; this was the last regular *multiple* slip in the British Isles, and was from the 7am Weston-super-Mare–Paddington. Into Didcot at 9.06am, the coaches went forward to Oxford. The slip coach is one of the Hawksworth conversions, coupled to a bow-end second-class (formerly third). Note the bow-end brake vehicle in departmental use on the far side.

The Laycock buckeye coupler on the 70ft composite dining cars, Diagram H.26.

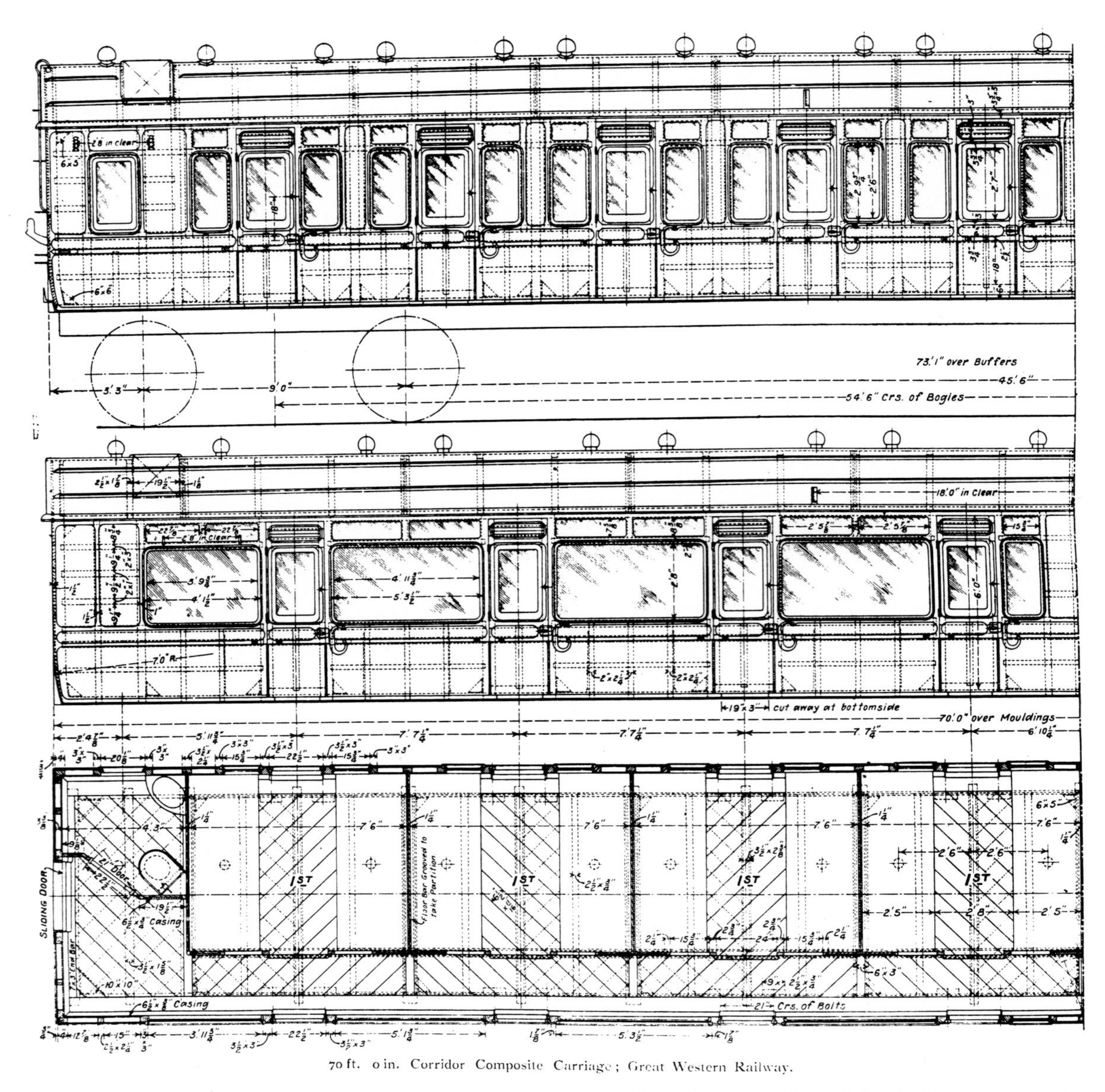

Constructional detail drawings of a GWR 70ft Toplight corridor composite.

steel body-panelling and an experimental fireproof floor. Others followed and, from 1913 onwards, bodyside steel-panelling and fireproof flooring became the rule. The standard 'Toplight' of 1914 had the compartment partitions formed of part corrugated-steel and part ordinary flush-steel panelling. The floor had an oak frame covered with corrugated steel and fireproofing material. Galvanised bodyside panelling was screwed onto the body framing after special treatment as, without this, the paint tended to peel off.

In early 1914, an experimental 57ft corridor third had been ordered which was completely fireproof, with steel body framing and both ends and body sides steel-panelled. It was not completed until 1921. Steel body framing was not adopted as standard, probably because it was felt that, with sufficient fireproofing, a wooden-framed coach was almost as good insurance against fire. An important development was the use of steel-panelling for roofs – a batch of non-corridor firsts produced in 1922 were prototypes in this respect – while all coaches now had steel-panelled ends.

The standard corridor and non-corridor stock built up to the early 1930s featured all these improvements, while the facilities for the production of steel roof-panelling were greatly improved. The most notable feature was the bow-ended outline that was adopted from the 1925 period which meant that what may be described as 57ft or 60ft body length coaches were 58ft 4½in or 61ft 4½in over the end panels. As from 1933, roof-panels were rivetted. Another development of some interest in 1927 was the adoption of slam-locks for compartment doors, but not for corridor and vestibule entry doors. The persistence with non-slam doorlocks on corridor doors was an anachronism which survived until nationalisation. It was argued that this practice was safer, as a door could not be only partly shut: in order to close it, the handle had to be fully turned.

Of more consequence was the introduction in 1929 of stock with the windows all but flush with the bodyside panelling. The new standard 60ft-plus coaches built between 1929 and 1933 had

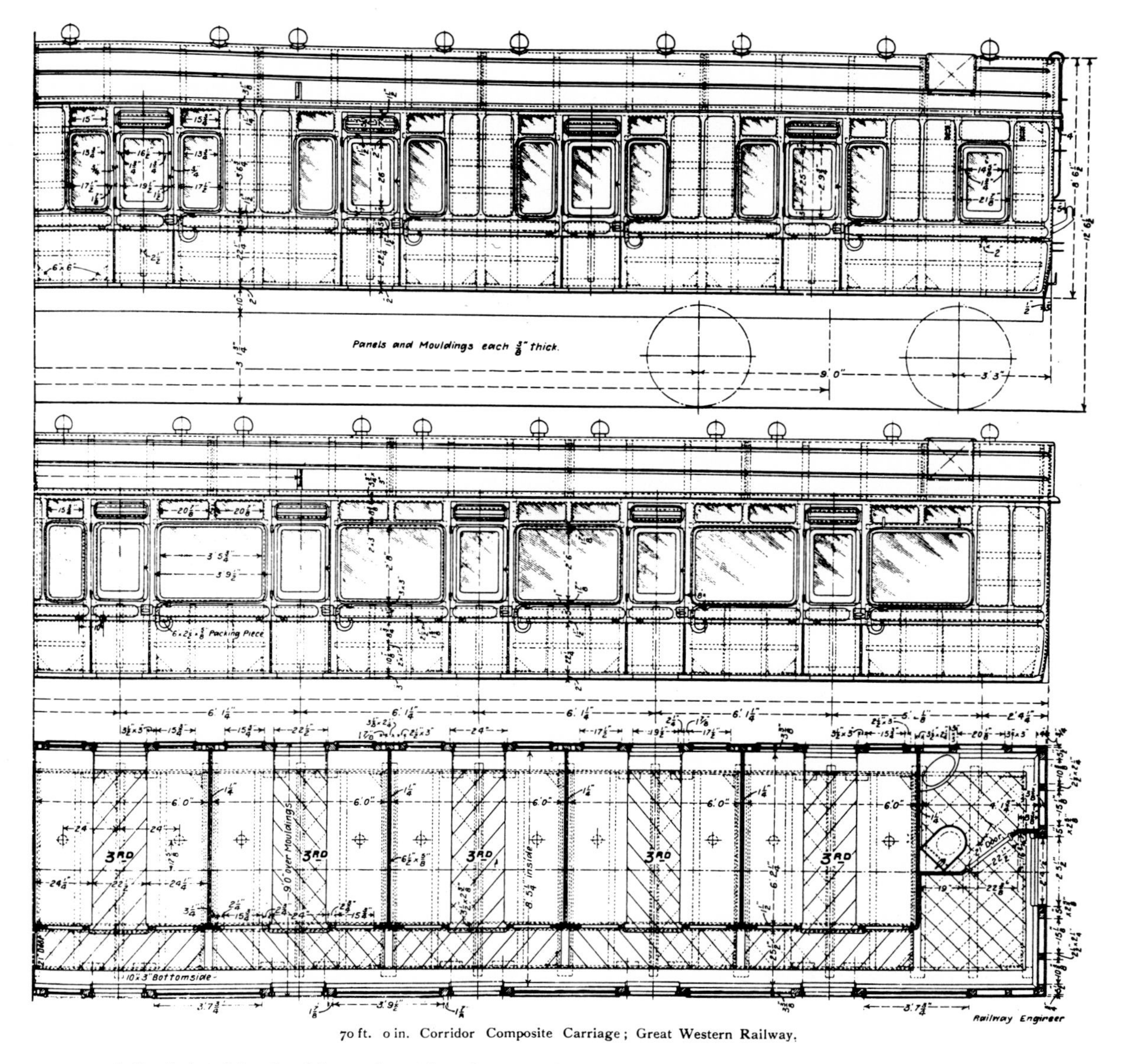

70 ft. 0 in. Corridor Composite Carriage; Great Western Railway.

unusual 'bulging' bodysides, the idea being that the body could be bulged out at below waist level to maximum width to allow more spacious seating, at the same time keeping the whole vehicle within the GWR general loading gauge. However, one of the big disadvantages of 9ft 3in width stock of this period was that it was restricted from running on a number of LMS and LNER routes. Another feature of the bodywork of this stock was that the roof was carried back sufficiently to form a gutter between it and the cornice plates. Body framing was of oak, teak and mahogany with bagac cantrails and oak or ash hoopsticks. The door handles and grips, which were chromium-plated in some cases, were recessed into the body-panelling in most of this 60ft-plus stock.

The remaining pre-war stock was constructed to the same principles, although the most important change was in the adoption of the end-vestibule layout for corridor stock, with resultant long bodyside frame members. For 1936, this was standard practice and did not incur the unpopularity that had greeted the 'Dreadnought' stock thirty years earlier. An important decision of 1937 was to build all future general service stock to an 8ft 11in waist width – identified by a yellow disc on the body ends – to allow greater route availability off GWR territory. Other details introduced with the 1936–40 standard stock included the adoption of large windows to the compartments with sliding ventilators, and some with the 'vane' wind-deflectors.

Direct assembly of the body on to the underframe was the notable change in construction technique introduced with the Hawksworth corridor and non-corridor stock after 1945. The underframes were fitted with steel brackets, into which the bottom ends of the body pillars were received, while the top ends fitted into similar steel brackets welded to steel cantrails – which were in themselves an innovation. For a start, this method of assembly eliminated the use of the long horizontal timber body members which were difficult to obtain at the time. The floor of the coaches, consisting of two thicknesses of laminated wood treated with asbestos with a sandwich filling of asbestos, was assembled directly onto the underframe instead of forming part of the body-unit. Ordinary mild-steel body panelling, screwed to the framing, was used for the standard vehicles

A good illustration of the direct-building method adopted for Hawksworth stock.

of this type; some had aluminium body panels. The roofs, which sloped down at the ends, were of normal rivetted construction, while the destination board brackets were mounted at cantrail level in LMS style. Direct assembly was not, of course, a unique system of construction, since something similar had been done by the LMS. Yet another change from normal practice was in the slab-sided profile, which meant that there were no curved body pillars which normally formed the 'tumblehome' body-side contour. The underframes of Hawksworth stock were of standard rivetted construction.

Quite apart from the employment of this method of wood and steel construction, experimental vehicles of part light-alloy materials were produced, as part of Swindon's research at that time into lightweight rolling stock, and the comparison of service experience with alternative materials. A corridor third, ordered in 1944, was built with a part aluminium underframe. Another vehicle had part aluminium body framing and window ventilators, while a batch of twenty-five coaches was completed with aluminium body panelling.

Availability of GWR passenger stock – in general
(dimensions given are length over buffers, width over waist)

73ft by 9ft 6in: Cannot be accepted by any other company. 'Red Triangle stock.' Must not work N of Wolverhampton or Hereford, E & W Valleys or Cambrian lines, and other local exceptions.

73ft by 9ft: Cannot be accepted by any other company except Cambrian lines – main lines only – and into Salisbury. Also permitted Yate to Standish Jc. Also local GWR restrictions.

70ft by 9ft 6in: Cannot be accepted by any other company. 'Red Triangle stock' similarly restricted as 73ft by 9ft 6in stock.

63ft 6in by 9ft 5¾in or 9ft 7in: 'Red Triangle stock.' Cannot be accepted by any other company. Must not work N of Wolverhampton or Leominster, over E & W Valleys or between Maindee and Little Mill Junctions. Until 1943, barred between Churchdown and Gloucester. Permitted south of Saltney Junction after 1945 (which meant in practice that they were just excluded from Chester) and to Pembroke Dock from 1939.

63ft 6½in by 9ft 3in: Not accepted at all by LNER or SR. Restricted major route acceptance by LMS.

63ft 6½in by 9ft or 60ft by 9ft: Fairly general acceptance by other railways, although not allowed on parts of ex-Midland lines or over parts of the SE&C section of SR.

64–67ft by 8ft 11in: 'Yellow Disc stock.' General acceptance by other railways, except certain LMS branches and Furness and Maryport & Carlisle lines, and various SE&C section routes.

Clerestory stock with lookouts was restricted to same extent as 9ft 3in width stock.

The 'Red Triangle' and 'Yellow Disc' markings were displayed on the ends of the vehicles. A small plate reading 'WXQ' denoted that the vehicle could work over the Weymouth Quay 'tramway'.

Passenger Comforts

The general evolution of the passenger coach to a layout and standard of comfort regarded as suitable until recently was achieved in virtually twenty years: from 1890 to 1910. The Birkenhead corridor set was the first train with throughout steam-heating and among the first with some form of communication between passenger and guard. Illumination in clerestory stock was provided by long pendants hanging below the level of the clerestory with fishtail burners fed by compressed oil-gas stored in cylinders under the coach. The first oil-gas plant on the GWR, at Swindon, was put into use early in 1893. All GWR restaurant cars, from the pioneer of 1896 to the very last, had gas cooking. Propane gas equipments were fitted to ex-GWR restaurant cars from c1955.

Steam heating was as notable an improvement in passenger comfort as decent lighting. Churchward, in a lecture given to the Swindon Junior Engineering Society in January 1896, mentioned that the heating surface for first-, second- and third-class compartments had been arrived at as follows:

First-class:	One inch of two-inch bore pipe per 3.6 cu ft of compartment.
Second-class:	One inch of two-inch bore pipe per 3.5 cu ft of compartment.
Third-class:	One inch of two-inch bore pipe per 3.0 cu ft of compartment.

The difference in constant heat was arrived at through consideration of the ability of the extra horsehair and trimmings in the higher classes to retain heat after the compartment had been initially warmed! A refinement of the first-class compartments during Dean's time was a thermometer, its presence being indicated by a button on the carriage door near the handle. Unfortunately, passengers found good use for them at home! The temperature of the compartments was normally maintained at the 55–60°F level. Footwarmers were out of general use by 1901 but available on special request until 1908. Non-corridor stock without steam-heating pipes was still being built up until 1901, while an oil-lit non-corridor coach was put into service as late as 1896, although gas lighting had been generally standardised since 1882.

Communication systems were improved, although what is now regarded as the standard system, with a chain partially enclosed in tubing at cantrail level and indicator discs at the ends of the coaches, was not introduced until the Milford boat sets of 1900–1. These sets were the first to bring the novelty of electric lighting to the ordinary passenger, although the first electrically-lit vehicles on the GWR were to be found in the 1897 Royal train. The rather orange glow of early electric lights was, however, inferior to gas lighting, the use of which was prolonged by the introduction for passenger coaches of the incandescent mantle in 1905, and the inverted burner in 1907. Although the railways were somewhat loath to scrap expensive oil-gas installations, the GWR built no new stock, excepting rail-motors and trailers, with gas lighting after 1911.

The proportions of incandescent gas and electrically-lit GWR passenger stock in 1910 and 1925 were as follows:

	1914	*1925*
Incandescent gas	52.7%	68.9%
Electric	10.8%	28.2%

Balance made up by flat-flame gas-lit stock

The early systems for electrically-lit stock are interesting: in 'Stone's' system, which was used for most of the pioneer vehicles with electric lighting, including the 1897 Royal Train, to prevent overcharging of the accumulators, once an optimum speed was attained by the train, the dynamo belt slipped from the driving shaft. The 'Leitner' system, which became standard from the late 1900s, was better in that the brightness of the lighting was self-regulating. In a number of the set trains, including some Fishguard boat-train sets of 1910, instead of independent lighting-generator sets, the brake vehicles acted as generator coaches, supplying current for the whole train. This rather unsatisfactory method was probably adopted on grounds of lower cost per vehicle than the 'self-lit' arrangements.

Unlike the other 'Big Four' companies, post-Grouping GWR stock did not have reading lights in either first- or third-class compartments. During the 1920s and 1930s, there were minor improvements to heating, lighting and communication. Graduated heat control was introduced and the communication cord was generally concealed, except for a short length over the large compartment windows. The 1935–39 Excursion sets had neat cube lightshades to all lights but, in general, all light bulbs were unadorned as, of course, they were in BR stock of the 1950s and early 1960s.

One of the most interesting of the unfulfilled post-war intentions concerned lighting. It was confidently announced in 1945 that all future main line passenger stock would be fluorescently lit: in contrast, 389 coaches were still gas-lit in 1948. The third-class corridor coaches which appeared from late 1946 were the first fluorescently-lit main-line stock in the country – London Transport was the pioneer for all types of stock, as some District Line cars had been fitted with fluorescent tubes in late 1944.

The system for the GWR coaches, which was developed jointly by Swindon and British Thomson-Houston, had the power taken from the existing lighting set and batteries which fed a motor-alternator set generating current at a frequency of 400 cycles. The high frequency was adopted to reduce the size and weight of underframe equipment, which added about ten hundredweight to the tare weight of the coach. In the first-class compartments, two tubes were placed behind the front of each luggage rack, with a single tube in the ceiling. In the third-class compartments there were two tubes in the ceiling only. In addition to ordinary all-third and composite corridor coaches – just half-a-dozen were fluorescently lit – one sleeping-car renovated in 1946 had fluorescent tubes. In the event, the new Hawksworth production-series standard coaches had normal filament lights and the only refinement was in the form of illuminated signs including the position of the toilet!

Apart from any general considerations, the idea of building all the new stock with fluorescent lighting seems to have been dropped because the system still needed perfection for non-electric stock, particularly when the batteries were not fully charged. Another important point was that the cold cathode tube had yet to be developed, and the earlier hot cathode tubes gave an unnatural reddish cast to the lighting which was unpleasant in the confines of a compartment, apart from their having a shorter life. It was 1951 before cold cathode lighting was installed experimentally in an open first of LMS design, and 1959 before BR produced stock with fluorescent lighting, in the shape of the St Pancras–Bedford diesel-multiple unit sets which made use of progress with transistorised equipment.

Coach Interiors

In spite of its obvious importance to passengers, not only in terms of comfort but as a general impression of rail travel, coach interior design has been a casually determined science until recently, and one neglected by railway historians. As to design, it is perhaps a reflection of general household taste during the period that few

Top:
The carved walnut seat-backs and morocco leather upholstered tip-up seats in the first-class saloon of Dreadnought restaurant car No 1575 – later 7575 and 9515. (Lot 1056 – Diagram H.8)

Above:
The interior of one of the saloons in nondescript brake saloon No 9110. (Lot 1400 – Diagram G.58) The side internal corridor is to the right. Note the central table with hinged flaps.

changes occurred in coach interior furnishings from 1890 to mid-1930, beyond simplification of materials, woodwork and features such as luggage-racks. The design features of the 'jazz-era' and chromium-plate mania made little impact on GWR stock beyond the 1935–39 Excursion sets and some restaurant cars. Post-war practice showed some interesting departures in the use of panelling materials and improvements in general features, including interior fittings in the lavatories.

As mentioned before, coach layouts were largely unaltered because public opinion was heavily in favour of the side-corridor arrangement. Passengers were also, it seems, thought to imagine a typical compartment as one with solid mahogany woodwork and sombre upholstery. Much of the enthusiastic reception of diesel railcars in the 1950s and 1960s was no doubt due to a departure from this concept.

To simplify description of GWR coach interiors in standard stock, the table on the next page summarises salient details. It is difficult to be accurate about interiors, and also interesting that there is no complete record of the materials used by the GWR at Swindon. For non-standard stock and specialised vehicles, similar details are given in the sections dealing with each design. Restaurant cars come largely into this category but some of the 1922–30 period vehicles can be described here as having the 'standard' woodwork of the period with brown cloth-covered seats for the first-class and brown hide tip-up seats in the third-class.

General improvements in design largely followed changes in materials, the adoption of more comfortable seating, such as the displacement of horsehair padding by springs for seat cushions in the late 1920s, and a steady betterment of the spartan facilities in lavatories. Woodwork sprayed with a cellulose varnish finish became standard in the early 1930s, but was later discarded in view of the fire-risk it presented. Vertically-fluted seat-backs came in during the mid-1930s, in place of the earlier horizontal stitching which produced bumps in the wrong places, catching the passenger across the back. Buttoned-in seat-backs only disappeared during the 1920s, and interior panelling largely deteriorated in finish during the 1920s and 1930s. The usual choice for interior panelling was walnut, offset by sycamore. Eventually, blockboard covered with a nondescript veneer was used for the compartment partition panelling in the mid-1930s. Over the years, many of the wood finishes lost their identity beneath thick coats of varnish or overall 'tarring' with cream or brown paint. From 1939, a green Rexine material was used instead of polished wood panelling in non-corridor first-class stock, and in the lavatories of corridor coaches.

In 1945, it was decided to renovate ninety restaurant cars built during 1922–39. The schemes were devised by an interior-decoration contractor and, although in keeping with contemporary taste in restaurant and café décor, were not popular with the general staff. Full details are given in Chapter 10. The original scheme was applied only to the first few restaurant cars. In the first-class saloons, new wood finishes of sapele veneer were applied, with decorative pink-tinted mirrors. Revolving pedestal-mounted chairs were an unusual feature for the GWR, while the centre panels of the ceilings were flat, with recessed lighting. The third-class saloons had ash panelling, tip-up seating, recessed lighting and pastel finishes to upholstery and curtains. Most of the renovated restaurant vehicles received a less flamboyant décor with bench-type leather seats and glass screens above the seat-backs. Contractors were also responsible for refurbishing a corridor composite of 1936–40 design.

Further renovation schemes were carried out on a handful of sleeping-cars, plastic finishes and modern fittings generally improving their appearance.

Post-war corridor stock had two styles of interior décor: one with wood veneer, the other with 'Holoplast' enamelled panelling. Both had greatly improved luggage racks without archaic bracket supports, while the 'Holoplast' scheme coaches had frameless mirrors only in place of photographs of prancing racehorses at Cheltenham races or sunny Salcombe, very much *à la* 1925. As an aside, it was remarkable that as late as 1966 surviving pre-war coaches still had GWR route maps showing some lines that had been closed for at least thirty years! One of the most important improvements in the Hawksworth stock concerned the lavatories, which were improved much beyond the ship-like simplicity and spartan discomfort of most previous stock. Laminated plastic was used for panelling and this concealed all the waterpipes. The floor was also finished in a more civilised fashion with mottled tiles, while the washbasin and pedestal were of primrose-coloured ware. The improvements appear to have been followed in the BR standard coach design.

A SUMMARY OF STANDARD COACH INTERIORS: 1890–1950

Period	Class	Woodwork/Wall Covering		Upholstery			Metalwork
		Primary Woodwork	Trim/ Inlay	First-Class	Second-Class	Third-Class	
Current in 1890-1895	1st	Walnut/oak	Dark walnut/ dark oak	Crimson plush	Rep	Rep	Brass
	2nd	Oak	Lincrusta Wax-cloth				
	3rd	Mahogany	—		Smoking compts. in leather		
c1896	1st } 2nd	Dark oak	Lincrusta	'Fancy' moquette or blue cloth	Velvet terry or rep.	Fawn rep.	Brass
	3rd	Mahogany	—		Smoking compts. in leather		
c1900	1st	Walnut	Sycamore	Dark green cloth or leather	Brown and white 'star' motif moquette	Dark red and white 'star'	Brass
	2nd	Mahogany	—				
	3rd	Oak	—		Smoking compts. in leather		
c1911	1st 3rd	Walnut Dark oak	Sycamore Light oak	Dark green cloth, green/gold trimmings	Blue and red rep. (some c1905, red and black rep. or maroon leather)		Brass
1922-1929	1st 3rd	Walnut Mahogany	Sycamore —	Dark brown cloth Gold trimmings	Red and black rep. 'Cauliflower' motif		Brass
1929	3rd	Mahogany or Walnut	Sycamore	Beige and black moquette	Grey and black moquette		Oxydised bronze
1936	1st } 3rd	Birchwood	Walnut	Blue and green 'Tartan'	Orange and brown 'fan' motif Gold and brown curtains		Oxydised bronze
1939 (non-cor)	1st		Green/blue	Rexine			
	3rd	—	—	—	Green		—
1946-c1948	1st 3rd	Maple Oak	— —	'Fruit-bowl' motif fawn on dark blue ground:smokers; dark red ground: non-smokers	Fawn filigree on dark blue ground: smokers; dark red ground: non-smokers		Oxydised bronze
c1948-c1950	1st } 3rd	Cream 'Holoplast' in compartments	Chocolate 'Holoplast' with cream horizontal lines	as above	as above		as above
		Chocolate 'Holoplast' in corridors	Cream horizontal lines				

Top Left:
A view along the corridor alongside the third-class compartments in a Diagram E.151 corridor composite of 'Sunshine' stock. Above the waistline the panels are birchwood, below is in walnut finish.

Above:
The interior of the dining saloon of a brake first-saloon to Diagram G.59 – Lot 1431. Walnut bodyside panelling, with upholstery in beige, with black and brown patterns.

Top Right:
The handsome interior of a Centenary first-class compartment, in this case brake composite No 6650 (Diagram E.150 – Lot 1539). The panelling is in light oak with figured panels above the seats, inlaid with walnut. The upholstery was of a blue, green and brown check pattern.

Above:
One of Hampton's first exercises in the renovation of GWR restaurant cars during the postwar years – No 9672, Diagram H.57 – Lot 1601. This is the first-class saloon. The walls are panelled in sapele, with peach-glass mirrors between the windows. The lighting consists of the circular opal bowls in the recessed 'false clerestory', with circular concealed lights in the ceiling above each table. Bronze and beige curtains, and revolving chairs mounted on pedestals. Chairs and tables were covered in smoke-blue hide.

One of the experimental interiors, in Hawksworth corridor third No 784. (Lot 1691 – Diagram C.82) Laminated plastic panelling, fluorescent lighting and non-standard upholstery. Note the curtains to the corridor partition windows.

Great Western Coach Liveries 1890–1947

The livery applied to the coaching stock of the GWR in the late 1890s was second to none from the point of view of its appeal and attractiveness to the beholder. Before turning to general changes, in this latest edition of *Great Western Coaches from 1890* some of the finer details of the GWR liveries applied over the years, ie brandings, insignia and other small items which more often than not do not appear on scale models or restored rolling stock are featured in accompanying drawings. If those details are incorporated, the finished vehicle (scale model or full-size) is that much closer to the genuine Swindon product.

It is fair to say that the generally termed 'chocolate and cream' livery was responsible for much of the popularity of GWR trains, particularly after the Grouping. However, the two-colour livery always had a popular following, not only because it was in keeping with the GWR tradition, but also because it was essentially an attractive combination of tones.

The two-colour livery can be traced back to 1864 when it was decided to paint white the roofs and all panels above the waist line. Because the oil varnishes made up from natural resins in those days were much darker than the synthetic varnish in use today, the white panels took a soft, creamy appearance. For this reason, the London & North Western Railway used a blued white for the upper panels of its two-colour livery. Thus the evolution of the GWR's distinctive scheme owed something to chance.

'Chocolate and cream' was established for posterity and its popularity was seldom in doubt. At a much later date, at the time of official deliberations during the late 1940s concerning the adoption of a standard passenger stock livery for the then new British Railways, chocolate and cream was still well liked. In the summer of 1950, *Trains Illustrated* ran a competition in the form of a ballot to determine the most popular livery; the GWR style of painting came out top with fifteen per cent more votes than the runner-up, which was the Southern's malachite green. The next most favoured two-colour scheme – BR's recently introduced crimson and cream – was some 25% behind in terms of readers' votes.

The livery applied from the early 1890s to the early 1900s was as follows: bottom panels, waist panels and body ends were finished in Windsor brown, together with the underframe. Windsor brown was a very dark, plain chocolate shade. The panels above the waist line were creamy white. The flat sections of the body mouldings were picked out with drop black. Then the edges of the moulding were lined with a ⅜in line of gold leaf. On the cream panel approximately 1in from the moulding, a ⅛in brown line was painted. The bolections (raised mouldings around the windows) and window droplights were varnished in natural wood: in most cases this was mahogany. The underframes were finished in Windsor brown, but bogie frames and general ironwork, together with the wheels, were black. If a vehicle was fitted with Mansell wheels the wheel-centres may have been varnished natural wood when new. Roofs would be finished with white lead paint. Numbering was in gold, shaded black and approximately 2in high, displayed in the panels below the cant-rail. Generally the number was displayed three times – two in the case of brake coaches – as symmetrically as possible. Class designations were in Egyptian letters shaded black. All letters and figures were in gold leaf. On the lower body panels, the GWR monogram was displayed two to each side – more often than not. There were two versions of this monogram quite different in design from each other. The ventilator bonnets were on each vane shaded from brown into cream. The area between the cant-rail and the roof rain-strip was painted a dull brown. This would almost certainly be body brown and without varnish. Body end mouldings were painted plain black.

A number of changes subsequently took place. The sides to the clerestory deck, the panelling of which was previously lined in the same style as the body, were painted Windsor brown following the adoption of unpanelled sides to the clerestory deck – from about 1898. Restaurant and sleeping cars had their designations on the waist panels to suit the vehicle in the same style of Egyptian letters as the class designations. A painting diagram for 1903, the result of research at Swindon in the early 1950s, shows some modifications to the basic livery. The ⅛in brown line on the cream panels was shown much closer to the moulding. Bolections and droplights were painted

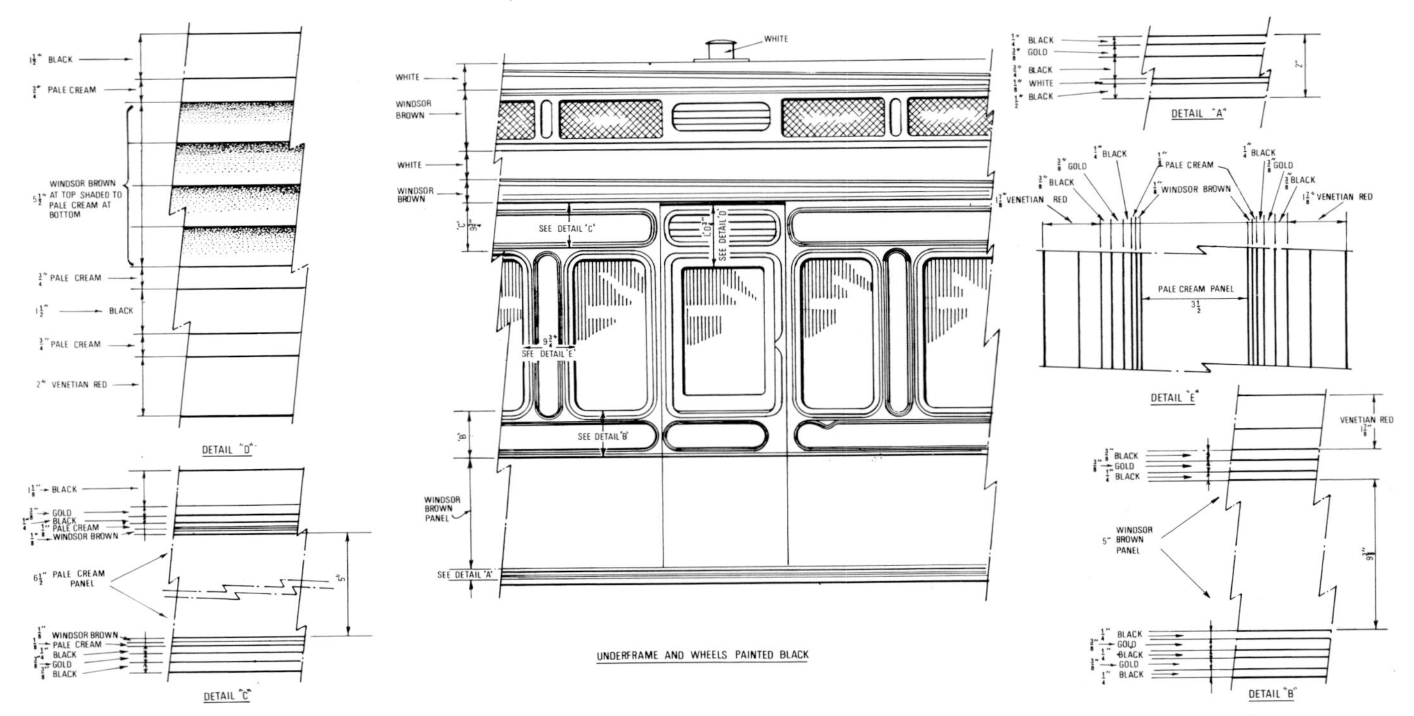

Livery scheme, c1903 as applied to Dean clerestory stock. The original drawing was prepared at Swindon, 1952, for filming work.

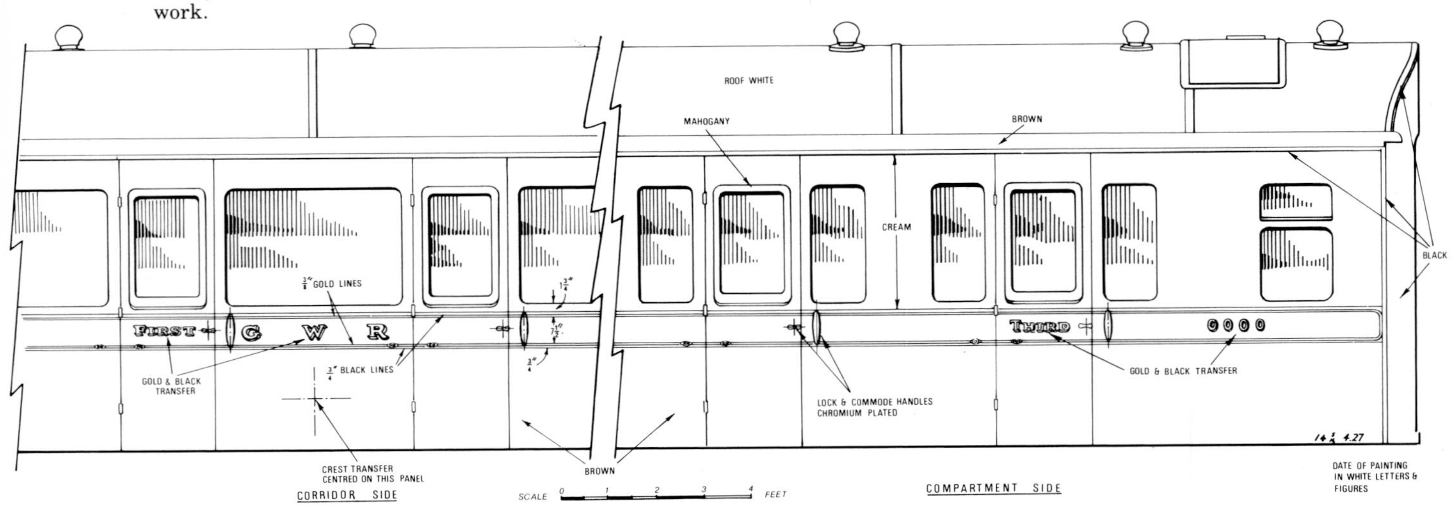

Livery scheme, 1930, as applied in this instance to 60ft bow-ended stock. Prepared from Swindon drawing 82868A dated February 1930.

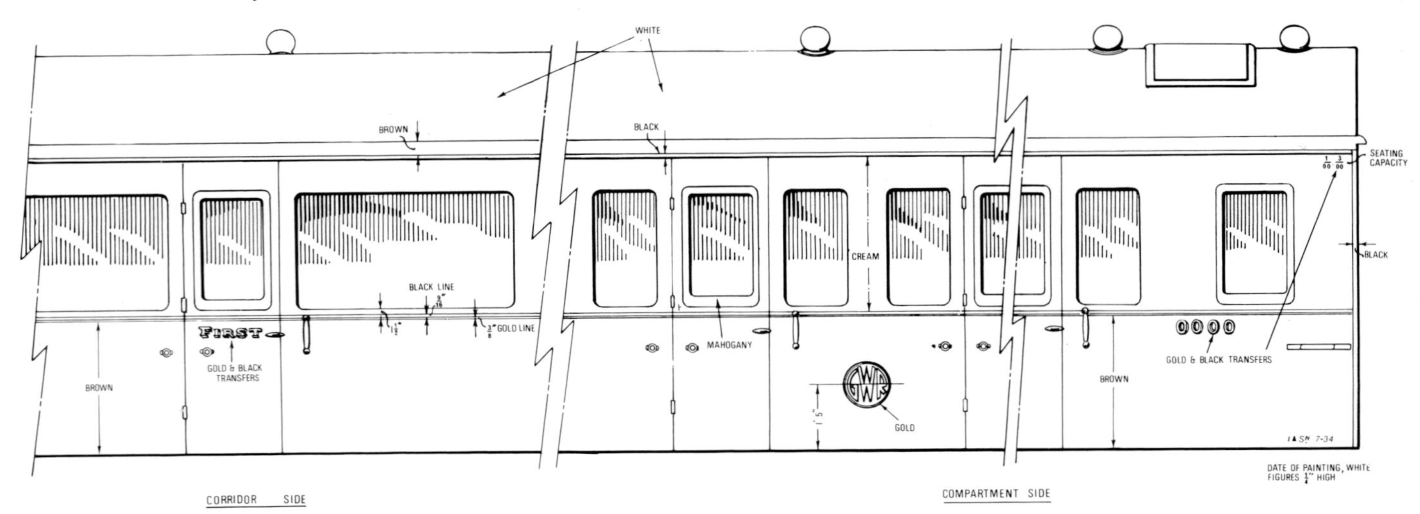

Livery scheme, 1934, as applied in this instance to 57ft stock. Prepared from Swindon drawing 101837, dated July 1934.

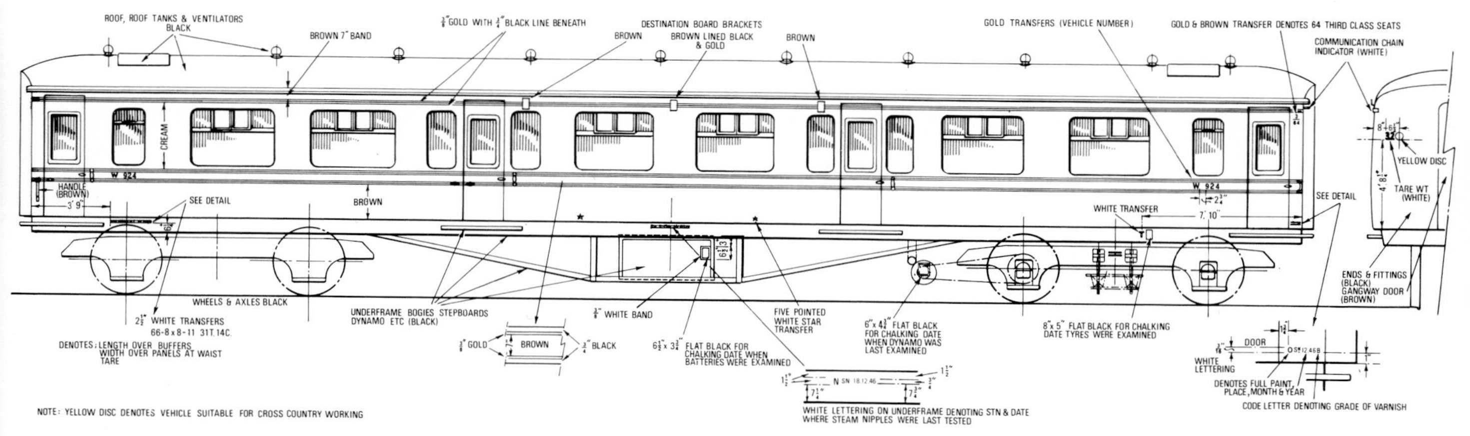

Livery scheme, 1947, as applied in this instance to Hawksworth corridor stock. The door droplights were painted maroon. Although dated January 1947, the original Swindon drawing, 124284B (as redrawn here) shows a BR prefix to the number.

Venetian red, although this would probably apply only to repainted vehicles whose fittings were by then badly stained. Underframes were painted black, in place of the previous Windsor brown.

Once G. J. Churchward was fully in command at Swindon, the winds of change blew with some force. One of the most noticeable traditions to suffer was of course the beautiful two-colour livery, as a result of a report on carriage cleaning dated November 1902 and referred to elsewhere. In criticising the existing state of affairs in general, the officers responsible concluded: 'A report shall also be prepared . . . [as] to whether the colours in which they [the coaches] are painted are the most suitable that can be devised'. This subsequent report, assuming it was completed, does not seem to have survived in the official archives. Shortly after the 1902 report, a number of coaches were put into traffic in a deep brown livery. However, it is not known whether this was the straight Windsor brown. After all, it was the cream that showed the dirt and grime, and not the brown.

The brown lake which was applied to some vehicles at this time would probably be a form of madder lake which was noted for colour fastness and durability and was available in rich, warm tones. In 1907, the two-colour livery was changed. Coach ends were now painted black, and coach numbers moved down to the waist bands. From about 1905, a much larger monogram replaced the one used throughout the 1890s: this would be the same that appeared on locomotive tenders. Shortly afterwards, the monogram was replaced by the well-known garter arms. It was possibly one of the best examples of the way that the science of heraldry was debased by our Victorian-Edwardian forefathers. One wonders who thought of putting the crests of the cities of London and Bristol halfway down the coach side instead of in their proper place above the respective city shields. At this time, steam rail-motors and auto-trailers were painted in the same manner as other vehicles, but for some reason carried very large fleet numbers and this practice was carried into the days of the GWR's diesel railcars.

From 1908, the two-colour livery was discontinued in favour of an overall colour described as a chocolate-lake. Lining and insignia remained much the same as before, but yellow ochre was used for lining from about 1907–1910. From 1912, a much deeper shade of chocolate was used for the basic scheme.

After 1913, with the adoption of steel body panelling for 'Toplight' stock, it was decided to paint imitation panels to represent the wooden mouldings used with the wooden body panels. This may seem strange to modern thinking, but it avoided a complete break in coach painting practice which went back to the days of the stage-coach. Another reason for painting these imitation panels would be to lessen the effect of cracking and chipping of paint around the steel panel joints and fixing points.

Victorian travel comfort – interior of a Dean non-corridor composite first-class compartment.

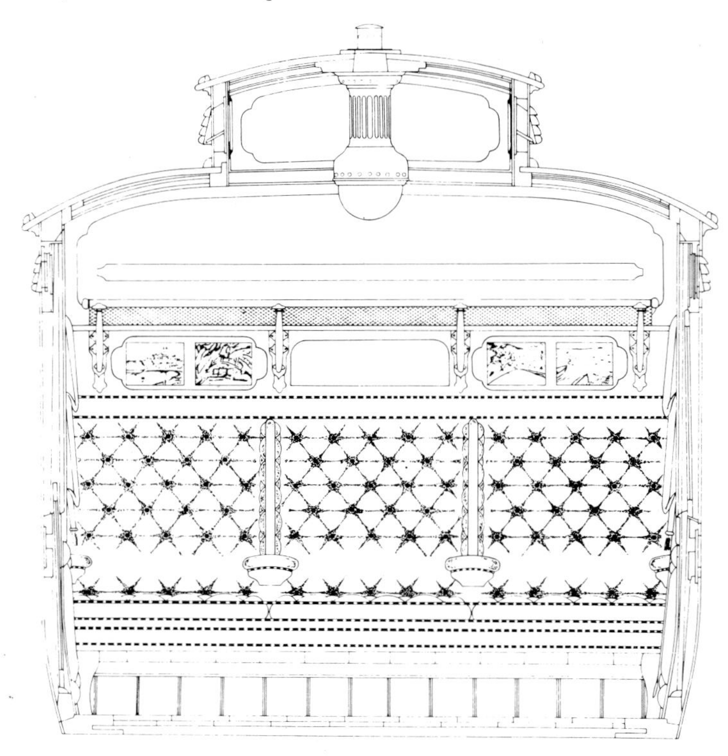

Top:
The effect of the false mouldings painted on steel panelled stock after 1923. The detail of the panels is shown in the photograph on page 23. The coach is brake third No 4915, a typical bow-ender. (Lot 1375 – Diagram D.95)

Above:
The later wartime livery on corridor third No 563. (Lot 1623 – Diagram C.77)

At this time, shortly before the First World War, after the normal application of primer stopping and fillings to the body sides, passenger stock was finished as follows: one coat ground colour; one coat of finishing lake, then four coats of coach varnish with denibbing or flatting taking place between coats. Compared with more recent practice, with the use of glossy or semi-glossy paints, the vehicles were finished in a final flat coat and then varnished. The imitation panels were set out with special templates. The gilding would be carried out using ribbon gold, a special type of gold leaf used for gilding and lining on transport vehicles of all types. The overall finish that resulted was expected to last up to ten years before repainting, but passenger stock employed on crack services would be given a 'flat and varnish' at regular intervals in the meantime.

Coaches repainted during the First World War do not seem to have emerged with any noticeable form of economy livery. From this time, clerestory stock had the clerestory deck-lights painted over. The first home-use ambulance trains supplied by, and continuing to remain in the ownership of the GWR, were painted in the full livery of the period. Later ambulance trains sold to the Government were outshopped in an unlined livery with the toplights painted over.

Following the First World War, maintenance had fallen into arrears and it was decided to restore the traditional two-colour livery. The first trains to appear in the old colours were the sets for the Cornish Riviera, ready for the start of the summer service in 1922. At this time, the well-known cream destination boards with black Egyptian letters were introduced.

The bow-ended, steel-panelled stock introduced from 1925 was at first painted with the imitation panels, but it was felt that this practice did not show off the modern lines of those vehicles, as well as adding to the cost of painting. From the middle of 1927, a much plainer livery was applied, and until around 1930 all lining appears to have been dispensed with. From about 1927 the garter arms was replaced by the heraldically more correct twin-shield device with the two city crests placed in their proper place over the respective shields. Having gone from the 'painted ladies' to the 'plain Janes', in 1930–3 we see a return to a generally simple lining scheme with double and single lining on the waist line. At this time it was decided to discontinue applying 'Third' to doors, but it had to be reintroduced with the new vestibule ('Sunshine') stock in 1936. In 1934, the 'shirt-button' roundel using the letters GWR was introduced, first appearing on buffet cars Nos 9631/2. Buffet cars were given a cream panel in which was emblazoned BUFFET CAR in gold-lined black. Nos 9631/2 also had a cream ground to their roundels, painted by hand, these cars being prototypes for the display of this device, and before a supply of transfers had been produced. Other special use vehicles had their designations displayed below the waist line in the standard 3⅛in Egyptian letters, gold, shaded

black. The 'Super Saloons' had their names in the centre of the lower panels, flanked either side by the twin-shield device, or roundel, depending on the period. One practice dropped in the 1930s was the use of painted seat indicator boards on the vehicle sides; their place was taken by boards carrying car letters instead. These were painted brown with a golden ochre 8in letter lined with a 3/16in black line. Letter boards seem to have appeared on TPO vans from about 1929/30. At this time, only two coats of varnish were applied instead of the four in earlier times. From 1935, some passenger brake vans appeared in an all-brown livery, but those used on front-line passenger work remained in the two-colour scheme. From the outbreak of the Second World War, roofs were no longer painted white because of the danger of being spotted from the air by enemy aircraft, but for some time after 1939, stock continued to be outshopped in the two-colour livery, but later in overall brown. In 1942, a wartime livery was introduced, using a red-brown shade of paint and the lining was a single 3/4in orange line along the waist.

With the appearance of the Hawksworth stock came the return of the two-colour livery. A new letter face was introduced, the Great Western's own version of Gill Sans. The GWR never could use other people's ideas without modifying them first! In the centre of the lower body panels, the words Great Western were incorporated with the arms of London and Bristol, this being the first time the company's name had appeared emblazoned on its rolling stock. Roofs were either painted black or dark-grey. Over the 1946–8 period, many variations were tried – and up to fifty have been recorded – before the move to a standard livery. With this final very smart look the Great Western Railway moved forward to become part of the new nationalised scheme.

The down Cornish Riviera Express behind a King in early BR days. The leading Hawksworth brake third (Diagram D.131) has the postwar double lining-out and 'Great Western' with coats of arms. Note the carriage identification plate.

After nationalisation, the chocolate and cream livery was at one time considered for a BR standard scheme. Some GWR-design coaches appeared with a large figure '1' – indicating first-class compartments – on the doors, the new GWR standard double-lining out and running numbers prefixed by 'W'. Other sets of GWR vehicles were painted in the short-lived experimental plum-and-spilt-milk livery. After the adoption of the crimson and cream style, some vehicles appeared with GW double lining out and W-style prefixed numbers on the left-hand side. From 1949 onwards, lined crimson became the standard livery for non-corridor vehicles but a number of GWR coaches of this type, as well as the majority of auto-trailers, were painted in the standard crimson and cream for the next couple of years.

Despite the adoption of the crimson and cream livery, most special-duty saloons were maintained in their old GWR livery. In 1956, as part of a current burst of Regionalistic free-licence, the Western Region painted a number of BR standard corridor coaches and ex-GWR restaurant cars in a deep brown and pale primrose livery for use on the named expresses. The 'Super Saloons' and inspection saloons were soon similarly painted. As from the autumn of 1962 this livery was discontinued, with the declining prestige of named services. Even in mid-1965, however, quite a few BR standard corridors, as well as the 'Super Saloons', still commemorated a livery that by then was one hundred years old.

4
VICTORIAN FINALE: 1890–1905

1. Paddington–Birkenhead Set: Built 1890–1
A notable landmark in the history of British rolling-stock was Dean's four-coach corridor set which, together with a bogie van, entered service on 7 March 1892, working up from Birkenhead in the morning and returning on the 1.30p.m. Paddington–Birkenhead.

This distinction afforded to the Birkenhead line shows the relative importance of the service at that date. This was the very first British train to have corridor connections between all the coaches in a set of side corridor vehicles – and, moreover, accommodation for all three classes. The American-built Pullman cars, a train of which first entered service in mid-1879 on the Midland Railway between St Pancras and Bradford, had through communication between the vehicles, but Dean's set was the prototype of what is regarded as the traditional British express train. The first British side-corridor coach was a six-wheel ECJS first, built at Doncaster in 1882.

As has been stressed before, its claim to be the first throughout side-corridor train in Britain must be qualified by the fact that passengers were not expected to move from one vehicle to another. In fact, the intercommunicating doors were locked and only opened by the guard with a normal coach key. Even then, he moved through the train only in response to a call on the electric bell from a passenger supposedly in distress. It all seems something of a publicity stunt, with the emphasis on the electric bell communication rather than the throughout corridor. In fact, what was recognised as more important was the internal corridor within the vehicles. The official explanation for the train reads as follows from *The Engineer* of 15 April 1892:

> The taste of English railway travellers has always inclined to the system of separate compartments rather than to large open cars on the American plan (i.e. Pullmans), and in this train the designers have combined the privacy of separate compartments with the *advantage of through communication* and access to toilet rooms on long journeys.

This does not make clear exactly to whose advantage the through communication was, but as the accounts published by *The Engineer* and *The GWR Magazine* both make great play with the passenger communication systems, it can be assumed that it was indeed for the guard to attend to the passengers.

Electric communication between passenger and guard was a great novelty, in theory, but, as will be shown later, it did not inspire nervous passengers to test its effectiveness. In each compartment or open section throughout the train there were pushbuttons which, if pressed, rang an electric bell in the brake third, where a recording instrument (presumably similar to those in hotels) indicated from which compartment the distress signal had come. The guard then set off to visit whichever one of the twenty-four compartments was concerned. In addition, there was a wire running along the gutter-rail throughout the train which, if pulled, made a full brake application. All this elaborate regard for passengers was slightly deflated when it was reported in *The GWR Magazine* for November 1892, first-hand from the guard of the train, that the communication wire had never been pulled and, more surprisingly, the electric bell had been sampled only once – by a small boy who had wanted to know what would happen if the button were pressed!

More important to the passengers was the installation throughout of steam heating in the train late in 1891, the regulation of which was controlled by the guard in his compartment.

An interesting sidelight on the 1890s is in the insistence on comparison with American practice – 'favourably compares with American standards of comfort, etc.' – yet, at the same time, stressing a preference for the British side-corridor arrangement. This was, of course, the time of sideways glances at American activities in general, and railways in particular, and Dean's train does appear to have been in some manner a counterblast to American innovations.

The first-, second- and third-class coaches were ordered in June 1890 and completed by November of that year. They were believed to have been marshalled at first with a standard 40ft passenger brake van at one end and a non-corridor clerestory brake third at the other. In this form it does not appear to have entered regular passenger service. In February 1891, a 50ft corridor brake third was ordered and completed in August. Even then, there is no record of the train going into use before the early months of 1892 and there seems to be no satisfactory explanation of the delay, beyond that of prolonged acceptance trials.

Constructionally, there were no unusual features, but the bodywork, beyond the novelty of side-corridors, was distinguished by a wider than normal clerestory and 'bay-windows' to the compartment, in the same style as the convertible sleeping-cars of 1890. The interior panelling was in walnut and satinwood. For some time, probably into the 1900s, the corridor connections to one side of the coach-ends were retained; the refitting with centrally-placed ones involved little more than a reduction in size of the lavatories at one end, and an altered seat arrangement at the other.

The internal layout of the coaches set the pattern for all standard one-class side-corridor clerestory vehicles with four or five side-corridor compartments and two open smoking sections. The brake third, however, had four side-corridor compartments and one smoking section: this was not perpetuated apart from the 1893–4 sets.

Unfortunately, very little is known about the subsequent existence of this prototype train, except that three of the coaches were withdrawn in 1932/3. The publicity importance of the train should not be overlooked and, of course, its apparent popularity (see below) and practicability saw the style perpetuated in standard stock. At a time when photographic reproductions were comparatively new in illustrated journals, *The GWR Magazine* published a two-page plate of the train, with Dean 2-2-2 No. 3003 at its head, *The Engineer* having published the same view to illustrate its article of 15 April 1892.

2. 'Cornishman' 1893 Series Sets

From an interview with Mr H. Lambert, general manager, Great Western Railway, published in *The GWR Magazine* December 1894:

> *Question*: 'What is your latest improvement?' *Answer*: 'The corridor train. We ran the first corridor to the North as an experiment [the 1892 train], intending to put it on in the West. But it grew into favour so much with the people in the North that we now run the corridor to both West and North, and also to South Wales.'

This being the official view of the public's reaction to the first corridor train, it was hardly surprising that a whole series of corridor coaches was ordered in February 1893 to grace, first of all the 'Cornishman', then South Wales and Penzance and Torquay expresses.

In comparison with the premier 1892 sets, the 'Cornishman' series discarded the bay-window outline and retained quarterlights along the corridors, as did the succeeding 'Ocean Mails' and 'South Wales Corridor' sets. They also had side-positioned corridor connections and, this time, with blank ends to the brake seconds and thirds vans. Separate ladies' and gentlemen's lavatories were provided, and this became a standard feature of Dean clerestory corridors. Also, in keeping with the 1892 train, the brake coaches had an end smoking open section. The newly developed 8ft 6in bogie constituted another difference.

The 'Cornishman', 10.15 a.m. out of Paddington to Penzance, with a through coach to Falmouth, was probably the most favoured of the crack GWR trains of the late 1890s, particularly as the big wrench of the abandonment of the broad gauge was being felt by staff and West Country passengers alike, and because of the possibility of competition by the LSWR. This six-coach train, with an additional tri-composite brake for Newquay in the summer, commenced running in the summer of 1894, although it is possible that the new coaches were used on the 'Cornishman' from the previous year. Passengers appear to have been permitted to walk through the train and, again, the electric bell system of communication was installed. From 1 October 1895, with the termination of the notorious Swindon refreshment rooms contract, the 'Cornishman' became the first train to be booked through Swindon without stopping, although no refreshments were as yet available on the train. On and from 20 July 1896, the 'Cornishman' was divided, for the summer season only; the first portion for Newquay ran from Paddington to Par, stopping only at Exeter, to change engines, and Plymouth. From the summer of 1896, one of the first dining-cars was included in the 'Cornishman' set. Not much is known of the Torquay and South Wales trains, but they seem to have remained as sets until the

The well-known and admirably posed official photograph of the pioneer GWR corridor train, before entering regular service in 1892. The locomotive is 3001 2-2-2 No 3003 (later named *Avalanche*), built in February 1892.

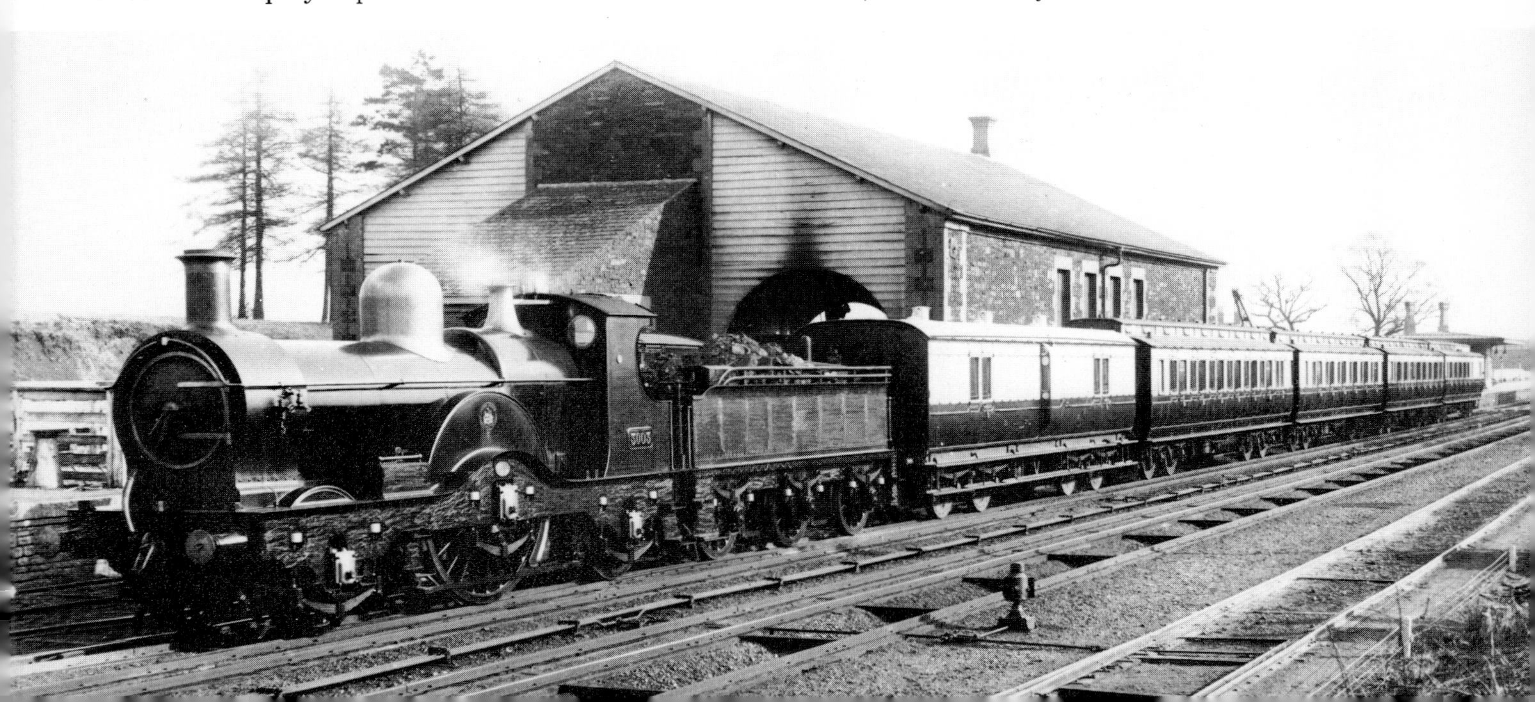

Cornishman stock corridor third No 2835. (Lot 691 – Diagram C.8) Note that the running number is repeated three times on the cantrail panels.

influx of elliptical roof stock in the late 1900s. One interesting feature of the sets was the comparatively small proportion of first- and second-class accommodation. In addition, the first/third composite was a rare type of clerestory corridor to be built before 1910.

The coaches themselves have been mentioned in passing and it has been remarked that they were the real prototypes for the standard Dean clerestory corridors. All the one-class coaches had the standard compartment/smoking-saloon arrangement, and so did the composites: a feature which the pre-production sets had in common with the 1892 premier train, 1896 'Ocean Special' and 'South Wales Corridor' sets. The clerestory itself reverted to the standard width in contrast to the wider variety on the 1892 coaches. The brake thirds were built as left and right-handed pairs, although the original formation of the 'Cornishman' included only one brake third. The reason was, primarily, that since the corridor connection was on one side only, and one end was blank, indiscriminate marshalling was not possible. These were the first 'handed' brakes and, curiously enough, the last were for the 'Cornishman's' successor, in the 'Centenary' stock of 1935. Most interesting of the coaches were the brake tri-composites with a corridor connection at one end and two fixed windows and a droplight at the other, for the use of the guard. Some of this batch were built as slip coaches (see page 44). Because of the first-class open saloon at the non-brake end, these coaches were referred to as the 'Falmouth coupé' type, as their first use was as through vehicles to that destination. Apart from their service on the 'Cornishman', they also appeared on boat-trains from Plymouth Docks, which were accorded the best vehicles.

After displacement from the principal services, the coaches were rebuilt with centre-position corridor connections, in common with the 1892 train. Other alterations were the re-positioning of the lavatory tanks in the roof and the fitting of electric lighting to a few. Nos. 3732/34 (Lot 797) ran for some time as brakes with pantry facilities. However, in December 1898, two thirds were converted to composite sleepers, reverting to ordinary coaches about 1910–11. In October 1905, the first of four was drastically converted to an auto-trailer with all centre-gangway seating. Of these, auto-trailer No 14 was still intact at Swindon in late 1956. More remarkable was the removal of the clerestory of an ex-second between 1916 and 1921, the only known instance of this being done. Withdrawal started in the mid-1930s and, by the outbreak of war, the majority had gone, including all the tri-composite brakes. The last brake third, No 2824, was condemned at Swindon in March 1940, but the ex-seconds survived to the very end of clerestory coaches, being withdrawn at the end of 1950, but possibly not in passenger service.

Official photograph of 3001 2-2-2 No 3006 *Courier* at the head of the first Cornishman set, in 1893/94. The formation comprises five corridor vehicles (brake second No 247 is leading and has no gangway at the van end). The last two vehicles are 'Falmouth' brake composites.

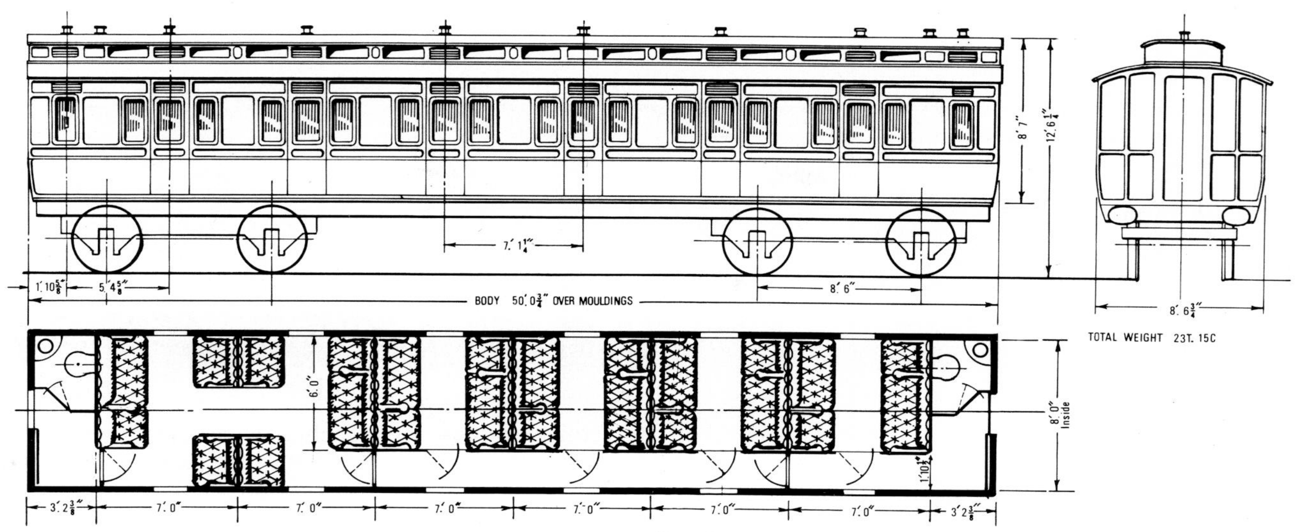

Drawing prepared from Swindon Diagram A.2 for the first-class coaches of Cornishman stock, Lot 693.

38ft 6in – 58ft Non-Corridor Clerestory Coaches: 1890–1905

At the beginning of the period, 'convertible' coaches were being produced with narrow-gauge bodies and broad-gauge bogies; non-corridor stock was general for all services and was without steam heating. By the early 1900s, corridor coaches were being produced for main-line services and non-corridor stock was built for suburban and local work and through coach services only. The external, as well as basic, details of the Dean non-corridor stock had varied little: the 6ft 4in bogie had been replaced by the 8ft 6in and finally 10ft types and clerestory features altered in various respects. But the amount of standardisation could be found in, say, 46ft 6in thirds built to one diagram from 1894–1902, a total of 328 coaches, varying in cost from £730, for the earliest lots, to £847 for the final examples with the refinements of steam heating and standard passenger alarms. This contrasted, however, with the many batches of brake composites, each differing in various ways. In the following section, types such as brake thirds and composites are dealt with separately, covering the 1890–1905 period.

Clerestory Types			*Dates – in general*
Clerestory	I	Upper deck and main deck, both single arc	pre-1890
	II	Upper deck single arc, lower deck three-centre arc	1891 (on earlier diagrams)
	III	Both decks three-centre arc	1890–1895*
		Panelled Clerestory	1895–1898*
		Unpanelled	1898–1904

*Vehicles completed later than this on earlier diagrams

Incidentally, there was another pattern of clerestory used for the 56ft sleeper cars to Lot 787, and the 1896–1903 dining cars, in which the sides to the clerestory deck were sloped at about 45°. Finally, there was the 'royal' clerestory with the clerestory deck rounding down smoothly at each end of the coach.

Finally, in 1905 two batches of thirds (Lot Nos 1077/80) on Diagram C.25 were built with elliptical roofs but were otherwise similar to clerestory vehicles. These survived as workmen's coaches in South Wales until condemned from late 1956–9.

Bogies

Dean	6ft 4in standard type	1890–1892
	8ft 6in (after 1895 on coaches less than 50ft body length only)	1892–1904
	10ft 0in standard type	1895–1904
	10ft 0in adapted in bolster form	1904–5

'Pseudo-Corridor' Ends

From 1896, Lot 813, non-corridor coaches hitherto with five-panel ends, were built with the same type of end as the corridor stock, with a recess in place of the corridor connection. This was to facilitate the conversion of non-corridor coaches to corridor stock at some possible future date. There is no definite evidence that this was ever done.

First/Seconds/Thirds/Third Brakes

Ordered in April 1890 under one lot number, 545, were some ten thirds and twenty-four brake thirds, with centre brake compartment, as broad gauge/standard gauge convertibles. The combination of types under one lot number was not unknown. The brake thirds were centre-compartment, the last of this arrangement except for some composites built up to late 1891. After conversion to standard-gauge coaches, the thirds, with a luggage compartment, became full thirds and the brake thirds had their right-hand compartments converted to luggage vans. They were withdrawn in the 1930s.

Most numerous were the 46ft 6¾in thirds with

Non-corridor brake tri-composite No 1141, built 1902. (Lot 983 – Diagram E.72)

eight compartments which had been built as express stock when the design first appeared in 1885 but which, by the early 1900s, and after some adaptations, had been drafted to secondary work. Coaches to Lot 572 of 1891 were built as convertibles, the last to be completed as such. From 1885 to 1902, as mentioned above, these thirds underwent few changes in design: those from 1894 onwards had 8ft 6in bogies, while the 1903–4 lots were of the 8ft 6¾in width. Indeed, Diagrams C.3, C.10 and C.22 comprised 640 coaches, mostly built in batches of ten or twenty with equal numbers of brake thirds. The pre-1893 thirds disappeared in the 1930s, the 1894–1902 series survived on workmen's trains until 1953 and the 1903–4 batches until 1955, in one or two cases with the centre compartment allocated for the guard's use. Several had been converted to parcels vans between 1939–45.

The 46ft 6¾in third (Diagram C.10) was developed into a ten-compartment version, 58ft long in 1904 (Diagram C.23), and, as already mentioned, was built in 1905 with an elliptical roof. In addition, the latter, and one batch of the clerestories, had a bolster bogie version of the 10ft Dean standard. The clerestory coaches finished their lives in workmen's trains, some with a centre guard's compartment, until 1957. Some C.10 diagram thirds and contemporary brake thirds, condemned early in the war, were pressed into service as temporary parcels vans. Three batches of 50ft eight-compartment seconds were built in 1901 for general secondary work: rather curiously, only some of the first two batches, but none of the third batch, were equipped with steam heating, and it would see that Lot 981, the third lot, was the last of ordinary service stock to be built new without it. They were withdrawn by 1957. Also used for secondary work were the three batches of seven-compartment firsts built 1897–1902. With the decline in demand for first-class accommodation and the construction of new suburban sets, Lot 985 was demoted to third class in 1938 and a further fifteen of the other two Lots were similarly declassed from 1941. They were withdrawn by 1955. Only the first of these types had been converted to electric lighting.

For the brake thirds of 1892–3 a body 48ft 6¾in in length was standardised with three, four and five passenger compartments and corresponding variations in luggage accommodation for different types of service requirements. They were withdrawn in pre-war days. From 1894 a 50ft brake third was standardised with either three, four or five compartments; those with the four, the most common, had luggage space equal to that of a six-wheel van. In 1897, the final type appeared, 8ft 6¾in wide and with a 10ft bogie; a little over a hundred of these were produced: about a fifth of the number of thirds built. Most of the 1894–97 coaches were withdrawn before the war, and the last of the final series had been condemned by mid-1951. None had been converted to electric lighting.

For incidental mention are two four-coach sets built in late 1898 for the 4.45 p.m. 'Afghan' from Paddington to Chester and Birkenhead, one of the important expresses of its day. The sets comprised two composites and two brake thirds designated semi-corridor. However, the brake thirds, five-compartment, side-corridor coaches with long corridor windows, certainly ran at a later date with corridor connections. The first/second composites were definitely non-corridor, with lavatory provision for all compartments. The building of non-corridor sets at a late date for an important express seems a little strange, and they are unlikely to have lasted on the service after the mid-1900s. All seem to have gone in pre-war days.

Composites/Brake Composites

Through-coach working over branches and other railways entered its most developed phase in the late Victorian period. Although the GWR was building corridor sets in some quantity by the late 1890s, the majority of its own secondary trains and a number of neighbouring railways' main expresses were still non-corridor and so the through-coach, nearly always a brake tri-composite, was semi-corridor. It also need hardly be mentioned that the corridor connections would have had little value, as the cross-country trains did not have restaurant cars for at least a decade, and, providing there was ample lavatory accommodation for each compartment, a through corridor was unnecessary. The first real 'fully-equipped' brake composite appeared in 1895, as noted below, but previous to that non-corridor main-line express stock was still being built.

The first two Lots under review were of the

standard Clerestory 3 type and were built as broad-gauge convertibles: the batches on the same Lot 544 differed as the first was a tri-composite and the second, a first and second composite with a luggage compartment. Lot 554 of late 1891 had the lavatories divided by a diagonal partition, which allowed the lavatory doors to be placed in the centre of the compartments, and made possible better-sized seats as the result of the more symmetrical layout. Lots 557/591/610 (1891) were similar to the second batch of Lot 544, still with the luggage compartment in the middle of the coach, but this old-style feature was absent from Lot 614 of 1892. Finally, Lots 634/658 of 1892 complete this series, being the last composites with 6ft 4in bogies and lavatory provision for first-class passengers only. All these composites and brake composites were withdrawn by 1939.

First of the new-layout brake composites were a pair of prototypes which appeared in late 1892 to Lot 630, to different diagrams and lengths, while No. 7290 was built with a 'royal' clerestory. For the first time, one compartment of both the first- and second-class accommodation had lavatory access. More unusual was the first-class coupé smoking-compartment at the right-hand end of the coach with chairs for two passengers who could benefit from three observation windows, similar to an inspection saloon, the centre one a droplight. They were also, most probably, the first coaches to be mounted on the standard 8ft 6in bogies. Both were withdrawn in 1938–39.

Following from these prototypes came a refined version with not only lavatory provision for all compartments, but with one of the two third-class lavatories projecting into the luggage space, the other being 'ladies only'. There were twenty-two vehicles in all, Lots 742/65 of ten each, Lot 748 (No. [6] 715) and Lot 749 (No. [6] 716).

Their original workings were between Plymouth, Bristol, Cardiff to Birkenhead and Manchester. *The Railway Engineer* was moved to remark that they were 'particularly fine', and that they had been on view at Paddington, possibly the first instance of such a presentation. Interestingly, they were the first coaches to have the familiar coloured photographs in the compartments, and Lot 749 was the earliest to have the standard 10ft bogie. All seem to have been withdrawn before 1939. An odd Lot was No. 846 of 1897, the only non-corridor second/third composites but with lavatory provision for all compartments.

The only other Lots with observation windows were diagrams Nos. E.44/52 – Lots 759/814, the earlier one with a side-corridor to the third-class compartments, the later one with one third-class compartment lavatory less. In addition, they were first- and third-class only, which suggests that they may have been built for through-working on to Cambrian or Midland metals, the only two railways to have abolished second-class accommodation at that date.

From 1897 (Lot 832) to 1904 (Lot 1058), the 53–58ft composites and brake composites were plainer, some without lavatory provision for all compartments, some with short connecting corridors without long windows on the corridor side, and without the observation ends and lavatory in the luggage van. Of particular note were four brake composites built in 1898, in matching pairs, for the new Birkenhead–Bournemouth through service which, four years later, ran as part of the new Newcastle–Bournemouth train via the recently opened Great Central Railway. Internal arrangements included the side-corridor to the third-class compartments, a lavatory in the luggage van and ladies' compartment. The luggage-van lavatories were removed from all the brake composites mentioned, at some time in the 1910s, in common with a similar reduction of facilities in the corridor composites. Almost all these composite brakes were extinct by 1939, but for a few which saw the early post-war days.

The splendid interior of saloon No 249, built 1894. (Lot 745 – Diagram G.3)

The interior of family saloon No 225, built 1900. (Lot 950 – Diagram G.33)

Slip Coaches

Normally similar to contemporary ordinary brake composites, the three standard diagrams of double-ended slip coaches differed only in body lengths, numbers of compartments and standard clerestory and bogie variations. Diagram F.10, Lots 844/975/1032, of 1897/1901/3, had lavatory provision for all compartments, unlike the earlier types, and are particularly interesting as Lot 844 was noted as being for 'Continental traffic'.

These four coaches were built for a through Birkenhead–Folkestone Harbour service, slipped at Reading from a Birmingham–Paddington train, worked forward to Tonbridge by stopping trains, then forward to Folkestone and from there on a Charing Cross boat-train to connect with the mid-day sailing to Boulogne. Again, returned by London express and stopping trains, the coach was attached at Reading to the midnight Paddington to Birkenhead train. Nos [7] 085-8 on the Birkenhead–Dover/Folkestone workings were slipped at Reading on the southbound journey until c1916. After 1909, with the revision of the slip apparatus, these clerestory slip coaches were given extra vacuum reservoirs by mounting two almost full-length cylinders along the top of the roof on either side of the clerestory. All these clerestory slip coaches were withdrawn before 1939.

Diagrams F.11 and F.12 were single-ended slip coaches of an unusual 38ft 6in body length. This meant that they had a reduced seating layout: one first-class, one second- and two third-class compartments. Nos [7] 089-92, the four vehicles involved, were built for a service which started in July 1898, originating at Liverpool Central (low level), over the Mersey Railway to Rock Ferry, thence via Reading (where they were slipped) to Folkestone Harbour.

There were also three types of single-ended slip coaches included in the normal brake composite batches of Lots 697, 742 and 765. The last two have been mentioned above. Lot 697 was known as the 'Falmouth coupé' type, as the first of the batch had formed part of the new 1894 'Cornishman' sets (see page 40). The only difference from the other coaches in these lots was that the brake-end had a droplight and slip apparatus was fitted.

Four, Six, Eight-Wheel Saloons: 1890–1904

The self-contained private hire and family saloons represented an age which died in the First World War. In the Victorian and, to a lesser extent, the Edwardian years, occasions such as Henley Regatta saw every GWR private saloon of any description pressed into use and supplemented with borrowed vehicles from other railways. Six-wheel saloons were built right up to 1898, probably because of their convenient size, and the first eight-wheel family saloons did not appear in any quantity until after 1896. Fifty-two saloons of various designs built before 1891 were converted to milk and parcels or fruit vans from 1920–8.

Four- and Six-Wheel Saloons: 1890–1898

Only one four-wheel saloon comes under notice and that is a first, built in 1890. It survived in original use until 1923 when it was converted to a fruit van and scrapped as such in 1933.

Two lots of clerestory roof six-wheelers were built in this period: ten coaches in all, four first saloons and six family saloons with two servants' second-class compartments and luggage accommodation. All were condemned in the 1930s, two becoming engineer's saloons.

Fifty-four three-centre roof, six-wheel third saloons were built to two diagrams from 1892–98. They had two open saloons divided centrally by a lavatory and WC, and all seem to have been withdrawn in the 1920s.

Eight-wheel Saloons: 1892–1904

The earliest saloon under review was a family carriage 38ft 6¾in long and built in 1892 to Lot 628. This contained a saloon, first-class compartment, servants' compartment and luggage space. Notably, it had sloping ends to the clerestory – 'royal' type – and at a later stage received gangways. As mentioned in Chapter 10, this coach, No 9043, passed to departmental use.

Much better known was the 56ft directors' saloon of 1894, No 249 (Lot 745), which possessed a kitchen with an oil-gas range and had two saloons, one of which was the dining-room, panelled in oak and furnished with revolving chairs. A special seat could be fitted to either end of the body to permit inspection of the track. Again, it was distinguished by a 'royal' clerestory and formed part of the Royal Train, when required. It was reclassified as a first-class saloon in 1935, and later passed to departmental use (see Chapter 10).

There were two lots of bogie family saloons with a guard's compartment, built in 1896 and 1899 respectively, only the later batch having gangways. They were the first ordinary saloons over 40ft in length and 8ft 6¾in wide and, as customary with earlier family carriages, had a servants' second-class compartment. Surviving into early post-war days, one had become an invalid saloon, another an engineer's inspection saloon, No 80971 (see Chapter 10).

From 1900–4, two designs of saloons were built, G.6 52ft 0¾in length first-class vehicles (Lots 980/1045), six in number, and ten invalid saloons on Diagram G.33 (Lots 950, 1027/46/51) of 47ft 6¾in length. The first-class saloons had an ordinary first-class compartment and a servants' compartment, in addition to the saloon and lavatories and WCs. The invalid saloons had two hammocks (1903 batch) and suspended couches (1904 Lots). All these survived into early post-war days, the invalid saloons having been converted to plain third-class. Ex-invalid saloon No 9029 was used on summer Saturdays in the late 1940s as the Paddington control coach. On the busiest summer weekends, various officers and inspectors were stationed in this vehicle and connected by phone to the control office to give on-the-spot directions regarding passenger movement control and train working. It is worth remembering that on those early post-war summer Saturdays, queues of passengers for trains stretched round from Paddington Station along Eastbourne Terrace, and passengers had to be turned away from certain over-subscribed trains! No 9029 was permanently designated as office accommodation in 1951, and scrapped around 1957.

Eight third-class party saloons, of two Lots on the same Diagram (G.18) were built in 1901–4 with accommodation in two saloons and 46ft 6¾in in length. The first lot had Westinghouse brake pipes for through workings, the other two coaches were stationed at Bristol. In 1915, the GWR turned out two nine-coach home-use ambulance trains, as described on page 67, the first and last coaches of each train being one of these saloons which were adapted initially as orderlies' accommodation and stores cars. In 1918, three of the saloons, Nos 9364-6, one classed as a pharmacy/ward car, were rebuilt with semi-elliptical roofs and 57ft 'Toplight' style bodywork, becoming once more third-class saloons in 1921. One was allocated to Paddington, the other two to Birmingham. In 1942, No 9364 was classified as a conference saloon for the SHAEF (Supreme Headquarters Allied Expeditionary Force) train. Both clerestory and rebuilt saloons survived into the late 1940s. No 9366 became a mobile office (internal user No 079016) and was shopped as recently as 1964.

45ft 0¾in Dynamometer Car No 790: 1901

Churchward's dynamometer car of 1901, built under the aegis of Dean, is probably the best known of these vehicles, even if it did not share the fame of the former North Eastern car which accompanied Gresley's *Mallard* on its record trip down Stoke bank. The GWR vehicle, of ordinary saloon outline with a 'royal' clerestory roof, was built for the purpose under Wagon Lot No 293 at a cost of £860, excluding the provision of internal recording equipment. No 790 had observation ends, side lookouts and an internal arrangement of two saloons with central 'offices'. Internal equipment included a Hallade recorder, and there was a retractable flangeless wheel for speed recording purposes. The GWR was, of course, the first British railway to carry out controlled road-testing of locomotives.

It was not until after the Second World War that the dynamometer car was put to extensive use. Its last GWR run was probably on the ATC high-speed special of October 1947 when 'Castle' No 5056 touched 96mph between Reading and Slough. At about this time the vehicle was fitted with metal-framed sliding ventilators to the body-side windows, and it was later numbered W7W.

Below:
The former GWR dynamometer car, out of traffic and seen as W7W at Swindon stock shed, August 1964.

Bottom:
A seven-coach set of four-wheel stock forming a train for Kidderminster, photographed at Stourbridge Junction behind 517 0-4-2T No 1477 in Edwardian days.

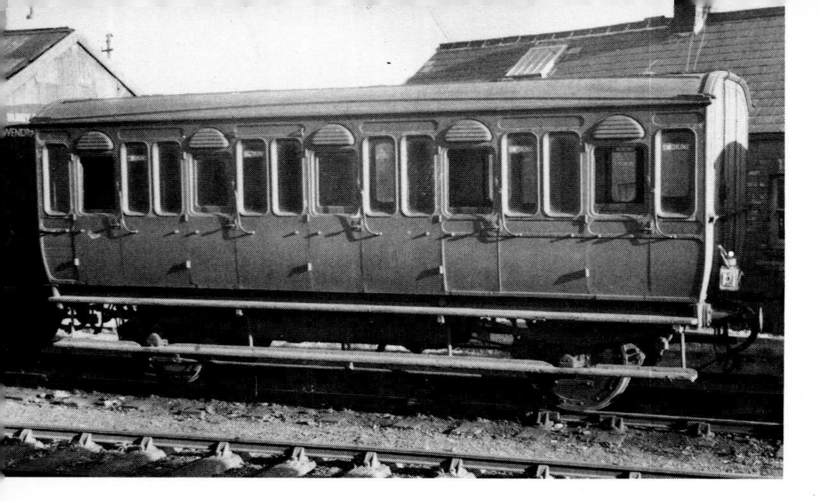

Late survivor: third No 2796, built 1898, at Burry Port, August 1951. (Lot 859 – Diagram S.17)

The locomotive exchanges of 1948 saw it behind the tenders of all the contesting locomotives on GWR territory from Bulleid Pacifics to the LNER 'O1' 2-8-0. After 1948, Swindon became the centre for the controlled road-testing of various types of locomotives, which included BR standard designs, an LNER 'V2' 2-6-2, and the famous tests of 'King' No 6001 on a 796-ton train. Other interludes were the tests of an LMR 'Duchess' 4-6-2 in 1955 and the first trials of the double-chimney 'Kings' and 'Castles' in 1956. The final full-scale road test with steam power was with a double-chimney BR 2-10-0, No 92178, in the early 1960s, which seems also to have been the finale of the 1901 dynamometer car as well. In 1961, the Western Region produced a new dynamometer car from the shell of a Hawksworth corridor third (see page 108) which was designed especially for the testing of diesel locomotives, but included apparatus from Churchward's car. Stripped of much of its interior, the old vehicle remained at Swindon Works after displacement and was subsequently purchased for preservation.

Four- and Six-Wheel Compartment Stock: 1890–1902

By the 1890s, the only four-wheel passenger stock being produced was for branch-line workings and suburban service, 602 being built between 1890 and 1902. Of these, no less than 200 were for the London suburban services: Hammersmith and City, Main Line and City, and some Middle Circle workings. In 1900–2, the Bristol local trains and the Ruabon–Dolgelley line were allocated several new sets each of four-wheel stock: among the last to be built by the GWR.

Structurally and in general appearance, the standard three-centre roof four-wheelers were not unusual. London suburban sets were, however, of reduced height and 8ft 6¾in width, and the coaches were close-coupled with short buffers. The most striking feature of these four-wheelers was in fact, the 'Holden' touch: in other words, the half-circle ventilators to the doors and narrow panels to the mouldings. This design lasted the twenty years from 1880 during which these four-wheelers were produced.

Apart from those displaced by the electrification of the Hammersmith and City, the London area sets remained until the 1920s. On disbandment of the sets, the individual coaches were generally rebuilt with standard-length buffers. By the late 1930s, however, the use of four-wheel coaches was generally restricted to the more out-of-the-way branch lines and workmen's trains in South Wales. Among those branches using four-wheelers in the 1930s were: the Wrington Vale light railway, the Highworth Branch and the Tanat Valley line. One line which had four-wheelers until the end was the Burry Port and Gwendraeth Valley. No bogie stock was used until the 1939 vehicles (see page 100). On the BPGV, four-wheelers were used until the withdrawal of passenger services in 1953, probably the very last vehicles of this type running in regular passenger service on British Railways. In the mid-1930s sixteen four-wheelers, including a former City service coach, were converted for use as camping coaches (see Chapter 10). A number of four-wheeled firsts and composites were redesignated thirds and workmen's thirds from c1933–9 and renumbered from 697 upwards. Others were appropriated for departmental use.

The only six-wheel compartment coaches were a batch of five, built in 1894, but otherwise similar to four-wheel stock.

Sleeping Cars: 1892–1897

50ft 0¾in Composite Day/Sleeper Clerestory Coaches: 1892/5 (Diagram J.4)

Of normal dimensions and outline as contemporary standard clerestory stock, these originally non-gangwayed coaches were built with either four or five first-class sleeping berths and two or three ordinary third-class compartments. There was no attendant. About 1896, two of the four cars built to this type were converted to corridor thirds with the usual centre-corridor smoking compartments. The other two were later, at some stage, refitted as ordinary corridor composites. All four coaches survived in converted form until the late 1940s.

56ft 0¾in First-Class Clerestory Sleeping-Cars: 1897

Among the best-known GWR coaches are the famous Dean 'bay-window' 50ft-body convertible sleeping-cars of 1890 which introduced a more civilized standard of comfort to sleeping-car travel. The 1897 coaches were 56ft in length, without the 'bay windows', and of somewhat similar appearance to the pioneer restaurant cars, including the sloping sides to the clerestory decks. Besides eight berths, and two sofas in an ordinary compartment, there was attendant's accommodation. There was one lavatory only, sandwiched between two compartments and so arranged that only one door could be opened at a time. The berths were, interestingly, not merely an elaborated 'bench-type' seat but were hung separately from the bodywork framing. The washbasin-top folded down to provide a table.

Here, therefore, was an important step forward in sleeping-car design, reflected generally in contemporary East and West Coast practice. It was, however, some step forward to the next new GWR sleepers – the massive 70ft vehicles of 1907. The 1897 vehicles survived until the late 1930s.

Standard 50–58ft Corridor Clerestory Stock: 1896–1904

Following the undoubted success of the first 1892 corridor train and the 'West of England' sets of the following year, the GWR produced corridor stock in quantity after 1896. Production was to a relatively standardised design which lasted until the last batch of clerestory corridor coaches appeared in 1904 (Lot 1050).

Differences between the series of clerestory corridors are best summarised, and it should be noted that the same differences, where applicable, are covered in the non-corridor clerestories' section on page 41.

Clerestory

Writers have not been kind to the GWR design of clerestory, dismissing it as box-like, which is possibly fair criticism in view of the Midland Railway varieties. One of the reasons for the GWR's less elegant design was the practice of making the clerestory appear as an appendage to the roof and not part of it. Clerestory types 2 and 3 are described in relation to the 1892–93 sets and non-corridor coaches. The post-1896 corridor coaches had three-centre arches to the upper and lower decks. Those built before 1899 had panelled sides to the clerestory, those after Lot 905 being unpanelled.

Window Layout

The 'Ocean Special' and 'South Wales' sets of 1896 had quarterlights, corresponding to the compartments, on the corridor side, but all subsequent coaches had long lights on the corridor side. The open smoking section of full first-, second- and third-class coaches had quarterlights on both body sides.

Lighting/Heating/Passenger Alarms

All were built with gas lighting and steam heating, probably just over a half being refitted with electric lighting. Those built after 1898, above Lot 870, and the 'Ocean Special' and 'South Wales' sets, had electric communication between passengers and guard, but only if connected up. Those built after 1900, Lot 940 and above, had the standard pull-down type of alarm, causing partial application of the brakes. Lot 870 and above had roof lavatory-tanks instead of the between-partitions arrangements.

Internal Layout

First-Class: Four side-corridor compartments, two centre-corridor smoking bays and two lavatories. The last were normally placed at either end of the side-corridor compartments, except for the 'Ocean Special' firsts which had the lavatory leading off from the smoking-saloon.

Second-Class: Five side-corridor compartments, two centre-corridor smoking bays, and two lavatories at either end of side-corridor compartments. Became third-class after 1910.

Third-Class: Five side-corridor compartments, three centre-corridor smoking bays, and two lavatories at either end of side-corridor compartments.

No full firsts, seconds or thirds were built new without two or three bays as a smoking-saloon, upholstered in leather. However, four Lots of second/third class composites, which were full side-corridors, as was standard practice, became all-thirds after 1910. The two sleeper/thirds built in 1892 and 1895 respectively, as converted to thirds, had the normal five compartments and three open bays, but with the latter arranged as two on the left and the other on the right of the coach.

Composites: All general service corridor composites were full side-corridor coaches, the two exceptions being mentioned below. All had the first or second compartments to the right of the body. All except Lot 987 and above (Diagram E.73) were built with four lavatories, arranged one at each end and two in the middle. It was a peculiarly Victorian practice to provide separate lavatories for the sexes; the two centre lavatories with adjoining compartments of each class were 'ladies only', with doors shutting off this section. From about the early 1900s this rather extravagant provision was discontinued and the final composites – and gradually, the earlier coaches – were altered to two end lavatories only. In the case of conversions, the resultant space became a

First-class sleeper No 243, later No 9039, built 1897. (Lot 787 – Diagram J.5) Note the sloping sides to the clerestory.

third-class compartment, although those altered in the 1910s produced substandard first-class compartments.

The final batches of all types had slightly narrower corridors with a correspondingly small increase in compartment size.

First of the 'production series' of the corridor clerestories were two eight-coach sets for 'Ocean Mails' expresses from Plymouth Millbay to Paddington, with generous accommodation for all classes. Of the baggage vans at each end of the sets, which were 48ft clerestory vehicles, one in each set was intended to be a pantry baggage-van. In March 1896, three dining-cars were ordered, one for the Cardiff service (see page 51), and two buffet brake seconds intended for this Cardiff train were switched to the 'Ocean Mails' sets in exchange for a second-class corridor. The idea of buffet luggage vans was dropped. A small detail, besides those already mentioned, was the absence of doors to one smoking-section bay as built, though these were cut through soon after; the same feature applied to the 'South Wales' set. The 'Ocean Mails' baggage vans had one central gangway at the guard's end and one side gangway. They were transferred to the Great Western TPO in the 1900s (see page 116). Finally they were demoted to luggage vans, losing their gangways in 1930·31, and survived until post-war days. Of the other coaches, withdrawal began in the late 1930s but the thirds lasted through to 1951.

The 'South Wales Corridor' train was originally intended, as mentioned above, to have had refreshments served from a buffet brake second but, instead, received the first restaurant car on the GWR. The coaches were the prototypes for the subsequent clerestory corridors, except for the composites which, unusually, had smoking saloons for both classes and two first-class compartments. The brake tri-composites seem originally to have been intended to be a non-corridor design.

A six-coach set was formed, including the restaurant car, and went into service on 11 May 1896 on the 9.58 a.m. Cardiff–Paddington, the front four coaches coming through from Swansea and the set returning as the 6.10 p.m. Paddington–Swansea. At Cardiff, the restaurant car and the rear third brake were detached, as well as a brake tri-composite on certain days, the two last vehicles going on to Swansea on a slow train. Although there were corridor gangways throughout the train, in common with earlier sets passengers were not encouraged to move from one coach to another and the occupants of the restaurant car remained there throughout the journey. Withdrawal of the coaches began in the late 1930s, most having gone by 1948, except some thirds which were withdrawn in 1951.

Not until 1898–99 were the standard coaches, with long corridor lights, turned out in anything like large numbers. One 1897 composite was rebuilt with a 'royal' clerestory but it was not allocated to a special working. A brake first, No. (8) 253, was built to work with a first-class restaurant-car, being centre-corridor, but was later demoted to a third brake, as were similar coaches, Nos. (8) 295-8 of 1900. The majority of coaches were formed into sets of four vehicles.

Corridor brake third No 2085, built 1900. (Lot 931 – Diagram D.30)

The large number of Lots constructed on capital account indicated the considerable re-stocking of the coach fleet and expansion of the GWR, as the fast expresses, part of the revolutionised train service of the late 1890s between Paddington–North Wales, Worcester and South Wales introduced by T. I. Allen when Superintendent of the Line, were formed of these new corridor sets. Half-a-dozen brake thirds built in 1900 were soon afterwards altered to pantry coaches, two compartments forming a small kitchen provided with tea and coffee-making facilities. They returned to normal brake thirds in the late 1930s. Three brake thirds were also branded to work between Cardiff and Neyland.

Becoming due for replacement in the 1940s, withdrawals began in the 1930s but the war, and subsequent restrictions on the building of new stock, meant that a number were in service until 1949–50. After this date there were still a few survivors in ordinary traffic: the very last being a 58ft first, No. 8316, built early in 1903 and withdrawn in 1953. Several survived into the early 1960s as camping coaches.

Prototypes of 70ft Standard Corridor Coaches: 1902–5

68ft 0¾in Brake Third No. 2400: 1902

A standard clerestory outline in appearance, No 2400 was built to a length of 68ft as a prototype for a range of coaches longer than the previously standard 56–58ft vehicles. This vehicle was used for vehicle riding experiments as a prelude to the production of the 'Whitewash Coach'.

With no modifications other than the removal of the lookouts, equipment with electric lighting, and remounting on 'American' equalised 9ft bogies, it was withdrawn in 1950.

69ft Brake Composites Nos. (7) 645-(7) 654: 1905

It has been stated that these elliptical-roofed coaches were intended to have been clerestories but, bearing in mind their late date of ordering and the fact that this Lot is isolated among 'Dreadnoughts', this appears doubtful. In view of the 68ft clerestory prototype above, and the two batches of elliptical-roofed non-corridor thirds (see page 41) it would seem that these composites were a hybrid of these two developments and an interim step in the evolution of a standard 70ft corridor coach. Nevertheless, they retained predominately clerestory design features. They had no toplights, lookouts with bullseye lenses (later removed), 5ft 6in third-class compartments, and were the 8ft 6¾in clerestory standard width. In addition, they were the last tri-composites with a lavatory for each class. Little altered, other than by the removal of the lookouts from some of the batch, they survived until 1953–6.

The compartment side of corridor composite No 1481 (later No 7481), built 1902. (Lot 986 – Diagram E.70) All but one compartment window has been blanked out by the photographer!

38ft 6in–56ft 0¾in Non-Corridor Three-Centre Roof Coaches: 1895–1898

These coaches, of non-standard lengths, were produced for branch-line working and, because of their humble duties, were not honoured with clerestories, no doubt because the expense of this fitting was not considered worthwhile. They had the same three-centre roof as the contemporary clerestories but, from the side elevation, had deeper panels over the windows than the clerestory types. Some had pseudo-corridor ends (see page 41) but, as the final Lots had five-panels ends, it wouid seem that conversion to corridor coaches was not considered.

Former broad-gauge frames and bogies were used for one of the two batches of four-compartment brake thirds that appeared in 1895–96, which explained the use of the old 6ft 4in wheelbase bogies. Also in 1895 came two other Lots of brake thirds with six and seven compartments. These and the earlier coaches appear to have been used on suburban services. Comparatively long-lived, they survived until 1949–50. During 1895–96, fifteen brake tri-composites were produced for branch line work, some formed as 'B' sets. One of them was built with oil lighting, probably the last bogie passenger vehicle so fitted, with the notable exception of Queen Victoria's 'rebuilt' saloon in the 1897 Royal Train. One or two survived to post-war days.

In 1897, three three-coach sets with steam heating were built for the Tenby and Pembroke line: all coaches were of 51ft length and the standard clerestory 8ft 6¾in width with 10ft wheelbase bogies. In post-war days, Nos 1963/4 were working the Culm Valley branch until replaced by the ex-Barry Railway 1921 vintage coaches. No 1965 was in service on the ex-Severn and Wye lines. Again, they were not extinct until late 1950. In 1898, fifteen composites and brake thirds were allocated to the Tondu and Bridgend area to work mostly as three-coach sets on such services as Tondu to Porthcawl, Blaengarw and Llynvi. During, and just after the First World War a number of both types were fitted for auto-working. The brake thirds were rebuilt with a driving-compartment with a centre narrow window flanked by two wide lights. Two composites, demoted to thirds, received through auto-working fittings for Bristol–Clifton–Avonmouth services formerly worked by steam rail-motor. Later they were transferred to such workings as the 'Marlow Donkey', between Marlow and Bourne End. All were withdrawn by 1950.

The Introduction of Dining-Cars

As a preliminary to description of the first dining-cars of 1896, it is possible to learn something of the official attitude to the employment of these vehicles from an interesting report produced by the traffic department, dated 1 July 1891. This also throws interesting light on the operation of dining-cars by other railways in the early days of these facilities. The first three GWR dining-cars were not ordered until March 1896 and the delay of five years would appear to be explained by the following points:

(i) 'The immovability of Jove', that is, to use Messrs Foxwell and Farrer's description, the general conservatism of GWR management at that time. This may be qualified by the fact that the 1891 Report did not hold out a particularly profitable future for dining-car services.

(ii) The main services on which the cars would be likely to be operated – from London to Cardiff, Bristol and the West of England – as stipulated by the lease of the refreshment rooms at Swindon, were required to stop there for passengers to take refreshments. Until the Swindon Junction Hotel Company, which owned the rooms, could be bought out or the contract rescinded, there would be little point in providing the dining-cars. This was mentioned in the report.

(iii) Preoccupation with the conversion of broad-gauge vehicles at Swindon and limited facilities for new construction, particularly in view of the reluctance of the traffic officers to recommend the introduction of dining-cars.

The brief of the traffic officers' report was: 'The views of the traffic officers as to the desirability of providing such accommodation, also an estimate of the cost of the vehicles, and of the special expenses which would have to be incurred in connection with the working of them.'

The pantry compartment facilities in brake third No 3423. It was built in 1900 and shortly afterwards converted for refreshment service. (Lot 955 – Diagram D.30)

Information was supplied by the GNR and LNWR, who operated, respectively, one dining-car in each direction between King's Cross and Leeds, King's Cross and Manchester, Euston and Manchester, Euston and Liverpool.

During the half-year ending 31 December 1890, 8,815 passengers were conveyed in the LNWR cars, 8,784 of whom dined, the average being fourteen per journey. Total gross receipts were £2,787 and costs £2,817, but this did not take into account the cost of the cars' construction, maintenance, fuel and lighting. 'If these had been included, the account would have shown a considerable loss, as the cars employed cost about £2,000 each,' noted the GWR report.

By contrast, the GNR had a rosier picture with less passengers (has the 'East Coast' always been more resourceful?) as the average number of passengers per journey was eleven in the Leeds cars, and eight in those to Manchester, with a profit of £428 from the former, and £105 from the latter. The GNR charged two shillings and sixpence (12½p) supplement on the Leeds service to keep non-diners out. The costs of operating the cars, as with those of the LNWR, excluded construction, maintenance, fuel and lighting.

In the event of the GWR providing dining-cars, the report continued, Dean estimated the cost of constructing a suitable vehicle giving dining accommodation for twelve persons, including two smoking side-compartments, lavatories and kitchen, at £2,000. However, the 1896 dining-cars provided dining accommodation for sixteen persons, cost £2,138, and were of 56ft body length. The staff costs, for a cook, attendant and page, were estimated at £195 per annum.

The traffic officers' concluding opinions were:

(i) Dining-cars could not be worked at a profit (taking the example of the LNWR and, probably, GNR).

(ii) They would not be made use of to a large extent. (Disproved in practice.)

(iii) They would add to the weight of trains, which would require additional engines or the running of relief trains. For instance, the LNWR ran a relief to the 4.10 p.m. Euston–Manchester. (Weight was indeed important in the days of 4-2-2s, but this factor seems to have been exaggerated.)

'On these grounds, the officers do not recommend the adoption of dining-cars on this company's line. If, however, the directors decide to provide such cars, they recommend they should be run as follows:

For Dinner
5.0 p.m. Paddington–Bristol
5.45 p.m. Paddington–Cardiff
For Luncheon
12.9 p.m. Bristol–Paddington
10.10 a.m. Cardiff–Paddington'

The report added that three cars would be needed, providing for one spare, and two sets of

staff. Temporary expedients, as suggested by a Refreshment Coaches Committee meeting on 25 October 1890, were that the availability of luncheon baskets should be made better known. To this end, notices should be placed in coaches and cards exhibited at refreshment rooms. Framed notices were suggested for first- and second-class cars, and unframed for third-class, at a total cost of £235 14s (£235,70) for 6,285. In addition, tables should be made available for passengers and a charge of sixpence made for their loan.

A 'Clifton Down' four-car set of auto-fitted, three-centre roof, non-corridor coaches. The leading vehicle is brake third No 3332 (rebuilt with driving cab), two composites are on each side of 517 0-4-2T No 833, and at the far end is a brake third. The set carries the post-1908 chocolate-lake livery.

56ft 0¾in Clerestory Dining-Cars: 1896–1903

Following some of the details mentioned in the 1891 report, the first three dining-cars, for first-class passengers only, appeared in mid-1896. There were three dining sections, seating sixteen passengers in all, with normal droplights to each bay. In addition to the kitchen/pantry, there were also two lavatories for the use of passengers who were, at first, expected to remain in the dining-car throughout the journey. The two gas cooking-stoves had different maximum temperatures. Electric bells were fitted to summon the attendants, in the usual style. Body construction was standard, except that the clerestory decks had sloping sides.

The saloons were panelled in walnut and satin wood, with gilt mouldings and carved door panels, in a somewhat more elaborate style than normal first-class stock. *The GWR Magazine* for June 1896 tells us that the car would be: 'Light and well-decorated, even without the additional features of mirror panels and flower vases.' The seats, the arm-rests of which could be raised, were upholstered in blue morocco leather, as were the table-tops. Of interest were the electro-plated fittings, probably quite a new form of finish at that time. The floor was covered in thick pile-carpeting, and normal pendant gas-lamps were installed.

The first 1896 car went into service on 11 May of that year, working up on the 9.58 a.m. Cardiff–Paddington, and returning on the 6.10 p.m. from the London end. It formed part of one of the 1896 'South Wales Corridor' sets (see page 48). The second car was put on a West of England service as far as Bristol only, as suggested in the 1891 report, and the third one was the spare.

Despite the obvious excellence of the dining-cars in themselves, *The Engineer* in its issue of 5 June 1896 greeted their introduction critically. It first remarked that the GWR had only just commenced dining-car facilities, which were first-class only at that, although the East and West Coast companies had found it advisable to run third-class cars as well. *Moore's Monthly Magazine* was quoted as suggesting that through corridor connection should be established to provide access to the dining-car and 'allow all passen-

First-class dining car No 237, built 1900. (Lot 929 – Diagram H.2) It was later No 9517 and subsequently reclassified as a saloon, No 9097 – Diagram G.53 – to be used by the Prince of Wales, later Edward VIII.

The interior of dining car No 9502, as converted to a café car in 1932.

gers, *irrespective of class*, the opportunity of lunching or dining en route'. *The Engineer* concluded that 'with the present restrictive arrangements, we are inclined to think the cars cannot be such a financial success as they would be if all the limitations were removed'. And then, with a sigh of resignation worthy of Queen Victoria herself, added, 'but it is the same with dining-cars as with hundreds of other things'.

The 1897 dining-car, No 235, was to the same diagram as the earlier three coaches and probably built to allow of an extension of dining-car facilities to other services. The pair of 1900 cars, Nos 236/7, were also on the same diagram as the 1896 batch. In the early 1900s, however, the 1896 and 1900 coaches were converted to composites with a total seating capacity of twenty-nine. Those of 1900 were built with two saloons only and, like No 235 of 1897, without lavatories. In 1914, two of the 1896 trio, now numbered Nos 9501/2, were marshalled in one of the two home ambulance trains of the GWR serving meals and refreshments. After 1918, No 9517 was reclassified as a dining-saloon (Diagram G.53) and renumbered 9097. With the influx of new restaurant cars in the 1929–31 period, the pioneer restaurant cars became surplus, and as they were considered uneconomic to modernise were withdrawn. Two were then reprieved, Nos 9502 and 9516, and refitted in early 1932 as 'Café Cars', as it was delicately put; in other words, snack-buffet cars. A rather makeshift 12ft buffet counter was installed, the remainder of the saloon providing seating accommodation for sixteen to nineteen passengers. From 5 July 1932, one was put on the 9.15 a.m. Paddington–Weston-super-Mare and 2.32 p.m. return; the other on the 9.45a.m. Paddington–Oxford, 11.21 a.m. Oxford–Birmingham and 4.5 p.m. Birmingham–Oxford–Paddington. Their apparent success stimulated the introduction of the 1934 'Quick-Lunch Bar Cars' (see page 88) Nos 9631/2 and 1936 Buffet/Thirds Nos 9643/4 (see page 98). Nos 9502 and 9516 were withdrawn as converted late in 1936. It is believed that even then the two Café Cars were retained for a short while in two exhibition trains for Messrs Fry's chocolates and HMV respectively.

Four more dining-cars of the same 56ft body length were ordered in mid-1902, and put into service on 1 January 1903. They were the first new GWR restaurant cars with meal facilities for all three classes in the one vehicle: one saloon first-class, the other second- and third-class. In contrast to the earlier coaches, the kitchen was in the centre of the body, setting the precedent for the majority of subsequent GWR restaurant cars. As with the 1896–1900 design, droplights to each seat bay provided ventilation and the coaches were gas-lit, although electric lighting might have been expected. The first-class saloon was panelled in walnut and sycamore, with walnut seat-ends. Again, upholstery was of blue morocco leather but, as part of the move towards more hygienic seating, there were loose, reversible cushions on woven-wire frames. The walnut tables were covered with blue morocco leather as before, while the floor was covered with blue Brussels carpet. Woodwork in the second- and third-class saloon was of polished mahogany. The seating, with arm-rests throughout, was upholstered in standard-patterned rep. The ceiling of this saloon was attractively painted with pale-blue lining on the white ground, the Milford boat-train saloons being similarly finished.

In the official photograph, a very prominent roofboard reading 'London–Newport–Cardiff Dining-Car' is shown mounted on No 1580, the first of the batch, as the first two three-class cars replaced the 1896 first-class-only vehicles on the Bristol and South Wales trains. The next two 1903 dining-cars were allocated to the Paddington–Torquay and Exeter services respectively.

One feature worth noting is that the average cost of each car, £1,770, was some £430 less than that of the 1896–7 vehicles. This 1903 batch had a comparatively short life of twenty-seven to thirty-three years, and the last survivor was withdrawn by 1936. It is likely that modernisation was not considered worthwhile in view of their small seating capacity, limited window area and clerestory outline. The body of No 7580 (9518) has been recovered for preservation.

The Royal Train of 1897

In early 1897, the GWR decided to replace the motley and antiquated Royal Train of the mid-Victorian age by a corridor train suitable for use by the Queen on her forthcoming Diamond Jubilee and, no less important, dignified and modern enough to represent the GWR. However, all plans for a straightforward replacement of the old train were soon baulked by a royal command to the GWR, via the Queen's secretary, that the old 1874 Queen's Saloon should not be replaced. Instead, Dean was required to remove the body

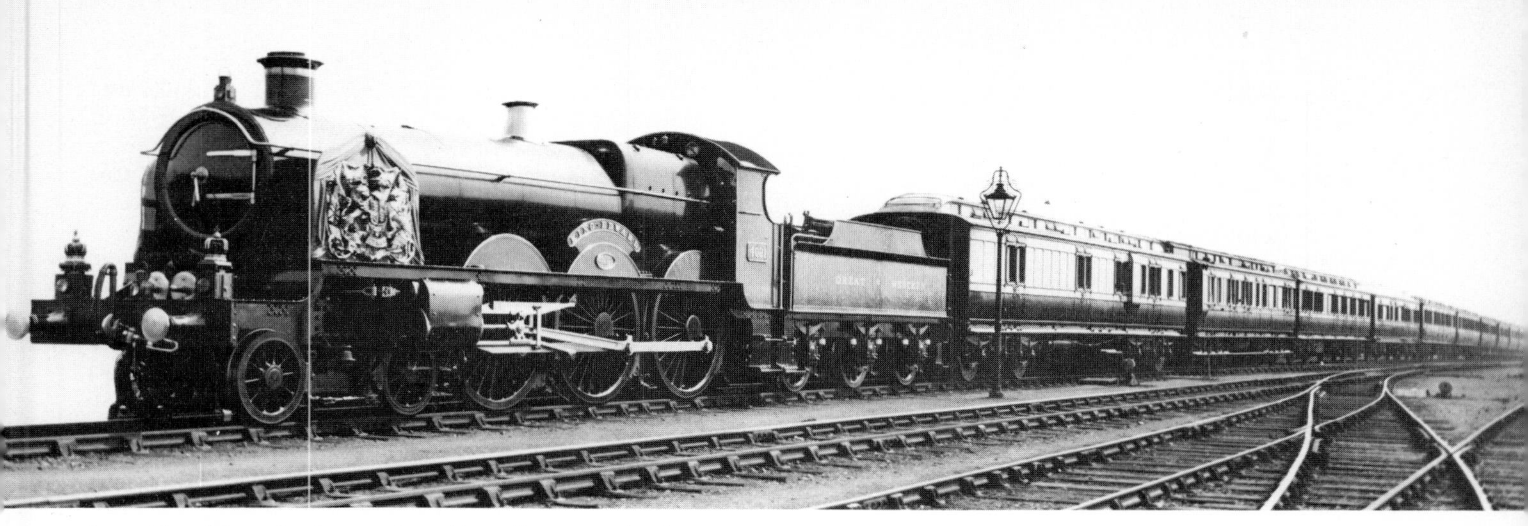

The 1897 Royal Train as formed for the funeral of King Edward VII in 1910. The second vehicle is a standard brake saloon, the rebuilt Queen's Saloon is fourth. The locomotive is Star 4-6-0 No 4021 *King Edward*.

from the old underframe, lengthen it to match the other 56–58ft Royal Train vehicles and bring it up to the outline of the new stock. How this was accomplished was well told in an interesting interview with Dean in the carriage shops at Swindon, published in *The Railway Magazine* of July 1897. Dean mentions his team's concern at seeing the 'empty, casklike structure' of the old Royal Saloon's body, and their wondering if it would ever be possible to make a reasonable vehicle out of it again!

The new train consisted of six coaches, formed as follows:

56ft Full Brake with Lavatory	No 1070
58ft Attendants' Saloon	No 234 (later No 9003)
54ft Queen's Saloon (rebuilt)	No 229 (later No 9001)
58ft Officials' Saloon	No 233 (later No 9002)
56ft First	No 283 (later No 8283)
56ft Full Brake with Lavatory	No 1069

In most respects, the new coaches were of standard construction but suitably embellished for royalty. They had Dean standard 10ft bogies but 'royal' clerestories and the novelty of electric lighting, being the first new vehicles with this form of illumination. The full brakes, with one lavatory each, did not have corridor connections at the outer ends, although these could have been fitted if required.

The other coaches all had internal doors sliding on ball-bearings, the design of L. R. Thomas, Dean's assistant, and were the first with roof water-tanks for the lavatories. The saloons, Nos 233/4, were straightforward enough, being upholstered in cream leather and decorated by the usual colour photographs. One of these saloons was redecorated in 1921 for the use of the Princess Royal and Viscount Lascelles.

The first, No 283, was described, somewhat pointedly, by Dean in the course of *The Railway Magazine* interview, as catering for 'peculiar idiosyncrasies of mighty persons', who presumably might want to hide themselves away in the compartments or smoking-saloon. It was, in fact, a standard first in layout with four side-corridor compartments and two open smoking-bays with the partitions up to cantrail level. Tables for meals could apparently be fitted in the open section.

The enlarged and virtually reconstructed Queen's Saloon, No 229, embodied most of the old 43ft coach, which had been built between 1872 and 1874. The main feature of the vehicle was the Queen's personal saloon which bulged out at the side and had a domed roof. The side framing of the body was mahogany, the floor being of oak and insulated by 300 pieces of cork laid on double-diagonal boards. The domed roof was a double one as there had been complaint, in the hot Jubilee year of 1887, that the saloon was too warm; so a second roof was put over the original one allowing an air space in between. The outer roof was made of cedar and was retained in the 1897 rebuilding. Internally, woodwork was in satinwood and sycamore panelling, with bevelled mirrors. The Queen's personal compartments were lined in white silk, her attendants' accommodation being in morocco leather. It is also worth recording that the curtain rods were supported by gold-painted figures of Atlas. Other features were a hand-painted ceiling and electric bells. The Queen herself decreed that the grandiose oil-lamp, which had several burners and an opal bowl, should be

Interior of first No 283, later No 8283, marshalled in the Royal Train. (Lot 839 – Diagram A.5)

retained in the central compartment but, elsewhere, the lighting was electric.

For Queen Victoria's funeral train in 1901, this saloon had its internal fittings removed to accommodate the coffin, and the interior hung with white and purple drapes. GWR Saloon No 223 accompanied this vehicle, both being incorporated in the LBSC Royal Train. The Queen's Saloon was used for the funeral of Edward VII in 1910, after which it lay unused until 1912, when the bodywork was scrapped and the frame used for the chief mechanical engineer's personal inspection saloon of that year No 9100 (see page 66). A section of the interior was preserved and is now at the Great Western Railway Museum, Swindon.

Until the early 1930s the remaining five vehicles, with composite No 7413 and the directors' saloon, constituted the GWR Royal Train but, by 1935, they had reached the end of their economic lives and were withdrawn. The full brakes, at about this time, had been converted to stores vans. After withdrawal, two saloons, Nos 9002/3, were bought for use as holiday accommodation on the Welsh coast at Helyg Fach, near Aberporth, for £30 each. By the early 1960s, after nearly thirty years' retirement, the bodies were still in sound condition, their doors sealed up, and one with a corrugated asbestos roof and the other also waterproofed. The interiors were still relatively untouched, retaining some of the leather upholstery, ornamental glass panelling, coloured pictures in the compartments, and gilded ceiling mouldings.

There both might have stayed but for the imaginative project of Madame Tussaud's Ltd to create a Royalty and Empire exhibition at Windsor and Eton Central station which opened to the public in spring of 1983. The centrepiece of the display is a train made up of Dean 4-2-2 No 3041 *The Queen* (a reproduction locomotive), 1897 Royal Train saloon No 9002 and a reproduction Queen's Saloon. The body of No 9002 was removed from Helyg Fach in the spring of 1982, then restored by Resco Railways Ltd and mounted on a shortened BR Mk 1 underframe. The Queen's Saloon, also produced by Resco, was 'new', mounted on another adapted underframe and including some secondhand body parts from a parcels van. The body of No 9003 remains on the Welsh coast.

55ft–58ft New Milford Boat-Train Stock: 1900–1

One of J. L. Wilkinson's main energies, when general manager, was the encouragement of Irish traffic. As a result, two centre-corridor 'tourist' sets were built for the New Milford boat-trains at the turn of the century. The first set permitted a tri-weekly service only, 6.25 a.m. New Milford–Paddington (arriving 1 p.m.) and 4.25 p.m. return (arriving 11 p.m.) on Tuesdays, Thursdays and Saturdays only. With the construction of the second set, a daily service was introduced. The sets were a novel venture which, unfortunately, did not come off. In view of the conservatism of British travellers this is not altogether surprising, and will be referred to later. They were the first GWR public-service set trains with electric lighting, and, moreover, the first on the GWR to have the modern system of a communication chain running just under the cantrail inside, and enclosed, except over the doors.

On 22 May 1900, exactly a year after the official order was placed, the first set of five coaches entered service. Outwardly, these centre-corridor coaches were not noticeably different from side-corridor clerestory stock as all seating bays had normal quarter and droplights. Constructionally, also, they did not differ from other bogie clerestory coaches. The second set was completed in April 1901 and was identical to the first, except for sliding luggage doors to the brake thirds: these were a unique feature on the GWR at that time.

Each vehicle was centre-corridor with two lavatories each and the usual one in the case of the brake thirds. The firsts, however, had one lavatory and one washbasin compartment at each end. The seating arrangements of the coaches differed. The first- and second-class had photograph panels and racks above the seats. The third-class had plain seats, like present-day open stock, with light parcels racks running along the bodyside at cantrail level, but without arm-rests to the seats, a bad feature not uncommon in GWR clerestory

One of the second series of New Milford boat train stock. Brake third No 3433 of 1901, with sliding doors to the luggage area. (Lot 964 – Diagram D.36)

Interior of New Milford boat train third No 2834. (Lot 936 – Diagram C.18) This provides a good view of a 'series 3' clerestory and the electroliers. No wonder the seats were regarded as uncomfortable!

open smoking sections. Tables could be fitted to each set of seats and, when not in use, were stored in the space between the backs of the seats behind panelled doors opened from the gangway. The second-class coaches had a small kitchen with a hot-water tank and 'household' stove. From this, a rather hardworked attendant served tea, coffee, sandwiches and cold meat meals to the whole train of five or six coaches. Doubtless the concept was derived from Pullman practice – but in economy style.

Internal decoration was generally similar to standard stock in the use of walnut and sycamore, mahogany and oak for the panelling of first-, second- and third-class respectively. Upholstery for the first-class was either dark green cloth or dark green morocco leather trimmed in gold and green braid, while the seconds and thirds had the seats covered in 'star motif' moquette. Ceilings in the first-class were the usual lincrusta with gold details but, in the seconds and thirds, the plain white surface was lined-out rather pleasantly in light blue. The electric lighting could either be full or half-on, and was controlled by the guard. Since the 'brake-vehicle' arrangement was adopted, it was necessary for the 'dependent' coaches to run always in the same order and so the number of the adjoining vehicle was painted on the ends of each coach.

'Anyone who knows Great Western carriages will admit that while it is possible to re-arrange their interiors, it is not very easy to increase their comfort.' So commented, rather obliquely, *The Railway Engineer* when reviewing the introduction of the first Milford set. Generally, however, opinion at that time was against open stock, particularly in the form of a whole set. Wilkinson was apparently aiming at the tourist trade to Ireland, and his policy later culminated in the Killarney excursions of the 1900s and later.

There can be little doubt that the open sets were not popular. Speaking at a debate of the GWR (London) Debating Society in 1920 on a motion, 'Should the compartment coach be abolished?' a Mr E. Robinson, MBE, had some hard things to say about the Milford sets. Referring to open stock, he maintained that they were uncomfortable, that the first-class accommodation of twenty-four was insufficient, and that the third-class seats were cramped and had poor luggage rack accommodation. He further said that there were occasions when passengers for Ireland arriving at Paddington had refused to travel in the centre-corridor train and had defected to the LNWR! *The Railway Engineer* review of 1900 said the five-coach set ran with a corridor-composite attached; presumably for loyal but anti-centre corridor passengers. Robinson also said that it was difficult at the time of the debate (1920) to find suitable services for them as they had, of course, been displaced on Irish boat-trains by more modern stock.

In fact, the sets preceded general practice by about twenty years. Soon after Grouping, the LMS introduced an open set on the St Pancras–Bradford service which proved equally unpopular. It was left to the LNER successfully to operate open sets with meals served to passengers at their seats on streamline services and the 'Hook Continental' and 'East Anglian' expresses. The GWR never again built open stock for ordinary services, except restaurant cars, and the only open sets were those of 1935–40 vintage designed for excursion use. By the late 1930s the Milford boat train sets were redundant and as they were then unsuitable for excursion work, withdrawal began. All except the thirds appear to have been condemned by 1939 and the final survivors went in early post-war days.

5
THE CHURCHWARD REVOLUTION 1903–1922

Steam Rail-Motors and Trailers: 1903–13
The story of the rail-motor boom of the 1900–14 period on British railways is well known and will not be elaborated except to point out that the GWR was an early exponent of rail-motors and also, in due course, operated the largest British fleet of these vehicles. The GWR also evolved its own distinctive variety of rail-motor, auto-trailer conversions of which survived until the late 1950s.

Trials were carried out in early 1903 with Dugald Drummond's LBSC/LSWR joint East Southsea service rail-motor No 1 between Stroud and Chalford. The first two GWR rail-motors, ordered in May 1903, differed quite considerably from Drummond's vehicle: the engine unit was considerably more powerful and enclosed as part of the coachwork, while the elliptical roof of the bodywork contrasted with the low-roofed Eastleigh product. The Swindon design was more realistic than Drummond's, which proved underpowered, although the GWR seemed to intend to use its railmotors on more arduous services. The GWR Nos 1/2 entered service on 12 October 1903, running between Chalford and Stonehouse, and serving a number of new halts built for the working.

A new outline, in the form of a high elliptical roof and large bodyside windows with ventilators, was introduced with these railcars and was soon to find expression in main-line stock with the 'Dreadnought' corridor coaches, the first of which entered service in 1904. Rail-motors Nos 1/2 had one large passenger saloon seating fifty-two, with an entrance from the other end to the engine unit through the driving compartment vestibule. A fixed set of steps on either side of this vestibule permitted access from rail level, since it was originally intended to pick up and put down passengers at level crossings as well as halts. The vestibule entrances were protected by collapsible iron gates.

Body framing was of Baltic and Canadian oak with vertical mahogany matchboarding for exterior body panelling. The interior was finished in polished oak, with seats and seat-backs formed of woven wire covered with rattan cane. This type of seating was much in vogue at the time. The large bodyside windows had spring roller blinds. For standing passengers there was a handrail, with leather straps, running through the saloon. This handrail was, in reality, a tube through which ran a cord allowing the driver to blow the whistle from the driving vestibule. The coach bodies were slab-sided and flat-ended, with three large windows at each end. The carrying bogies were of a specially-designed 8ft bolster type. Nos 1/2 cost £1,738 each, the carriage department's work accounting for £728 of this.

By May 1904, new services were started with rail-motors Nos 3–14 between Millbay, Saltash and Plympton, Westbourne Park and Southall via Greenford and on the Brentford branch. Nos 3–14 were the same as Nos 1/2 with the same slab sides with matchboarding but were 59ft 6in in length. In December 1904, two trailers were built to match these rail-motors, one 59ft 6in, the other 70ft, and both 9ft wide. By September of the same year, further cars, Nos 17–28, were put into service on London area workings, supplementing the existing timetables.

All the above rail-motors, except Nos 1/2, were of the 'Suburban' type, but the first two and various subsequent batches were known as the 'Branch' type. The sole difference was that the 'Branch' type had accommodation for luggage and light goods.

The other differences between the batches of rail-motors concerned the driving wheel diameter of the engine units (Nos 1/2, 3ft 6in; Nos 3–36, 3ft 6½in and Nos 37–99, 4ft). There were variations in the capacity of the coal bunkers, too: Nos 1/2, 10cwt; Nos 3–83, 15cwt and Nos 84–99, 30cwt. In all, there were 112 engine units for 99 coach bodies.

Auto-trailers Nos 1–28 comprised a mixture of types, including the converted clerestory coaches mentioned on page 40. One distinctive feature of all the purpose-built vehicles was the provision of large oval-faced buffers, fitted because of the 70ft length of most coaches and designed to obviate buffer-locking on lines with severe curvature.

Motor cars Nos 29–40, put into service in late 1904 and early 1905, were the 'Branch' types but, more important, were of a different body design, three were 70ft in length, the others 59ft 6in. The bodies were slightly reduced in height with a standard elliptical roof, curved lower body panels, and bow-ends. The 70ft vehicles had two passenger saloons, one smoking, one non-smoking, those with the 59ft 6in body having one saloon only. Four-a-side transverse seating was predominant in the saloons either flanked, or interspersed by longitudinal 'benches' accommodating eight or ten passengers. The bodyside windows had bolection mouldings and square-framed frosted toplights above, and there were usually three pairs of droplights on each side, although the arrangement of windows varied. In addition, there was a central vestibule providing entry other than through the end driving vestibule. Retractable steps were worked by levers in the vestibules. This description covers most of the rail-motors and trailers built, although individual batches require mention.

Rail-motors Nos 59/60 and Trailers Nos 9/10 were built with gangways to their inner ends to work as two-car sets on Plymouth area branches: they were of the 'Branch' type. In the 1910s, Trailers Nos 3/6 were similarly fitted to work as a two-car set, as later were Nos 4/5. In 1905, the first experiments were carried out with auto-trailer working with 0-4-2Ts and, in the Plymouth area, two two-car trailer sets worked with the locomotive sandwiched between. These trailer pairs were used in this form rather than with the rail-motors. In most cases one car provided the smoking accommodation while the other was a non-smoker.

From 15 May 1904, all the old passenger stock working on the Lambourn Valley Railway was withdrawn and replaced by two rail-motors. In August 1905, Trailers Nos 7/8 were built for this service, forming the tail-load in addition to the usual horseboxes. They were among the first to have incandescent gas lighting. Unfortunately, it is not possible to give a full list of the progressive introduction of new rail-motor services but, in 1905 for instance, rail-motors started between Acton and Park Royal, Ruabon and Dolgelley, Weymouth and Dorchester, Trowbridge, Westbury and Patney. An interesting service which started on summer Sundays in 1904 was that between Addison Road, Kensington and Acton.

Two 'odd-men-out' of the rail-motor fleet were Nos 15/16, built in late 1905 by Kerr Stuart. Swindon seems to have had no hand in their design: the engine unit was separate from the coach body with a high domed roof, while the coachwork was low-roofed with two central entrance doors each side and seating for forty-eight. The carrying bogie had inside bearings to the wheels, a not unusual feature of 'proprietary' rail-motors. In comparison with the GWR standard cars, the Kerr Stuart vehicles were considerably less powerful and it seems surprising that these comparatively underpowered cars should have been added to the GWR fleet. Electric

One of the first two GWR rail-motors (Lot 1037 – Diagrams A/A.1), which went into service in October 1903, running between Chalford and Stonehouse.

lighting was to have been fitted but this was not proceeded with and all standard GWR rail-motors and trailers built up to 1913 were gas-lit. Nos. 15/16 were built with a steam brake only, but were fitted with vacuum before entering service. In spite of their uniqueness, the Kerr Stuart cars survived the first rail-motor withdrawals late in the First World War, though No 15 was sold in 1920. It ended up on the Nidd Valley Light Railway and was not scrapped until 1937. No 16 was also withdrawn in 1920, but reinstated, and lasted until 1927 when it was sold to the Port of London Authority for use on its dockland passenger workings. It was scrapped the following year.

Rail-motors Nos 61–72 introduced neater turn-under steps for the central double vestibule doors fitted to these cars, while Nos 73–80, although a standard GWR design, were built by the Gloucester Railway C. & W. Co who seemed to have used the design for its rail-motors ordered by the Cardiff Railway in 1911. Further rail-motors, Nos 81–3 of 1907, Nos 84–90 and 91–99 of 1908, differed very little from the Nos 61–72 batch although they had single sliding entrance doors in the centre of the body and larger cab windows. The final batch, Nos 91–99, cost £2,175 against the £1,900 of the earlier 70ft cars. Although as originally built, the whistle on the engine unit could be sounded by the driver from the front cab, the more familiar gong on the front end, operated by a pedal, was later fitted. There was electric bell communication between driver and fireman.

There was more variety with trailers, most of which were turned out after about 1906. The most numerous were diagram 'L' of which thirty 70ft

Steam rail-motor No 43 (built 1905, Lot 1079) with trailer No 55, built 1908. (Lot 1141 – Diagram L)

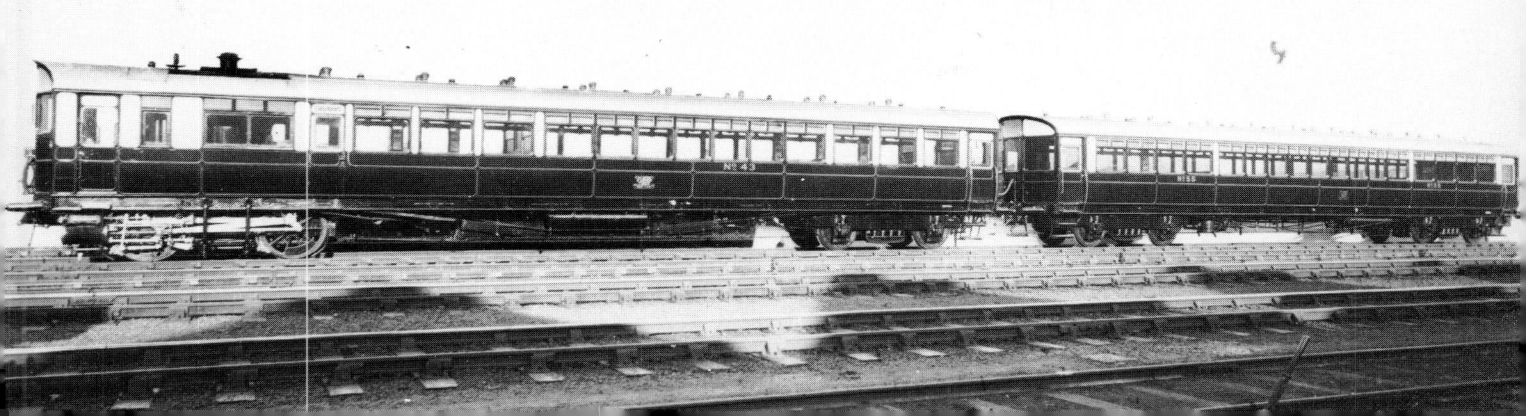

seventy-six-seat coaches were produced. Nos 71/2 and 73/4 were built to work in gangwayed pairs in the Plymouth district and remained on Plymouth–Saltash–Liskeard workings all their lives. Nos 73/4 had no driving cabs. All Nos 75–98 were gangwayed and, of these, Nos 75–80 were without driving cabs. Nos 93–98 usually worked in pairs. The distinguishing feature of the Nos 71–98 batch was the fact that they had no droplights between the large bodyside windows.

Without doubt, one of the most peculiar vehicles produced by a British railway was trailer No 48 built in March 1907. Difficulty with loading and unloading passengers on suburban lines had been encountered, as there were usually only two passenger doors on each side of the trailer or rail-motor. As an experiment aimed at improving passenger movement, twelve sets of four-a-side back-to-back seats, five feet apart and accommodating ninety-six passengers, were placed down the centre of the body, with circulating space on either side of them. Not only was this supposed to permit easier entry and exit at stops, but also to help the conductor-guard in issuing tickets. Corresponding with the spaces between the seats each side were eleven normal-width sliding doors and, in addition, two end doors. The sliding doors were all operated by the conductor-guard, at first by a lever, and then by a wheel! The experiment was, apparently, a total failure as, on several occasions, passengers were trapped and stuck fast in the doorways when the guard tried to shut the doors. In outward appearance, No 48 most nearly resembled the 'Concertina' corridor coaches, as the recessed sliding doors and large windows without ventilators produced the same effect as the corridor-sides of those coaches. It was not long before No 48 was rebuilt with end passenger access, but retaining the narrow quarterlights. This trailer survived into the 1950s.

Six rail-motor trailers were 1905 conversions from clerestory corridor coaches, three from 1893 'West of England' thirds, and the other three from standard 1899 thirds. Details of individual identities are given in Chapter 10. The interior was completely altered with a driving cab fitted at one end. The non-smoking section had eight-and-a-half transverse seating bays with a centre gangway and two longitudinal benches on each side. The smoking-section had six full and two half-bays with a centre gangway. Four of these coaches retained one lavatory compartment, which reduced their seating capacity by two to sixty-five.

Below:
The interior of the unsuccessful trailer No 48, built 1907. Note the sliding doors and 'island' plywood-covered seats.

Bottom:
Steam rail-motor No 85, built 1908 (Lot 1140 – Diagram R) working from Reading to Didcot, with a clerestory trailer in tow.

Rail-motors converted to Auto-trailers: 1915–1936

It has been pointed out that auto-train services were developed from 1905 along with the rail-motors, more notably on higher density services with the engine hauling three or four trailers. In many cases, of course, the rail-motors had encouraged new traffic beyond their capacity and that of one trailer – their maximum practicable load. From 1915 onwards, the rail-motors were progressively rebuilt as auto-trailers. This does not seem to have been a case of withdrawals when the boilers wore out, as coach and engine-unit were taken out of service separately. From 1920–23 and 1927–30, withdrawal and subsequent conversion to auto-trailers was at its height. In January 1935, seventeen rail-motors were still in traffic, ranging from No 30 of 1905 to the final batch. The last service worked by these machines was that between Neath (Canal Side) and Court Sart, which was withdrawn from 16 September 1935. However, of the seventeen remaining in 1935, only seven were subsequently converted to trailers, this process ceasing with the emergence of trailers Nos 210–15 in February 1936.

Actual conversion involved more than the use of the space vacated by the redundant engine-unit for extra seating and a guard's and luggage compartment; in some cases the bodies were mounted on new bogies of 7ft or 9ft standard types. In fact, for the earlier rail-motors considerable alterations to the bodywork were needed, with the insertion of new sections. In many cases the ventilators over the bodyside windows, as well as the bodyside mouldings, were sheeted over with steel panels. All the original rail-motors and trailers had been built with, and retained, gas lighting, which was kept in all but a very few conversions. As late as 1925, two trailers still had flat-flame gas lights. Altogether, eighty-five GWR rail-motors were rebuilt as trailers and, in addition, the four Gloucester RCW-built vehicles for the Cardiff Railway, which closely resembled the GWR design. During the period of conversion, therefore, only three batches of trailers were built new – Nos 159–180/7–96 inclusive.

Nearly all the original trailers and conversions survived into post-war days, by which time, like much other old GWR stock, they were in dire need of replacement. However, it was not until 1951 that the Western Region built new trailers, Nos 220–34, and the oldest examples could be withdrawn. From this date onwards, branch-line closures also enabled further withdrawals to be made. In 1954, however, a number of the original pairs of trailers – Nos 3/4 and 5/6 for instance – were on the Exe Valley line and around the Plymouth area. By late 1958, only a handful of rail-motor conversions or original trailers remained and, with the dieselisation of some of the London area workings, these were then withdrawn. The very last, still gas-lit, was a 59ft 6in trailer, No 211, formerly rail-motor No 81, which was withdrawn early in 1959. However, a number of trailers remained in departmental stock, including several 70ft examples. An interesting survivor in departmental use at Monmouth Troy, at least until 1962, was trailer No 118 converted from one of the early straight-sided rail-motors, No 22 of 1904. Possibly the last 70ft trailer on BR was No 12, withdrawn when in internal use at Old Oak Common in 1966.

68ft–70ft 'Dreadnought' Corridor Stock: 1904–1907

If the domeless, taper-boiler 'Atbaras', 'Cities' and 4-6-0 No 100 ushered in Churchward's new locomotive era for the GWR and shocked traditionalists, then it is fair to say the same for the

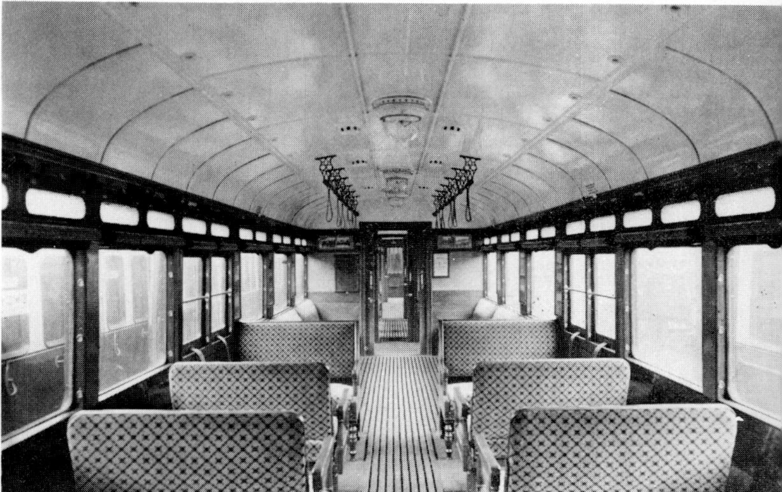

Top:
Auto-trailer No 81 at Princes Risborough, July 1947. (Lot 1198 – Diagram U)

Above:
The interior of auto-trailer No 200, converted in 1933 on Lot 1511 to Diagram A26, from rail-motor No 58.

Below:
Evidence that the GWR did not always work strictly to plan! 51xx 2-6-2T No 5114 leaves King's Sutton with a stopping train made up of auto-trailer No 11 (Lot 1097) and cattle wagon.

The 10.10am Paddington–Penzance near Twyford in the summer of 1904 with a Dreadnought restaurant car fourth in the formation.

'Dreadnoughts' in respect of coaches. They were truly revolutionary. Dean's neat clerestory outline was thrown aside, the new coaches being the first main-line stock without clerestories. But, apart from that, the massiveness of the bodies and their near-70ft length was their most impressive feature. The 'clipper' bodies, bulging out to a 9ft 6in width, made full use of the old broad-gauge loading gauge. Churchward had a difficult time overcoming conservatism which jibbed at the thought of 70-footers. It was argued that the locking-bars in use over the system would have to be renewed, but this was countered by the CME pointing out that the minimal cost of this – £50,000 – was outweighed by operating advantages. The 'Dreadnoughts' went through.

The only previous 60ft-plus coach was the experimental clerestory brake third of 1902, No 2400 (see page 49), which appears to have been built as the precursor of a fleet of larger coaches.

The name 'Dreadnought' was, obviously, derived from the pre-Great War series of all-big-gun battleships, the first of which was launched in 1906. The same tag was also applied, less explicably, to the Metropolitan Railway steam-hauled suburban coaches of 1910–12 and 1920–23 and various other vehicles. The GWR 'Dreadnoughts' were probably the largest coaches in all time to run on British railways – a distinction achieved by the sheer bulk of their 70ft by 9ft 6in bodies.

First to appear was a restaurant car, No 9515 (ex-1575), in May 1904, and this was followed three months later by three more, Nos 9512–4 (ex-1572-4). These vehicles were not accompanied by batches of corridor coaches and at first ran in clerestory sets, as did Nos 9509–9511 (ex-1569–71) completed in January 1905. The numbering backwards was rather an unusual feature. The new 'Dreadnoughts' added to the number of composite-first, second and third-class dining-cars in service, of which there were fourteen by late 1904. They had a central kitchen and one first-class saloon, while the other saloon combined second- and third-class. Electric lighting 'from ornate electroliers' was installed. Other notable features by that date were the electric fans in the saloons and the refrigerator in the kitchen – heralding the beginning of the electric age in GWR coaches. Heating could be regulated by passengers, a feature not extended to ordinary coaches for about ten years, and the heating pipes were concealed by brass grids.

The internal furnishings, highest and best Edwardian, are worth mentioning in detail. Sliding internal doors shut off the saloons from vestibules and kitchen. The first-class saloon, seating eighteen, had the usual gleaming white lincrusta ceiling with raised gold-painted decoration. Woodwork was American walnut with sycamore panels – an almost standard favourite. The large windows with frosted-glass toplights above set a pattern for future generations of GWR dining-cars. Brass racks with coloured photographs below were, of course, standard. The tables, in mahogany and covered in green morocco leather, were removable and adorned with electric bell-pushes which added to the wonder of electricity. The seat frames, in carved walnut, contained tip-up, green morocco-leather-covered seats and there were no arm-rests. Finally, the floor was covered with green Brussels carpet.

Second/third-class saloons had less elaborate woodwork which was predominantly the traditional mahogany, a birchwood veneer ceiling with gold lining, and red leather upholstery. Blue carpeting completed the furnishing.

As mentioned above, the new restaurant cars of 1904 were marshalled in the front-line Dean clerestory sets. From 1 July 1904, the GWR introduced a new 10.10 a.m. Paddington–Penzance limited express running non-stop to Plymouth via Pylle Hill loop, Bristol, the return train arriving in Paddington at 5 p.m. The new train, which could claim the longest non-stop run in the world, consisted of seven coaches: a five-coach clerestory set, a 'Dreadnought' dining-car, and a tri-composite for Falmouth. This train officially became the 'Cornish Riviera Limited' in the following year when it received a full 'Dreadnought' set.

Nos 9509–9515, the first type of 'Dreadnought' restaurant car, were modernised in 1939/40, receiving flush steel panelling above the waist and larger windows with sliding metal-framed ventilators. Apart from that, there had been few modifications, although No 9511 had been fitted with 'American' six-wheel bogies soon after being built. After the war, all returned quickly to top-line express work but withdrawals began in 1952 and all, except two with Pullman gangway adaptors which went in 1959, were withdrawn by 1956.

In mid-1905, the ordinary 'Dreadnought'

coaches appeared. Original intentions were for only two sets including second-class coaches but, early in 1905, the orders were changed to three sets with first and third accommodation only, as it was decided in that year to withdraw second-class from 'limited express' trains between Paddington and Penzance. Three seven-coach sets were built to commence service from the summer timetable of 1905 on the recently-named 'Cornish Riviera Limited' which was still a summer-only train and which inaugurated seat-reservation.

The new coaches had the same 'clipper' bodies as the first batches of restaurant cars, with recessed end and central doorways. The first noticeable change was the absence of compartment-side doors and entry was by end and central vestibules only.

There were many bitter criticisms of the 'Dreadnought' sets on the 'Cornish Riviera Limited', revealing yet again traditional British conservatism. It was noticeable that, in order to have ample space for the three vestibules in the thirds and composites, space equal to one compartment had to be sacrificed – in comparison to the later 'Concertinas' – and that the lavatories, in particular, and compartments were correspondingly rather cramped for a 70ft vehicle. A particularly interesting discussion of the pros and cons of the 'Dreadnoughts' took place in the stimulating and well-argued debate of the GWR (London) Debating Society in the 1920–21 session referred to on page 55. The motion, it will be recalled, was: 'Should the compartment coach be abolished?' and a Mr Bulkeley, putting forward the case for open coaches, referred to the 'Dreadnoughts'. He suggested that this stock, which he called the finest in England, should have its interiors stripped and rebuilt to a centre-gangway layout, seating seventy-six for the thirds as against seventy-two in practice. The fundamental mistake, he said, had probably been in providing compartments without side doors.

Mr E. Robinson, defending the compartment coach, let fly against the 'Dreadnoughts', alleging that they had been most unpopular with passengers as there had been much scrambling in the vestibules when de-training travellers had met en-training crowds. In fact, to effect some measure of control, the doors had to be marked 'Entrance' and 'Exit' but, even then, complaints had continued to come in. Dissatisfaction is evident as the 'Dreadnoughts' only lasted from 1905 to about 1914, on the 'Cornish Riviera Limited' and were replaced by 70ft 'Toplight' stock. The fact that the 'Dreadnoughts' were not multiplied, even as a modified design, is indicative of official reaction to the complaints. But it is only fair to point out that the 'Concertinas' were ordered in mid-1905, just as the 'Dreadnoughts' were going into service. One can only conclude that, magnificent though the 'Dreadnoughts' were, and although the design was advanced for its day, they were not appreciated. Nor was the 'Cornish Riviera' perhaps the best testing ground for a completely new layout which did not come to that train for another thirty years in the 'Centenary' stock.

Of the other innovations, more unusual was the arrangement whereby the corridors 'crossed' from one side of the coach to the other, divided by the central vestibule. The object was to provide outside corner-seats on both sides of the train and also, allegedly, to distribute passengers' weight more evenly. Most interestingly, the either-side corridors were incorporated into the design of the BR second-class side-corridor coaches in the XP64 train set of 1964 – an interesting 'throw-back'.

Also notable, as previously remarked, was the absence of exterior doors to the compartments but, unfortunately, this did not allow the provision of large windows. Ventilation, it seems, was something of a problem and, rather than use a large window with hinged toplights, a normal droplight was inserted between ordinary quarterlights. The last batch of thirds, Lot 1098, had wider droplights than the rest.

In *The Railway Engineer* for November 1905 it was mentioned that compartment doors could not be fitted because these vehicles were too wide. The answer to this one seems to be provided by the appearance of the 'Concertinas', with individual recesses for each bodyside door. The same issue of *The Railway Engineer* also states that brass bars were fixed over the droplights but there is no record of this in practice.

The increased height in the compartments made possible by the elliptical roofs was something worth remarking about at the time, as the height inside from floor to ceiling was 8ft 0¾in.

The Cornish Riviera Limited in 1905, seen near Uphill headed by 4-4-2 No 173 *Robins Bolitho*, built in March of that year. The restaurant car is third in this formation of Dreadnought stock.

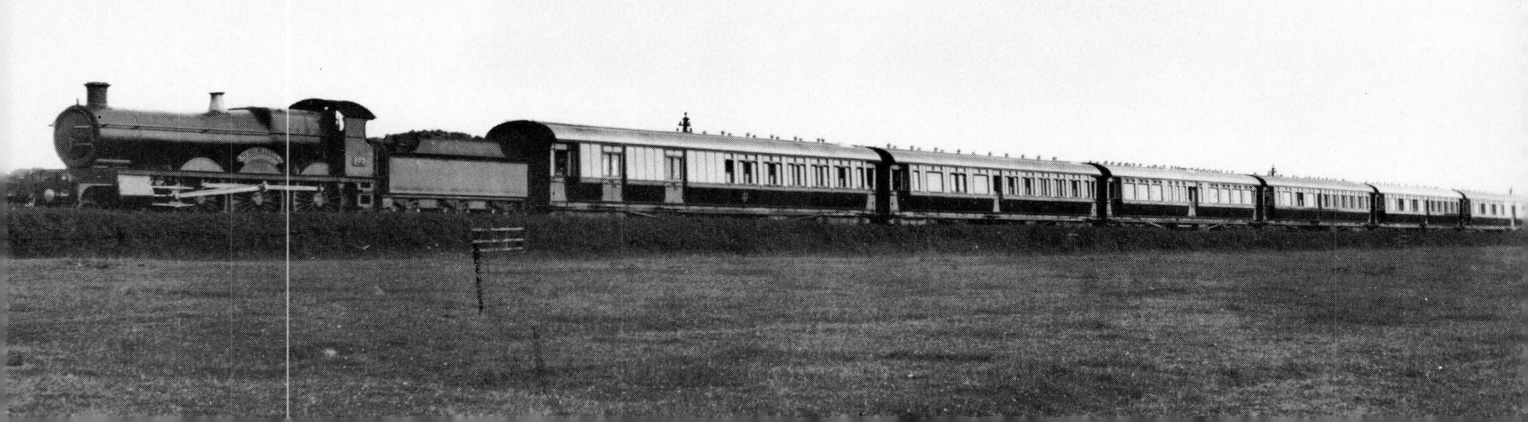

Dreadnought third No 3277, for excursion use and fitted with gas lighting. (Lot 1084 – Diagram C.24)

The ceilings in the ordinary coaches were all three-ply birchwood, the joins in the panelling being covered by gold mouldings. The first-class corridors were panelled in polished American walnut matchboarding below the windows and sycamore panels above, and compartment panelling was in the same walnut. Upholstery was either dark green or dark blue cloth set off by 'handsome' antimacassars for non-smoking compartments, and morocco leather for smokers. This seems to be about the last time on the GWR that distinction was made by materials in this way. The third-class corridor coaches had the usual oak panelling and uncomfortable, if hygienic, seats of woven wire, covered in red and black wool rep, with maroon leather in smoking compartments. Mention is made specifically of photographs in third-class compartments, for the first-class seems to have had white enamelled panels above the seats. As originally built, sliding doors shut off the corridors from the vestibules but these were soon removed.

Of the individual batches which entered service between June and September 1905, the composites, Nos (7) 639–(7) 644, seem to have been the first to appear. Seven-coach 'Cornish Riviera' sets were formed: two each of brake thirds, thirds and composites and one composite dining-car. Soon after 1906, with the 'Cornish Riviera' running via Westbury, slip coaches of 70ft 'Concertina' design were added to the 'Dreadnoughts' and slipped at four different points. Three six-coach 'Excursion' sets were also built and, being of less importance, were gas-lit, conversion to electric light taking place from 1927–30. The lengths of the different types varied: brake-thirds were 70ft, although originally intended to be 68ft, the thirds were 69ft, and the composites 68ft. The diners were 68ft for the earlier vehicles, Nos 9509–15; Nos 9505–8 were 70ft.

The brake thirds had the unusual feature of the guard's door put in place of the end vestibule door, a very awkward position. It was also found at first that the luggage compartment double doors would not open right back, so new, narrower doors were hung, leaving the old hinges in place. Nos 3467/72 were converted in 1912 to buffet third brakes with a kitchen/pantry in place of two compartments with an extra door on each side. They returned to their original state in 1937. In 1926, No 3476 was damaged by fire and given a new body of the 70ft 1922 'South Wales' design, only 9ft wide and of all-steel construction – including the compartment partitions. The composites were not altered in later days, although No 7641 had some 'Beclawat' frameless drop-type windows fitted in early 1931. The first GWR coaches to be built with the drop-type windows were the 'Centenary' and 'Excursion' sets of 1935 but both types had them replaced in due course. Composites Nos 7640/1 were the last ordinary 'Dreadnought' coaches to go out of service – in 1956.

There were three batches of thirds, the final one being general spares and equipped with electric lighting. Although on the same diagrams as previously mentioned, there were some differences in droplight width between vehicles. Originally, the spares, Nos 3291–3300, were to form the last ten of the second batch but, when re-ordered in April 1905, the lot was given to an outside contractor – the Birmingham Railway Carriage and Wagon Company.

With the influx of new 60ft standard coaches in the 1936–40 period, the 'Dreadnoughts' went into decline. After the war, most were relegated to relief sets and stopping trains. At the same time, a large number of 'Dreadnoughts' going for repair had their toplights sheeted over by steel panels which changed their appearance to some extent. Withdrawals began in 1949 and few 'Dreadnoughts' were in service after 1953, the final examples going in 1956. Two, Nos 3298/9, were reconditioned in 1954 to serve as sleepers for dining-car crews working on lodging turns to Newquay. No 3299 was most fortunately saved from breaking-up by David Rouse in 1964, and is now preserved at Didcot Railway Centre.

The restaurant cars for the 'Dreadnought' 'Cornish Riviera' sets were Nos 9505–8 and were very similar to the earlier batches but of 70ft length. They also had a fractionally larger third-class saloon and were of reduced height. Nos 9505–8 were modernised from the late 1930s, like Nos 9509–19. No 9506 was completely destroyed during the bombing of Paddington in 1941 and not replaced. The others remained in service until 1954–56.

Not immediately recognizable as 'Dreadnoughts', but most easily classed as such, were the four first-class sleeping cars, Nos 9082–5 (originally Nos 237–240) of 1907. Claims were made for

Dreadnought restaurant car No 9515, as outshopped in August 1940, having received six-wheel bogies and new windows with airstream ventilators. Note that the roof is painted grey. (Lot 1056 – Diagram H.8)

them as 'the finest sleeping-cars in the country' (Mr Marillier, 1906), but there was little mention of them in the technical railway press. They were 70ft vehicles with recessed doorways and slab sides and a width over the waist of 9ft. On the corridor side there were long windows, and on the compartment side two windows to each compartment. A gauze blind could be drawn down over the droplight at night in addition to curtains.

A surprising feature was the use of wood for solebars, headstocks, and for the framing of the American six-wheel bogies with a view to reducing vibration and noise. Internally, the coaches were panelled in walnut and sycamore with sliding doors to vestibules and compartments. One innovation was a washstand which, by bringing down a lid, could be converted to a writing-desk while, in addition, there was a folding table across the berth. The cars were electrically-lit, there were electric bells in the compartments, and the attendant had a well-equipped kitchen. Their whole appearance was obviously derived from American practice and, at an average cost of £3,169, these were the most expensive passenger coaches built up to that date by the GWR. Two were allocated to the 9.50 p.m. Paddington–Penzance, and 8.45 p.m. return, and the other pair to the midnight Paddington–Truro train. Their lives were shorter than those of the restaurant cars: two went in 1935 and the other two in the following year. It is possible that, like the restaurant cars, they were considered for modernisation but condemned as odd men out in a fleet otherwise of 56–60ft sleeping cars.

70ft 'Concertina' Corridor Stock: 1906–1907

It would seem that while the GWR might have shied away from the revolutionary aspects of the 'Dreadnoughts', there was the additional factor that their 9ft 6in width precluded their use in general and on South Wales expresses in particular. And so a design of more traditional layout and with a higher seating capacity was produced. This, modified, became the standard 'Toplight' 70ft type. In appearance the 'Concertinas' were almost as striking as the 'Dreadnoughts' for, in order to keep the extreme body width as near as possible to 9ft, to satisfy loading-gauge restrictions, all body-side doors were recessed. The resultant 'in-and-out' effect inspired the tag 'Concertina'. Another nickname sometimes mentioned is 'bay-window', but this is completely misleading as it was a case of the doors being recessed rather than the windows bulging out, in contrast to the Dean 'bay-windows' (page 38). As with the 'Dreadnoughts', they had hammered glass toplights over the windows. The panelling on the side of the body reached up to the cantrail and was generally about a foot wide. Internally, a standard side-corridor layout was adopted, with compartment-side doors. All except the last batch of restaurant cars were, in contrast to the 'Dreadnoughts', built with gas lighting.

Apart from the initial pre-production batch of thirds all the 'Concertinas', like the 'Dreadnoughts', were booked to capital expenditure, which gives some indication of the expansion of the GWR in the Edwardian era. The initial batches, in particular, were drafted to form set trains on the premier expresses, notably the Paddington–Neyland service, a duty on which the third brakes appeared until withdrawn in 1956.

First-class sleeping car No 9082 of 1907. (Lot 1123 – Diagram J.6)

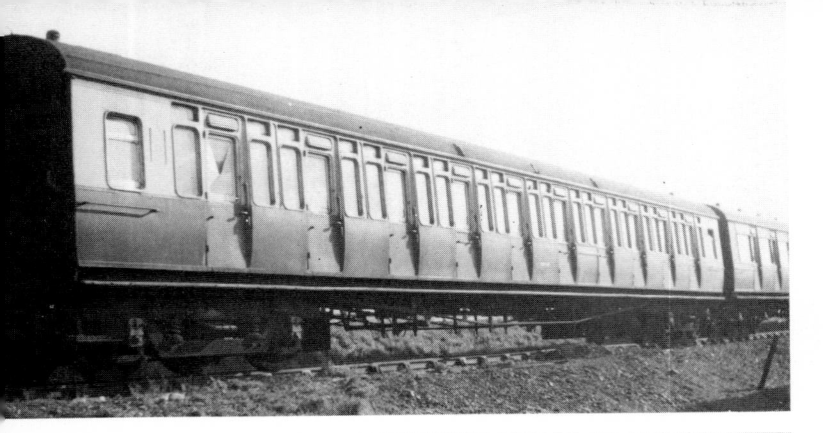

Top:
Concertina third No 2417 (Lot 1107 – Diagram C.27) lying condemned at Goodrington in February 1957. It had retained its original equalised beam bogies.

Above:
Concertina No 7695 in BR livery at Carmarthen in 1951. The slip gear was removed in 1941 and not reinstated. (Lot 1117 – Diagram F.13)

Third brake No 2419 of the first batch had a kitchen fitted in the place of two compartments for buffet service, but was converted in 1938. The remainder survived on express service until 1950–56.

Probably the best known of all the slip-coaches were the 'Concertina' tri-composites, Nos 7685–7699. These were used, principally, on the Bristol line and West of England slip workings. The slip gear was removed from Nos 7685–99 between October 1940 and 1941; from 1946–50, Nos 7685/7/8/9/98/99 were re-equipped, the others finding employment on branch line work. The four re-instated as slip coaches found their most regular duty on the Weymouth slip from the 3.30 p.m. Paddington–Plymouth. No 7698, with body in a graceful arc, saw this working out in January 1959, but was then transferred to the Paddington–Bicester slip working alternately with 1916 70ft slip No 7990, until the autumn of that year.

The restaurant cars, too, were less massive vehicles than the 'Dreadnought' coaches and, in contrast, had end kitchens. The general layout of the 'Concertina' restaurant cars was adhered to until 1923. Each seating bay had a droplight flanked by wide quarterlights in similar style to the compartment side windows of the 'Dreadnoughts' but with gauze shields that could be pulled down to prevent draughts. The second batch of diners, Nos 405/6, had conventional dining-room tables with loose chairs, all in mahogany, and covered in green Spanish antique buffalo leather. Also of note was a partition dividing the passenger saloon from the kitchen, with a curtain in place of a door. At head-level there were transparent coloured photographs.

The two other batches had high-backed settees and Nos 405/6 were similarly fitted in 1936. Larger windows, with sliding ventilators and steel panelling above the waist, improved their looks in the pre-war modernisation programme mentioned in Chapter 10. After the war, most received adaptors for Pullman gangways; those that did not were scrapped in 1954–55. The remainder were relegated to lesser jobs after this date, only a few being repainted in lined maroon. All had gone by 1960, except No 9526 which was scrapped in 1961. No 9527 lingered on in temporary service use at Swindon MPD until at least late 1962.

Nos 9534–7 of Lot 1131 were technically 'Concertinas' while Nos 9538–45, of the same lot and diagram, did not have recessed doors and are classed as 70ft 'Toplight' coaches and dealt with in that section. Nos 9534–7 were single-vestibule coaches with loose chairs for seating. All were modernised in 1936–38. All had gone between 1957–58, except No 9534, withdrawn in 1960, which had been damaged by enemy action in 1942 and, on rebuilding, the body was modernised and six-wheel bogies later fitted.

56ft–57ft 'Toplight' Corridor Stock: 1907–1920

These vehicles, with their 70ft counterparts, were the most typical GWR Edwardian coaches and most could be distinguished, in both lengths, by their oblong hammered-glass toplights above quarter and full-size windows and full panelling above the waist. Coaches built towards the end of the period, together with rebuilds, lacked either or both of these features.

Of those as originally built, there were four basic types:

1. 'Bars 1': 56ft and 57ft body length. 'American type' 8ft bogies (some later received Churchward light-type 9ft). Initial batches and 1909 slip coaches originally gas-lit, rest built with electric lighting. Built 1907–1911.
2. 'Bars 1': 56ft body length. Churchward heavy and light-type 9ft bogies as built. All built with electric lighting, 1911.
3. 'Bars 2': 57ft body length. Churchward heavy and light-type 9ft bogies as built. All built with electric lighting, 1912–1913.
4. 'Multibar' and steel-panelled, with toplights but no mouldings above waist. 8ft 11¼in wide only. Churchward heavy and light-type 9ft bogies as built, 1914–1920.

The designations 'Bars 1', 'Bars 2' and 'Multibar' refer to differences in underframe bracing and, at the same time, denote variations in mouldings as detailed on page 71.

This 56/57ft stock was built simultaneously

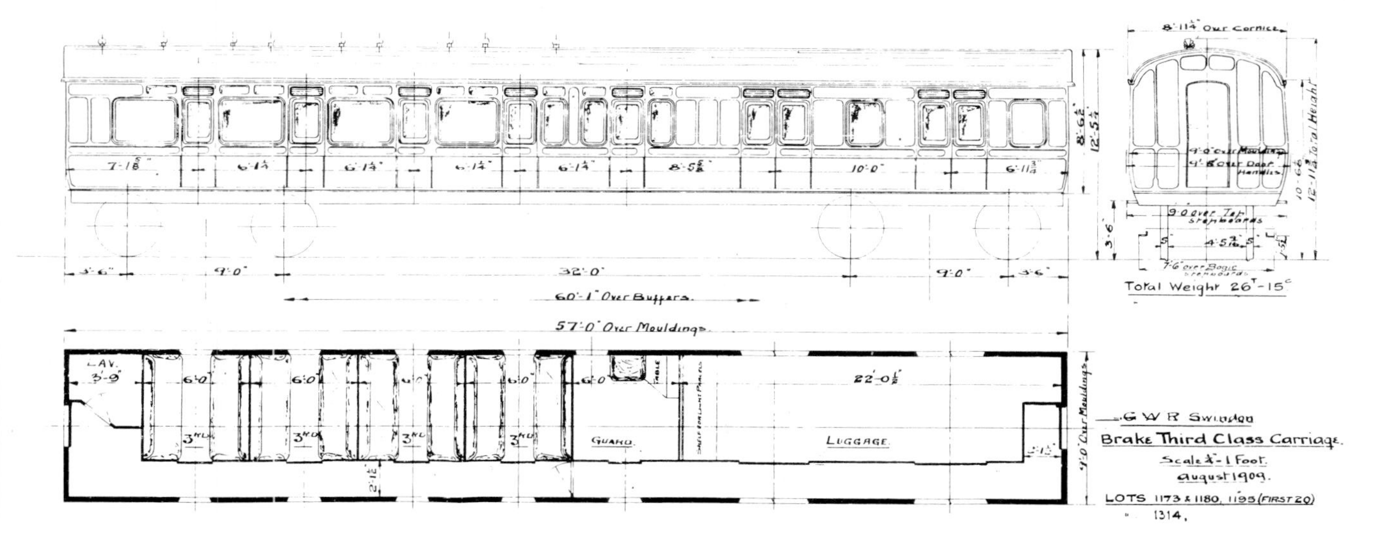

Swindon Diagram D.47, for brake thirds of Bars 1 pattern covering Lots 1173/80/95, some of which went for ambulance train service. This facsimile of the GWR diagram is of one of the better drawings. As these were primarily for operating and identification purposes, strict accuracy of detail was not necessary.

with the 70ft stock for service on 'second string' expresses on which 70ft stock was not suitable and for through 'cross-country' working. The 70ft vehicles were, for the most part, in sets working out of Paddington.

First Lots of Bars 1 stock differed particularly in having incandescent-gas lighting. Another interesting detail in the first series of third brakes was the absence of a door dividing the guard's and luggage compartments from the rest of the coaches, a feature soon rectified. Lots 1138/45 had second-class accommodation, but thereafter the 'Toplights' were first and/or third-class only. Electric lighting was made standard for this type after Lots 1146–9, of which series two composites were notable in being among the first GWR coaches with hot and cold water taps in the lavatories. The restaurant cars to match these series, Nos 9546–51, Lot 1149, were undistinguished and with one unclassed saloon. Nos 9546–8/50 were used on overseas ambulance trains in the Second World War and fitted with air brakes. With little alteration, apart from sliding ventilators being fitted to two in 1947–58, they survived until 1958–60.

Of the thirds and third brakes, built 1907–09, all except twelve were sold to the Government after the outbreak of the First World War and converted at Swindon into ambulance trains. Their subsequent re-purchase after 1919 is dealt with on page 67. All the other types lasted a full forty years except for a few war casualties, until the large deliveries of BR standard stock began from 1954 onwards: they were almost extinct in normal service by 1960.

Lot 1166 comprised two different types of slip coaches. The first batch had first- and third-class corridors on opposite sides, with central lavatories which were inadequately small, but the second lot had the corridors on one side. They were probably the first to have the improved slip apparatus of 1909 (see page 23). A number of both batches was built so that corridor connections could be fitted at a later date. No 8000 was completed in this state but was apparently found unsuitable.

Lot 1150, of 1908, comprised single-ended slip coaches with electric lighting and, by evidence of compartment size and other details, appears to have been intended as a first- and second-class composite brake type. Both Lots 1150/66 lost their slip apparatus after the outbreak of the Second World War and Nos 7103/07/7995 were used with CCTs to form mobile fire units from January 1941. None of these 57ft slips regained their slip gear in post-war years. From Lot 1171 onwards, the light-type bogies were fitted in all but a few cases and on-off heating control was standardised with hot and cold water taps in the lavatories.

Of Lots 1173/4, two were built as kitchen brake thirds with only two seating compartments, but retaining ordinary numbers although on restaurant car diagrams. They were intended to be used for the service of refreshments on short distance expresses. No 2365 was converted back to a standard brake third in 1937, No 2355 in 1936. No 2360, of Lot 1174, became the famous 'Whitewash Coach' in 1932 and is described in full on page 69. A number of thirds were sold in 1917–18 to the Government, converted for US Army ambulance trains along with Bars 2 coaches, and later repurchased. The majority of coaches of these Bars 1 1910/11 series remained in service until 1954 and, although withdrawn in large numbers up to 1957, a number of brake thirds were retained for departmental use. Six thirds were refitted as camping coaches in 1957–58, as detailed in Chapter 10.

From 1912–14, the Bars 2 pattern 'Toplights' were the standard type. As an example of the work in progress during December 1913, 88 ordinary coaches, two sleeping cars and 23 CCTs and scenery trucks were under construction. Of Lots 1193–5, two of the composites, Nos 7562/6, and an unidentified restaurant car were fitted with Laycock automatic couplers in 1922 as

A handsome picture of Toplight Bars 1 corridor third No 3663 in chocolate-lake livery. (Lot 1153 – Diagram C.28)

prototypes for the 70ft 'South Wales' sets of that year (see page 75). Nos 7562/6 had an automatic coupler at the first-class end. Numbers of thirds from this series, together with Bars 1 coaches, were sold to the Government in 1917–18 for conversion into US Army ambulance trains. Complementary brake thirds were, however, retained.

During the Second World War, several brake thirds saw service in emergency evacuation trains. Thirty-eight thirds were converted to camping-coaches in 1957–58, the period when the majority were withdrawn from ordinary stock. Lots 1200–3, consisting of a few vehicles each, were replacements for new vehicles that had been destroyed in the Swindon paintshop fire of 1911. Brake composite No 7583 is of importance as it was the first coach on the GWR to have external steel bodyside panelling. This innovation was quickly applied, simultaneously with trials of fireproof flooring. An isolated Lot of brake composites of 1913, No 1212, included three single-ended slips numbered, unusually, in the 6xxx series.

Finally came the immediately pre-war type distinguished by steel bodyside panelling with an almost complete absence of mouldings, but including bolections round the windows and the usual toplights. Although these vehicles all had the normal wooden and canvas roofs as standard, two thirds were built with steel roofs as prototypes for future construction. The windows and droplights were also set lower in the bodyside.

Third No 3948, Lot 1248 of 1921, was a prototype for all-steel construction. All the framing, panelling and partitions were of steel and the body lacked the customary turn-under ends. It had a central cantilever underframe, constructed on the Livesey-Gould principle, with rolled steel sections in which the channel beams forming the central girders were trussed with transverse cantilevers. Lot 1256 had wooden body panelling with the same outline as the steel-panelled coaches and were building during 1915–16. They were then requisitioned for ambulance use and did not enter normal service until after the war. Lot 1269 had various coaches with different types of flooring as part of the experiments in developing fireproof, sound-proofed floors.

Special Coaches: 57ft Third Saloon, No 9055: 1912

This vehicle, an ordinary private-hire saloon, was of normal Toplight 'Bars 2' appearance and was built to replace an earlier vehicle of the same designation. The interior comprised two large open saloons, an ordinary eight-seat compartment and seated forty-four, two lavatories, and a luggage compartment to carry refreshments. It remained as a nondescript saloon until withdrawn in the 1950s, ending its life as an MPD office at Shrewsbury, and was later preserved.

54ft Special Saloon, No 9100: 1912

No 9100 was constructed using the frame and bogies of the old 1874–97 Queen's Saloon, No 9001, as the CME's personal saloon. In general appearance, it was a normal semi-elliptical roof 'Toplight' of rather LNW appearance. The interior consisted of two open saloons, one kitchen, one guard's compartment and a lavatory. It was modernised and redesignated a first-class saloon in 1927 and reclassed as a third-class saloon in 1931. Finally, it was numbered in the service vehicle series and condemned in the 1950s.

56ft 11in Nondescript Brake Third Saloons, Nos 9369–71: 1923

Although ordered in 1914, these steel-panelled, normal dimension vehicles were not completed until 1923. They were without toplights or ventilators over the doors. Built for general excursion and private-hire use, the three were allocated to Bristol, Paddington and Cardiff respectively. Interior arrangements consisted of two large open saloons, one ordinary compartment seating eight, a guard's compartment, and two lavatories, with a side corridor. Normal gangways were fitted at both ends. Comparison can be made with the 1929 vehicles (see page 83).

All three were extant until the 1950s: of the

three, one became an MPD office at Shrewsbury (see No 9055 above) and another finished as a grounded body at Swindon Works. No 9369 has been preserved.

57ft Sleeper/Third Coaches, Nos 7596/7600: 1921
Entering service in January 1922, these coaches were allocated to the 9.15 p.m. Paddington–Neyland and 6.30 p.m. return, providing four single first-class sleeping-berths and three ordinary third-class compartments seating twenty-four. Interestingly, the first-class compartments were equipped with venetian blinds and electric fans. In contrast to similar day/sleeping all-third coaches of 1928, there was an attendant's compartment and a pantry. Externally, they were Bars 2 wood-panelled 'Toplights'; this, and the fact that they were of 56ft body length, suggests that they may have been ambulance conversions, possibly from Lot 1256 of 1915–16. Later renumbered Nos 9092/3, they remained unaltered until 1942, when No 9093 was rebuilt as a sleeper first with seven berths and two lavatories for the wartime 'Alive Train' in company with No 9079 of 1929. It also received some steel panelling and sliding ventilators, and was in use for Royal Train duties as late as 1958.

First-class sleeping car No 9091, as photographed in June 1914. (Lot 1218 – Diagram J.8)

56ft 11in First Sleeping-Cars, Nos 9090/1: 1914
Among the first steel-panelled 'Toplights' were these sleeper firsts with one double and eight single berths, lavatory, and the usual kitchen/attendant's compartment. They were fitted with six-wheel bogies in 1939, and modernised in the late 1940s as part of the general renovation scheme. Both were withdrawn in the 1950s.

Ex-LSWR 56ft First-Class Sleeping-Cars, GWR, Nos 9086–9089, purchased 1910
Built in 1908, under the Surrey Warner *aegis* on the LSWR, these coaches were allocated to the Plymouth Stonepool–Waterloo boat-trains at the height of the fierce competition with the GWR for Transatlantic liner traffic. Externally, they followed the contemporary LSWR standard outline. Internally, they slept nine, in one double and seven single berths. The panelling was in oak, with mahogany vestibules. As many times recounted with relish, they had high-Edwardian brass bedsteads. In May 1910, the LSWR and GWR entered into an agreement for the pooling of Plymouth to London boat passengers, the GWR operating the trains. The LSWR sleepers, Nos 39–42, were thereupon sold to the GWR. They were built with Stone's electric lighting and had hot and cold water in the compartments. While being repainted, Nos 39/40 were burnt out in 1911 in the Swindon paintshop fire, but the other two, which were used on the Paddington–Penzance sleeper service, survived until 1928 and 1931 respectively.

Repurchased 56ft 11in and 57ft Corridor 'Toplight' Ambulance Coaches: Rebuilt 1920–26
As described in the previous section, a number of 'Toplight' corridor thirds and brake thirds were sold to the Government and converted or, newly built as ambulance coaches for use in Britain and on the Continent. In all, 181 Bars 1, Bars 2 and steel-panelled varieties were refitted, slightly less than half being brake thirds.

The GWR supplied 238 vehicles for sixteen ambulance trains, four of these being for home service. Plans for conversion of vehicles for home-use ambulance trains had been in existence at the outbreak of war and, early in 1915, the GWR supplied two trains, each comprising nine vehicles: six 40ft passenger brake vans, a restaurant car, and two clerestory saloon brakes. In 1915, at six weeks' notice, the GWR supplied another home-use train, conversion being financed with funds raised by the United Kingdom Flour Millers; this consisted of seven 'Toplight' brake thirds. Early in the same year, an 'Ambulance Trains for the Continent' subcommittee of the Railway Executive Committee was formed, which drew up conversion plans for new ambulance trains. These were to be formed of sixteen coaches: a brake coach (infectious cases), staff coach, one kitchen/officers' coach, nine ward coaches, pharmacy coach, kitchen/mess coach, personnel coach and brake/stores coach.

F. W. Marillier, carriage manager at Swindon during this time, was on the committee and designed the folding bunks which could also serve as seats for sitting cases. It was suggested by the committee and agreed to by the Government that

Star 4-6-0 No 4037 *Queen Philippa* heads a 16-car ambulance train of Toplight stock, near Rushey Platt, Swindon.

the railways' compensation for supplying vehicles for ambulance trains should be an amount equal to their original cost, plus the cost of conversion, and transport to destination. The first home-use trains were painted in standard fully-lined-out GWR livery, including crests. Later sets lost their original owners' identities, having been sold to the Government.

The first three trains for the Continent were exhibited at GWR stations before going into use. Altogether, the GWR turned out eight sixteen-coach trains during 1915–16, the majority of the 'Toplights' involved having been ordered as ordinary thirds and third brakes in 1915 and completed as ambulance coaches. Their external appearance – steel-panelled and with toplights – bore no obvious sign of being converted from ordinary passenger coaches. With the entry of the USA into the war in 1917, four further sets were produced by the GWR late that year. These trains were equipped with Westinghouse and vacuum brakes, internal telephones and, at least the first few, with Pullman gangways.

Of the 181 ambulance coaches, 148 have been definitely identified and their re-conversion accounted for, while a less certain case can be made for another dozen. The majority of these vehicles, purchased back from the Government, were renovated or rebuilt largely to their original state and, while some emerged without toplights and were largely steel-panelled, others retained full body mouldings; this, no doubt, depended upon their condition on return. The numbers allocated to them did not necessarily correspond to their original series or diagrams and, in many cases, a particular batch of numbers was used for the second time. It would also seem that those coaches in poor or damaged condition, which were left until 1921–22 before being rebuilt, were ones which changed their identities from thirds to third brakes or passenger brake vans (Lots 1326/32/44). Lot 1325 should be mentioned as steel-panelled coaches without any toplights. Three pharmacy and ward cars became nondescript saloons, described later, while four four-wheeled milk train brakes (Nos 1397–1400, of 1921) were made from presumably two vehicles. One infectious cases vehicle reappeared in the guise of two six-wheel milk train brakes (Nos 503/99) in 1921.

Lot books also suggest that twelve bow-ended thirds, Nos 4545–4556 of Lot 1352, had underframes from re-purchased vehicles, though there is no evidence from the diagrams to support this.

As late as January 1926, there appeared a unique vehicle of the sort that added to the interest of GWR coaches. Using a re-purchased underframe, No 4377, an isolated number to Diagram C.55, had a new flat-ended turn-under body, betraying its 'Toplight' origin, but was otherwise similar to the bow-ended 1923–29 standards, being fully steel-panelled and having a steel roof. It was badly damaged in the Norton Fitzwarren accident of November 1940 and cut-up at Swindon.

Details of the re-purchased vehicles cannot be given in full owing to lack of space, but Lot numbers between 1279 and 1366 cover the vehicles involved and their original Bars 1/2 or Multibar origin.

The war-service 'Toplights' survived as long as the batches from which they were drawn, and were extinct by 1960. The majority of 'Toplight' camping-coaches came from these re-purchased thirds and were largely steel-panelled vehicles without toplights. Various brake thirds were retained, in faded crimson and cream BR livery, for extended periods of temporary use by engineering and signalling departments until the early 1960s.

56ft Re-purchased Coaches Converted to Nondescript Third Saloons, Nos 9372–9374: 1921

Three pharmacy and ward cars from ambulance trains of unknown origin, possibly Bars 1 thirds, were turned out as forty-seater saloons for general use, two being allocated to Paddington and the third to Birmingham. Internally, with two saloons, an ordinary compartment, guard's compartment and two lavatories, they were similar to Lot 1250 of 1923. Lasting until the 1950s, No. 9373 was definitely condemned, No 9372 became a mobile defence school, and No 9374 a grounded body at Swindon Works.

46ft 6¾in Re-purchased Ex-Clerestory Saloons, Rebuilt and Re-numbered 9364–6: 1921
Three clerestory saloons, the pharmacy and ward cars in the first home-use ambulance trains, were rebuilt in 1921. Originally built in 1901 and 1904, they are described on page 45.

48–60ft Non-Corridor 'Toplight' Stock: 1908–1922

56ft 11in/57ft Suburban Coaches
Not many 'Toplight' non-corridor coaches were produced in comparison with clerestory types and Collett-era vehicles of the late 1920s. All those built, except the first-class coaches, formed London and Birmingham suburban sets. The 1908 batch of firsts was unique with a body length of 60ft and spacious compartments 7ft 4in between the partitions and pseudo-corridor panelled ends. Bodywork was of Bars 1 type. They were withdrawn between 1952 and 1958. Four-coach sets of Bars 2 type consisting of two third brakes and two composites were allocated to the Birmingham area in 1911. Surviving in these sets until the early 1950s, they were withdrawn in 1954–55.

The odd coach No 8263 of 1912, an eight-compartment Bars 2 type first, was built to replace a seven-compartment first of 1897. The original bearer of the number was destroyed in the Swindon paintshop fire of 1911. In contrast to the 1908 firsts, and in common with the latter vehicles, it had 6ft 11in partition-to-partition compartments. Running as a full third in later days after the war, it survived until 1955.

Multibar, steel-panelled 56ft 11¼in-body four-coach sets were built for the London area services in 1913, but were otherwise similar to the 1911 trains. They lasted until the arrival of BR non-corridors in 1954–56. London and Birmingham again received a new series of 'Toplight' coaches in 1922, bringing the respective totals to ten and eight sets. The brake thirds were similar to the 1911 sets, having six compartments to the seven of the 1913 series. In post-war days, the sets were split up but two London area coaches survived on their original duties until 1957. Some brake thirds and thirds had been re-numbered from 1953 to avoid confusion with BR standard stock allocated to the WR. One of these, No 3422, survived until late 1959 around Swindon and was probably the last of its type.

Without toplights, the 1922 batch of firsts included the first production coaches with steel roofs, anticipating the 'South Wales' 70ft stock of that year, but half the lot had wood and canvas roofs. One minor distinction was that they were the last 'Toplights' (without toplights) to be built, and one of their number was the last of this outline in service. During and after the Second World War many were derated to all-thirds, some not being reinstated as firsts until 1953. In August 1959, three were still active on Newbury race specials (two marked 'Return to Paddington') but were withdrawn soon after. No 8076 outlived the others by some time. It survived until withdrawn in December 1962 during the purge of Birmingham area non-corridor stock, and remained at the Hollinswood (Oakengates) dump of condemned coaches as late as August 1963.

48ft Main Line and City Sets: 1920–21
To replace gas-lit four-wheeled stock built from 1893 to 1898, six new 'Toplight' sets were ordered in 1913, but the lot was cancelled in 1915. The old four-wheeled coaches had an extended lease of life until after the war, when the six-coach steel-panelled 'Toplight' close-coupled trains appeared. Their short length, small compartments and narrow width gave them a more antique appearance than was justified by their date of construction. There were roller-blind destination indicators on each side of the third brakes.

Although the through GWR City service to Liverpool Street (Metropolitan) was withdrawn in 1939, these sets continued on London suburban services, working as far out as Oxford, until 1956–57. They were not, however, finished with. One third, a composite, and two brake thirds were appropriated for use on workmen's trains between Glyncorrwg and South Pit Halt on the former South Wales Mineral Railway, a service of two workmen's trains each way with speed restrictions of 10 and 20 m.p.h.! In 1961, they were fitted with propane gas lighting, as were the ex-Barry Railway brakes on the Hemyock branch, in view of the low speeds involved. The third was withdrawn in 1962, but the others remained until 1964. In the light of the purge of all non-standard coaches, the authorities at Swindon were rather surprised when they found these gas-lit 'Toplights' still extant – even if each of them was only in service for twenty-two minutes a day! The trains between Glyncorrwg and South Pit Halt were withdrawn on 30 October 1964. However, two of the brake thirds, Nos 3755/6, were then purchased for preservation.

1920/21 Main Line and City stock exiled to the former South Wales Mineral Railway for workmen's trains, seen at South Pit Halt, July 1958. The brake is No 3755, the third, No 3910. (Lots 1275/74)

The 'Whitewash Coach': 1932
Shortly after the Grouping, experiments were carried out by the GWR in an attempt to evolve a steadier-riding, light standard bogie. Obviously, as vehicle riding characteristics are dependent on

The 'Whitewash Coach' in its most recent guise, repanelled, on B4 bogies and in blue and grey livery, but still numbered DW139. It is seen at the rear of a Penzance–Paddington track testing special near Totnes, March 1982.

the condition and maintenance of track, experiments covered the civil engineer's provinces as well. The outcome of the bogie experiments was the production of the 7ft wheelbase design, but the research department at Swindon continued track-testing with a train of standard coaches which had been selected and maintained as steady-riding vehicles. The precursor of the 'Whitewash Coach' was to be found in these experiments in which staff from the experimental department stood by the lavatory pans of each coach and, when they struck a rough stretch of track, tipped part of their can of whitewash down the pan! Each participant had a differently-coloured mixture. One coach involved in this train was 70ft clerestory No 2400 (see page 49).

One of the coaches in this train was a 'Toplight' brake third, No 2360 of 1911, which had been fitted with 7ft bogies. Following the success of the empirical tests mentioned above, this vehicle was selected as a track-testing car to be run over the system on a regular basis behind normal trains and under the supervision of the chief mechanical engineer. Converted in 1932, No 2360 was stripped internally except for the two front compartments and lavatory. Observation windows were placed at the brake end. The whitewash operating equipment was positioned in place of the guard's compartment and connected to a tank of the liquid. In the centre of the coach, a standard Hallade track-recorder was placed, independent of the whitewash apparatus. There was a recessed section of body panelling on each side with a lookout for the operators. Speedometers were fitted at the brake end of the coach. When a test was in progress the divisional engineer's staff and inspectors of the section under the examination would keep their eyes on the track from this end.

The whitewash apparatus, possibly a unique piece of equipment, was directly connected to the bogies and automatically operated by their movement over the track rather than by the general oscillation of both bogies and bodywork. Coming on to a rough stretch of track, the movement of each lurch of the bogies was transmitted by electrical impulses. The primary coil was attached to the bogie bolster, with the field strength kept constant; a secondary coil slid within the primary coil and was activated by the action of the bogie frames. With violent 'hunting' over the stretch of track, the action of the secondary coil generated electrical impulses, transmitted through relays, acting on a solenoid operating a flap valve. Each exceptional lurch was sufficient to open this valve and deposit, through a pipe, about a quart of whitewash over the track, while simultaneously a horn was sounded in the coach. Obviously, with a train moving at a reasonable speed, the drop began about 60ft ahead of the bad spot causing the action, the deposit covering the track for about a hundred feet.

The Hallade recorder, meanwhile, was maintaining a continuous graph of the journey and showing on four separate lines: brake and rolling, lateral movements, alignment and super-elevation, vertical movements and the location of each whitewash 'drop'. After a report was produced on the section of track covered, it was up to the local permanent-way inspectors and gang to work on their 'bad spot'. As the last vehicle of the train, the 'Whitewash Coach' was subject to the inevitable lateral swinging, particularly while going round curves, but this action was transmitted to the bodywork rather than the bogies.

Remaining with its original brake third number and outwardly a normal 'Toplight' with full panelling and hammered-glass lights, the coach was fitted with gas tanks, heaters and cooking facilities in December 1948, transferred to the wagon stock, and numbered W139, at the same time being repainted in crimson and cream with the legend 'Track Testing Car' painted on the recessed section of body panelling. Still in use in the 1960s, by now painted lined maroon, it continued to be worked on an annual programme of track-testing involving two or three days running each week.

Unique and something of an institution, even though by no means well known, the erstwhile 'Whitewash Coach' was one of those special Swindon products that managed to survive in changed circumstances. It would be a pity not to include a ganger's story about an incident in which the coach was involved, a story dating from the 1960s. An acquaintance was in Slough West Box, shortly before it was abolished, and, when photographing an up Worcester train, noticed that the last vehicle was the 'Whitewash Coach', by then in maroon livery and identifiable only by the initiated. A few moments later the signal-box door was flung open and an enraged ganger came in.

'Did you see the last coach on that express?'

'No,' said the signalman.

'Yes,' said the enthusiast, 'that was the track-recording coach – W139.'

'That's right, it's the second time the blighter's done it in a fortnight and we'd only just finished cleaning up after the first time.'

In the mid-1970s, DW139 was given a thorough examination when it was found that its body framing was in remarkably good condition and needed little in the way of repairs. At the same time, the exterior was repanelled. In 1980, the Hallade recorder was replaced by more modern equipment and No DW139 was remounted on B4 bogies. In this condition it is cleared for running up to 100 mph, usually formed in a special train of modern vehicles, and works to a programme inspecting all WR main lines (and the Waterloo–Exeter route throughout) twice a year.

Vehicle from Lot 1174, diagram number D.46, new diagram D.114 then Q.21 (1950).

Bars 1, Bars 2 and Multibar 'Toplight' Designations: applicable to 56ft–70ft Stock

The above terms distinguished between differences in underframe bracing, at the same time corresponding to altered bodyside mouldings and panelling. Otherwise, 'Toplights' had canvas and wood roofs, raised (bolection) mouldings round the windows; in other words, window pans, two hammered-glass lights (toplights) over corridor-side windows and one over each compartment-side quarterlight. All doors had louvred ventilators above the droplights. Later batches differed in these respects. With Bars 1 and 2 vehicles, the body ends were generally panelled, with raised mouldings; with steel-panelled coaches, the ends were similarly steel-panelled. Another distinguishing feature was the way in which the ends turned inwards to the headstocks; all but one 'Toplight', all-steel third No 3948, was built in this way.

70ft Toplight corridor brake first No 8178 was built for the Cunard boat trains. The installation above the gangway was part of the 'brake vehicle' lighting system. (Lot 1182 – Diagram A.11)

70ft Toplight corridor composite No 7782 was outshopped in January 1923, having been facelifted by having the toplights removed, and quarterlights and doors raised. Improved upholstery, luggage racks and lavatories were also fitted. (Lot 1276 – Diagram E.102)

Bars 1: Underframes braced with flat bars. Only those panel mouldings between compartment windows reached the cantrail, elsewhere horizontal eaves panels were formed. On the corridor side, only one toplight over each end window.
Bars 2: Bar trussing again, but differently positioned. All panels, including those at body ends, reached up to cantrail. Two toplights over each end window.
Multibar: Generally without mouldings. Two toplights over end windows. Underframe trussing round in section for earlier (mostly prewar) coaches, rigid non-adjustable angle-irons for later series. Majority steel-panelled, some without toplights.

A number of coaches having their bodywork destroyed by enemy action during the Second World War were rebuilt with flush steel-panelled bodies similar to 1933–35 standard 57ft stock (see Chapter 10).

69ft 11¼in/70ft 'Toplight' Corridor and Non-Corridor Stock: 1908–1922

Following the appearance of the 57ft 'Toplight' corridor coaches in 1907, 70ft counterparts, developed from the 'Concertina' design, appeared in 1908. As with the 57ft coaches there were three categories: Bars 1 (1908–11), Bars 2 (1912–13) and steel-panelled 69ft 11¼in body (1914–22).

The first Lot was non-standard: first and second composites with gas lighting, but, from the thirds on Lot 1154 of 1909 onwards, all but one vehicle had electric lighting. Lot 1154 was also the first with the heavy-duty 9ft bogie introduced in 1909, but subsequent Lots were variously turned out with this bogie as well as the 'American' equalised type.

In late 1910, two eleven-coach trains of all-first coaches were built for the Cunard boat-trains from Fishguard which had commenced running in August 1909. Each set comprised eight firsts, a restaurant car (9552–5 series) and a brake first at one end and a twelve-wheel baggage van at the other. The Cunard liners, with their first-class Transatlantic passengers, ceased to call at Fishguard after 1914 and the sets were disbanded. One set had the 'brake vehicle' system of Stone's electric lighting.

Solitary buffet brake first, No. 8303 of 1911, for the Plymouth boat-trains, may have been built with gas lighting to be in keeping with the 1896 clerestory 'Ocean Special' sets. It remained on this work until at least 1930. The majority of the 70ft 'Toplights' survived until the mid-1950s except for three brake firsts of 1910, Nos 8178–8180. These lasted until 1961 for use on the 'members only' Newbury race specials, No 8179 being one of the few 'Toplights' of either 57ft or 70ft length to be repainted in lined maroon, an approximation to the livery in which they were turned out when new. Their longevity was best explained by the absence of brake firsts of GWR and BR design – of suitable capacity – until the building of two BR standard vehicles in 1960, but these replacements lacked the style imparted to the Newbury trains by the 70-footers.

Bars 2 design vehicles were built in better balanced series of Lots with some, Lots 1207/8/10,

70ft Toplight restaurant car W9542W, at Old Oak Common, May 1957, in carmine and cream livery. Partly repanelled and with airstream ventilators, but retaining its original bogies. (Lot 1131 – Diagram H.15)

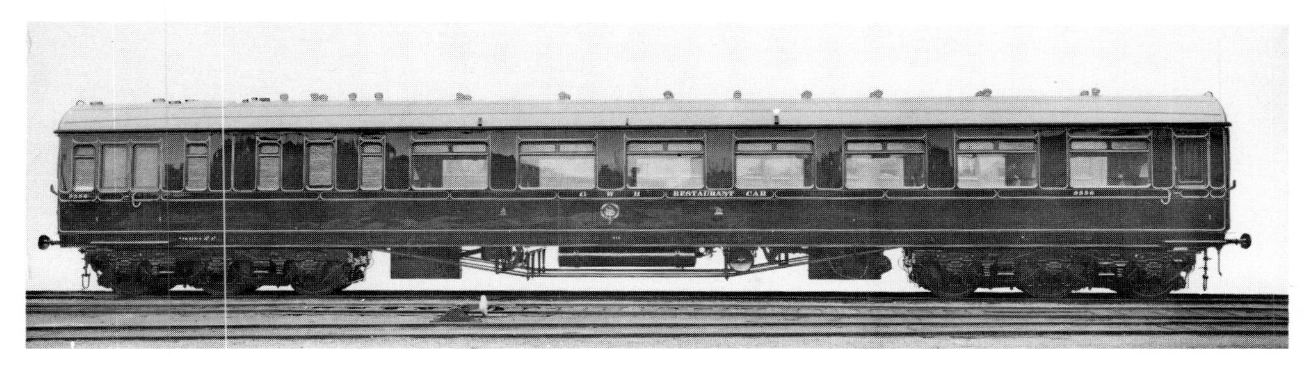

turned out as sets. As with the 57ft designs, various coaches had fireproof floors and steel panelling. Eight-coach sets of this design replaced the 'Dreadnought' 'Cornish Riviera' sets in 1913–14, but included the 'Dreadnought' restaurant cars and with additional 'Concertina' slip coaches. In July 1922, these 'Cornish Riviera' sets were the first complete trains to be repainted in chocolate and cream.

Again, as with the 57ft coaches, the immediate pre-war and post-war batches were steel-panelled Multibar underframe coaches to an 8ft 11¼in width. Included in the pre-war lots were four double-ended slip coaches, Nos 7990–3, completed in 1916. These lost their slip-gear by 1942, No 7991 becoming an all-third, but were re-equipped from 1949, No 7993 as late as 1954. All except No 7990 were withdrawn before 1958 but this vehicle survived on the Bicester slip off the 5.10 p.m. Paddington–Wolverhampton until 1959. The final 1921 lots had syphonic-flushing in all the lavatories and were mounted on the heavy-type 9ft bogies. Composite No 7782, from Lot 1276, was the prototype for post-1923 stock, and was rebuilt by having its quarterlights raised, new doors fitted, the toplights panelled over and the bolection mouldings removed. The interior was also modified, with new-type luggage racks and the seats retrimmed with a new pattern of upholstery. No 7782 entered service in this form in January 1923, painted in chocolate and cream livery.

The batch of brake composites, Nos 7788–7797 of 1922, were specifically mentioned as having 'Midland Railway-type' w.c.s and washbasins, but why the Reid-era appointments on the MR were particularly noteworthy is not clear! The first-class compartments also had a flowered-patterned upholstery which was not common on the GWR. These were the last 70ft 'Toplights' to be constructed.

70ft restaurant car No 9556, in chocolate-lake livery, shown in the official photograph dated July 1913. With six-wheel equalised beam bogies, this H.22 vehicle had a look of the Lancashire & Yorkshire Railway about it. It was repanelled and modernised internally 1936 and 1938, as seen below.

As with the 1908–13 built coaches, withdrawal of the later seventy-footers was concentrated between 1955–58, except for first No 8324, which was used on the 6.55 p.m. Paddington–Fishguard in 1956–57. It was then repainted in lined maroon, like brake first No 8179 of 1910, and retained for Newbury race-train use until 1961.

Four seventy-footers suffered from wartime damage and were rebuilt with 69ft 6in by 8ft 11¼in flush steel-panelled bodies (see Chapter 10).

The first 70ft 'Toplights' were eight restaurant-cars, Nos 9538–9545 of 1907, their Lot No 1131 covering also Nos 9534–7, technically belonging to 'Concertina' series vehicles. Nos 9538–9545 were general service coaches having two unclassed saloons with loose chairs. In 1936, the first examples were modernised, receiving flush steel panelling above the waistline and larger, modern windows with sliding ventilators. All other mouldings were generally retained. They were not greatly altered internally, except for the substitution of high-backed settees for the chairs. Some remained in front-line service until 1961; of these, No 9543 had been repainted chocolate and cream in the late 1950s and was used on the 'Cheltenham Spa Express' until that date. No 9540 worked on the fast 1.15 p.m. Paddington–Bristol until June 1961: the 1.15 p.m. was a lightweight seven-coach train on which a 70-footer saved using an adjacent open-second for meal service. Its fifty-four years' work on main-line expresses is

No 9556, with standard 12-wheel bogies and as modernised in 1936.

70ft non-corridor Toplight brake third No 1071, as built. (Lot 1227 – Diagram D.55)

perhaps an unchallengeable record, the 1905 'Dreadnought' contenders having been relegated to relief work before withdrawal.

The 1911 restaurant cars, Nos 9552–5, were built for the Fishguard boat-trains. The saloon, which had high-backed seats, was divided by partitions, while the bodysides had large windows similar to the 'Dreadnoughts'. No 9554 was built with six-wheel bogies. All were modernised in 1936–38 and withdrawn in 1958.

No 9556, built 1913, and Nos 9557–9561, built 1922, were austere slab-sided coaches. The 1913 vehicle had 70ft by 9ft dimensions which, with the later five, were reduced to 8ft 11¼in width and ¾in less in length. No 9556 had six-wheel bogies, as built. All were refurbished by Hamptons from 1947. In 1954, No 9560 was converted to a buffet-restaurant car with one saloon including a bar serving light refreshments and normal restaurant service to the seated passengers. All of this series were withdrawn between 1958–61.

69ft 11¼in 'Toplight' Non-Corridor Sets: 1913

Without doubt, the only 70ft non-corridor coaches to run on an English railway were these four four-coach sets for Birmingham suburban services. They were also the first of the Multibar underframe, steel-panelled body 'Toplight' design which had become standard for both corridor and non-corridor coaches of both 57ft and 70ft lengths from 1913. Both Lots of these coaches had fireproof floors; the first time these had been fitted to whole batches of vehicles on the GWR. Despite their impressiveness, however, the train length/passenger and total weight/passenger ratios were disappointing and inferior to the standard four-coach 57ft body sets.

The sets survived until 1955–57, and at least one of them had been transferred to Worcester some time before.

70ft Toplight corridor composite No 7762, lying condemned at Blackthorn, April 1957. It has been partially repanelled. (Lot 1210 – Diagram E.93)

6

THE BOW-ENDED ERA: 1922–1934

70ft Stock 1922 – 1925 (South Wales)
These coaches marked an interesting point in post-Grouping policy: they were the last 70ft stock, thus ending one era, and were the first new post-war coaches to be painted in the reintroduced brown and cream livery. Moreover, they preceded a period of conservative design with limited inspiration. The original 'South Wales' sets were the first on the GWR to be fitted with buckeye, or automatic, couplers and Pullman gangways, and their prototypes appear to be the 'Toplight' 57ft composites mentioned on page 65.

Having ventured into the use of buckeye couplers, the system was different to that adopted by that great exponent of these fittings, Gresley. Instead of the push-in buffers, also standard for BR coaches, the hinged, drop-down type were fitted. Nor were the Pullman gangways of the LNER type, though they were equipped with adaptors for coupling to other GWR standard vehicles. Rather than involve the reader in a complicated description, the layout is shown in diagram form:

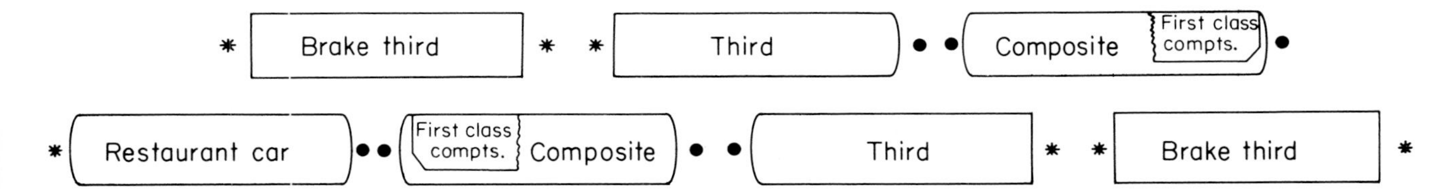

Arrangement of buckeye-fitted 70ft South Wales set. *Indicates flat ends and screw couplers. •Indicates bow-ends and buckeye couplers.

South Wales 1922 Sets
The limited day-to-day capacity of a seven-coach set was overcome by providing screw-couplings between the brake thirds and thirds, thus making it possible to strengthen the set with ordinary coaches without the use of adaptors. Care was also taken, as in other set trains, to keep the internal corridor running continuously on one side of the train by building left and right-handed brake coaches. The first-class passengers were also given easy access to the restaurant car.

Later sets built in 1924 introduced three further varieties: with formations identical to the above, those with bow ends and buckeyes only within the set, and sets with screw couplings and standard gangways throughout. These variants made up a total of twelve different types of 70ft coaches, covering thirds, brake thirds and composites, to achieve operating requirements! The rigid standardisation of the locomotive department did not influence the carriage and wagon side and this is a good example not only of this, but also of the drawbacks of set trains.

The first two South Wales sets, resplendent in the 'old' livery, went into service on the 3.35 p.m. Paddington–Swansea and 12 noon return on 17 May 1923. Before the inaugural Press trip, the train was inspected at Paddington by Viscount Churchill, accompanied by W. A. Stanier. Before the return from Swansea, the Press was given a demonstration of uncoupling and coupling. Contemporary journals carried suitable notices and photographs of the occasion. The first vehicles to lose their buckeye couplers and Pullman gangways seem to have been converted in early 1931, and the only published record of the demise of the GWR buckeye couplers, about 1933–34, was in a reply to a question in *The Railway Magazine* during 1935.

The restaurant cars for these sets, Nos 9568–9573, and also for the 1924 batches, Nos 9574–9577, were similar in general outline and dimensions to the other coaches. Except for Nos 9572/3 which had screw couplings, they were fitted with the buckeye couplers at both ends. The interiors were without special interest and had tip-up leather seating and the usual electric fans and attendants' bells. In the late 1930s, three received six-wheel bogies, which made Nos 9573/4, at 49 tons tare probably the heaviest unpowered coaches in the British Isles. Nos 9572/3 were painted in the experimental plum-and-spilt-milk livery in 1948 for the 'Cornish Riviera' and were internally renovated after the Second World War. The batch was extinguished in 1962: No 9574, one of two painted WR chocolate and cream in 1956 for the 'Torbay Express', was used for the 11.55 a.m. Paddington–South Wales until June 1961.

In addition, forty-five thirds were built as part of the stepped-up 1923 building programme

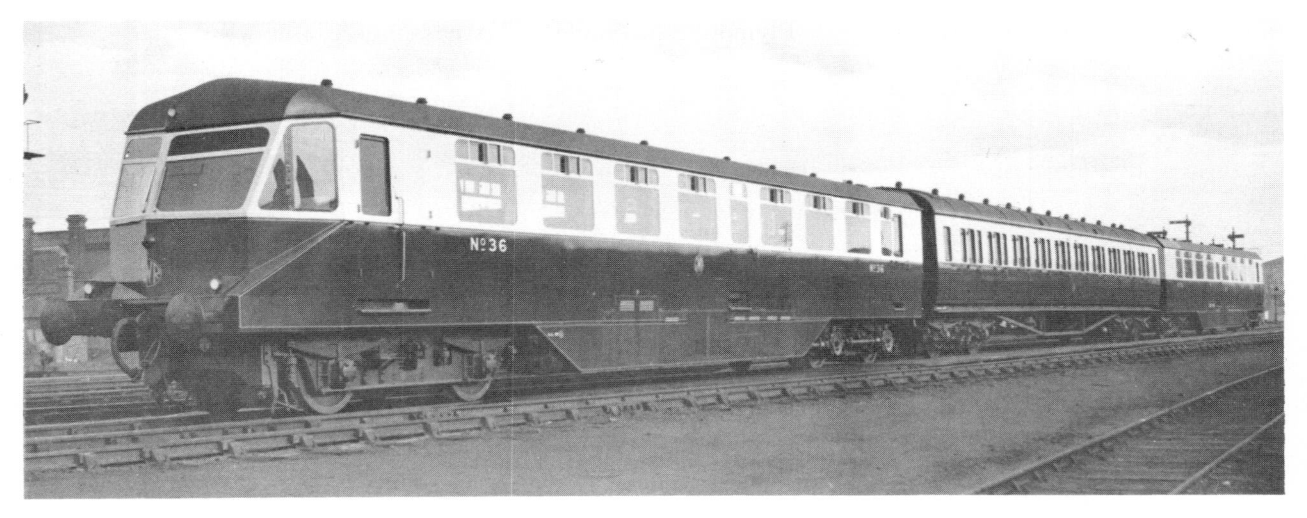

The three-car set produced during the second world war with GWR railcars Nos 36 and 35 and 70ft corridor third 4509. It worked between Bristol and Weymouth.

following Grouping, making a grand total of 127 coaches, of which ten were restaurant cars. The bow-ended vehicles were 71ft 4½in long over the bodies. The famous GWR booklet, *The 10.30 Limited*, published in September 1923, thus featured stock replaced a few months later. By the next year the new coaches had arrived on the premier train and will be familiar from photographs of the LNER's A1 Pacific working on the 'Cornish Riviera' during the locomotive exchanges of 1925. Mention should also be made here of the 'Dreadnought' brake third No 3476, described further on page 62, which in 1926 received an all-steel body including, even, steel compartment partitions, to 'South Wales' outline and dimensions, after its original bodywork had been destroyed by fire.

In 1929, the 70-footers were displaced from the 'Cornish Riviera' by 60ft-plus flush-panelled body coaches (see page 81) and dispersed to general service, probably because there were no matching 70ft brake composites or slip coaches. As to modifications, one or two vehicles received equalised beam bogies, and third No 4509 was adapted for working with GWR railcars Nos 35/6 in October 1941. Withdrawal of this 70ft stock began in earnest during 1957, but only then was it taken off everyday service on expresses, and examples were still in evidence in relief sets until the early 1960s. In 1959, a 1924 composite, No 7942, was marshalled in a London area semi-fast set, looking rather out of place among short-length compartment coaches.

Several survivors were contained in a relief set which consisted of a later design 60ft brake third, 70ft thirds Nos 4736, 4728, 4715, two later 60ft composites, and thirds Nos 4730, 4729 and 4741. This set, but with one or two other 70ft thirds originally, had been formed in 1958. One of its last duties was performed on a summer Saturday Kingswear branch-London train whose seating capacity of 612 was probably the greatest of any nine-coach corridor express at that time. This set, which must have been the last of its kind in the country with 70ft coaches, survived until the end

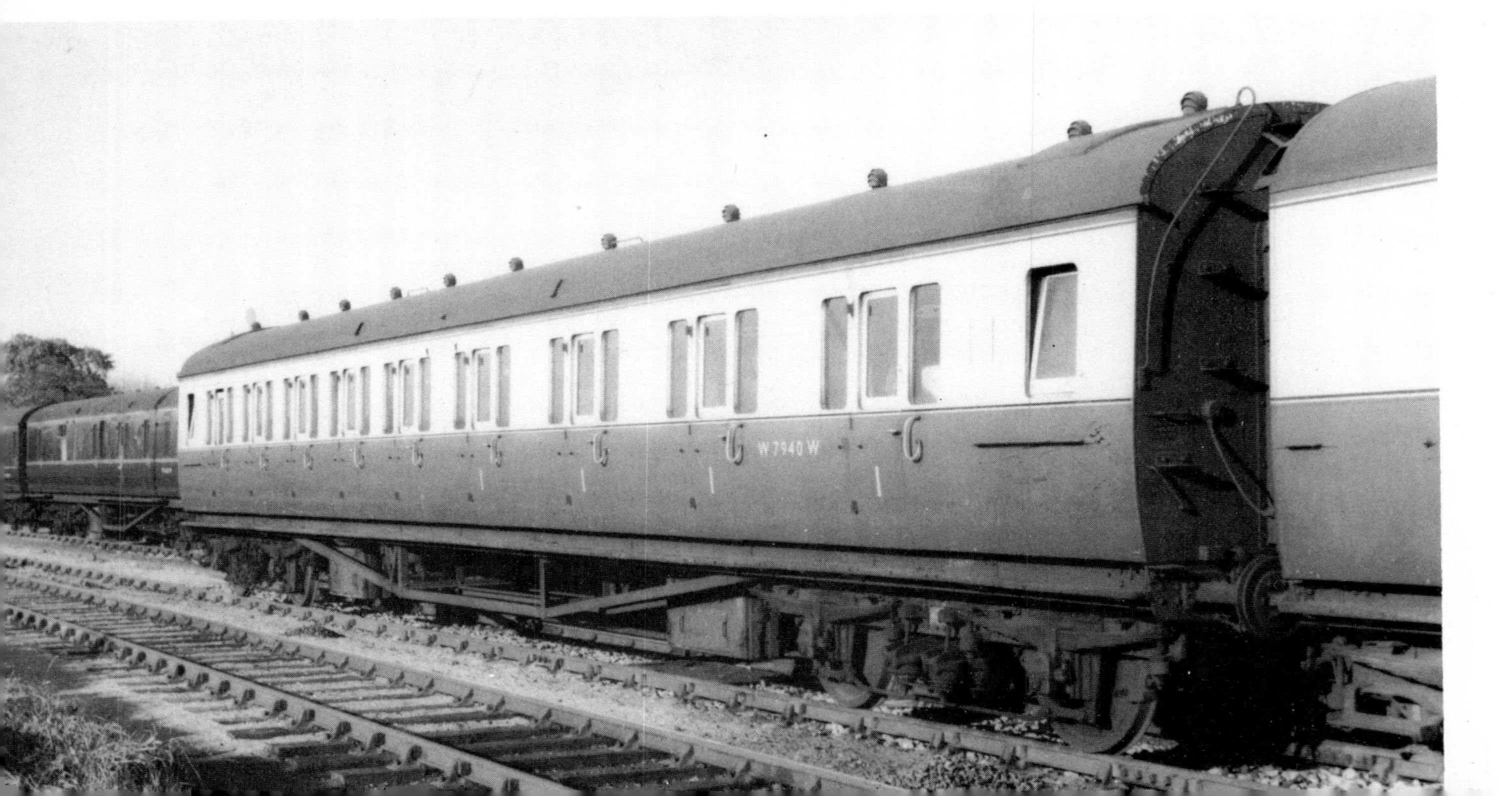

70ft corridor composite W7940W at Henley, October 1958. (Lot 1319 – Diagram E.111)

of 1961. The last few coaches disappeared in 1962, and when No 4748 was withdrawn in January 1963 this effectively finished the history of the GWR's 70ft era.

Standard 57ft Corridor Stock (58ft 4½in over bow ends): 1923–1929

Some months after the introduction of the modernised, steel-panelled outline for 70ft coaches a 57ft design of the same appearance was produced. Apart from a cleaner exterior appearance, higher waistline and plainer internal finish, they were generally similar to the later batches of 'Toplight' stock. Modified, the Churchward-period standard 57ft coaches thus lasted as the basic GWR design for nearly thirty years. Uninspiring, but of robust construction, the standard coaches of the 1920s were used on the majority of important expresses until the late 1930s, and both the 'Cheltenham Flyer' and 'Bristolian' were formed of this stock for some time after introduction.

The first three Lots, Nos 1322–4, were, in effect, a pre-production series with the Churchward elliptical roof, flat ends (and so of 57ft length over end panels) and the light-type 9ft bogie. Eighteen of the brake composites were originally dual-fitted to enable them to work through on cross-country services.

From late 1925, with the introduction of the suspended gangway, the familiar bow-ended profile and 7ft bogied standard vehicle was produced. All were built for general service. Some were originally formed into six-coach sets (Lots 1351–3 and 1373–5) while Lots 1411/2 (to 8ft 10¼in width) were marshalled as eight-coach all-third-class excursion sets. Three other peculiarities were Nos 5140–5142, which were originally built as third-class sleeper coaches with three four-berth and five ordinary day compartments (see page 86). All three were converted in 1935: No 5141 to a composite sleeper, while the other two reverted to a standard third-class corridor layout.

Two six-coach sets were turned out in April 1929, made up of vehicles featuring a cleaner exterior appearance, with the windows nearly flush with the panelling, instead of recessed as previously. The coaches were brake thirds, Nos 5133–6; thirds, 5177–80, and composites 6101–4. This modification in panelling was adopted for the 61ft 4½in vehicles built from that date.

A number of brake thirds (Lots 1399, 1412) and some other vehicles of this type, including restaurant cars No 9562 et seq, were converted to form casualty evacuation trains in September 1939, some later reformed into ambulance trains at York Works. They were returned to normal traffic from 1945. Six brake thirds of Lots 1353/4 and several thirds were used as stores/office cars in overseas ambulance trains during World War 2.

Withdrawals commenced in the late 1950s, with a large number sent for scrapping in 1959. By the following year, there were many conversions for departmental service, both thirds and brake thirds. The contraction of the WR passenger stock fleet during 1962 saw the large-scale withdrawal of these bow-enders, although a number had been outshopped from Swindon in the previous year.

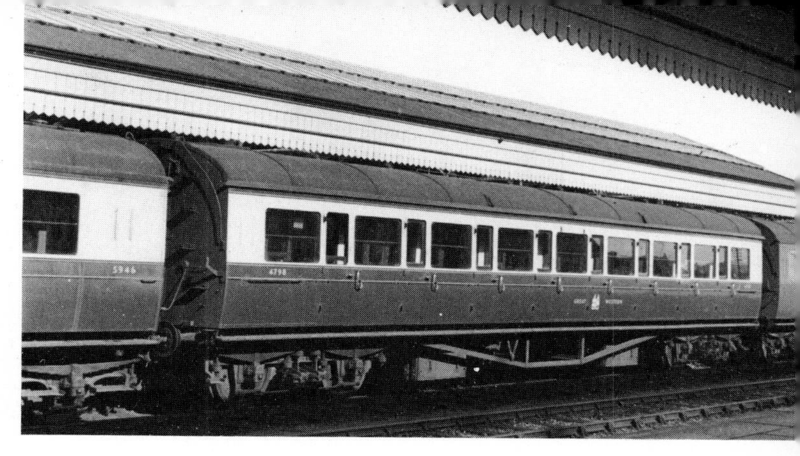

Top:
58ft 4½in bow-end corridor third No 4798, in postwar livery, at Aberystwyth, August 1948. (Lot 1369 – Diagram C.54)

Above:
The down Bristolian near Bathampton in 1936, headed by partially streamlined King No 6014 *King Henry VII*. The train consists of recently over hauled 58ft 4½in bow-end corridor stock and includes one of the Quick-Lunch-Bar cars.

There were two lots of contemporary restaurant cars: flat-ended 57ft-long body and 8ft 6in-width composite diners, Nos 9562–9567, for general service on cross-country trains, and bow-ended 9ft-width composite diners, Nos 9578–9581. The first lot, apart from the fitting of sliding metal frame ventilators, remained in more or less their original condition until withdrawn in 1960–61: some were redecorated from 1947. Nos 9562–9567 had 9ft wheelbase bogies as built, and received the 7ft wheelbase type in 1928.

The second batch, Nos 9578–81, was condemned by 1961, except for No 9580. In March 1952 this coach was converted to an unclassed buffet car with 12 seats and four bar-stools, and in 1960 underwent a further transformation to become an engineer's inspection saloon. It was painted in lined-out chocolate and cream and renumbered DW 150266. Later carrying the BR blue paint scheme, it was repainted in 1982 to an approximation of GWR livery. No DW150266, is based at Reading as a signal and telecommunication department inspection saloon at the time of writing.

Bow-end non-corridor brake third No 5528, built 1928. (Lot 1392 – Diagram D.101)

Standard Non-Corridor Stock: 1924–1929

To the same profile as the early Collett-era corridor stock, four Lots covering conventional flat-ended non-corridor coaches were constructed in 1924 for general service. The following year, four-coach, bow-ended and originally permanently-coupled sets for suburban duties were constructed, their only point of interest being the curved seats fitting the bow-end contour of both the brake thirds and composites. The sets for general service did not have this unique feature and, as with all subsequent bow-ended, non-corridor stock, false walls were fitted at the ends of the coaches. During the next three years, further suburban sets with the newly-developed 7ft bogie were built to cover Chester, Birmingham and South Wales Valleys services. A number of composites were downgraded to all-thirds from late 1953. Displaced by dieselisation, all this stock was withdrawn gradually from 1958 and extinguished in 1962.

The 'B' sets were probably the most interesting of the non-corridor coaches of the inter-war period. They were two close-coupled brake composites in permanent formation for branch-line and cross-country stopping services. The majority were initially allocated to the Bristol Division and this number included the original batches with flat ends, on 9ft bogies and later bow-ended vehicles. One peculiarity was the position of the first-class compartment – at the centre-coupler end for the first batch, and therefore subject to buffeting and grinding over curves! For the second batch it was then placed in the centre of the coach – away from the helping hand of the guard – and, finally, for the flush-sided coaches (see page 82), placed next but one to the guard. The two 1929 sets were allocated to the Looe branch, although originally destined for Bristol, and had 7ft bogies. Incidentally, the Looe branch was originally restricted to coaches with bogies with this wheelbase, and besides the two 'B' sets, two 1931 brake thirds and a 1937 brake composite specially mounted on 7ft bogies were allocated there. The earlier 'B' sets were withdrawn up to 1962.

Articulated Corridor and Suburban Stock: 1925

For a railway committed to the use of fixed formations for express trains, articulation offered advantages in length, weight and space. The LNER, although making great use of articulation, had at an early stage abandoned articulated trains for general service. The six GWR eight-car sets were prototypes and the experiment was not to be repeated.

But there was no doubt that the GWR made the most of the trains when first introduced. The prototype set was completed during the summer of 1925 and, together with the inevitable 'Castle' – in this case the rebuilt *Great Bear* – represented the GWR at the Stockton & Darlington Centenary Exhibition in July 1925 with headboards announcing the 'New Articulated Express Passenger Train'. The other seven sets appeared by October and went into service on Paddington to Birkenhead, Paddington to South Wales expresses, and Channel Islands boat trains, while the

Articulated corridor stock of 1925 made up as an eight-coach train: third-class triplet leading, restaurant car triplet and first-class twin. The locomotive is Castle No 4085 *Berkeley Castle*, built May 1925.

first set was also used on the Plymouth ocean-liner boat-trains.

The original formations of the sets are shown in diagram form below:

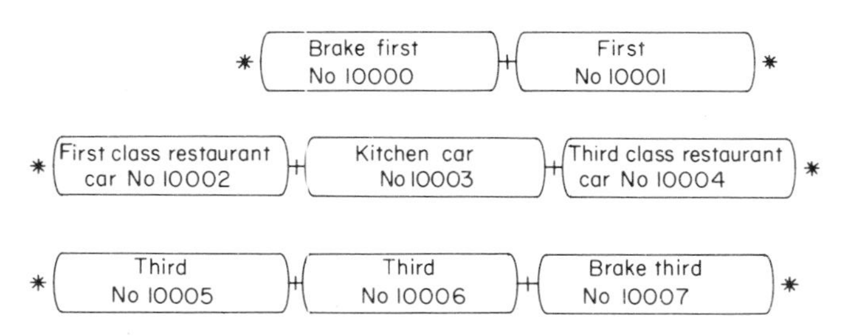

Arrangement of articulated corridor stock set. *Indicates screw couplings. +Indicates articulation bogie and ratchet couplings.

First and third-class were kept rigidly apart by the kitchen car, and it is interesting that all first-class passengers could be accommodated for meals in the restaurant car in the first four sets. The capacity of the first-class diner was, no doubt, in excess of the requirements, but it does emphasise that the articulated trains were built for front-line express work. It was not long before the restaurant triplets were replaced by one or two full-length cars and two 70ft classless diners were substituted on the 6.10 p.m. Paddington–Wolverhampton.

In their construction, the vehicles were otherwise standard with the contemporary corridor stock although of shorter body length, and made use of the 7ft bogie for the first time on passenger coaches. For the five later sets, buckeye couplers were fitted on the ends of the pairs and triplets within the set but these, of course, disappeared upon rebuilding. Ratchet couplings were used between each articulated coach. The vehicles were allotted numbers from 100xx onwards; not only a new series but one that was numerically significant.

The subsequent history of the articulated corridor sets was disappointing. Until the arrival of the flush-sided 60ft-plus stock in 1930, they remained on first-line expresses but were then demoted to working on Cheltenham and Weymouth trains. By 1935, their usefulness was limited and all the coaches were rebuilt in 1936/7 to approximately the 57ft body length of their contemporaries of the 1920s. This was achieved by splicing additional frame lengths and adding new body sections. The 7ft bogies were retained. As rebuilt, the thirds and third brakes were indistinguishable from standard stock, but the firsts were the only ones of their outline since none of this type was built new from 'Toplight' days until 1937. In addition, the first brakes were the only post-Grouping examples in the GWR's fleet. Withdrawal of the rebuilds did not take place until the late 1950s and the thirds and third brakes were active until 1963.

The restaurant cars in the triplets were open saloons with standard high-backed seats, the leather covered tip-up variety being provided in the third-class cars. The two of the sets had classless saloons, far more sensible than the original outmoded arrangement of the other sets. When the articulated sets were disbanded in 1935, two dining-car triplets were appropriated for the second excursion set of that year (see page 93 until the delivery of new open thirds in 1936. During that year and up to the middle of 1937, the restaurant cars were rebuilt as separate vehicles; to a 58ft body length with the ex-first-class coaches remaining as such. Diners from the last two triplets became open thirds, the others retaining their original classification and receiving metal-framed sliding ventilators.

The kitchen cars were retained as such until 1956, when they were rebuilt at Swindon as cafeteria cars for party work. The layout, as modified, featured a central kitchen, with a saloon on each side including a counter and table with high bar-stools. Two bodyside windows were provided on each side for the saloons, some kitchen windows were blocked up and an end vestibule formed at each end. In this condition their tare weight was 36 tons. These cars were a frequent sight in the London area on excursions from the provinces until withdrawn in 1961/62.

Four first-class diners used on the Birmingham route (Nos 9647/8/50/51) were fitted with six-wheel bogies in 1938/39. Third-class diners Nos 9650/1/4/5 were reclassified as open thirds in 1952. In early 1957, No 9653 was appropriated for use as a mess car, No DW150032, in the first of the two WR emergency control trains described on page 90. No 9654 was similarly taken out of traffic for the second control train in 1962. The remaining ex-triplet dining cars remained in service until 1961. When the control trains were disbanded in 1979, Nos 9653/54 were acquired by the National Railway Museum for preservation and both were removed to the Severn Valley Railway for restoration.

A down local train leaves Paddington in 1927 behind Metropolitan 2-4-0T No 3565. Its train consists of a clerestory tri-composite brake and two non-corridor articulated triplets.

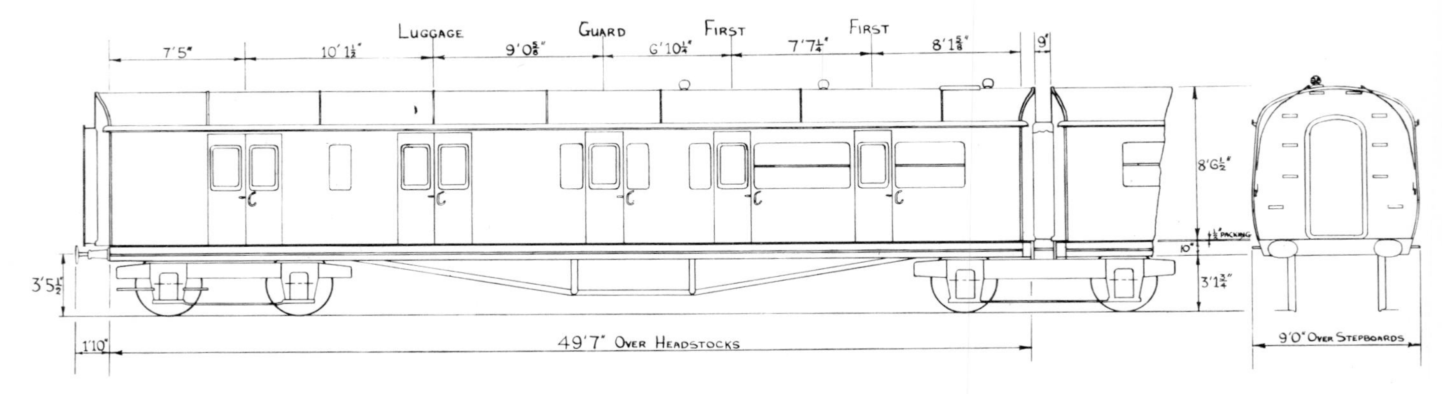

Articulated brake first and first of articulated corridor twin. (Diagrams A.17/A.16 – Lots 1364/63)

The articulated suburban stock did not receive the widespread publicity of the corridor vehicles, ironically and lasted in their original condition. Basically, the design adopted for the vehicles forming the three six-coach sets, comprising two triplets, built in 1925, represented the contemporary post-1923 non-corridor body scaled down to Metro gauge dimensions. Like the Gresley articulated stock, this resulted in cramped compartments with 'sit-up-and-beg' seating. The only advantages of using articulation came with the reduced overall length and weight of each set, the former admittedly a basic statistic for operating over the 'Widened Lines', but the twenty per cent saving in weight and length, in comparison with standard six-coach 57ft-body coaches, was offset by a reduction of twelve per cent in passenger accommodation.

The three suburban sets did not suffer the conversion process of the corridor stock, and were presumably considered not to have the disadvantage of corridor set formations. With the termination of the through GWR trains to Liverpool Street (Metropolitan) as from 15 September 1939, the three sets remained on London suburban services and saw no further alterations, other than the fitting of thermostatically controlled heaters in the second set. All the composites were downgraded to thirds during the Second World War and were reinstated as composites in 1949/50. The last duties of the sets were outside the London Division, around Bristol and in South Wales. Two sets were withdrawn in November 1957 and the last (coaches 9813–8) in July 1960.

The sets were originally lettered 'Local C' sets Nos 7/8/9 respectively, and were subject to a number of local restrictions on working, on account of an overall width of 9ft 2in for their stepboards and undersides above rail level.

Standard Corridor Stock: 1929–1933

These coaches marked some advance in external design as they were the first GWR vehicles, other than the two six-coach 57ft length bow-ended sets also built in 1929, with the windows almost flush with the body panelling. The exteriors of the coaches were now free from window ledges and protruding door and commode handles, since the latter were recessed into the panelling. The most striking feature of the design was the 'bulging' body side profile, an attempt to obtain the maxi-

THE REBUILDING OF THE ARTICULATED CORRIDOR SETS

ORDINARY COACHES

Original No	New No	Type	Length over Ends	Altered Weight	Rebuilding Date
10000/8/16/24/32/40	8017–8022	First Brake	58ft 3¾in	31t 4c	7/36–7/37
10001/9/17/25/33/41	8011–8016	First	55ft 4¾in	31t 11c	7/36–7/37
10007/15/23/31/9/47	4202–4207	Third Brake	58ft 0¾in	30t 15c	7/36–4/37
10005/6/13/4/21/2/9	4190–4201	Third	59ft 8¾in	31t 7/10c	7/36–4/37
10030/7/8/45/6					

RESTAURANT CARS

Original Nos	Type as Rebuilt	New No	Seats	Altered Weight	Date
10003/11/9/27/35/43	Kitchen Car	9657–9662	—	41t 11c -43t 7c	1937
altered by BR to	Cafeteria Cars	9657–9662		36t 0c	1956
10002/10/26/42	Diner First	9645–9648	48	31t 7c	6/36–3/37
10004/12/28/44	Diner Third	9649–9652	64	31t 9c	6/36–3/37
10018/20/34/36	Diner Third	9655/3/6/4	56	31t 12c -32t 2c	4/36

Two dining triplets, one Nos 10018–20, allocated in April 1935 to GWR VT No 2 (see page 93). Replaced 1936 and rebuilt as indicated.

61ft 4½in bow-end corridor brake composite No 6088, with Paddington-Falmouth destination board for the Cornish Riviera. This illustrates the 'Plain Jane' livery referred to in Chapter 3. (Lot 1425 – Diagram E.138)

mum width at seat level in the compartments and corridors compatible with the loading gauge. Internally, the layout and furnishings showed no advance on previous designs. The other development was the increase of body length to 60ft, 61ft 4½in over the bow ends.

'Cornish Riviera' 9ft 5¾in/9ft 7in wide coaches: 1929–30

For the summer service in 1929, new stock to the new 60ft length and of increased width was built for the 'Cornish Riviera', 'Torbay Express' and principal Paddington–West of England trains.

The dining and kitchen cars were to 9ft 7in width; the other coaches were 9ft 5¾in wide. To quote the GWR *General Appendix to the Rule Book* (1936), 'Coaching stock of these dimensions, which is distinguished by a red triangle placed at each end of the vehicle, *cannot be accepted by any other Company*'. It could only be accepted on specified GWR routes, and in the main was restricted to Paddington–Penzance via Westbury or Bristol; Paddington–Fishguard, Neyland and Milford Haven (to Pembroke Dock from 1939), and Paddington–Oxley Sidings (Wolverhampton) via Bicester and Oxford (allowed south of Saltney Junction after 1945).

From 8 July 1929, the 'Cornish Riviera' resumed non-stop running to Plymouth and was accelerated to a four-hour timing from Paddington.

The original formation of the train in the down direction was:

Coach No		*Destination*
1	Van brake third	Penzance
2	Third-class	Penzance
3	Third-class	Penzance
4	Third-class dining saloon	Penzance
5	Kitchen car	Penzance
6	Composite dining saloon	Penzance
7	Composite	Penzance
8	Van brake third	Penzance
9	Brake composite	St Ives
10	Brake composite	Falmouth
11	Brake composite	Plymouth
12	Slip composite	Weymouth
13	Brake composite	Weymouth

Tare weight: 449 tons
Seating capacity: 428

This stock, probably because it was produced for premier GWR services, had the heavy 9ft bogie in preference to the otherwise standard 7ft variety, which suggests that the latter, even in the official view, had limitations in riding qualities. Sceptical interest is aroused by the Vita-glass windows with which these coaches were fitted. In the famous *Cheltenham Flyer* book of 1934, published the year before this stock was displaced on the 'Cornish Riviera Express', a description of the windows ran: '. . . but perhaps I ought to mention that these coaches are glazed with Vita-glass, which admits the health-giving ultra-violet rays of the sun which ordinary glass excludes. No wonder the "Cornish Riviera Express" has been called "the aristocrat of railway trains!".'

The start of a slightly later vogue was anticipated by the chromium plating of the neatly

No 9587, one of the handsome 61ft 4½in composite dining cars used on the Cornish Riviera and West of England services. As rebuilt with sliding ventilators in 1938/39. (Lot 1421 – Diagram H.36)

61ft 4½in, 9ft width bow-end corridor second (formerly third-class) W5245W, from the compartment side, at Penzance, 1958. (Lot 1423 – Diagram C.60)

recessed door handles and grips. Two additional six-coach general service sets were built in 1930, to Lots 1433–5.

The slip coaches which covered the Weymouth working on the 'Cornish Riviera Express' and the Taunton slip off the 'Torbay Express' were the first to be built after the Grouping. These vehicles, Nos 7898–7900, lost their slip gear in 1940/41, but although the first was restored with slip gear in December 1947 the other two were not re-equipped until 1952. All three were condemned in 1959.

The dining and kitchen cars inaugurated a handsome new outline for these types of vehicle which was followed by catering vehicles built in 1931/32, although those were of reduced width. The 1929 train had a greater proportion of restaurant facilities for third-class passengers, a sign of the times. Apart from internal redecoration and the fitting of sliding ventilators, most vehicles remained as built and were withdrawn from 1957–62. No 9595, however, was taken into use for staff accommodation at Laira (Plymouth) and did not reappear in normal service after the war. It was withdrawn still carrying its 1930s livery in 1957. Two of the kitchen cars received six-wheeled bogies. Third diner No 9590 was redesignated as an open third in 1952.

The other types of this 9ft 5¾in width stock were withdrawn between 1959 and 1962.

General Service 9ft and 9ft 3in-wide Coaches: 1930–33

With a similar outline to the 'Cornish Riviera' 1929 stock, general service coaches 61ft 4½in over the bow-ends and with 9ft and 9ft 3in-wide bodies appeared in 1930. Other improvements covered seating – increased seat widths, with springs in the cushions and larger compartment dimensions. The bulged sides of the body were accentuated in the 9ft 3in-width design: as a result, the outside doors had to have extremely wide hinges at the tops to enable the door to hang correctly. The 9ft wide vehicles (Lots 1423/36–38/66) were primarily intended for use on cross-country services such as Torquay–Bradford, Birkenhead and Wolverhampton to Deal and Hastings. Changes to the general design were instituted with the thirds to Lot 1489. All this batch were fitted with the pressed steel 9ft wheelbase bogie, and Nos 5744–78 had flat ends and were 60ft in length over the end panels. All earlier vehicles had 7ft wheelbase bogies.

No changes of any interest were made to these coaches, which were in general service until withdrawal began in 1959. As with the 1923–29 standard corridor stock, a number were overhauled until 1961, but the sudden reduction in the WR passenger-stock fleet in 1962 resulted in the complete condemnation of the design by late 1963.

Standard Non-Corridor Stock: 1930–1933

Suburban Sets

To the same outline as the 1929–33 corridor stock, 61ft 4½in non-corridor coaches of 9ft 3in width were put into service from late 1930 in the form of set trains for South Wales, Birmingham and London suburban services. Additionally two Lots, only 9ft wide over the waist, were built for general service.

The five-coach South Wales sets had composites with five first-class compartments, to preserve the normal percentage of about twenty per cent for this accommodation. In general, the compartment coaches inherited from the 'Valleys' railways were in need of replacement, not only by virtue of their age but also because of their sub-standard condition.

Composite No 6353, of 1930, was of interest as one bogie was fitted with Timken roller bearings, which it retained until withdrawn in 1960. About the same time as No 6353 had appeared, the Metropolitan Railway had put a number of roller-bearing equipped 'T' stock coaches into service. Two general service third brakes, Nos 5650 and 5668, were allocated to the Looe branch.

Despite dieselisation of the Birmingham and South Wales suburban service in 1958, the majority of these coaches remained in service until 1960, and final extinction did not take place until December 1963.

'B' Sets

The branch lines received their allocation of 61ft 4½in flush-panelled 'bulging side' 9ft 3in width non-corridor coaches at the same time. In comparison with the 1923–29 batches (see page 78) these series, although permanently coupled, were fitted with short buffers; earlier 'B' Set brake composites were without them. In addition, the longer bodies allowed slightly more spacious third-class compartments and the luggage space was increased. The 1933 sets were built with the heavy 9ft bogie. Allocation was predominantly to the Bristol Division, and a favoured centre was Taunton, which used them on the Minehead, Yeovil, Chard branches and some main-line stopping trains. Until 1962, they were also staple provision on the Barnstaple line, working through to Ilfracombe and Torrington during the summer, both destinations over sixty miles from Taunton. By this time, they were often supplemented by a corridor composite brake which, in the latter days, was an ex-slip coach of pre-war or Hawksworth design.

The Bristol Division sets were also used on the main line stopping trains and, since these formed running-in turns for ex-works express locomotives, there was frequently the incongruous sight at Reading of a spotless 'King' on a dingy 'B' set. A set from the Bristol area strayed on to the S & D line in the 1960s, working on Bath to Templecombe trains. One of the last 'B' set survivors was noticeably out of place under the 25 kV electrification at Crewe on Wellington–Crewe trains in mid-1963.

Although they gave very useful service, the 'B' sets were not really the most satisfactory stock for branch lines, particularly as they were often employed on fairly long turns as noted above. Most survived the initial dieselisation schemes, but the closure of branch lines hastened their demise after 1959, although all were not withdrawn until December 1963.

Saloons: 1929–1931

Nondescript Brake Saloons: 1929

This batch of ten side-corridor saloons with one ordinary compartment was built for private hire and excursion work, and they were similar to vehicles of 'Toplight' outline which had been built in 1923 (see page 66). The designation 'nondescript' was literal, and meant that they were unclassed. Internally, the two saloons bore some resemblance to Underground surface stock cars, with inward facing bench-type seats and Edwardian mahogany woodwork. Additionally, their clumsy folding tables restricted movement. The single compartment was identical with those in contemporary side-corridor coaches. Their original duties are not known, but the delivery of BR standard open thirds in the 1950s resulted in the allocation of two each of these brake saloons for the five excursion sets. They were on this work until the arrival of BR standard open brake thirds. Despite their non-standard layout, they survived this displacement and continued in general relief and excursion work until late 1961, but by the middle of the following year all had been condemned. One was used in a commercial television exhibition train in the early 1960s and was subsequently preserved. Their main interest in later years was the fact that they were the last open saloons in general service on the WR, carrying the word 'Saloon' in bold sans-serif lettering below one of the pairs of large windows.

Brake First Saloons: 1930
(61ft 4½in over bow ends, 9ft wide, Lot 1431)

Originally built as self-contained saloons for first-class private hire, these bow-ended 'bulging-side' coaches were to the same outline as the 1930–33 general service stock. Of particular interest were the large observation windows in the bow ends, a large central kitchen and pantry, and the Pullman-type dining saloon. As with the nondescript brake third saloons, a separate first-class compartment was provided. Internal panelling was in walnut veneer and all seating was upholstered in patterned beige moquette.

No 9005 was modernised with sliding ventilators set in larger windows in 1938, and No. 9004 in 1942. In 1947, in common with other saloons and restaurant cars, the vehicles were generally modernised, the side-corridor compartment was dispensed with, and the smaller saloon enlarged. As a result, the seating accommodation was reduced by four.

Right:
A four-coach set of 61ft 2in body non-corridor stock leads this stopping train headed by a Saint 4-6-0 in the 1930s.

Below:
In private ownership, saloon No 9004 is seen as repainted in post-war GWR livery, being employed as an observation saloon on the Inverness-Kyle of Lochalsh line, at Inverness in August 1983.

In BR days, the chocolate and cream livery was maintained and the coaches reserved for VIP use. No 9005 went for modernisation in 1961, in the course of which its underframe was replaced by that from brake second No 5301 and it was further distinguished by receiving the newly developed, Swindon designed B4-type bogies. No 9005 was used as the WR General Manager's saloon, later being painted in BR blue livery and fitted with air braking. Withdrawn in 1974, its interior was stripped and the B4 bogies replaced by a set of BR1 examples which then made it out of gauge. In this form it was moved to Didcot after acquisition by the Great Western Society. Subsequently, it has been mounted on 9ft wheelbase bogies and now awaits restoration.

No 9004 was regularly used for Royal VIPs until transferred to the former North Eastern Region as the Chief Civil Engineer's saloon in March 1963. On withdrawal in 1972, it was purchased by William McAlpine for private use on BR metals, and from the late 1970s has seen regular use as an observation saloon on the Inverness–Kyle of Lochalsh ordinary passenger services, latterly resplendent in post-war GWR livery.

'Super Saloons': 1931

These coaches are among the most famous of all GWR vehicles, not only because of their exclusiveness but also for their distinctive outline. Although 'Super Saloon' was the official designation, they were familiarly known as 'Pullmans', 'Cunard' or 'Ocean Saloon' stock. When the Plymouth boat-trains were no longer operated, they appeared refined and well turned-out in Newbury race-trains and for private hire duties.

Their introduction was an interesting sidelight on the importance of the Plymouth boat-trains and the GWR's experiment with the use of Pullman cars. More lucrative than the Fishguard route, traffic through Plymouth docks was increasing in the 1920s: in 1921, 354 liners called and 13,170 passengers were landed, but by 1930 these figures had risen to 684 and 38,472 respectively. This was due to the current vogue in sea travel and cruises, and before modernisation at Southampton in 1934. The high-class clientèle from the liners, and the lengthy journey involved, called for special vehicles, and the GWR started running Pullmans in the Ocean Liner expresses from May 1929. However, to make greater use of the Pullman contract, the fleet was increased to allow operation of a regular, if uninspiringly run service, 'The Torquay Pullman'. The latter's failure, and the obvious unprofitability of using Pullmans for the boat-trains only, saw the end of the GWR's Pullman association as from 1 January 1931 when, ironically enough, the cars departed for the Southampton boat-trains which later contributed to the end of the Plymouth service.

The 'Super Saloons' were, without doubt, the GWR's personally-styled Pullmans, more spacious, non-Americanised, and considerably more modern in specification. The bulging sides and recessed doorways had their forerunners in the 1929 'Riviera' three-coach restaurant car sets (see page 82), and the width inside was a clear 9ft. Their extreme body width dimension was 9ft 7in and, with the 1935 'Centenary' stock, they were among the widest of all main-line coaches in Britain, and naturally branded as Red Triangle vehicles.

The order for these vehicles read as follows: 'The underframes, bogies, shell bodies to be built by Carriage Department, Swindon. Two saloons to be panelled and equipped with furnishings and fittings by Messrs Trollope & Sons. Six saloons to be panelled in GWR standard finish by the Carriage Department, Swindon, and Messrs Trollope & Sons a/c to be charged to this order.' (*From*

'Super Saloon' No 9117, as converted with catering facilities. (Lot 1471 – Diagram G.61)

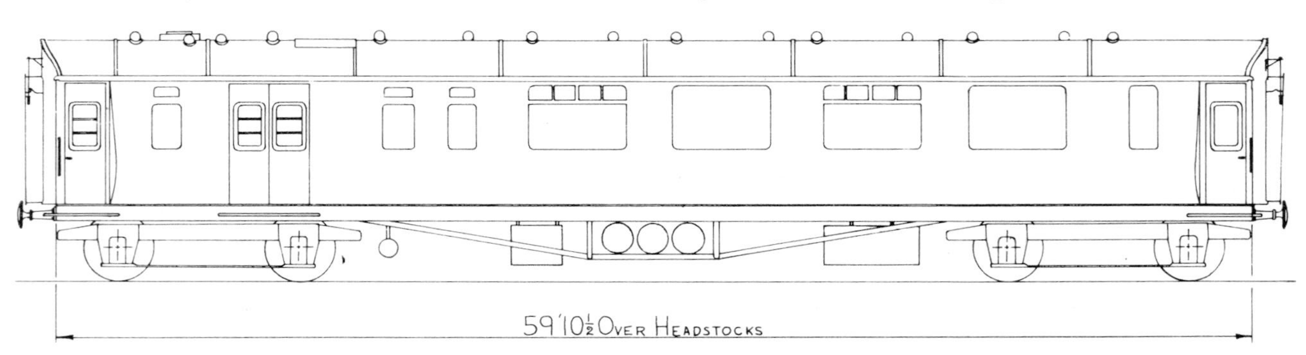

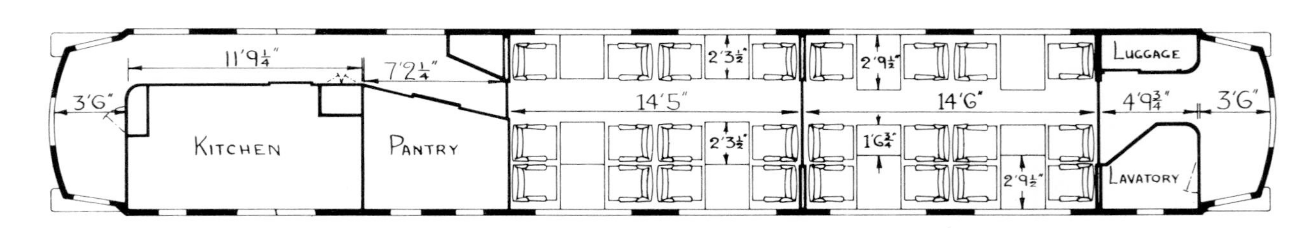

'Super Saloon' No 9116 *Duchess of York*, as built, with Beclawat windows with glass ventilators. (Lot 1471 – Diagram G.61)

Carriage Department Swindon Lot Books.)

The bodies were bow-ended, with recessed entrance doors unusually hinged on the right-hand side and set at an angle of 30° to the sides. This permitted ample step accommodation for passengers, and if a door opened during a journey it would still be within the loading gauge. Construction was otherwise standard to a dimension over the bow-ends of 61ft 4½in and heavy 9ft bogies were fitted.

Interior furnishing was luxurious and certainly up to Pullman standard, if not better: the saloons, separated by sliding doors, and Pullman coupé compartment were panelled in highly-polished light French walnut veneer, and Nos 9111/2 had dark, figured, burr walnut panels between the windows. The later vehicles had large scenic photographs in this position and on the coupé bulkhead, this constituting the main difference between the completely Trollope-furnished and Swindon/Trollope coaches. The ceilings were covered with stippled vellum. Neat ceiling light fittings were installed, as well as Pullman-type table lamps. The tables were not rigidly fixed to the floor but hinged to the bodyside. There were two types of chairs: those in the large saloon were straight-backed, those in the small saloon round-backed. Being moveable, seating accommodation could be changed according to demand. The large saloon normally sat three-a-side. The coupé compartment had no windows on the corridor side. Upholstery was in brown patterned moquette for most of the coaches, although one or two of the GWR-furnished saloons had blue coverings.

Other furnishing notes included silk damask curtains, a combined curtain-box and bar-luggage rack, and carpeting in dark brown Wilton. The original window arrangements were interesting: the alternate large bodyside windows were opened by a large car-type winder and all had sliding plate-glass louvred ventilators. The naming of the vehicles after the Royal Family and the inscriptions in Pullman-type lettering increased their prestige. But the prestige had to be paid for as the supplementary charge for the saloons was ten shillings (50p) in addition to the first-class fare. This was high by comparison with Pullman rates, as well as with the contemporary 'Silver Jubilee' express of the LNER which, under almost the same conditions, had a five shillings (25p) charge.

The 'Super Saloons' made their debut in November 1931, when Nos 9111/2 were used by a party of guests of the French Line (CGT) travelling from Le Havre to London on the occasion of the maiden voyage of the *Colombie*. The other coaches entered service soon after, the last being outshopped in May 1932. When only a small party was travelling, it was a disadvantage to have to provide a separate kitchen car so, in 1935, Nos 9117/8 were rebuilt with catering facilities in place of the coupé compartment. This meant reducing the large saloon to almost the same size as the smaller one. Other detail differences included the fitting of metal-framed ventilators to alternate saloon windows in place of the original arrangements, and the standardisation of square-backed chairs. During the post-war renovation of vehicles, when private furnishers refurbished the interiors, rust, and rust and grey material was used for the chairs and curtains. The remaining 'Super Saloons' were then fitted with new windows, with deep sliding ventilators and radiused corners. No further alterations were made.

The best-known Plymouth boat-train formation comprised five 'Super Saloons' and two passenger brake vans. However, the usual load when the fastest running was put up was five coaches, three of which would be 'Super Saloons'. On other occasions, heavier trains were run – up to nine and thirteen-coach loads – including the 1937 kitchen cars and other restaurant cars for the use of third-class passengers. A typical 'Ocean Liner' formation reported in late 1956 comprised a bogie brake, Hawksworth brake composite, two second corridors, restaurant second No 9626, 'Super Saloon' No 9115, kitchen car No 9663, 'Super Saloons' Nos 9113/2 and a bogie brake. The 'Super Saloons' began to be repainted in WR chocolate and cream livery from 1957, No 9111 later being outshopped in BR maroon.

As from the end of 1962, as British Railways could no longer deal with liners at Plymouth, the

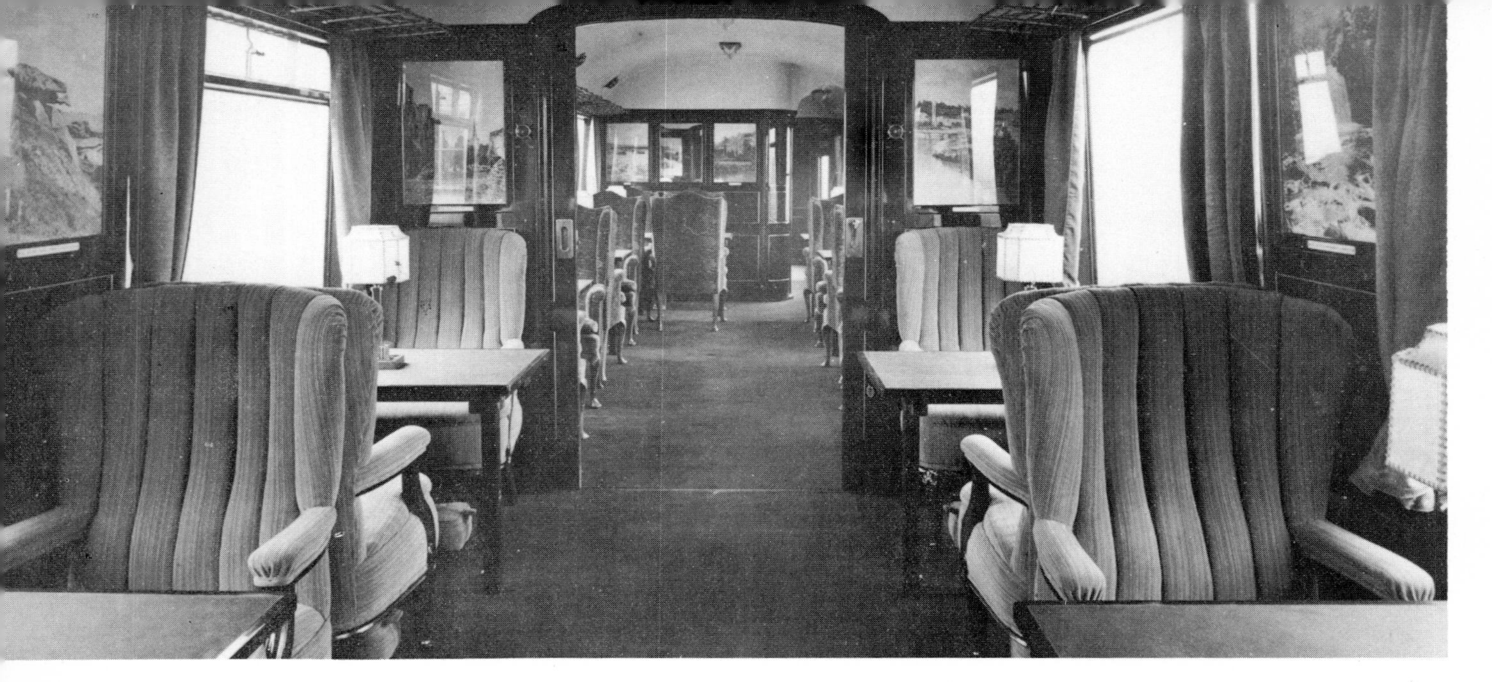

The small saloon of a 'Super Saloon', as originally furnished.

famous boat-trains similarly passed away. In the next three or four years, fairly extensive use was made of the 'Super Saloons' in line with the Western Region's policy of encouraging first-class party travel, and by employing them on Newbury Racecourse specials.

In the past, they played their part in a number of special occasions such as the GWR 'Centenary' special to Bristol in 1935, the GWR high-speed Automatic Train Control special of October 1947, and the Press run to and from Swindon Works in March 1960 on the occasion of the completion and naming of the last new steam locomotive, 2-10-0 No 92220 *Evening Star*. By October 1965, the first two were taken out of traffic, although the remainder were at work into the next year, and subsequently five 'Super Saloons' were purchased for preservation. During the mid/late 1970s, the examples based at Didcot were used on charter excursions over BR main lines, including a journey over the Central Wales route.

Saloon names: 9111 *King George*, 9112 *Queen Mary*, 9113 *Prince of Wales*, 9114 *Duke of York*, 9115 *Duke of Gloucester*, 9116 *Duchess of York*, 9117 *Princess Mary*, 9118 *Princess Elizabeth*. Names removed in early BR days.

Sleeping Cars: 1929–1934

58ft 4½in Day/Sleeper Thirds Nos 5140–5142: 1929

It is relevant at this stage to refer to the provision of sleeping car facilities during the Second World War. From December 1942, sleeping cars were barred to civilian travellers but ten vehicles were still in use for military and Government passengers on services from Paddington to Plymouth, Penzance, Neyland and Newquay at the end of hostilities. On 17 September 1945, the Government agreed to release a proportion of sleeping car accommodation on those routes to civilians, and subsequently full facilities were restored.

In March 1929, bow-ended coaches Nos 5140-2, with five ordinary and three sleeping, couchette-type compartments were put into service on the 9.25pm Paddington – Neyland and 6.30pm back.

Nos 5140–2 were the first vehicles providing *all* third-class sleeping accommodation on the GWR. In 1922, as mentioned on page 67, the Neyland service had been allocated a sleeping-car with first-class berths and ordinary third-class compartments, so the 1929 vehicles were not the first day/sleeping coaches. Now, however, it was intended to provide one of these thirds in addition to a first-class sleeping-car. Their introduction is important in marking a further step in the increase in facilities for the third-class passenger, and it represented a transitional step to GWR third-class sleeping cars. The sleeping compartments, without doors on the compartment side, had four bunks each furnished with a mattress, two pillows and a rug, all obtained for a rather expensive six-shilling (30p) supplement, particularly as there was no attendant.

Whatever the public reaction may have been, this cautious gesture was superseded by the quick appearance of all-third-class cars in the May of the same year and the following year. The day/sleepers survived until 1935 when Nos 5140/2 became standard eight-compartment thirds and No 5141 was converted to a sleeper composite and renumbered 9079. In 1942, it was rebuilt as a first-sleeper for use in the SHAEF train in Europe and, after being 'demobbed' in 1947, was refurnished by Hamptons and altered as a six-berth first-class vehicle. It was condemned in 1962.

61ft 4½in Third-class Sleeping-Cars Nos 9094–9096: 1929. Nos 9069–74: 1930
(Diagram J.11)

Only two months after the appearance of day/sleeper coaches Nos 5140–2, these bow-ended coaches, 61ft 4½in by 9ft 7in and to Red Triangle restriction, were put into service on the 9.50 p.m. Paddington–Bristol–Penzance and 8.35 p.m. return.

Externally, they set the style for the other 1930–3 sleeping cars with contemporary 'bulging-sides', large corridor-side windows in the style of the standard corridor coaches, and recessed doorways. Accommodation was provided in four-berth compartments with hinged top berths, and no attendant. Nos 9069–74 therefore provided the same type of facilities as the 1929 cars. Nos 9070–2 were rebuilt with attendants' compartments in 1955. British Railways, to improve third-class sleeping-car travel, built cars with two berths only with full bedding and, at the same time, withdrew all pre-nationalisation cars with four berths and limited facilities. These cars were then withdrawn in 1960–61, the body of No 9069 becoming a houseboat on the Thames near Goring, and was still extant in 1983.

61ft 4½in First-class Sleeping Cars Nos 9080/1/6–8: 1930, Nos 9065–8: 1931
(Diagram J.12)
These were the first post-Grouping first-class cars and were outwardly of the same appearance and dimensions as the third-class vehicles. It should be mentioned that the corridor-side windows were not flush with the body panelling, unlike the contemporary corridor stock. The first-class cars were mounted on six-wheel bogies but the third-class vehicles described above were on heavy-type 9ft bogies. The first-class cars had proper sound insulation in the usual form of double floors.

The interiors of the coaches were dull and it was not surprising that, with the post-war renovation schemes for coaches, No 9065/6 were completely redecorated in plastic panelling as prototypes. The walls and corridor were panelled in cream plastic with walnut doors and mouldings. Each compartment was differently furnished – one even with figured gold fabric for wall coverings! Ashtrays, tables and light fixtures were all finished in plastics, and the whole coach had brown carpeting. Forming part of a 'post-war intentions' train, one of these conversions was exhibited at Paddington in November 1946. No 9087 was modernised with plastic finishes in 1949.

No 9086, damaged during the war, was rebuilt in 1945 with a body to the original dimensions and with sliding window ventilators.

All these J.12 diagram cars were withdrawn in 1960–61.

61ft 4½in Composite Sleeping-Car No 9075: 1931
(Diagram J.13)
Similar in general design to the first-class cars described above, No 9075 was the only composite sleeping-car to be built new by the GWR, although joined in 1935 by the rebuilt No 9079 (see above). It was condemned in 1961.

57ft Third-class Sleeping-Cars Nos 9076–8: 1934
Flat-ended, and with a width of 9ft, these coaches were built for working on the Manchester–Plymouth service, previously without sleeping-cars and, like the 1929 vehicles, they had no attendant's compartment as built, although they were modified to include one in 1952. All three coaches were withdrawn late in 1962.

No further sleeping-cars were built during this

One of the couchette-type compartments in sleeper/day corridor third No 5140. (Lot 1395 – Diagram J.10)

A first-class berth of sleeper composite No 9079, as refurnished by Hampton's.

period, although cancelled 1938 orders included two new cars – a third and a composite. The 1951 Hawksworth vehicles (Nos 9082–5) were the only post-war sleeping-cars built (see page 112) and were first-class only.

Restaurant and Buffet Cars: 1931–1934

61ft 4½in Composite Restaurant Cars Nos 9601–9610: 1931

These restaurant cars had an end kitchen but were not otherwise unusual. Following the same 'bulging' side outline and appearance of the contemporary bow-ended corridor stock, they were of 9ft width and built for service on cross-country trains. Their internal furnishings were unremarkable.

Remaining as built until the post-war renovation schemes, the cars were then fitted with shallow-framed sliding ventilators and the interiors were renovated. In BR days, they continued in general service. After 1957, with the delivery of new BR standard cars, the batch was seconded to relief train work and Newbury race specials all, generally, based on London. Withdrawal started from the end of 1961, following the delivery of further BR restaurant-buffet cars. Although without any special distinctions, this batch was a very useful type and gave good service.

Nos 9603/5/6 were appropriated for use as work study offices after withdrawal, and No 9605 was subsequently acquired by the National Railway Museum for preservation, but its general condition is poor.

61ft 4½in First and Third Restaurant Cars Nos 9611–9630: 1932

With the same outline as the above composite cars but of 9ft 3in width, pairs of diners, comprising a kitchen/first dining saloon and a third-class saloon, were built for general service. No unusual features marked these vehicles and internal furnishings were standard.

Before 1939, the first and third-class cars were run together, normally with the same digits paired. New windows with shallow sliding ventilators had been fitted to all except Nos 9614/9/24/9. On the outbreak of war, all the pairs were taken out of traffic, the firsts then going for storage at Great Somerford, later to be joined by the thirds when restaurant car facilities were suspended. Subsequently, the thirds were back into general traffic. By May 1949, all 20 coaches had been returned to service and were gradually modernised in the revised Hampton style with green leather settee-type seats and frameless seat-back screens in fluted glass. No 9614 retained its original hinged window ventilators until 1952.

From September 1953, Nos 9611–13 were converted to buffet cars, with two bays of double seats for eight passengers on one side of the saloon and a buffet counter opposite. The windows on that side were blanked off. Usually they worked with a third (second)-class dining saloon.

These fine vehicles continued to operate as restaurant car pairs in the early/mid-1950s, being progressively converted from oil-gas to propane gas cooking equipment. From the summer of 1956, they began to be outshopped in WR chocolate and cream livery for use on the principal express trains. So they remained until 1961/62 when WR restaurant services were reorganised and the survivors of the two batches were withdrawn, all going by 1963. First-class car No 9615, with two second-class diners, passed to departmental use in South Wales, and by the early 1970s Nos 9615/27 had been recovered by the Severn Valley Railway. After expensive re-equipment of No 9615, travellers can once again enjoy the pleasure of dining in the two-car set formed in the 'Severn Valley Limited'.

57ft 'Quick-Lunch-Bar Cars' Nos 9631–9632: 1934

Among the most interesting of GWR restaurant cars to be built, and with one of the most remarkable interior layouts, were these two decisively-named vehicles. They were among the first coaches to carry the GWR 'shirt-button' monogram introduced during 1934.

Externally, they were probably the ugliest of all GWR catering cars with a 57ft flat-ended body and high-placed windows for the benefit of passengers seated at the high stools. Internally, apart from a pantry at one end, the space was taken up by a long buffet counter placed down the middle of the coach. Twelve high stools along this counter provided the sole seating accommodation. Showcases were placed on the counter, all metalwork of which was chromium-plated. The windows behind the counter were of frosted-glass with clear-glass ventilators. The floor was covered with square rubber tiles, and steam-heating pipes were co-

61ft 4½in body restaurant car pair: first class/kitchen car No 9611 (left) and third-class car No 9621. As built. (Lots 1468/69 – Diagrams H.39/H.40)

vered by a grille running down the corridor side of the car. Internal decoration was in green and fawn with the usual sycamore wood panels. As built, both cars had Thermotank pressure ventilation with fixed windows, converted to sliding vents in 1938/39.

One vehicle was first put into service on the 9.45 a.m. Paddington–Stourbridge and an afternoon return Worcester train, the second one working up from Bristol on the 9 a.m. Paddington train, returning again in the afternoon. One was later used for some time on the 'Bristolian' and the other, as recounted by George Behrend in *Gone With Regret*, was used on the 6 p.m. Paddington–Weymouth where, apparently, there were not so many quick lunches served as 'more Scotch whisky than I have ever seen drunk on any other British train; for connoisseurs of the drink knew all about GWR special whisky!'

In post-war days, most of their work was on excursion and relief trains, and they were based on London. No alterations of any interest were made to these vehicles. No 9631 was withdrawn for preservation at the end of 1961 and arrived at Nine Elms Goods Yard on 12 April 1962 for the final stage of its journey to the Museum of British Transport at Triangle Place, Clapham. The

View from behind the full-length counter of 'Quick-Lunch-Bar' car No 9631, as built with fixed windows. (Lot 1518 – Diagram H.41)

vehicle was restored as near as possible to the condition in which it entered service on 9 July 1934. No 9632 survived until late 1963; probably one of its last journeys was made on 20 April 1963 when it was marshalled in the annual special train from Paddington to Minffordd for the Festiniog Railway Society, hauled by the restored *Flying Scotsman*. No 9631 subsequently moved on loan from the National Collection to the Severn Valley Railway, and after refurbishing has been used with Nos 9615/27 on the 'Severn Valley Limited'.

Corridor and Non-Corridor Stock: 1933–1936

The vehicles completed during these years were probably the most undistinguished of GWR coaches. Standard practice was followed through-

57ft corridor brake composite No 6583, compartment side. This Lot had droplights to each of the luggage compartment doors. Built 1933. (Lot 1491 – Diagram E.146)

57ft corridor brake third No 5878. (Lot 1514 – Diagram D.118)

out, nothing of interest was applied to the designs and the corridor stock could only claim one distinction, that of being the last traditional side-corridor type with outside access to every compartment. They were also the last 57ft-body corridor coaches for the GWR and were of 9ft width, their dimensions allowing them unrestricted running on lines of the other 'Big Four' companies. Other design details were that only four corridor-side doors were provided, the bow end was discarded and only reintroduced, in a modified form, in the Hawksworth corridor design. The body sides were straight with standard curved bottom panels. Inwardly, there were few differences, none any improvement on previous styles. The design featured a higher waistline than previously and so the windows on both non-corridor and corridor-coaches were high-placed, limiting the passengers' view.

Only five diagrams covered the corridor stock types, with D.116 (brake third) and E.146 (brake composite) being identified by the provision of two droplights each side to the luggage compartment doors, D.116 and E.148 having one droplight each side only in this position.

The history of the corridor stock was relatively uneventful, although a number of brake thirds were used for overseas ambulance trains. Brake composite No 6582 ran with an ex-GWR railcar pair in the Bristol area during the 1950s. In March 1957, seconds Nos 5848/56 and 5929 were withdrawn from service to undergo conversion to form the WR's first emergency control train. This was intended to provide a complete railway control office which could be dispersed to a rural area during wartime conditions. The set was made up of two generator cars (Siphon Gs) to supply 220–240V ac current to telecommunications equipment installed in the former second-class corridor coaches which were gutted, rewired and equipped with telephones, switchboards and support gear. Some doors were sealed up and double doors provided at the extreme ends of the bodies. An ex-articulated diner was included as a mess room (see page 79). The conversions seem to have been completed by the summer of 1957 and thereafter the train's existence was a well-kept secret, all vehicles being painted in standard crimson and cream livery (until 1963) but numbered in the DW 150027–32 series. A second train was formed in 1962, this time with one generator van (Siphon G), two corridor seconds, Nos 5813/63, and former restaurant car No 9654. All were numbered in the DW 150xxx series. By the late 1970s, the two trains were stored at Craven Arms and were offered for sale in December 1979. The five 1934/35 corridor seconds have all been acquired for preservation.

Corridor second No 5918 was the subject of an unusual experiment, c1964, presumably undertaken at Swindon, when it was fitted with unusual plate-framed bogies. It is not thought to have run in ordinary traffic and was derelict at Bristol East depot by 1965.

Only three types of non-corridor coach were produced: third, brake third and brake composite to three diagrams – C.66, D.117 and E.147. The last two were 57ft over the body ends, the thirds, 55ft 3½in. All were of 9ft width. Further batches of the non-corridor 'B' sets were built, to the large numbers completed from 1924–33. The 'B' sets saw service mostly in the South Wales and Bristol areas, although dieselisation caused some to be transferred to Taunton and West Wales to make up deficiencies of earlier withdrawn sets.

Experiments with welding-up body ends were

Diagram of non-corridor brake composite (as formed in B sets). (Diagram E.147 – Lots 1494/1505/23/50)

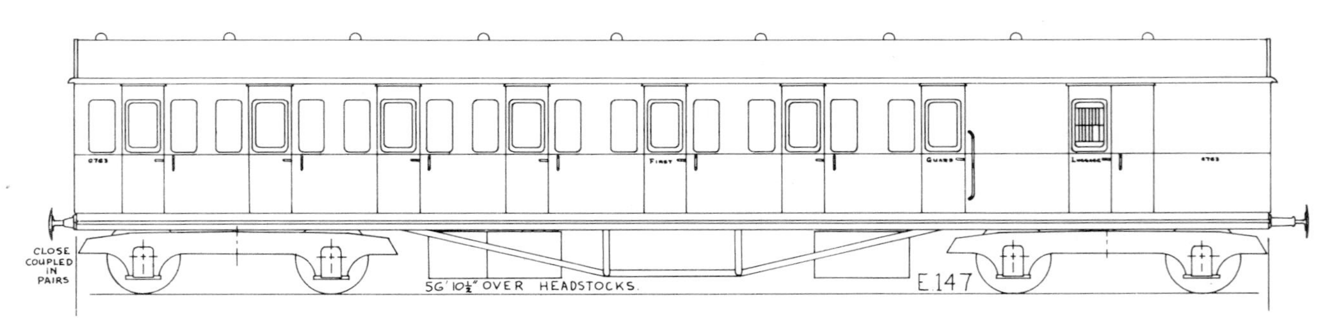

One of the 57ft B sets forms an Andover Junction–Swindon train in the 1930s, near Red Post Junction, behind 45xx 2-6-2T No 4566.

carried out with a batch of brake thirds but, unfortunately, no details are known.

Brake thirds Nos 4350/64 (Lot 1525) were converted in 1935 as auto-trailers with one large end window and the usual control equipment. Brake composites Nos 6818/20 (Lot 1550) were built new as auto-trailers.

From 1953, the reorganisation of Cardiff Valleys services saw a number of workings diagrammed for auto-train operation. By September 1954, 19 thirds and brake thirds of the 1933–35 and 1936–40 non-corridor stock varieties had been equipped for auto-working, the thirds being classed as intermediate trailers with through auto equipment, and the brakes being rebuilt with a driving cab, control gear, and large end window. Details are shown in Chapter 10. From 1955, further conversions of brake thirds took place (from Lots 1493, 1507/25/52). As converted, they were designated Diagram A.44 and renumbered in the auto-trailer series from 245 onwards, and are listed in Chapter 10.

Withdrawal of non-corridor stock began in 1958 but the corridor coaches were almost all intact until the winter of 1962. During that year, both varieties suffered heavy withdrawals, some corridor coaches going to service stock. As mentioned elsewhere, all non-corridor stock was generally extinguished in 1963, but, even well into 1964, a few corridor coaches remained. Several have been preserved.

Auto-Trailers: 1929–1933

The steam rail-motors' power-units had reached the end of their economic lives between 1920 and the late 1930s and, additionally, their disadvantages in operation and maintenance hastened the condemnation of the power-units and the conversion of the coach-bodies as auto-trailers for push-and-pull work with 0-4-2Ts and 0-6-0PTs (see page 58). The number of auto-train saloons of new construction during this period is, therefore, small and, pre-war, only three batches were built. The rail-motor conversions are given in the sections dealing with the original vehicles.

59ft 6in Nos 159–170: 1929 (Diagram A.27)

These bow-ended saloons had inset windows with inward opening hammered-glass ventilators. To cater for over-crowding, there were eight tip-up seats available. The interior, comprising two saloons, was unremarkable, with heavy mahogany seats of the normal type, mahogany window frames and panelling above the seats. The remaining exposed woodwork was tongue and grooved boards finished in ochre stippling.

Built for general branch line service, the coaches were still in service until 1959–60, at which time about five were based on Plymouth.

62ft 8in Nos 171–180: 1930 (Diagram A.28)

Of increased length and with three saloons, these coaches were similar to Nos 159-170 in general appearance and interior detail, and were built for general branch line service.

They remained in service until 1958–60, the

59ft 6in body auto-trailer W161W, condemned and at Laira Junction, July 1960. (Lot 1394 – Diagram A.27)

majority being in the South Wales area on lines that lost their services at that time.

62ft 8in Nos 187–196: 1933 (Diagram A.30)
Of the same general appearance as the preceding batch – Nos 171-180 – Nos 187-196 had one distinction of being the first flush-body panelled auto-saloons, but with the same hammered-glass ventilators above the windows. There were no other details of interest. Built for branch line service, the batch remained in general use until 1961; from 1959 onwards a number had gone to Plymouth to replace earlier withdrawn cars.

62ft 8in body auto-trailer No 187, as built. (Lot 1480 – Diagram A.30)

7
PRE-WAR MODERNITY: 1935–40

Excursion Stock: 1935–1940
These sets were important as the first modern GWR coaches and also as the first GWR excursion open stock at a time when all the other 'Big Four' companies had already built many of this type. The GWR emphasised that they were for excursion and party-hire traffic only and capable of having meal service to every seat. Until well into BR days, the idea that the centre-corridor coach was a non-common user vehicle persisted on the former GWR. The Silver Jubilee celebrations no doubt indicated that the sets would not be short of work but, appropriately, their début was made on specials from the Midlands to Wembley for the FA Cup Final on 27 April 1935.

Externally, they set a new line for the GWR, with spacious windows of the 'Beclawat' drop-type – also fitted to the 'Centenary' stock which appeared a little later. A surprising feature of the first two sets was the amount of space, half of each the brake coaches, devoted to luggage accommodation. Presumably this was intended to cater for holiday baggage on summer reliefs or, more likely, liquid refreshments on party outings. As regards the catering vehicles, for the first set, known as Vestibuled Train No 1, these were a pair of specially-built kitchen cars, Nos 9633/4, but the second set, VT No 2, coaches Nos 4569/70/3/4, was given two triplets of two ex-diners and a kitchen car each, from the 1925 articulated sets which were being disbanded. The ex-diners served as temporary open thirds until the 1936 batch of new open thirds was available. In actual fact, the sets frequently ran as eight-coach sets, or less, without restaurant cars. During the early days of service there were disputes with catering staff over the difficulty of maintaining an adequate service of meals throughout the trains.

Internally, a suitable and contemporary décor was adopted. Eight bays in open thirds were divided by partitions, without sliding doors, the GWR monogram dominating the glass in the partitions. All surfaces above seat level were panelled in light birchwood with mahogany trim and inlays. All other woodwork was polished mahogany. The upholstery was a new standard pattern probably used for the first time in this stock. Light fittings were concealed in white opaque glass cubes, certainly an attractive refinement in this era, but no corridor stock had similar lights, unfortunately. *The GWR Magazine*, in an article on the new sets, drew attention to the fact that 'there is a complete absence of curves in the design of the fittings, the decorative effects being obtained by angular and rectangular designs'. The whole effect was cheerful and bright – in tones of orange and brown – and was as successful an attempt as any at designing an excursion train interior without the spartan effect of similar LNER Tourist sets.

In 1936 an isolated batch of open coaches (Lot 1558) was put in service as spares and to make up the formation of the second set, so permitting the articulated triplets to be withdrawn for rebuilding. The new batch differed from the earlier sets in having fixed windows with deep sliding ventilators. The originals were similarly rebuilt from 1938–44, although as a minor difference their lower window corners were rounded.

The next two sets, which appeared in 1937, conformed to the outline of contemporary side-corridor stock and, for these, spare open thirds were built. At the same time, six kitchen cars, Nos 9663–9668, with the standard outline were built for excursion use (see page 101). Two trains were formed, VT No 3: 1298/9, 1274/5/8/9, with 9663/4, and VT No 4: 1300/1, 1280–2/4/6, with 9665/6.

After the GWR decision to build coaches to a loading gauge to suit cross-country running, the 1938 set was built to Yellow Disc dimensions, but otherwise unchanged, VT No 5: 1541/2, 1530–5, 9669/70. These three 1937/8 sets had a half-bay at each end. The 1939–40 vehicles (Lots 1625/43/4)

An early view of the 1935 Excursion stock set, with open third No 4565 nearest. (Lot 1530 – Diagram C.68)

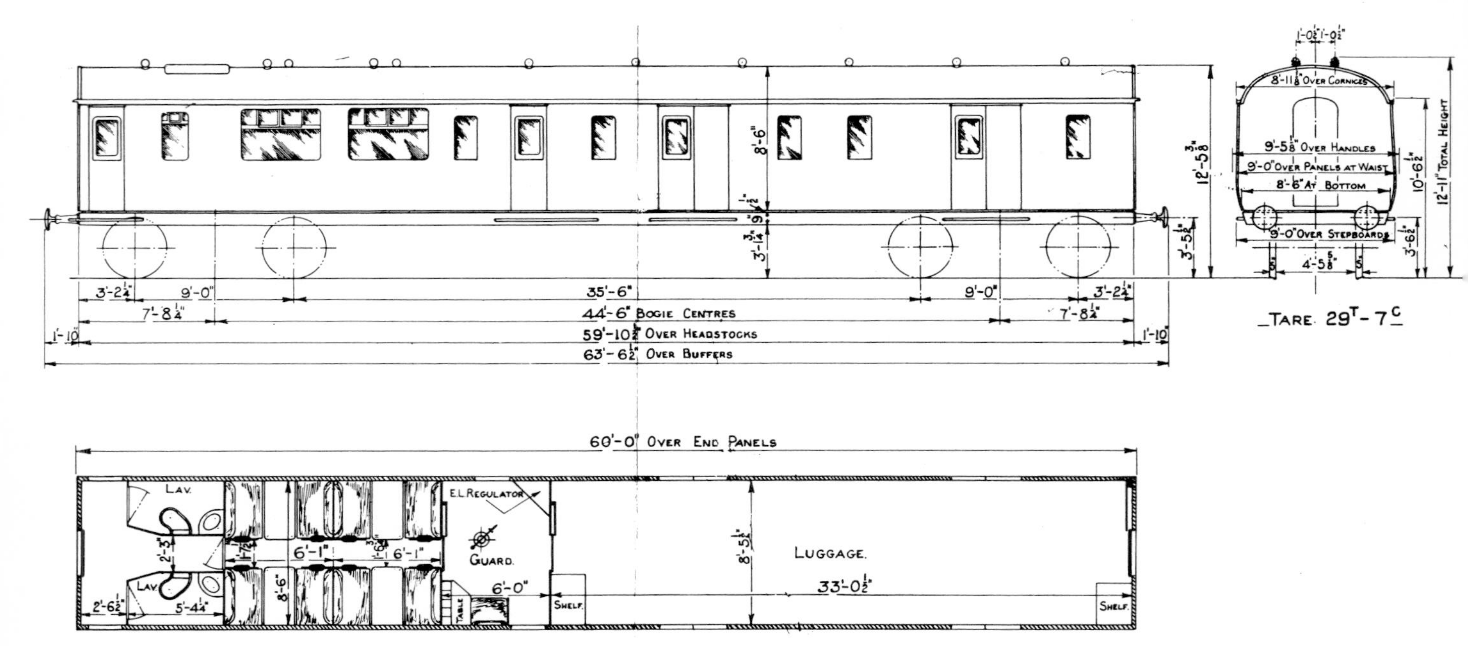

Drawing of Excursion Stock brake third, from Swindon Diagram D.119 – Lot 1531.

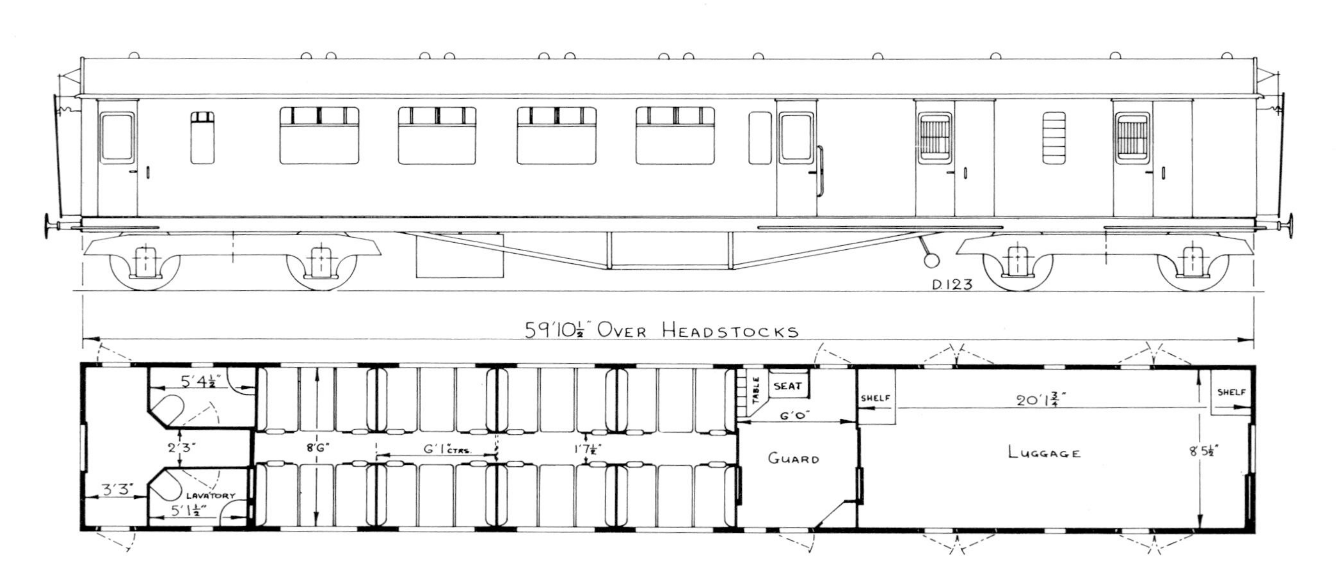

Drawing of Excursion Stock brake third, from Swindon Diagram D.123 – Lot 1576.

are not believed to have run in formations, and one coach at least was almost immediately marshalled in a casualty evacuation train. During the war several of the open thirds from Lot 1530 were converted for conveying sitting-case casualties in overseas ambulance trains and were used as far afield as Austria.

The subsequent life of the 1935–40 excursion stock was uneventful, the coaches remaining in original condition generally, although in some cases the birchwood panelling was repainted cream and some of the tables received laminated plastic surfaces.

The vehicles from Lots 1591/92 (except No 1536) made up the 11-coach Newport No 2 excursion set in the 1950s. In April 1957 Nos 1532/41 were burnt out at Abergavenny Junction, victims of a case of arson, and other coaches were badly scorched, but by September 1959 the two complete casualties were back in traffic with new bodies to the original design.

Early 1964 also saw at least one set, the earlier 1937 one, outshopped with BR standard horizontally-striped upholstery and blue curtains. Nos 628/37/46/9 of the 1940 set were fitted up with a public address system as part of the Western Region's radio train. In later years the sets included in their formation the motley cafeteria cars allocated to the Western Region. The formerly articulated kitchen cars, rebuilt as cafeteria cars at Swindon in BR days, were used

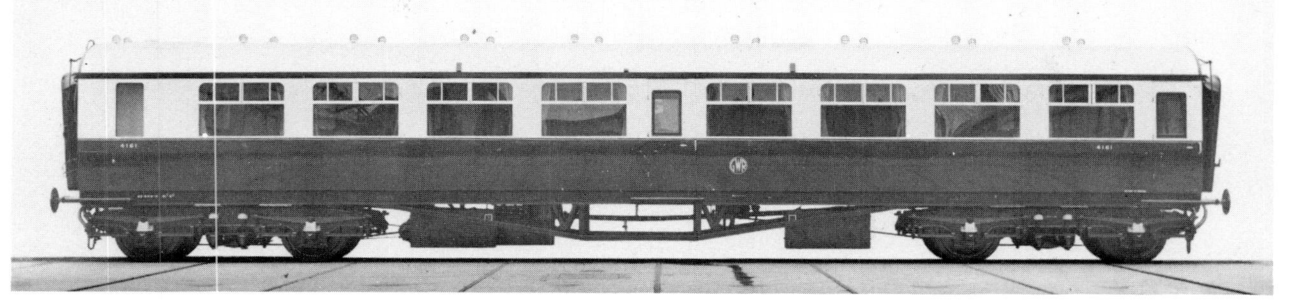

Open third No 4161, built 1936. (Lot 1558 – Diagram C.71)

with the South Wales-based open sets. In BR days the open coaches were frequently seen in normal service; one, for instance, was paired for some time in the early 1960s with a BR restaurant buffet on the Paddington–Worcester trains, and was used as restaurant accommodation. Most of the first 1935 set were withdrawn in late 1962. The remainder were in use until 1963–64 but were all extinct by late 1966.

'Centenary' Stock: 1935

The GWR celebrated the centenary of its foundation with great zest and, not surprisingly, the crack 'Cornish Riviera Express' received appropriate attention. It was re-styled the 'Cornish Riviera Limited' and from 8 July, the beginning of the summer 1935 timetable, carried booked-seat passengers only, making its first passenger stop at Plymouth, normally, and at St Erth on summer Saturdays. More important, a completely new set of rolling-stock had inaugurated the service.

Ten-coach sets were normally employed on the 'Limited' although spares allowed thirteen-coach maximum formations. At the outset, only one new set was available, but the second set arrived at the end of July and then worked alternately.

The standard formation was: brake third, third, third, third diner, first diner/kitchen, composite, brake third, third, brake composite, brake composite. The brake thirds Nos 4577/80 were left-hand, and Nos 4575/6/8/9, right-hand.

Anticipating the streamliners of the LMS and LNER, the GWR unforgivably added weird projections to 'King' 4-6-0 No 6014, which was photographed hauling the new set for publicity material.

Body design closely followed the impressive outlines of the 'Super Saloons' and 1929 'Riviera' restaurant cars, and was to Red Triangle restrictions with recessed doors. The frames were exaggeratedly described by *The GWR Magazine* as 'massive', but they were no more so than other restaurant cars and saloons, although the general bulk of their outline did make them look out of place in later years when running in normal rakes. The brake thirds were the last on the GWR to be built with handed bodies for a set train.

The only significant change subsequently made to the coaches concerned the windows. The amount of underturn caused by the bulging sides presented problems with opening windows and the drop-type 'Beclawat' fitting, standard for early

An interior view of a coach in one of the later Excursion Stock sets. Note the half-bay extreme right.

Centenary third No 4582, in original condition. Note the Red Triangle on the body end. (Lot 1537 – Diagram C.69)

Maunsell SR open stock, was at first installed. However, in 1936, visors were fitted to the compartment windows, and alternate fixed windows with sliding ventilators were put in the corridor side. During 1938 the compartment side windows were altered and the drop-type lights replaced by a fixed window and sliding ventilators. The alterations to the windows were funded under the Government Guaranteed Loan scheme to the main line railways.

When built, they were the first GWR coaches to have large compartment windows and, as a result, access was from the corridor only; the 'Centenary' sets preceded the standardisation of this feature from 1936. Other improvements later to become standard were the recessing of the housings for the blinds in the corridor partitions and the concealment of the greater portion of the communication chain. The luggage-racks were of a simpler design than previously, with less clumsy supports but, unfortunately, this was not standardised.

Interior panelling was in light, quartered oak with walnut inlay trim in the first-class compartments, and gaboon mahogany in the thirds. The traditional photographs were sensibly discarded in favour of inset oval mirrors, though again this was not made general practice. Rayon curtains in either gold and green, or brown and blue colour schemes were fitted to the wide windows in not only the firsts but also the third-class for probably the first time. The third-class curtains were of brown and gold colouring. A new upholstery design was introduced, which was standardised, and a more satisfactorily padded 'fluted' seat-back also made its first appearance. Other details of interest were the use of GWR monogram-patterned pile carpeting in both corridor and compartments in the first-class, and horsehair rugs in the thirds. With these refinements, a more modern approach towards interior furnishings had been made and was expressed in the 1936 standard coaches. Overall, the 'Centenary' stock was greatly superior to other 'Big Four' corridor coaches, and noticeably less fussy than the LNER's 'Silver Jubilee' set.

The four restaurant cars, Nos 9635–8, for the sets were to the standard GWR specifications, with the same general furnishings as the coaches but introducing table lamps. Tip-up seats were fitted in the thirds. Also notable was the use of stainless-steel sheeting to line the kitchens.

At the outbreak of war, the set formations were officially abandoned, but the sets continued to work on the 'Cornish Riviera Express' until 1941 when the possibility of diversion over emergency

The interior of Centenary first-class restaurant/kitchen car No 9635, as built.

Corridor third No 4312 of 'Sunshine' stock. (Lot 1554 – Diagram C.70)

routes, probably unable to take these 9ft 7in vehicles, saw their removal. A 1940 photograph shows the combined 'Cornish Riviera' and 'Torbay Express' with a front section of 'Centenary' coaches. Branded as Red Triangle restriction vehicles, they were shown as barred north of Saltney Junction from 1945; previously they were not to work north of Wolverhampton, Oxley Sidings.

On the outbreak of war the restaurant cars were withdrawn and returned to traffic after renovation in 1947. These received the Mark 2 Hampton interior scheme with buff leather upholstery for the first-class seats and brown in the third-class. The glass screen at the seat-backs had a ground-glass design featuring waterfowl. Shallower sliding ventilators than normal were fitted to these cars.

Post-war days did not see the 'Centenary' stock restored to the 'Cornish Riviera', which was then composed of a wide variety of stock, including new Hawksworth coaches, until replaced by 'plum-and-spilt milk' livery rakes of 1938 stock. In the early 1950s, one set of 'Centenary' coaches was used between Weston-super-Mare and Paddington while the diner pairs were working between Paddington and Shrewsbury. From then onwards, the 'Centenary' coaches were used on all types of working and, like the pre-war élite stock of the LMS and LNER, ended their lives in reliefs and slow trains.

The restaurant cars were among the last of GWR design in regular service. In late 1961 they were still at work on Weston-super-Mare, Wolverhampton and Plymouth trains, being based on Old Oak and used at weekends on Newbury Racecourse specials. Contention over the *last* of a particular instance can be expected but, with little doubt, No 9636 was the final GWR restaurant car on a regular daily working out of Paddington on the 6.45 p.m. to Weston-super-Mare until the autumn of 1962. By the late autumn of that year all four cars were condemned and stood near Cholsey for some time. Fortunately, efforts were made to preserve one of the restaurant cars in 1963 and No 9635 was acquired.

Of the other coaches, all were in service until 1962 and were then gradually withdrawn, becoming extinct in 1964.

Standard Corridor Coaches: 1936–1940

1936 Corridor Design

This design marked an important step forward in GWR corridor coach practice for standard stock, introducing large windows extending almost to the cantrail on the corridor side, end entrance vestibules and large compartment-side windows. The adoption of this layout afforded greater possibilities for internal design. These corridor coaches, built 1936/37, were frequently referred to as 'Sunshine' stock on account of their increased window space, also as 'New-Type' stock. The first vehicle into traffic was third No 4304, officially completed on 31 December 1935. Lot 1553 was completed during March 1936.

The vehicles built during the 1936–40 period are curiously varied and, in many ways, non-standard, particularly in regard to length. Generally, it is more convenient to refer to lot numbers in clarifying these differences.

Lots 1553–5/9/60 comprised one type with large windows and a low waistline on the corridor side. The large windows were opposite the compartments, which improved the passengers' view. The

Corridor brake third No 1593, built 1937. This type had an end vestibule, and droplights (but not doors) between the corridor-side windows. (Lot 1574 – Diagram D.124)

other type, Lots 1557, 1571–4/81/2, had a high waistline, with the corridor side windows without sliding ventilators, interspersed with droplights (not doors) and extending almost to the cantrail height. No 6859 (Lot 1557) received five doors on the corridor side on rebuilding in 1942. The low-waist design, with the door droplights finishing a foot or so above the waistline, featured a non-standard paint scheme with the 'First' and 'Third' designations and running number transfers uniquely placed on cream paintwork. This stock, to 9ft width, was restricted from general running over other 'Big Four' companies' lines. Apart from the more generous window-space, both outside and in corridor partitions, deep metal-framed ventilators were fitted, with hinged vanes to deflect direct draughts and prevent cinders from entering the compartment. The improved finish of the interior fittings was dealt with in Chapter 3. These coaches were allocated to the 'Bristolian' and the 'Cheltenham Flyer' during late 1936 but not in set formations.

Lot 1556 covered two buffet cars, Nos 9643/44, in which half the body comprised a buffet with counter, high stools, and pantry, and the other half, three third-class compartments and a lavatory. After the Second World War, the pair were used on the Weymouth line but were not popular with the operators and were soon relegated to relief work. In 1955, Nos 9643/44 were rebuilt, the compartments being converted to a three-bay unclassed saloon and curiously designated buffet-restaurant cars although without kitchen facilities. In this form they were employed on the Penzance–Swansea service, continuing in use between Swansea and Plymouth until 1962, and withdrawn the next year. The other coaches were in general service until 1962 and were extinct by the end of 1964. No 4319 was damaged by enemy action and rebuilt with a new body in 1949. No 4329 was allocated to the SHAEF 'alive' train.

A well-known model of brake composite No 6484, in post-war livery with 'Cornish Riviera' roof-boards and coupled to a fine model of 'King' No 6000, was on display at Paddington station until removed for exhibition in the National Railway Museum.

1938 Corridor Design

More noticeable changes were made in this design, which standardised the layout for all the remaining pre-war corridor coaches which was used with only slight differences, for the Hawksworth post-war vehicles. Also important was the fact that the design was within the more restricted loading-gauges of the LNER and LMS as the result of a policy decision of late 1937, the vehicles being identified by a yellow disc on the body-ends. Gangway adaptors for coupling to buckeye stock were also fitted as standard in the later batches. An improvement on the 1936 design was better illumination of the vestibules, and whereas entry in the earlier design had been by the end vestibules only, the arrangement of four doors on the corridor side was now reintroduced. In later batches of composites, brake composites and brake thirds, one compartment had entry from the compartment side with flanking quarterlights. Internally, the panelling above the seats was improved in appearance and less clumsy rack supports were fitted.

One interesting point was the obvious attempt to clear up the number series: Lot 1589 of 1937, for instance, in thirty vehicles covered the number range from 6355 to 6829! Later Lots were deferred in view of wartime restrictions, although it is worth noting that orders for some were placed up to 1940. One of the deferred lots comprised three slip coaches, no doubt to be similar to the 1938-built Nos 7069–7074 of standard double-ended type. Of these, No 7071 was used during the last months of the Bicester 'slip' off the 5.10 pm from Paddington, while the remainder, after their original use had ended, were allocated to Taunton and used on various workings on local branches. Three of the 7069–74 batch had been repainted in chocolate and cream livery in 1956. Interest surrounds the number of corridor and non-corridor coaches of this design ordered in 1938–40 but whose construction was deferred

Corridor first No W8093W, built 1938. Note the roof rain-strip. At Birmingham Snow Hill, September 1956. (Lot 1586 – Diagram A.22)

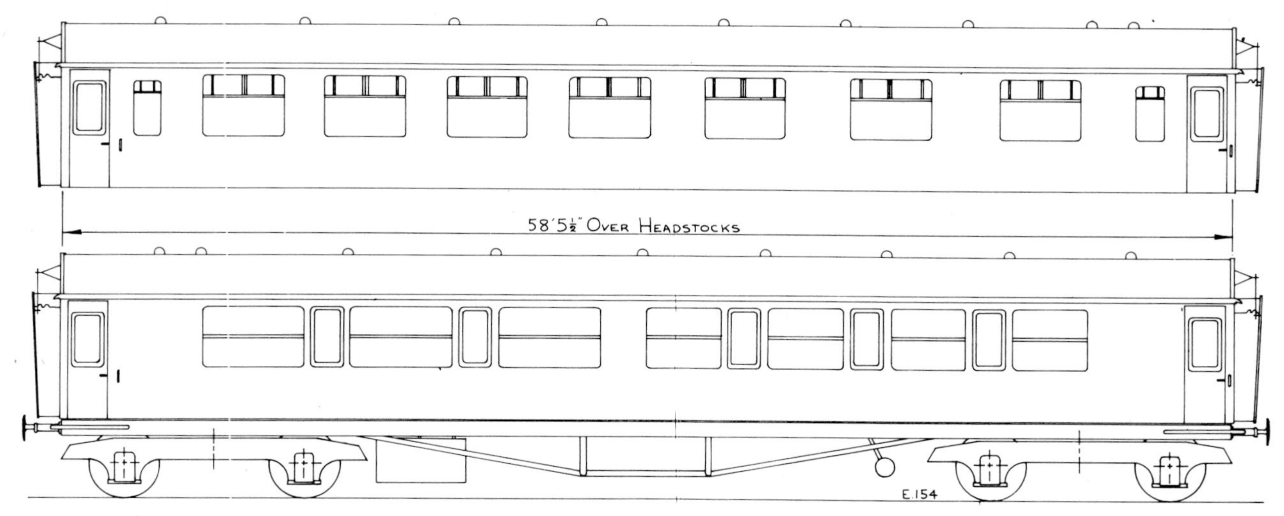

Drawing of 58ft 7in body corridor composite, from Swindon Diagram E.154 – Lot 1571.

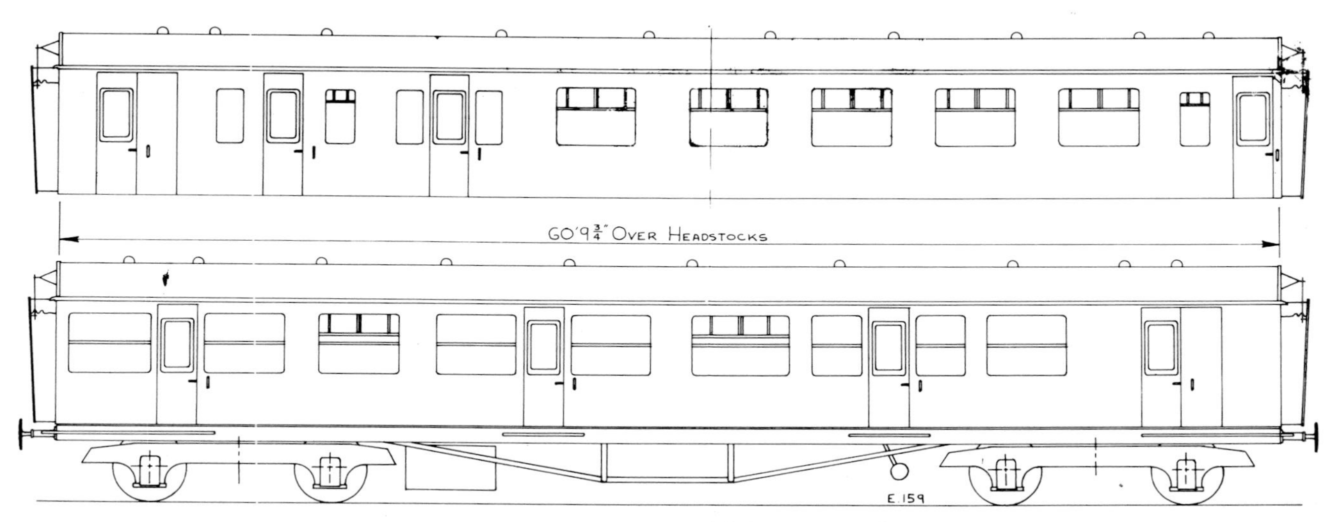

Drawing of Yellow Disc corridor brake composite, from Swindon Diagram E.159 – Lots 1589/90/1622/40.

with the onset of the Second World War. Details are given in the Lot List, but the most noteworthy cancellations included two sleeping cars and the three slip coaches already mentioned.

Subsequent changes to these vehicles were few. Composite No 7022 was equipped in the late 1940s with fluorescent tubes throughout as part of the post-war coach modernisation plan, while another composite coach, No 6302, was completely redecorated by an outside contractor as a prototype for similar conversions. No general application of this modernisation was ever carried out. Third No 1096 had a long association from 1942–61 with the GWR diesel railcar pairs, Nos W37/W38, then later W33/W38, and in 1960 all three vehicles were outshopped in BR green diesel unit livery. Only a year later the diesel cars were withdrawn and No 1096 reverted to standard maroon livery.

It was a pity that the Western Region did not manage to modernise these coaches in the 1950s. In many ways they were still modern although their internal décor did not come up to contemporary standards. Apart from war damage, none was withdrawn until August 1962, when No 525 was demolished in the Torquay accident. Late in 1963 more general withdrawals took place and the majority were condemned in 1964, only a few vehicles surviving by mid-1966.

A number of these corridor vehicles survived to be preserved by the Great Western Society, Severn Valley Railway and others. Some were used in the GWS Vintage Train, and the SVR examples have been in regular operation from the early 1970s, probably achieving the most mileage run by any pre-nationalisation preserved stock. They have proved most successful and easy to maintain.

1937–40 Non-corridor design

The standard compartment stock of this period followed the lower waistline of the contemporary corridor vehicle designs, and was of 8ft 11in width. There were two principal types, thirds (Diagram C75) of 55ft 3½in length and brake thirds (Diagram D125), 57ft over the body panels. As noted in Chapter 10, thirds from three Lots built to C75 were converted as intermediate auto-trailers from 1953. By 1963, all of the two diagrams C75 and D125 had been withdrawn except for a handful working to the Royal Navy

Non-corridor first No 8034. (Lot 1566 – Diagram A.21)

depot, Trecwn, near Fishguard.

The other types of this stock included composites to Diagram E.156, 59ft 3½in long over the panels, and brake composites, Diagram E.157 and 161, 57ft long. Lot 1566 comprised ten first-class vehicles, Nos 8033–42, Diagram A.21, distinguished by rain-strips on the roof, as were some of the thirds and composites. Most ran at some time post-1956 as seconds, and No 8040 was the first to be withdrawn, in 1957.

Six coaches, two each of brake composite, third and third brake, were built in 1939 for the Highworth branch near Swindon. This had a restricted loading-gauge and, to conform, these vehicles had their ventilators positioned well down on the roof. Churchward light-type 9ft bogies were recovered from earlier vehicles, no doubt to save cost. The pair of brake composites formed the normal service, while the four brake thirds and thirds comprised the Swindon to Highworth staff train. When a replacement was sought for the ex-Barry Railway gas-lit brake thirds used latterly on the Hemyock branch, No 1239 was tested on this line but was deemed unsuitable and postwar LNER-design vehicles appropriated instead, duly converted to propane gas lighting because speeds were too low to charge batteries.

Most intriguing of all these coaches were the seven Burry Port and Gwendraeth Valley section vehicles completed in the same year. This line had never previously used bogie coaches and its severely restricted loading-gauge necessitated the new stock being eighteen inches lower than standard and three inches narrower in overall width. Although otherwise modern steel-panelled coaches, their reduced height gave them an old-fashioned appearance reminiscent of LBSC vehicles. References in the railway press at various times have implied that they were rebuilds but this is not so. Neither were they cut down from standard coaches already in service. As with the Highworth branch coaches, they were mounted on Churchward 9ft bogies from older stock, a fact which may have influenced the suggestion of rebuilding. After the withdrawal of passenger services on the BPGV in 1953, the coaches were transferred elsewhere in South Wales – to Tredegar, for instance – and three, Nos 1324–26, on hire to the Royal Navy for working to Trecwn. No 1324 was overhauled at Swindon in 1963. This trio saw the limelight when they were used for filming at Bath Green Park in 1965 in company with an ex- LMS '3F' 0-6-0T, thereafter returning to Trecwn.

60ft First and Third Restaurant Cars Nos 9639–9642: 1935

These four 9ft width restaurant cars, formed in the customary two-coach sets, were mentioned in the 1935 building programme, but no reference was made to their duties and there was only a passing reference to the most interesting feature that one set would be fully air-conditioned. Why these rather nondescript coaches were so fitted while the 'Centenary' restaurant cars built in the same year were ignored is rather curious. Good

Non-corridor brake composite No W6265W, in unlined BR maroon livery. This was used on the Looe branch, and accordingly fitted with 7ft wheelbase bogies.

Above:
A Burry Port & Gwendraeth Valley section train at Burry Port, August 1951. The locomotive is 16xx 0-6-0PT No 1618, and the coaches, brake third No 1325, third No 1329 and brake third No 1326, of the special BPGV profile stock. (Lots 1611/12 – Diagrams D.129 and C.80)

Right:
The air-duct between air-conditioned restaurant cars Nos 9640/42 is noticeable above the gangway connections. (Lots 1533/32 – Diagrams H.48/H.47)

publicity could have been made of 'air-conditioned restaurant cars on the 'Cornish Riviera Limited' ', but possibly Swindon was being cautious with this new-fangled idea. In any event, no subsequent pre-war coaches were fitted with full air-conditioning.

Externally, they were not striking, having 60ft flat-ended bodies of the same profile as the contemporary 'Excursion Stock'. The air-conditioned pair with Stone's equipment (Nos 9640/2) had a conspicuous air-duct above the corridor connections between the vehicles, which had large windows without any sliding ventilators. This latter feature distinguishes them as the first fully air-conditioned coaches on a British railway, as the Gresley 'Silver Jubilee' sets which entered service three months before had a pressure ventilation system only, with sliding ventilators above the windows. Additionally, the air-conditioned coaches had conspicuous grilles on the bodysides. Internally, there were no interesting features and furnishings were standard. Nos 9639/41 originally had drop-type windows, being refitted with fixed windows and 'Beclawat' sliding ventilators in 1937.

The two pairs operated from Old Oak in general service, mostly on specials and relief trains, and resumed such duties from 1947. The air-conditioned pair received double-glazed windows with sliding ventilators in 1954 but retained the Stone's equipment. All four were redecorated in the Mk 2 Hampton's style. Before condemnation in the autumn of 1962, the vehicles saw use on relief trains and Newbury Racecourse specials.

60ft/60ft 11in Kitchen Cars Nos 9663–9670: 1937–38

Built primarily for use in the GWR excursion sets – 'Vestibuled Trains' Nos 3/4 – the six 1937 cars Nos 9663–8 of 9ft body width (Diagram H.54) were ordered shortly after the open thirds forming these sets. Two kitchen cars were allocated to each set in order to provide meals at every seat and the details of the excursion trains can be found on page 93. Their profile was the same as the open thirds and they had four-wheeled bogies. The usual catering equipment was installed and was capable of serving full meals on a large scale. Staff facilities included a rest compartment and two lavatories and, to match the adjoining vehicles, the corridor was panelled in walnut veneer, rather than a more suitable paint finish.

For the last excursion set, VT No 5, two twelve-wheel cars were built, Nos 9669/70, (Dia-

The interior of the third-class saloon in restaurant car No 9674, as built. These vehicles were refurnished in Hampton's style in early post-war years. (Lot 1601 – Diagram H.57)

gram H.56) of the same 60ft 11½in body length as the later open thirds and of 8ft 11in width. Otherwise the facilities were the same as the 1937 cars and probably their only notable feature was the high tare weight of 47 tons 18 cwt.

Two spare eight-wheel cars were later used in the 'Plymouth Ocean Liner' expresses when ordinary formations were run. In BR days, Nos 9663/7 were liveried in WR chocolate and cream for this work. In 1954, when the Western Region excursion sets were re-formed and a motley collection of cafeteria cars assembled for working in these trains, the VT kitchen cars found other work. Much of this was on holiday relief trains but, in common with many other restaurant cars previously described, they were used on Newbury Racecourse trains, the patrons of which expected a full lunch on the down journey. Nos 9663/8 continued on varied special train work until December 1962, when all the H.54 cars were condemned. Only a short while before, one had worked in a Rugby International Special from Wales to Murrayfield, Scotland, as a last fling.

The two twelve-wheel cars survived the purge of late 1962 and continued on much the same duties as before, including the Newbury trains. It is probably worth recording that No 9669, in place of the usual BR 19xx series diner/kitchen car, appeared in the up 'Cornish Riviera Express' on 21 March 1964, possibly the last occasion that a GWR restaurant car was used on this train. Nos 9669/70 were in service in late 1964, and withdrawn the next year.

60ft 11in Restaurant Cars Nos 9671–9675: 1938
Reverting to the earlier layout of a central kitchen, these 'Yellow Disc' general service cars were intended for use on cross-country services and lighter formation trains. Internal decoration was in walnut and mahogany with leather-trimmed shoulder-height seats in both saloons.

After the war, No 9672 was selected as one of the prototypes for the intended renovation of all restaurant cars. Although, admittedly, the refurbishing was very thorough and novel, the GWR used this as an opportunity to publicise No 9672 as a new post-war design. The interior scheme was devised by Hampton & Sons and is described on page 32. No 9672 went into service on 8 February 1946, by which time twenty-six restaurant car services had been restored. Nos 9671/4/5 were also renovated to the same style. No 9673 played its part in European history by forming part of the mobile headquarters of the Allied forces in France and Germany, conveying General Eisenhower and his staff. In 1947 this car had four bronze plaques fitted in the saloons to commemorate its notable wartime exploits and went into use on the 'Torbay Express'. Three plaques were stolen while in service. The fourth was removed on withdrawal but it is not known if it has survived. The vehicles continued on top-link duties until 1960 – Nos 9672/3 having received WR chocolate and cream livery – thereafter finding work on relief services until all were withdrawn during the purge of GWR restaurant cars in October 1962.

60ft 11in Buffet Cars Nos 9676–9680: 1938
The final type of the twelve-wheel 'yellow-disc' catering vehicles were these buffet cars for cross-country services. Nos 9676–80 were the only GWR buffet cars capable of generally unrestricted running over the northern railways' lines.

Two interior schemes were applied – three coaches had teak saloon panelling and two were in walnut. The internal layout was practical, the buffet counter having eight high seats, as well as ordinary bench-type seats with tables, seating twenty. One interesting facility was an 'intercom' between the buffet counter and kitchen.

Buffet car No 9676, as built. (Lot 1602 – Diagram H.55)

Walnut panelling in one interior scheme was set off by red leather upholstery for stools and seats; in the other, teak panelling was relieved by green moquette seating. Tables and the counter for both schemes had cream-coloured composition tops with chromium-plated trim. The heating pipes running along one side of the cars had oxydised-bronze grilles.

Post-war renovation schemes did not affect them and they continued on their pre-war duties. In 1954, with the restoration of the 'Bristolian', one of the batch was included in its formation and, in 1956, No 9677 was repainted WR chocolate and cream for this train. No 9678 was later similarly liveried. No 9677 remained on the 'Bristolian' until June 1961, when it was replaced by BR standard Pressed Steel-built restaurant-buffet, W1646, which saw out the end of the non-stop Bristol to Paddington schedule of this train.

Although by 1962 the batch was generally employed on relief and excursion work, No 9676 is believed to have kept to a Plymouth–Bristol and return diagram until the September of that year and with 'Centenary' kitchen-first No 9636 (see page 97) was probably the last GWR restaurant car in regular express service.

No 9680 was condemned in the autumn of 1962 but, in 1964, the others were still in use on excursions. By early 1965, only Nos 9676/9 remained, with contemporary kitchen cars, Nos 9669/70, the last GWR catering vehicles in service.

Special Saloons: 1940 and 1944/45

The four vehicles under the above heading were specialised, self-contained saloons for VIP travel; the 1945 coaches were allocated for Royal Train duties.

Nos 9001/2 were ordered in 1938 as saloons for railway and government VIPs making daytime journeys and, like previous vehicles such as Nos 9004/5 (page 83), had a coupé compartment, day saloon, pantry and kitchen. Radio-receiving equipment was installed in the main saloon in late 1944 for wartime duties, with extensions to the coupé compartment and dining saloon, reducing the seating by four, to 20 seats.

Externally, they followed the same lines as the 1938 buffet cars and, like them, were mounted on six-wheel bogies with the same standard 60ft 11¼in body of 8ft 11in width. In the dining saloon, fixed seating was provided but the coupé and main saloon had settees and armchairs with small tables. The original interiors were rather spartan, panelled mostly in light wood, but were repanelled and refurnished in 1953.

The attractive interior of buffet car No 9679, as built. The panelling was in walnut, and the seats upholstered in red leather. (Lot 1602 – Diagram H.55)

During the war, Nos 9001/2 were used by Government officials and Service chiefs but, post-war, they found comparatively little use until mid-1963. It was then decided to advertise them for hire as executive suites in which business firms could hold conferences en route to visit factories and installations, or on tours of inspection. To this end, the coupé compartment was adapted for secretaries' use, and the dining-saloon equipped with a large table and movable chairs for meetings and meals. The WR advertised them as new saloons, which was not strictly true. The first duty for one of these 'boardrooms on wheels' was when the then Lord Mayor of London, Sir Ralph Perring, visited South Wales on an official tour in May 1963. Both coaches were painted chocolate and cream c1960.

The two other saloons, Nos 9006/7, were ordered in 1943 under the same specification as Nos 9001/2 but with sleeping accommodation to overcome the deficiency of the earlier vehicles in this respect. Use was made of two underframes from war-damaged 1938 60ft 11¼in body standard coaches: that from third No 1133 being used for No 9006, built November 1944, and that from

Special saloon No 9002, as built. (Lot 1626 – Diagram G.62)

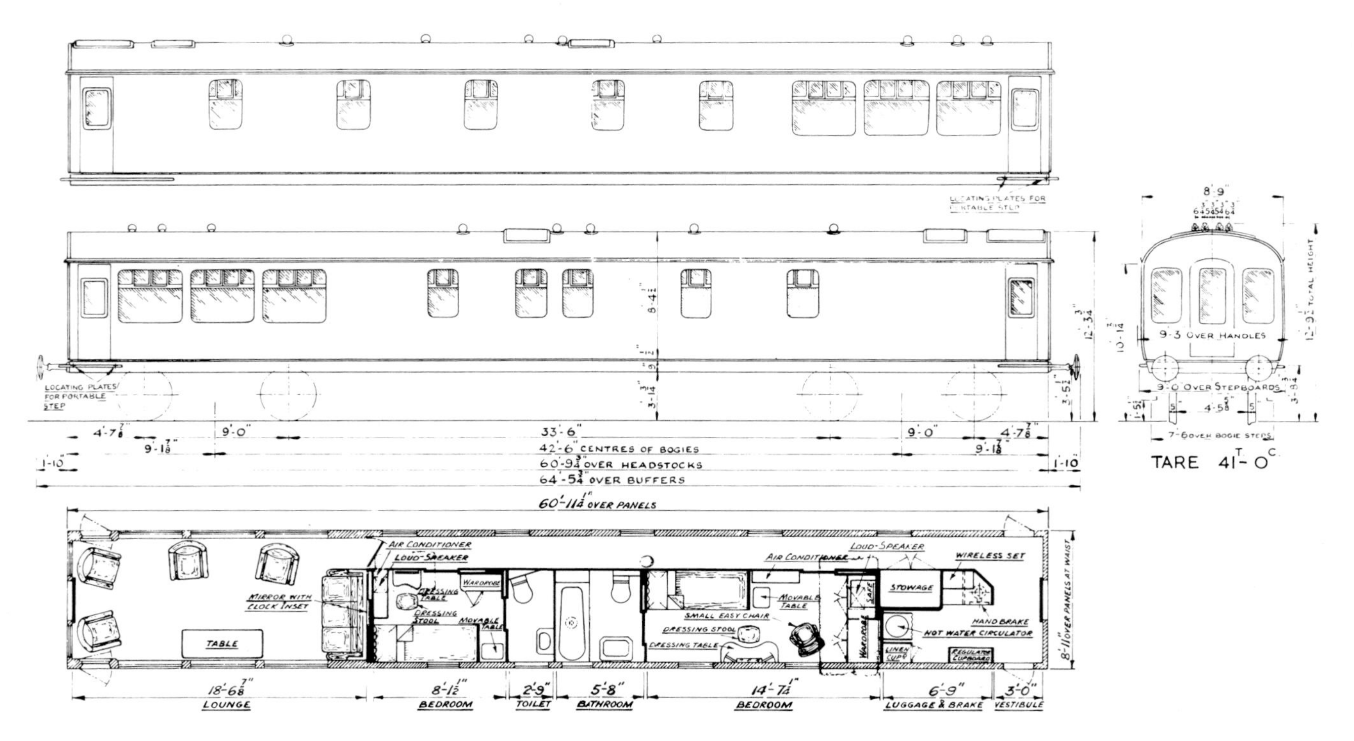

Swindon Diagram G.65 – vehicle No 9007 to Lot 1673.

brake third No 1598 for No 9007, completed December 1945. The two vehicles differed and worked as a set. No 9006 was equipped with two bedrooms, a bathroom, a small end-saloon seating seven on easy chairs and settees, a dining-room seating eight, an attendant's sleeping compartment and a fair-sized kitchen, including a refrigerator. No 9007 had no catering facilities but a lounge, two large bedrooms for use by the most distinguished travellers, and stowage space, which was in reality the 'guard's compartment'. Radio-receiving equipment with loudspeakers in each compartment was provided in both vehicles. Observation windows were fitted at the saloon ends.

In 1948, when the GWR decided to form a new Royal Train, Nos 9006/7 were internally refitted and provided with pressure ventilation, the set being completed by brake composites Nos 7372/7 of Hawksworth standard corridor stock. In 1949–50 the saloons were fitted for receiving portable steps and, in 1955, both were internally refurnished and repainted in the Royal claret livery, with numbers painted on the underframe only. The two brake composites remained in chocolate and cream livery.

This set was maintained as the WR-based Royal Train until about the mid-1960s, but by the 1970s Nos 9006/7 were maintained by Wolverton Works, used by HM the Queen Mother until 1979. Both vehicles have been claimed by the National Railway Museum for preservation and first went on display on 19 July 1984.

Vale of Rheidol stock: 1923/38 (1ft 11⅝in gauge)

Soon after Grouping, the GWR built four new open coaches for this line, open above the waist with wire mesh screens above and with large glazed windows at the ends. Except for No 4999, recently converted as a Vista Car, the entrances are at each end, with the seating in transverse, reversible wooden benches. Access is by means of tip-up seats fitting across the gangway, giving a total capacity of 48 seats. Canvas sheets hung from the roof can be let down for protection in bad

The GWR Royal Train in 1946, headed by Castle No 5056 *Earl of Powis*. The formation comprises a 60ft 11¼in length corridor brake composite, special saloon No 9006 or 9007, special saloons Nos 9001/02 and two 60ft 11¼in corridor coaches.

weather, and footboards are fitted. In 1938, the underframes and running gear of three Vale of Rheidol Light Railway 1902-vintage open coaches were used for the construction of replacement open stock generally similar to the 1923 design to Lot 1618.

The original VoR closed coaches were replaced by nine new steel-panelled vehicles in time for the 1938 summer season. Seven thirds and two brake thirds were supplied by Swindon, on new underframes, but retaining bogies recovered from the withdrawn stock; officially they were regarded as rebuilds. Large bodyside windows with only three doors a side enable passengers to enjoy the beauties of the Rheidol Valley. The wooden seats are arranged transversely (for alterations, see below) and each door opens into a 'compartment'. Neither heating nor lighting were provided when new as winter passenger services had been discontinued as from 1 January 1931. Three four-wheel brake vans were also produced in 1938.

The VoR line stock was painted in standard GWR livery, thereafter BR crimson and cream until 1955, being repainted WR-style chocolate and cream for the 1956 season. An unhappy Cambrian Railways-style bronze green paint scheme was used from 1964–68, replaced by standard BR blue paintwork; this was lined out in black and white from the late 1970s. By then the coaches were no longer maintained by Swindon and were usually overhauled or repainted at Shrewsbury station.

As a result of commercial sponsorship, the London Midland Region was able to introduce a series of improvements for the VoR stock in June 1983. Most striking, if not particularly handsome, is the conversion by Chester C & W shops of open coach M4999 to a Vista Car. It now has deep picture windows on the 'valley side' and is also glazed on the other side. All seats now face the picture windows and are upholstered. The brake seconds Nos M4995/6 were converted to brake composites with the 'compartment' furthest from the brake now containing 24 first-class upholstered seats. Nos 4995/9, with 'opens' Nos 4149/4997 and 'closed' coaches Nos 4143/4/7 and 4994, now carry chocolate and cream livery, ostensibly their original scheme with shirt-button GWR monograms although the numbers are wrongly placed about 18in above the solebars.

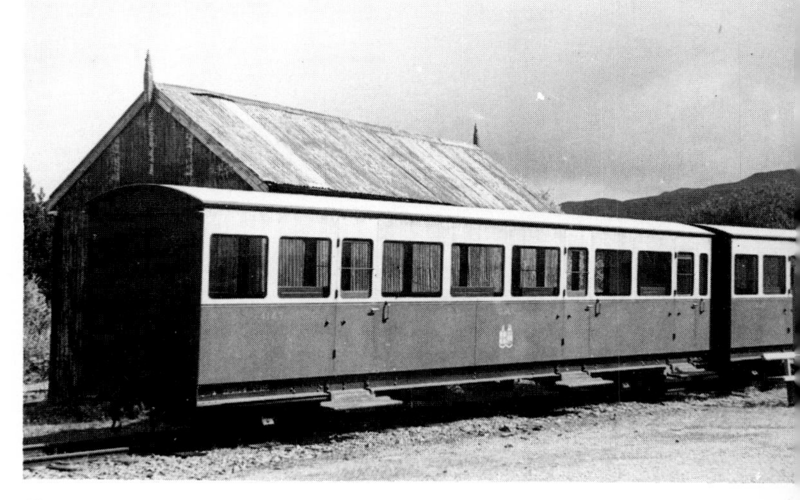

Top:
Royal Train saloon No W9006W, in BR claret livery. (Lot 1673 – Diagram G.64).

Above:
Vale of Rheidol third No 4143 in GWR livery, at Devil's Bridge, August 1948. Designation 'G.W.R.' above coats of arms. (Lot 1615 – Diagram C.78)

Vale of Rheidol brake third No 4995, as converted by BR to a brake composite, and painted in GWR-style livery in 1983. At Aberystwyth, June 1983. (Lot 1616 – Diagram D.128)

8

POST-WAR HOPES FRUSTRATED: 1944–1954

Hawksworth Stock: 1944–1954
Indicative of the forward-looking spirit of the GWR after the war, the Hawksworth-designed coaches introduced and embodied many interesting developments and experiments. As the end of the Second World War became apparent, plans were made for the construction of a new design of corridor coach, the Lots for all types being issued in October 1944, and including a prototype with an aluminium underframe. By late 1945, details had appeared in the railway technical press of the new stock, attention being drawn to the most interesting fact that fluorescent lighting would be fitted in all these coaches.

It was expected in October 1945 that 260 new fluorescently-lit main-line coaches would be built under the 1946 building programme at the rate of one a week. Not surprisingly, this figure proved impossible of achievement. Shortage of men and materials resulted in construction falling well behind schedule, and recourse was made to rolling stock contractors. It is fair to say that the impending 1947 Transport Act discouraged the railways from continuing many experiments, in the shareholders' interests.

The restrictions curtailed the general application of fluorescent-lighting and special interior finishes. The original specification for the latter included 'Empire veneers' for panelling and specially-woven materials for internal furnishing. Only the prototypes featured these.

After the Lots had been placed in 1944, the GWR and British Thomson-Houston collaborated on the development of fluorescent lighting. The manufacturer had already equipped an LPTB District Line 1938 stock car in October 1944, but main-line stock required special attention. Details of the lighting installation are given on page 29. Besides five third-class coaches of this stock, composite No 7022 of 1938 was also fitted throughout with fluorescent tubes.

The experiments with fluorescent lighting appeared to have died under nationalisation, although the vehicles so equipped, except in one case, retained it. Until the early 1960s, fluorescent lighting was uncommon in BR standard stock because difficulty was experienced with the weight and size of the necessary equipment. Additionally, the quality of the light was unsatisfactory in the GWR experiments, being harsh and colour biased, in contrast to original publicity which asserted that the 'fluorescent tubes will give an even daylight effect, without glare or shadow over a whole compartment'.

Yet another innovation was the use of laminated plastic panelling which, again, did not extend beyond various prototypes. This material, known under its trade name of 'Formica', offered a cheaper and more durable alternative to the traditional wood veneer which was in short supply at the time, and third No 784 was so panelled in 1948. The colour scheme was a venturesome combination of duckegg blue and iron grey. No 797 was finished throughout in cream. One or two other coaches had imitation wood grain panelling, as later used in BR diesel railcars. The Hawksworth sleeping-cars also had plastic panelling, as mentioned on page 112.

Also important was the more economical and speedy method of sectionalised construction which is dealt with on page 27. The experiments with the use of light alloy both for panelling and for some components of the frame of the 1944-ordered prototype third No 2239 are interesting and again did not receive attention with a view to further development by BR until the 1960s. Several other coaches of this type had aluminium body panelling.

The Hawksworth look of the post-war GWR. This was one of the most common livery schemes in the variety that was a feature in the period before Nationalisation. This is corridor brake third No 833, officially released to traffic on 6 December 1947. (Lot 1692 – Diagram D.131)

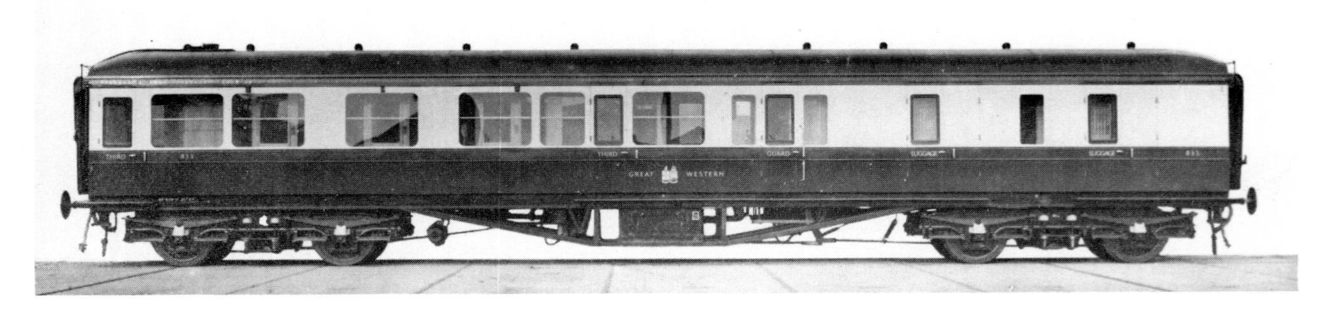

Double lining-out on corridor brake composite No W7383 (no 'W' suffix to number), built 1948. (Lot 1690 – Diagram E.164)

Although the Hawksworth stock brought a new profile to the GWR – a slab-sided box with sloping roof ends – the basic layout was the same as the 1938 stock, although advantage was taken of the increased body length from 60 to 64ft to have bigger vestibules and larger compartments as measured between partitions. The destination-board brackets were moved, as mentioned elsewhere, from the roof to below the cantrail in LMS style. If the sloping roof ends suggested the LNER, one lady shareholder was not impressed: she was adamant that the large windows, LNER-style, allowed such a wide view of the countryside rushing past and so much sun to enter the compartments, that train-sickness was inevitable!

The interiors of the standard production batches of the corridor coaches followed two schemes: oak veneer or 'Holoplast' enamelled hardboard. The first scheme was applied to the earlier Lots and was a revised version of the 'Empire veneers', while the second one was the result of economising with materials and lasted extremely well. Both are described on page 31. The experimental interior finishes made use of red satinay and African cherry in third-class compartments, while Australian maple was used in the firsts. The 'specially woven material' was ordinary cut-moquette of filigree patterns of purple-grey or green colouring. All other detail and refinements were made standard, as related on page 31.

Although publicity concerning the introduction of the new stock was widespread in mid-1945, the first coach to the new design, No 796, was not completed until August 1946 and by the end of that year only 20 had been delivered. From early to mid-1947, another 30 had been completed although Nos 781–804 did not enter traffic in numerical order and the fluorescently-lit examples generally appeared later.

An exhibition of modern GWR stock, mostly conversions, to indicate future trends was held at Paddington on 5 November 1946. Oil-burning 'Castle' No 5091 *Cleeve Abbey*, demonstrating the abortive fuel experiment on the locomotive side, was coupled to a train consisting of a fluorescently-lit third No 790, refurnished composite No 7022, also with fluorescent tubes, two other renovated vehicles with ordinary lighting, a restaurant car in the 967x series and a sleeping-car.

Swindon Diagram C.83, for non-corridor thirds covering Lots 1693, 1712/26/39/45/48.

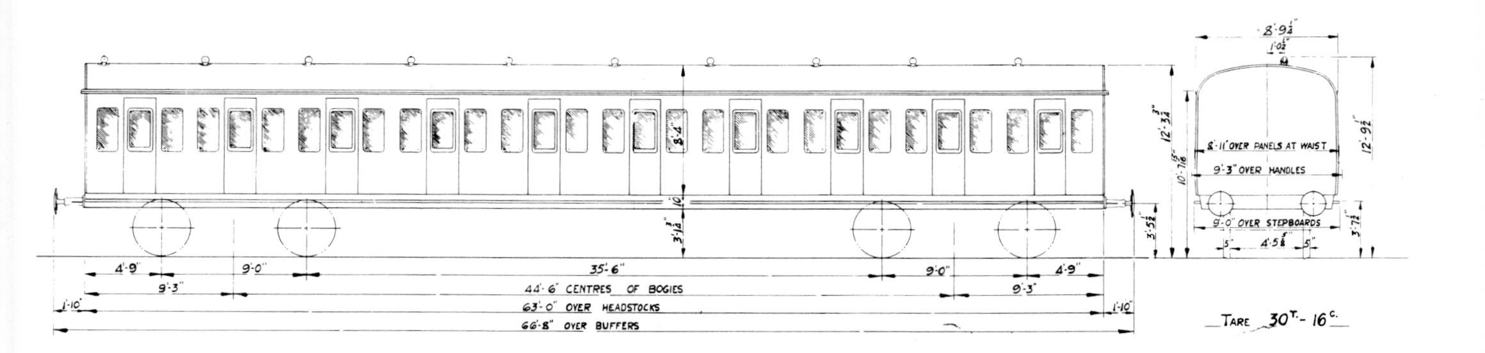

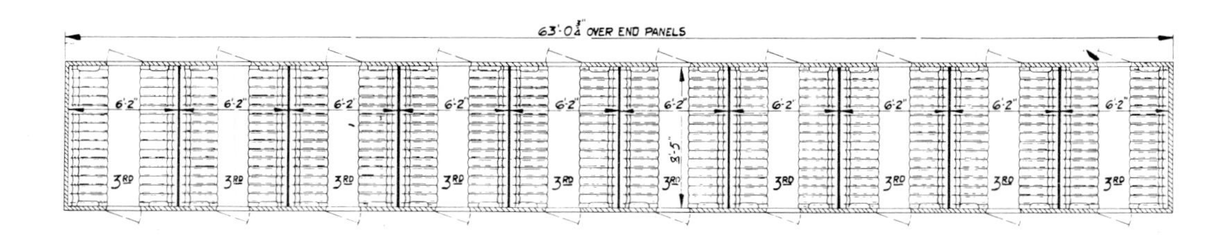

Holoplast cream panelling with trim either in dark brown of the same material, or dark, polished wood. Note the neat design of the alloy section luggage rack, and the coved ceiling. The upholstery was not a standard type. This is a third-class compartment in one of the early Hawksworth vehicles.

First-class compartment with exterior door in corridor composite No 7252. Some attractive veneered panelling with inlaid trim, and recessed pictures and mirrors. The 'fruit-bowl' uncut moquette was fawn on a dark-blue ground in smoking compartments such as this. (Lot 1689 – Diagram E.163)

The new coaches coming into service were painted in the new GWR livery with Swindon's Gill Sans lettering but there were several variations in style. Although there was a general shortage of modern vehicles, the Hawksworth stock was not drafted to form set trains on services, possibly because of the slowness of delivery even with the aid of three contractors, the Gloucester Railway Carriage Company, Birmingham RC&W and Metro-Cammell. The 'Cornish Riviera' had a number of Hawksworth coaches in its formation until it was allocated a set train of older stock in the experimental plum-and-spilt-milk livery during 1948. Although set trains of Hawksworth stock were made up in the early 1950s and appeared on Birmingham–West of England services and also Birkenhead–Bournemouth, at the same time stopping and branch-line trains included Hawksworth corridor stock!

Brake composites Nos 7372/7, built in 1948, were used from the start by Old Oak Common on special work and were then formed in the WR-based Royal Train with saloons No 9006/7. They were turned out in GWR livery and were maintained as such until c1957 when they were repainted in the WR chocolate and cream scheme. Both have been preserved.

The 'Bristolian' as re-introduced in 1954 was formed of Hawksworth stock with a 967x twelve-wheel buffet car until 1956, when the former were displaced by chocolate-and-cream painted BR standard stock. From this date onwards, the majority of main-line Western Region trains were formed of BR standard stock. One curious conversion in 1958 was that of three brake composites to slip coaches. At this time there were only three such workings, only one of which, the Weymouth slip off the down 'Cornish Riviera Express' at Heywood Road Junction, warranted the painting of these conversions in chocolate and cream with the BR crest. There were already three of the 1938 slip coaches so painted.

The Hawksworth slip-coach conversions, Nos 7374–6, were used on the last days of the two remaining slips: at Didcot off the 7 a.m. Weston-super-Mare–Paddington in June 1960, and the very last in the world, No 7374 with two ordinary coaches at Bicester off the 5.10 p.m. Paddington–Wolverhampton on 9 September 1960. Still remaining in chocolate and cream livery, the conversions were transferred to Taunton in early 1961, with the slip-gear removed, for use on the lines to Barnstaple, Minehead and Chard, and for main-line stopping services.

An important conversion took place during 1961 when third No 796, built in 1946, was used as the shell of the new Western Region dynamometer car to replace the Churchward vehicle of 1901. This was an occasion for stressing the continued independence of Swindon, and the vehicle was liveried in WR chocolate and cream with the GWR coat of arms prominently displayed in the conference room. The new dynamometer car was primarily intended for testing new diesel

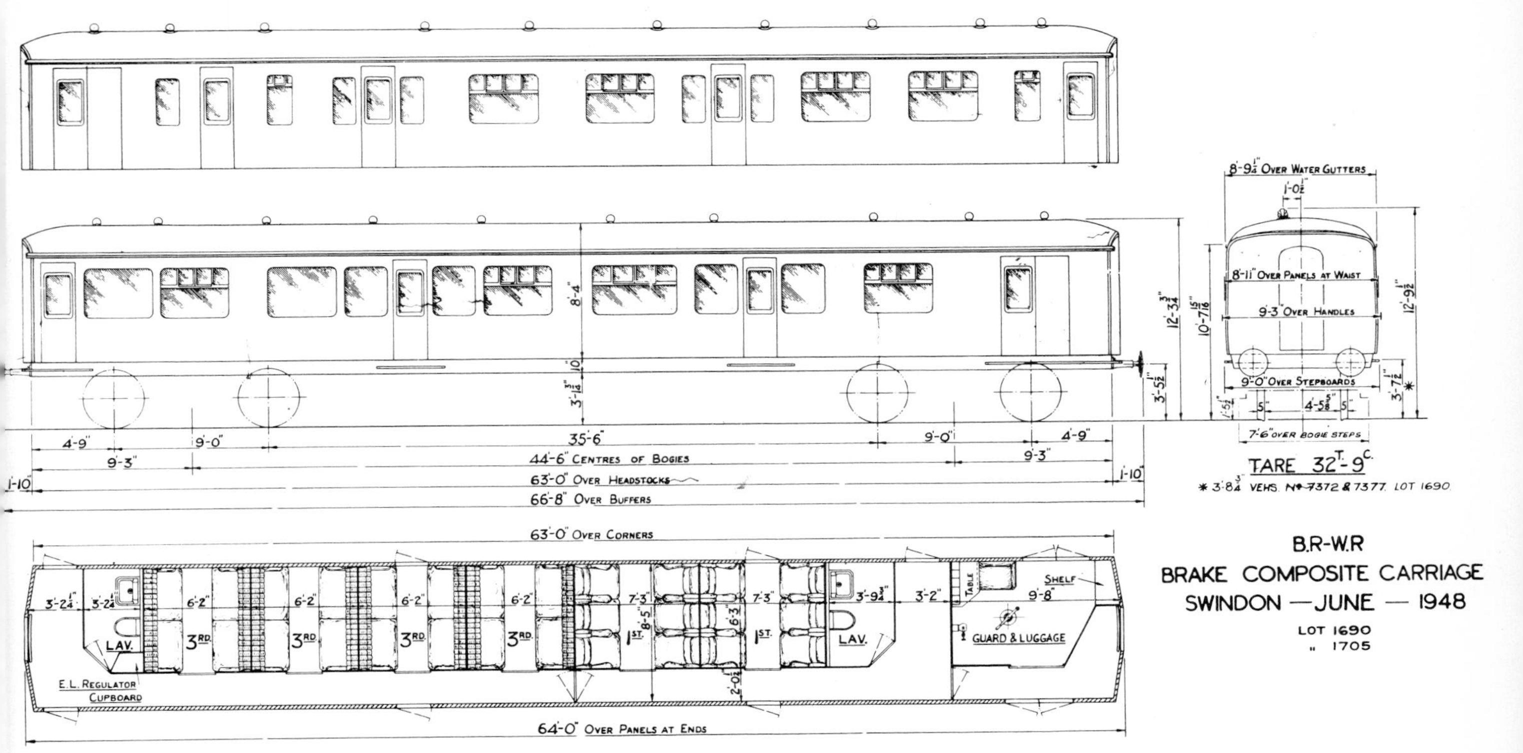

Swindon Diagram E.164, for corridor brake composites covering Lots 1690, 1705/38.

power but was also used in trials with a mechanical-stoker-fitted National Coal Board 0-6-0ST in early 1963. Some apparatus from the old Churchward vehicle was installed in the 1961 car. Numbered DW150192, the dynamometer car was transferred to the Railway Technical Centre after 1967 and remained in use until 1983 when it was withdrawn and acquired for preservation.

Another interesting use was found for three composites which were repainted in late 1961-early 1962 in diesel multiple-unit Brunswick green with cream lining for use as trailers, classified TCL, in three-car Western Region 'Cross-Country' diesel sets which covered, principally, an up Westbury to Paddington train, an out-and-back trip to Oxford and return on the then 6.5 p.m. Paddington–Westbury, which was a replacement for the withdrawn evening Paddington to Weymouth train. The standard dark green diesel-unit livery of these conversions clashed badly with the older lighter green of the sets in which they were working! No other alterations were made to the coaches, apart from the fitting of jumper cables for through control. All were condemned by May 1967.

Withdrawal of Hawksworth corridor coaches began early in 1965, and with the closure of carriage overhaul facilities at Swindon the responsibility for shopping was transferred to Wolverton Works. This works dealt with many of this stock during the next two years, a number being overhauled and the upholstery retrimmed. During 1966, Nos 1719 and 2135 were repainted in the BR grey and blue livery, but the Hawksworth stock was under sentence and all were scheduled for official withdrawal at the end of December 1967. Eighteen brake thirds were converted for departmental service, Nos DW150390–407. Several Hawksworth corridor coaches have survived for preservation.

The compartment coaches, also constructed by the same direct building method and with the same outline, began to appear from late 1947 onwards. Of interest were the thirds seating a hundred passengers and all types could take advantage of the increased body length for more spacious compartments. Generally it was not until 1950–51 that these coaches appeared in quantity and, for the greater part, were allocated to the London and Birmingham Division suburban services. Three contractors helped to complete the orders, including uniquely for the GWR, R. Y. Pickering & Co. Lot 1777 is of importance, historically, for being the last GWR Lot covering passenger coaches to be issued, and among the last non-standard types to be built by BR: comprising ten brake composites to form five 'B' sets in the Plymouth area. Apart from damaged vehicles, they had the shortest life of all GWR coaches, as they were withdrawn, after eight years' service, in 1962.

The dieselisation of the suburban services from 1958, and progressive closure of branch lines, made the Hawksworth compartment stock redundant from the early 1960s. By 1961, only the Birmingham area had regular locomotive-hauled suburban services and, in 1962, it was decided to make use of holiday relief corridor sets for this work. Consequently, withdrawals began heavily from 1962. The decision to eliminate all non-corridor stock on the Western Region by the end of 1963 – and this included BR standard coaches – saw their virtual extinction by this date, though a few survivors lingered on into 1964.

Eighty composites, built at Swindon for the LMR in 1952–53, should be considered separately

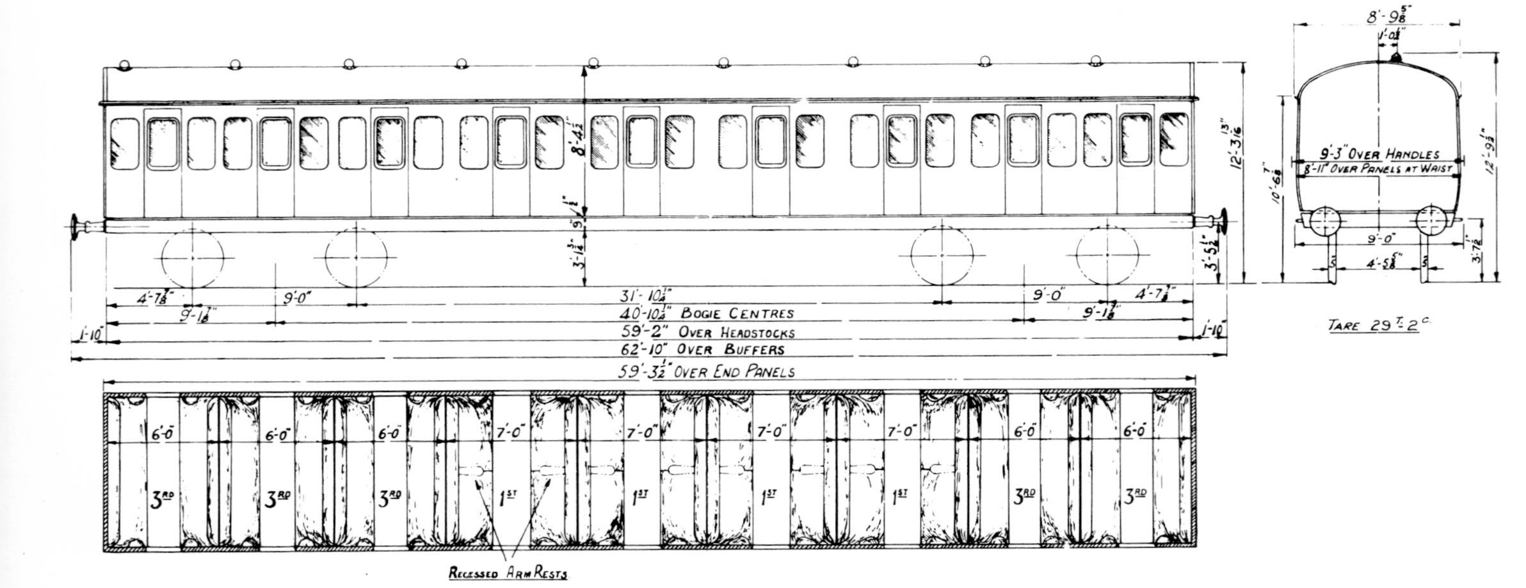

Swindon Diagram E.156, for non-corridor composites built for the London Midland Region, Lots 1749/72. This was a pre-war design also covering Lots 1567/96, 1630.

as they were 59ft 3½in body vehicles built to Diagram E.156 first issued in 1937. At this time Derby and Wolverton Works were heavily committed with the construction of BR standard corridor coaches and the BR standard non-corridor designs did not appear until 1955. The virtual standardisation of 57ft body non-corridor coaches on the London Midland Region possibly ruled out the use of the 63ft-body Hawksworth design. The eighty composites were only slightly different in width and height over gutters to the pre-war coaches to the same diagram and had tumblehome body panels above the solebars, in contrast to the slab-sided Hawksworth coaches. The interior finish followed the post-war style. To indicate their LMR ownership they were given LMS non-corridor series numbers (16797–16876) with the 'M' prefix, the 'W' suffix denoting Swindon's responsibility for maintenance; some were tentatively allocated GW-series Nos 7209–22/4-44. They were not withdrawn at the end of 1963, following the Western Region's policy, and in mid-1965 could still be seen in the LMR Manchester area, finally disappearing in late 1967.

Experimental Coaches, etc.

Thirds Nos 784/97. Laminated plastic panelling prototypes. No 784 also with fluorescent lighting.

Third No 790. Fluorescent lighting prototype. Also with Empire veneer panelling. Nos 783/94/5 also with fluorescent lighting.

The May 1961 conversion of Hawksworth corridor second (formerly third-class) W796W (Lot 1691 – Diagram C.82), originally outshopped in August 1946. The livery is WR chocolate and cream.

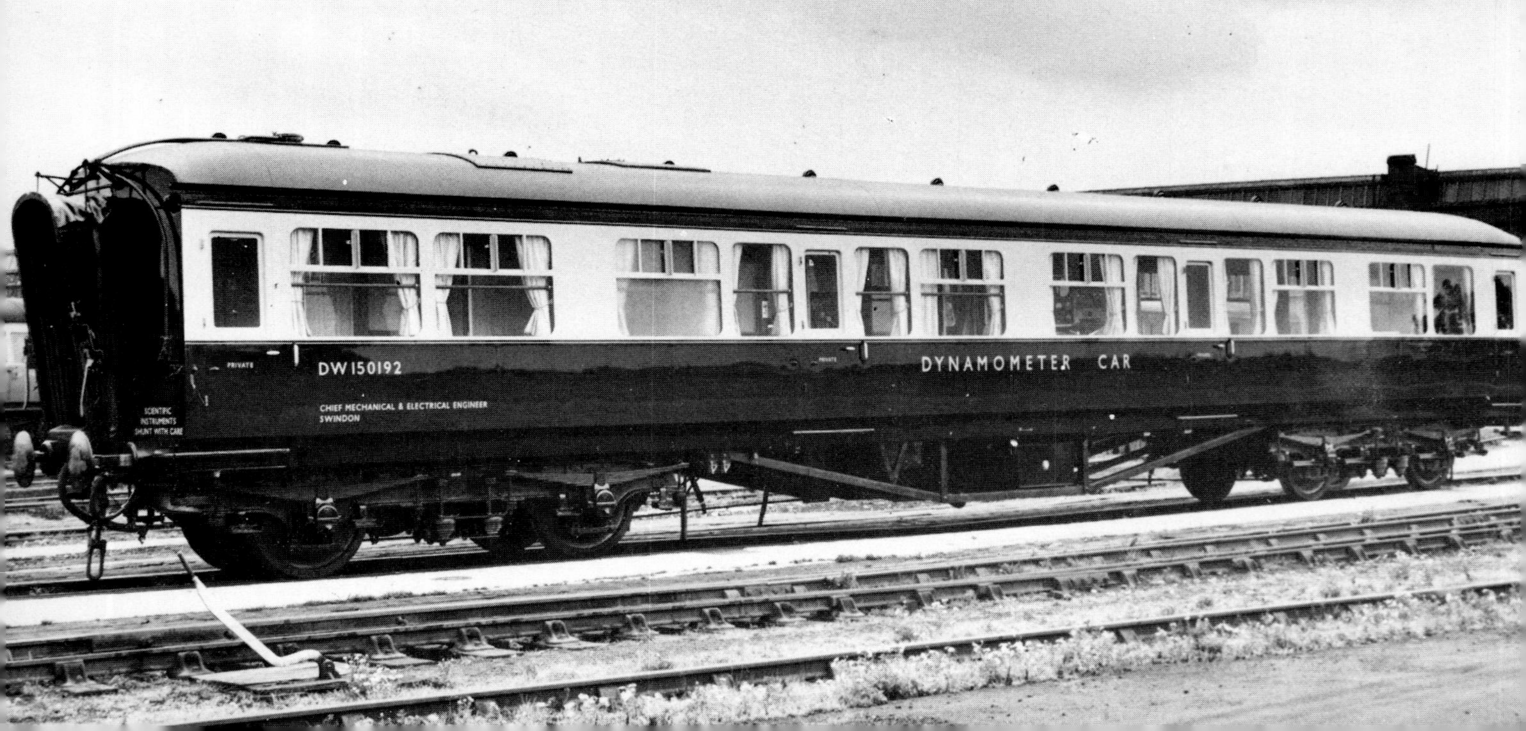

Corridor brake composite W7376W, converted in BR days as a slip coach, and seen at Oxford in May 1963 with slip gear removed. It is in BR lined maroon livery with the yellow cant-rail stripe recently applied to denote first-class accommodation. (Lot 1690 – Diagram E.164)

Third No 804. Decolite flooring. Weight: 31 tons 14 cwt. All other Hawksworth coaches had wood-sandwich floors (see page 27).

Third No 813. Aluminium body panelling and window ventilators. Weight: 30 tons. Some of Lot 1735 similarly finished.

Third No 2239. With part-aluminium underframe, also aluminium body panels and laminated plastic panelling. Weight: 27 tons 12 cwt.

Brake third No 2259 and first No 8060. Withdrawn from probable damage, 1958 and 1961 respectively.

Proposed 'Automat' Buffet Car: 1945

The most intriguing of all the abortive post-war GWR intentions was the automatic-buffet car. Just how far the idea proceeded is not clear; certainly no lot was issued to cover the construction of any such vehicle and it is only possible to conclude that, in view of post-war shortages, it was too much of a novelty to be given precedence over the building of standard coaches.

Only one definite announcement seems to have been made by the GWR and this was featured in *The Railway Gazette* of 4 January 1946 and *The Engineer* of 11 January. *The Railway Gazette* gave some prominence to the proposed vehicle and illustrated the paragraph by an interesting, but apparently unofficial, artist's impression reproduced on page 112. The vehicle would have been seemingly a full-length automatic-buffet and not in the manner of the cubicle in the BR standard corridor second auto-buffet converted in 1961 for use on the 'Cambrian Coast Express' between Shrewsbury and Aberystwyth. There would have been 'many hundreds of snack compartments' (so it was reported) supplying 'varieties of sandwiches, salads, savouries, cakes, fruit, chocolate, confectionery, ice cream, cigarettes, matches, stamps, medical requisites, and even drinks, complete with wax cups'. The practical, non-edible supplies are worth noting. All could be obtained for sixpence (2½p) or a shilling (5p) each, which seems rather optimistic. The journal commented that 'the new cars will be brought into service as soon as food conditions permit and will probably be put into use on short main-line services'. Exactly what services seems questionable, in view of the GWR's provision of restaurant and full buffet-car service on some short-distance main-line semi-fast services, but, possibly, they could

Non-corridor brake third No W416. (Lot 1694 – Diagram D.132)

Non-corridor third No W2646, built Birmingham RC&W, and outshopped in BR lined carmine livery. (Lot 1745 – Diagram C.83)

have worked between Paddington and Oxford, or Bristol and Swansea.

The artist's impression gives as much detail as is known except that it implies the use of shaded tungsten lights instead of the intended fluorescent tubes. The interior decoration would have been in contrasting sycamore veneers for the walls, with coloured rubber flooring. The project was wittily summed up in the verse reproduced (right), which appeared in *The Railway Gazette* of 4 February 1946.

No new restaurant cars were built after the war by the GWR and the only evidence of trends in this direction lies in the extensive renovation of older cars.

Artist's impression of the proposed GWR automat buffet car.

Contemporary Comment in Verse

('Tailpiece' by W.E.N. from *The Railway Gazette*, 8.2.46)

The new Great Western proposition
Is in that railway's high tradition,
It now intends to introduce
The Automat for meal-time use.

Here passengers may eat and drink,
Here bags will rustle, glasses clink,
And ice-cream portions may be got
By dropping coins into a slot.

You want a postage stamp en route,
Or matches for the old cheroot?
These also will be there for sale
And coins will bring them without fail.

When Automats are in full swing,
You need not for a waiter ring,
But help yourself to something hot
By putting sixpence in the slot.

Be sure, Great Western Railway, that
We'll patronise your Automat,
But when we're short of proper cash,
How shall we get a lemon-dash?

Hawksworth Sleeping-Cars: 1951

The only special-duty Hawksworth outline passenger coaches were the four first-class sleeping-cars Nos 9082–85, built to the standard 64ft body length, but of 9ft 1¾in width. These were ten-berth cars, with the usual attendant's compartment, and interesting as they were equipped with Stone's pressure ventilation. Apart from two restaurant cars, No 9640/2, and Royal saloons, Nos 9006/7, they were the only GWR-built coaches with some form of air-conditioning.

Interior panelling was in laminated plastic throughout: green and beige in the corridors and

First-class sleeping car W9085W, in BR lined maroon livery with yellow stripe denoting first-class accommodation, at Old Oak Common, c1964. (Lot 1702 – Diagram J.18)

ivory in the compartments. A number of other fittings were also plastic, while all metalwork was in satin-silver finish.

By August 1964, Nos 9082–85 were in use on the West Wales–Paddington sleeping car service and were overhauled at Swindon in the August of that year, among the last vehicles to be so treated at the Works, reportedly because they were not passed to run outside former GWR territory. The four sleeping cars remained in traffic until early 1970 when all were withdrawn and acquired for preservation.

Auto-Train Saloons: 1951–1954

Having brought a new look and fresh thoughts to standard post-war GWR coaches, attention was turned to auto-train saloons, the first to be built new for over fifteen years. By the early 1950s the rail-motor conversions were not only nearing the end of their economic lives but were spartan and unattractive to travellers, while the cars built new in the early 1930s were little better.

The new saloons, Nos 220–234, had the same slab-sided profile as the standard corridor and non-corridor stock, with large bodyside windows and very deep ventilators. The interior was also changed, the usual arrangement of longitudinal bench seats being replaced by Underground-type back-to-back benches. All woodwork below window-level, including the seat frames, was in dark oak finish, off-white Holoplast panelling being used elsewhere. Two peculiarities were Nos 220/21, intended to be the first of a class with bird names, which were named *Wren* and *Thrush*, the titles being displayed below the middle windows in sans-serif lettering. The two names were also carried by Pullman first-class kitchen cars built in 1960 for the East Coast route. *Wren* and *Thrush* were sent to work on the frequent and busy Ealing Broadway to Greenford 'auto', among other duties. The others were widely dispersed but with a bias towards the London and Gloucester areas and Churston–Brixham. Most originally appeared in crimson and cream livery.

In 1952, No 221, *Thrush*, was internally renovated, the heavy wooden fittings being replaced by diesel railcar type metal-framed seats upholstered in deep green striped material. All internal surfaces were panelled in pastel laminated plastic. The result was most satisfactory – producing a thoroughly modern vehicle and anticipating the imminent flood of diesel railcars with similar interiors. No 221 returned to Southall and the named pair remained in the London Division until dieselisation of the Ealing–Greenford and West Drayton–Staines 'autos' in 1959.

In 1954, the year railcars began appearing in quantity on other Regions, the Western Region built a further ten auto-coaches with the same interior as the renovated No 221 but with seating increased by a further ten. These ten, Nos 235–244, were the last coaches built new to a non-BR standard design, although not of pre-nationalisation origin as the original batch had been ordered and designed in 1951. These again went to the London area, also to Tiverton and Newton Abbot. From 1958–59 onwards, when the lined maroon livery was extended to non-corridor stock, all surviving auto-saloons due for repainting had the lining-out above the windows carried round under the roof curves at the ends.

After 1959, the post-war saloons were covering the majority of the surviving push-and-pull services with the compartment brake third trailers on the remainder.

The last two or three years of Western Region auto-train working were not without interest. From 1 January 1963, when the Western Region gained control of the ex-LSW lines west of Salisbury, there was still push-and-pull working with Maunsell two-car sets on the Yeovil Junction to Yeovil Town and Seaton Junction to Seaton services. Despite imminent dieselisation, the Western Region imposed the old GWR system of

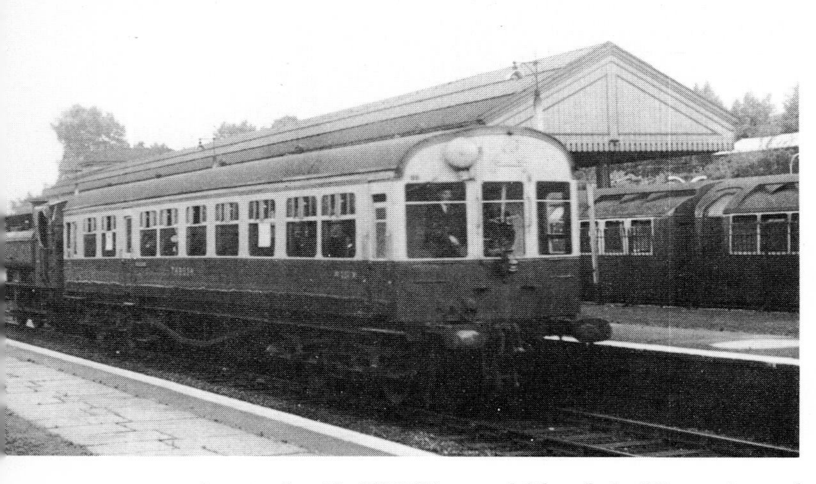

Auto-trailer No W221W, named *Thrush*, in BR carmine and cream livery, at Ealing Broadway, June 1952. (Lot 1736 – Diagram A40)

auto train working on these lines and sent 64xx 0-6-0PTs from Laira (Plymouth) with trailers Nos 233/5/8/40/1/3 in March 1963 to take over their workings. After some trouble, the 64xx locomotives were introduced on the Yeovil line but the Seaton branch reverted to ordinary working until dieselised. In October 1963 the last rites were exercised on the Exe Valley line, until then auto-worked, incongruously using 'North British' diesels and corridor coaches. The once numerous auto-train working in Devon ended with the withdrawal of the Tiverton–Tiverton Junction service in October 1964 and the only West Country survivor was on ex-LSW territory. The Yeovil Town to Junction working probably provided the last example of the GWR auto-trains. In place of diesel railcars, 14xx 0-4-2Ts and saloon auto-trailers appeared on the Seaton Junction to Seaton service in February 1965.

The Dudley to Old Hill workmen's service returned to steam auto-trains once its sentence of execution had been passed while, among the others, the Berkeley Road–Sharpness truncated service remained in splendid isolation with one compartment auto-coach and few passengers to the end. The most notable of the surviving auto-workings was that between Gloucester and Chalford which ceased on 31 October 1964; this route had seen the first rail-motors in 1903. In North Wales, the LMR replaced the 14xx 0-4-2Ts at Oswestry by Class '2' 2-6-0s to rid itself of that particular class until a two-car diesel set arrived for the Gobowen service.

By 1964, with few workings remaining for them, withdrawal of the post-war auto-coaches began, several becoming departmental vehicles. However, the Great Western Society purchased No 231 and five others were preserved by the Dart Valley Railway. No 239 was retained for service use by Swindon, subsequently being transferred to the Railway Technical Centre where it was used as a test car, in red and blue livery, numbered ADW 150375.

Engineer's Inspection Saloons: 1948

The use of passenger stock saloons for departmental duties is dealt with in Chapter 10, and at the end of the Second World War the older vehicles, including some aged Bristol & Exeter Railway conversions, needed replacement. Six new inspection saloons for use by divisional engineers were built during 1948. These were 52ft long and 8ft 11in wide, carried on pressed steel 9ft wheelbase bogies, with bodywork generally similar to the pre-war corridor stock. The usual layout of a saloon at each end was followed, with large end windows, and warning gongs and access steps were provided. A galley, lavatory and guard's brake were included amidships. These vehicles were outshopped in post-war GWR chocolate and cream livery, and allocated initially to Newport, Neath, Shrewsbury, Wolverhampton, Bristol and Taunton. All survived until the early 1970s, by then most still carrying WR chocolate and cream livery. Nos 80969/72/4 were withdrawn in 1972/3 and acquired for preservation. By 1983 Nos 80970/5/6 still remained with BR.

The former Taunton Division engineer's inspection saloon, still wearing badly weathered WR chocolate and cream livery, as TDW80976. At Guide Bridge, Manchester, in September 1978. (Lot 1701 – Diagram Q.13)

9

TPO VEHICLES AND SERVICES; PASSENGER BRAKE VANS, 'OCEAN MAILS' VANS AND BULLION VANS

Readers are recommended to consult The Railway Philatelic Group's excellent two-volume history, *TPO. A History of the TPOs of Great Britain, Parts 1/2* for full details of the evolution and development of Travelling Post Office services operated by the GWR. As an introduction to the history of the TPO vehicles, a brief history of the GWR TPOs and sorting tenders and carriages and their services seems appropriate.

Great Western TPO
This only assumed its present Paddington–Plymouth–Penzance through working as from 1 January 1902. Additional new stock provided in 1905, replacement vehicles in 1929 and 1933, with subsequent conversions. The GWR vehicles were replaced by BR Mark 1 standard stock in 1959. Withdrawn as a TPO operation with bag tenders only after 21 September 1940. Sorting operations recommenced as from 1 October 1945.

Truro–Falmouth Sorting Tender
In connection with Great Western TPO. Duty discontinued in 1916.

Plymouth–Bristol TPO
Major acceleration and reorganisation of West of England and South Wales–North mail workings took place in 1891. In October 1895, the TPO became Bristol (dep 6.15 a.m.) – Plymouth; Plymouth (dep 3.55 p.m.) – Bristol workings, in connection with the Normanton TPO. Extended to/from Penzance, February 1896, withdrawn beyond Plymouth, August 1916. Bristol and Penzance and return working 1922–28, to and from Plymouth only from March 1930. Suspended 21 September 1940, restored 21 May 1948. Discontinued after 3 March 1972.

Plymouth–Bristol TPO (Foreign Mails)
By 1895, to Bristol (or London) conveying Cape and West Indian mails. By 1914, occasional operation, both ways Plymouth–Bristol, or to/from London. From 1915 and after the First World War, American mails conveyed, Plymouth–Bristol (or London).

London and Bristol Sorting Carriage
Out 5.30 a.m. from Paddington, 3 p.m. return. Up working suspended 1917–32. Thereafter, up from Bristol at 6.8 p.m. Suspended September 1940 and not restored.

Bristol and Exeter TPO (Day)
Conveyed on the 9 a.m. ex-Paddington from Bristol, returning empty.

South Wales TPO (Night)
Swansea–Gloucester, December 1891, to New Milford, January 1892. From Carmarthen, December 1924, to/from Bristol from July 1925 to connect with the Great Western TPO, Bristol dep 1.5 a.m., Carmarthen arr 5.8 a.m.; dep 8.10 p.m., Bristol arr 12.2 a.m. Bag tender London–Neyland conveyed from 1928. Additional bag tenders included from 1932. TPO operations suspended on 21 September 1940, restored 6 May 1946. Ran to Milford Haven until February 1969, thereafter to/from Carmarthen.

The Bristol & Exeter TPO (Day) was allocated a 48ft passenger/mail brake No 2083, later converted for mail purposes only and renumbered 839 as seen here, with nets and delivery arms. (Lot 735, replacement of earlier written-off vehicle – Diagram L.12)

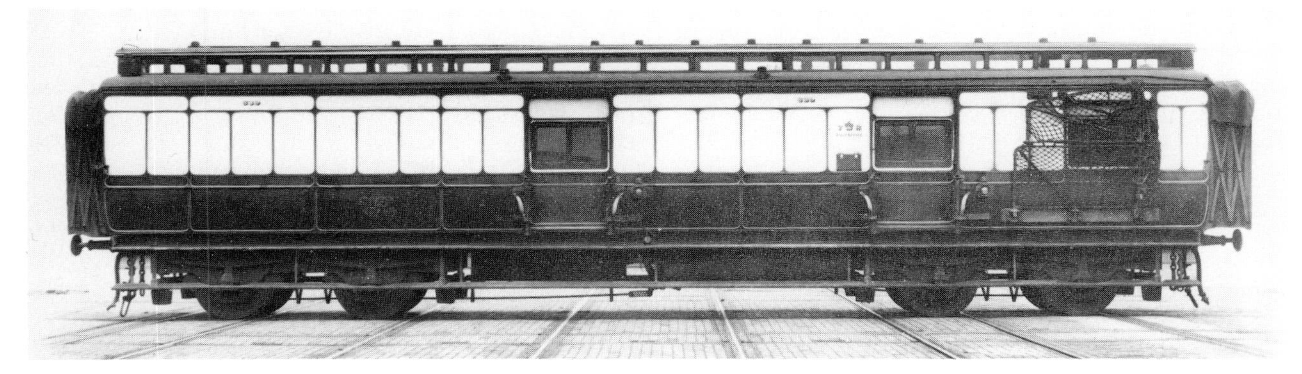

The interior of parcel sorting and bag tender No 853, built 1888 (not described in this book) used on the London and Plymouth TPO.

South Wales TPO (North Mail)
Commenced 1884 between Gloucester and New Milford, connecting with the Midland TPO. Gloucester dep 5.15 a.m., New Milford arr 11.40 a.m.; dep 1.5 p.m. Gloucester arr 7.55 p.m., weekdays only. Letter and parcels sorting. By 1915, used two 40ft vehicles (alternately). To/from Swansea from 6 November 1916. Discontinued 27 October 1923.

Cardiff–Crewe TPO
Started 4 October 1920, previously Cardiff–Shrewsbury–York, the two services having been split. Ceased September 1940, restored 7 October 1946.

Carmarthen and Newcastle Emlyn Sorting Carriage
Carmarthen–Llandyssul and return, connecting out of South Wales TPO. New vehicles 1891/92. Extended to Newcastle Emlyn, July 1895. Discontinued May 1904.

Shrewsbury–Aberystwyth Sorting Carriage
Started 1883 by Cambrian Railways, service suspended 1917–July 1919. Designated Shrewsbury–Aberystwyth Sorting Carriage and vice versa, September 1930. New vehicle with net and arms, 1933.

TPO and associated vehicles 1891–1947

28ft 0¾in four-wheel sorting and luggage vans Nos 490/1/9, 500, 1891/2
Four of these clerestory vehicles were built, Nos 499/500 (1891) and Nos 490/91 (1892). Nos 491/500, Truro–Falmouth; Nos 490/99 Carmarthen–Llandyssul (Newcastle Emlyn). The last two vehicles were converted to full brakes.

46ft 6in parcel sorting vans and bag tenders, Nos 846/59–61; 1892/4
Clerestory vans generally similar in outline to contemporary passenger stock. Gangwayed, with delivery arms and nets, and gas-lit. Used on South Wales TPO (night). Nos 843/44 of 1884 and No 859 were letter sorting vans only, two in operation, one spare. Nos 846/60/61, two in operation, one spare. Not shown in 1935 list of vehicles held by the Post Office archives.

40ft 0¾in Foreign Mail vans Nos 862–5: 1892
Clerestory, gas-lit and gangwayed. Nos 864/5 fitted with nets and delivery arms by November 1894. Allocated to Plymouth–Bristol TPO (Foreign Mails) but by November 1894 Nos 864/5 were shown as allocated to the Great Western TPO. Nos 821–4/37 allocated to this service by 1905, thereafter No 862 spare for special mails on South Wales service, and No 863 usually worked with slip van No 837, slipped at Bedminster for Bristol. No 863 transferred to South Wales TPO (North Mail) in March 1917, No 864/5 on this service c1915. No 862 spare for Bristol–Exeter TPO (Day) by that date, transferred to Cardiff–Crewe TPO with Nos 864/5 by August 1916. Not shown on 1935 list of vehicles held by the Post Office archives.

48ft 0¾in Ocean Mails/Stowage Vans Nos 1062–5: 1896
The originally intended use of these vans is described on page 48. They appear to have been transferred for use as stowage vans on the Great Western TPO from early 1915. They had one central gangway one end, while that at the other end was offset. On displacement from the Great Western TPO they became non-corridor.

54ft 0¾in TPO Vans Nos 1125–8: 1903
Among the few clerestory-roofed bogie luggage and brake vans, these vehicles had offset gangways to serve as brake-ends to TPO trains. For a time, No 1128 was a spare for one of the GW TPO sorting-vans while, in later days, No 1125 was lettered '10.10 p.m. Postal Paddington–Penzance' as the GW TPO brake van. All were allocated to Old Oak Common, and scrapped by the mid-1950s, the last clerestory TPO vehicles in stock.

48ft/48ft 6¾in Sorting carriages with passenger accommodation
On some Post Office workings, combined sorting and passenger accommodation vehicles were provided by the GWR. The London and Bristol Sorting Carriage used No 2085, originally built as a 36ft vehicle, rebuilt to longer length in 1889. In November 1894, No 2085 was working on this service with another having been lengthened from 46ft 6¾in. No 2085 had originally included two passenger compartments and both vehicles were gas-lit with a lavatory, gangways at each end and nets and delivery arms. Nos 2085/2xxx were renumbered 842/5 by 1894, following the removal of their passenger accommodation. Both were in use on the service until it was withdrawn in 1917.

The Bristol and Exeter TPO (Day) was allocated

48ft brake No 2083, originally with three passenger compartments. This vehicle was built in 1894, using the underframe of an earlier vehicle of that number which had been destroyed by fire. No 2083 had nets and delivery arms, and had lost its passenger accommodation and was renumbered 839 by 1894. It was used on this working until 1917.

On the Plymouth–Bristol TPO, there were three such vehicles (one spare), Nos 2080/84/86, originally to 30ft 6in, lengthened to 48ft in 1889 (2080–1892). Originally there were three passenger compartments in each vehicle, and nets and delivery arms were fitted. They became, in order, Nos 838/40/1 by 1894, and remained at work during the First World War, probably until replaced by the 1933–built TPOs Nos 799/800.

Elliptical-roof 68ft/70ft Stock: 1904–1910

Among the very first elliptical-roof main-line stock built by the GWR were five ocean mails vans ordered in January 1904 for the prestige Plymouth–Bristol/London Ocean Mails trains. By virtue of their outline and dimensions, they rank as part of the 68ft 'Dreadnought' series vehicles described on page 59.

Four were side-corridor stowage vans, Nos 821–4, and one of these, No 823, had a guard's compartment. These were allocated to Plymouth for working the Plymouth–Bristol TPO (Foreign Mails). With the arrival of 57ft ocean mails vans in 1928, two were demoted to general use and mounted on 7ft bogies. During 1955, Nos 821/2 lost their gangways, and all four in the batch survived into the 1950s.

The other vehicle, No 837, also ordered in January 1904, was not completed until the following January and was unique in being an Ocean Mails slip van, used on the Plymouth–Bristol TPO (Foreign Mails) and slipped at Bedminster for Bristol traffic when the service was extended to Paddington. Originally built with gangways at both ends, with the usual guard's slip compartment, it was later modified with a side gangway at one end only and a lavatory was installed. It also had a wired-glass top to the roof, a feature followed in the 1905 TPO stock and, unlike Nos 821–4, No 837 had three recessed folding doors each side, as against sliding ones. The usual 'Ocean Mails special' formation was five vans, of which two were slipped at Bedminster for Bristol, the remainder continuing to London. No 837 lost its slip apparatus about 1917, but retained the windows at one end and, in the 1940s, became non-corridor.

In March 1905, a number of 70ft length by 8ft 6in width TPO vehicles were ordered, and came into service in the autumn of the same year. This was to provide more modern facilities for the Great Western TPO which had been earlier reorganised. The orders comprised five stowage vans, Nos 825–9, and three letter-mail sorting vans with four delivery arms and one net: Nos 830–2. The rest of the Great Western TPO consisted of earlier vehicles, some of which were converted to double apparatus vans. Nos 834–6 had wired-glass skylights to the roofs. In 1942 Nos 830–2 had the delivery arms removed and the net recesses sheeted over. Displaced by the 1947 Hawksworth TPOs, they were then withdrawn.

With mail traffic coming off Atlantic liners *via* Fishguard, two 70ft centre-gangway vans, Nos 874/5, with sliding doors and guards' compartments, were built in 1908. They were stationed at Old Oak Common and Fishguard respectively. In 1910, two twenty-ton capacity baggage vans were built with four sliding doors each side and mounted on twelve-wheel bogies. They were numbered 876/7 and when their purpose was ended after the First World War they became newspaper vans. Other 70ft ocean mail vans, Nos 1203–6, were built in 1910. Nos 1201/2 of this batch were stowage vans with electric lighting. All except No 1206 later became newspaper vans. None of the above formed part of the TPO fleet as such.

No 833 was an oddity – a 70ft newspaper van with outside body framing in 'Siphon' van fashion – with sliding doors and a guard's compartment. It received 7ft bogies in the late 1920s and survived into the 1940s, then going to Oxford MPD, for internal use.

46ft 6in–57ft Steel-panelled TPOs: 1927–1947

All pre-1946 TPOs were basically similar to the 1933–35 standard corridor stock but of 57ft, or less, length, 8ft 6in width and with flat body ends. The whole series were mounted on the standard 7ft bogies.

The Great Western TPO formation at Old Oak Common in 1905 behind Churchward 4-4-2 No 183. The leading vehicle is a Diagram K.9 (Lot 793) brake van (without guard's lookouts), with 70ft Diagram L.13 TPO vehicle next, then 1883-built letter-sorting van and another L.13 70-footer. The rest of the train is difficult to identify.

Collecting van with full pick-up equipment for the Great Western TPO – No 795. (Lot 1499 – Diagram L.21)

Nos 806–8 were 57ft sorting vans with guard's compartment, recessed sliding doors both sides, delivery arms and a near-side net and were completed in 1929 for the Great Western TPO. The apparatus was removed about 1956. Replaced by BR standard stock in 1959, they were transferred to the Southern Region in 1960 and painted green. In common with other South Eastern Division locomotive-hauled stock, they were fitted with electric heating in 1961–62.

In 1932, Nos 848/9, 57ft bag tenders, with nearside sliding doors, without nets and delivery arms, were built for the Paddington–Neyland working conveyed on the South Wales TPO (Night). After 1956, they ran between Bristol and Neyland.

February 1933 saw the ordering of seventeen TPO vans, of varying types, Nos 793–6 57-footers, the rest 50ft in length, except Nos 815–7 which were only 46ft 6in long. They entered service between late 1933 and early 1934 and virtually displaced all the clerestory sorting and pick-up delivery vehicles. Nos 793–5 were collecting vans, with recessed sliding doors both sides, and with full equipment for the Great Western TPO. They were reduced to stowage vans in 1953. No 796, without nets or apparatus but with a lavatory, was a spare for the Bristol–Carmarthen service at first but, later in the 1930s was the Cambrian main-line spare to No 797, at Shrewsbury.

Nos 797–800, with nets and delivery apparatus, were allocated as follows: 797 (Shrewsbury–Aberystwyth); 798 (London–Bristol day working) and 799/800 (Plymouth–Bristol TPO). The last two had electric apparatus for interior heating when standing at Bristol, and were also regarded as cover for No 798. They were used on this working until condemned in 1968.

Nos 801–3 for the Cardiff–Crewe working were sorting vans with nets and delivery apparatus, two working, one spare vehicle at Cardiff, also with lavatories and electric interior radiators.

Nos 812–4, with guard's compartment, were for the Great Western TPO and as built had neither nets nor delivery apparatus. No 814 was destroyed at Hay Lane, Swindon, in 1940, and an identical replacement vehicle was built on Lot 1666. All were fitted with delivery apparatus in November 1946.

Nos 815–7 were bag tenders, without apparatus or nets, working Paddington–Neyland and return (two vehicles in traffic). After 1956, they operated to and from Bristol only.

Late Fee posting boxes were fitted to Nos 796, 797–800, 815–7 and 848/9. Those vehicles without nets or delivery apparatus were so designed that it was possible for them to be so converted at a later date, as indeed was the case with Nos 812–4.

To replace Nos 1063–5, the 1896 Ocean Mails vans used for stowage on the Great Western TPO, 61ft 4½in passenger brake vans Nos 39, 81 and 1177 were appropriated for use as stowage vans in the Great Western TPO.

In 1945, all TPO vehicles remained in chocolate and cream livery, except Nos 81, 812/3, 1125–8/77.

Nos 793/4/5/8, 812/3/4 of the above vehicles were displaced from the Great Western TPO in 1959, as were Nos 806–8. Of these, the first four were transferred with vans Nos 39/81/1177 to the London Midland Region, for use on the 'West Coast Postal'. They were not the vehicles that were ransacked in the Great Mail Train Robbery of 1963! In fact, it was because they were being fitted with extra precautions at the time of the robbery that a less adequately protected vehicle was in the formation. Nos 812–4 were reallocated to the South Eastern Division of the Southern Region, painted green and fitted with electric heating. All the above vehicles were withdrawn by about 1972, when Nos 813/4 returned to the Western Region and were converted to Enparts vans. No 814 has been preserved.

Five post-war TPOs only were built, sorting vans Nos 843–847 of 1946/47, of standard Hawksworth outline, and turned out in post-war chocolate and cream livery. These were allocated to the Great Western TPO. Upon displacement, Nos 846/7 went to the SR, where they were repainted green and fitted with electric heating, while No 844 went to the London Midland Region and Nos 843/5 to the North Eastern Region, to cover the working between Edinburgh and York. No 843 was soon remounted on Gresley 8ft 6in bogies. The last survivor was E844W, withdrawn in 1975. In late 1948, Lot 1730 was issued, but subsequently cancelled, to cover the building of five brake vans of Hawksworth design with offset gangways, for use with TPO vans.

28–48ft Luggage and Passenger Brake Vans: 1890–1906

The majority of this category of vehicle were the three-centre roof 40ft-body bogie vans of Dean era design with 8ft 6in bogies. A few four-wheel vans, of 28–31ft length, were also built but call for little reference. The other vehicles include a batch of six 48ft 6¾in passenger brake vans and six 46ft 6¾in newspaper vans, both designs of similar outline to the 40ft vans but with wider panelling.

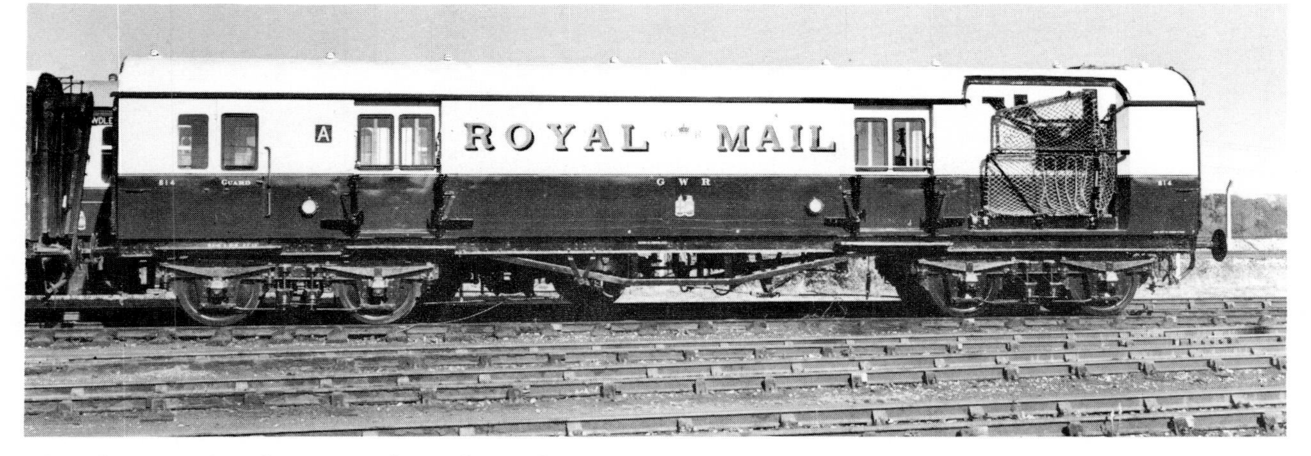

Not a GWR official photograph, but an example of the fine restoration work of the Great Western Society. This is an unusual TPO vehicle: No 814, a replacement for the original destroyed in 1940, and turned out in the same year to Lot 1666 on Diagram L.23. The collecting equipment was added in post-war days. At Didcot, September 1979.

The absence of a clerestory from the 40ft vans, and others, has surprised some people, but this feature made construction more expensive. TPO vehicles (see page 116) of this period did, however, have clerestory roofs. A number of the later batches of vans were corridor vehicles, some built with a lavatory as part of the guard's compartment. From the late 1890s gas lighting and steam heating became standard fitments for new vehicles, as later did electric communication. Final 1904–06 lots had bolster and equalised bogies in place of the hitherto standard Dean 8ft 6in type.

Scrapping began in the 1930s but quite a number survived until post-war days, including some as stores vans.

56ft 11¼in–57ft 'Toplight' Corridor Passenger Brake Vans: 1912–1925

Only forty-six 'Toplight' passenger brake vans, of 56ft 11in and 57ft lengths, were built as such, although the total was increased by fifteen with rebuilt ambulance coaches in 1924–25. Following the standard 'Toplight' corridor coach outline and construction, the various batches of the passenger brake vans differed very little, although the 57ft body vehicles had wooden body panelling with mouldings. The remainder were steel-panelled, but with the characteristic toplights below the cantrail.

Ex-ambulance rebuilds of 1924–25 were to the 56ft 11¼in and 57ft-body lengths, following their original passenger coach body dimensions with steel-panelled bodies and toplights, and were of the same appearance as the other vehicles described above.

In the 1940s a number of these passenger brake vans had gas heating installed in the guard's compartment for use when there was no steam heating available. The lower panel of the guards door was also painted bright yellow. Apart from these, no other modifications appear to have been made.

These passenger brake vans were the last of the 'Toplights' to remain in general service, the later examples lasting until 1961–62. They were among the last vehicles on the old 9ft equalised bogies, although a batch of 'Siphon Gs' on these 'American' bogies was not withdrawn until 1962–63.

Corridor Passenger/Parcels Brake Vans and Vans: 1925–1951

Among the first of the bow-ended passenger vehicles was Lot 1346, part of a series of passenger vans completed during 1925–26 and probably the first vehicles with the newly-developed 7ft bogies. Lot 1346, Nos 1169–1174, were well known to observers as they carried the large legend 'Ocean Mails' and were allocated to Plymouth, replacing the five 1904 'Dreadnought' vehicles Nos 821–4/37 (see page 117). Following wartime use as ordinary vans, Nos 1170–4 resumed Ocean Mails duties in 1949. Their external appearance, with recessed windows, followed that of the contemporary 1923–29 corridor and compartment stock. Withdrawal began in 1962.

The 1930–3 vehicles, 61ft 4½in over the bow ends and 9ft wide, followed the 'bulging side' profile of the 1929–33 standard corridor and compartment stock. To Lots 1413/62/81, they were of 15 tons capacity and mounted on 7ft wheelbase bogies. Number series 3–57, Lot 1462, comprised passenger brake vans with a guard's compartment, denoted by the number series. The vans, Nos 1175–84, were the first with slam locks to all doors. Of this series, three, already mentioned, were transferred to the LMR and included in each of the 'West Coast Postal' sets. These bogie brakes survived to c1966/7.

The passenger brake vans constructed from 1934 to 1936, of which there were sixty to Diagram K.41 and 57ft in length, had a cheaper and heavier design of 9ft bogie than the pressed-steel type used for contemporary passenger coaches. This was of single bolster design with coil springs. The general outline, quarterlights and high waistline followed the 1933–36 corridor and compartment stock. One batch, Nos 181–200 of 1935, had a corridor partition the length of the vehicle which protected the contents and also provided a gangway for passengers when the van was marshalled in the middle of a passenger train.

Standard 40ft body Dean period passenger brake van No 231. (Lot 1075 – Diagram K.15 as built) converted to a sleet-cutter van – note fittings on the bogie. Westinghouse brake fitted.

The guard's compartment of one of the 1897 Royal Train brake vans, No 1070. (Lot 838 – Diagram K.12) Note the electric lights and cooking equipment.

The Diagram K.41 vehicles were withdrawn by 1974.

Those built from 1937–40 were to the same profile and quarterlights of the 1938 corridor stock, 57ft long and only 8ft 11in in width. All were to Diagram K.42. Of these, Nos 121–30 were the first of their type to have food heaters in the guard's compartment. Nos 61–70, to Diagram K.44, had a full-length internal partition and, on the corridor side, two large windows flanking the door opposite the guard's compartment. These vehicles were finished from an order placed in 1939 for corridor composites, and so were 59ft 10in long and 8ft 11in wide.

At the end of 1973, only seven of the vans to Diagrams K.42/44 had been withdrawn, and by this time all carried the plain BR blue livery. Some had their gangway connections removed. By late 1977, only half a dozen remained in traffic, and a reduction in the non-passenger vehicle fleet during 1978 saw their extinction by the end of that year.

Forty-five passenger brake vans, to 64ft body length and of the characteristic Hawksworth outline, were built from 1949–51, to Diagrams K.45/46. Withdrawals started in the early 1970s, by which time a number had lost their gangway connections. All were taken out of traffic by 1979.

In common with most GWR passenger brake vans, a number of the above vehicles of all types were allocated to particular workings and carried prominent designations such as 'To work 8.55 p.m. Paddington–Cardiff, 1.48 p.m. Cardiff–Paddington'; 'Paddington and York LNE' and 'Swansea and Nottingham'.

Also included in the number series for passenger brake vans, Ocean Mails vans, TPOs and the like were the three lots of bullion vans, to Lots 996, 1139 and 1220. These were built for the conveyance of gold bullion to/from the United States via Plymouth. The resulting solution in rolling stock design terms was intriguing: to carry 12 or 16 tons (the latter, No 878 of Lot 1220) of high-value material in security produced a vehicle 36ft long, 8ft wide, between 6ft $5\frac{13}{16}$in and 6ft $11\frac{7}{8}$in high (the batches varied) with double doors on one side only; (Lot 996 single doors). Heavy-duty equalised beam bogies were fitted. All caried passenger stock livery and were withdrawn during the 1950s, the last, No 878, going in 1959.

Earlier six-wheeled vehicles were built in 1893, No 799 (Lot 665), 26ft $8\frac{1}{2}$in by 7ft 11in wide, and two Lots on the same diagram, Nos 797/798 (Lot 842, built 1897) and Nos 795/6 (Lot 866, built 1898). These had three-centre roofs.

10
MISCELLANY

In a work of this nature, having covered the general history of rolling stock, in necessarily general, and one hopes readable fashion, it is inevitable that there are a number of specialised subjects, demanding greater detail, which it seems sensible to gather together in a miscellaneous chapter. What follows appears to be well worth recording in order to satisfy the specialist, and to give as much detail on the past and subsequent identities of some of the conversions and alterations that so characterised the history of GWR passenger rolling stock.

Camping Coaches

Four, six and eight-wheeled vehicles were converted to act as camping coaches from 1931–58, the series 9935–99 being complete by 1939. Post-war conversions started in 1951/52; after Nos 9900–35, later vehicles had progressively lower numbers. Several camping coaches later passed to service use.

Running No as converted	Converted	Former type (Diag No/*Lot No*/Running No)	Condemned
Pre-war conversions			
9978/9	1935	*E17/*411*/6861/2	
9980	1935	*E28/*470*/7043	
9981–5	1931–5	*U27/*286*/6196, 6218/23/44/5	From 1/50
9986–91	1931–5	*U19/*302*/6787/91/4/8/9, 6803	From 1/50
9992	11/1931	*U28/*287*/6874	1/54
9993	11/1931	*U20/*327*/6889	
9994	11/1931	*U21/*330*/6907	11/53
9995–7	11 & 12/1931	*U21/*341*/6914/23/31	From 8/44
9998	1931–5	U6/*818*/7885	
9999	1931–5	*E23/*461*/6729	
9935/6	c1935–9	T35/*731*/2634/5	From 11/48
9937–9	,,	T35/*738*/2657/60/3	
9940	,,	T49/*582*/416	
9941	,,	T36/*978*/957	
9942	,,	T33/*589*/912	
9943	,,	T49/*582*/475	
9944	,,	T50/*582*/411	6/51
9945	,,	T33/*589*/913	
9946	,,	T36/*978*/951	
9947/8	,,	T37/*978*/949/56	
9949	,,	T32/*589*/935	
9950–4	,,	E33/*591*/7367–70/2	
9955–9	,,	E32/*557*/7390/5/7/8, 7400 (9959 was E33)	
9960/1	,,	E33/*610*/7402/3	
9962–5	11/34–1/35	*U29/*370*/6820/2/3/7	From 3/52
9966–9	1/35	*E17/*411*/6850/3/6/8 (9966 was E18)	
9970/1	1/35	*E26/*470*/7044/6 (9971 was E27)	
9972–6	1/35	E27/*544*/7050/2/4/5/8 (9976 was E28)	From 9/49
9977	2/35	*U29/*370*/6818	
		*Built before 1890.	
Post-war conversions			
9900/5	1952	A7 (*1001*/8315 (*1007*/8321	
9901/2/4/6/7/8		E72 (*1030*/7492 (*1040*/7508 (*994*/7484 (*987*/7472 (*987*/7474 (*1040*/7502	
9903	1952	E70/*986*/7463	
9909	,,	C17/*1020*/3243	
9910	,,	C79/*932*/338	Former first-class No 8291
9911/3/5/8/9) 9930–4)	,, ,,	C30/*1167*/2424/2/5/6/7 2430/5/29/32/3	
9912/4/6/7) 9920–9)		C31/*1286*/3632 *1312*/2463 *1286*/3630 *1311*/2457	

(continued on page 122)

Running No as converted	Converted	Former type (Diag No/*Lot No*/Running No)	Condemned
		1311/2458/60/59/62	
		1312/2468	
		1311/2456/61	
		1312/2476	
		1286/3629/34	
9885/6	1957	C35/*1256*/3963	
9888/97		*1295*/3665	
		1313/3668	
		1256/3969	
9887/90/1	1957	C31/*1289*/3639	
9894/8		*1194*/2522 (identity in doubt)	
		1292/3655	
		1172/2448	
		1289/3642	
9889/92/3/5/6/9	1957	C32/*1234*/2578	
		1312/2454	
		1269/3896	
		1234/2576	
		1246/3933	
		1246/3914	
9875/6/81	1958	C35/*1256*/3950	
		1256/3951	
		1256/3980	
9877	1958	C31/*1289*/3637	
9878–80/2–4	1958	C32/*1269*/3888	
		1234/2573	
		1286/3631	
		1269/3885	
		1246/3917	
		1269/3898	

Nos 9879–86 were the first to be outshopped (on conversion) in WR chocolate and cream livery. Other WR camping coaches were similarly painted when shopped at a later date. 9869–74, converted at Swindon in 1962, were former Pullman cars. Kitchen cars *Alicante* (Schedule No 47) and *Mimosa* (Schedule No 50) became 9874/69; parlour car No 97 (ex-*Calais*), No 9870; brakes *Aurora, Flora* and *Juno* (Schedule Nos 153–5), Nos 9873/1/2. In 1983, all remained at their original site, Marazion, under the control of the British Railways Staff Association.

Engineers' Saloons

Nearly all the saloons used by the GWR Engineer's Department were converted from vehicles formerly in revenue earning stock. Before 1948, the notable exception was the Taunton Engineer's Department saloon, No 6479, converted on Lot 1170 (Diagram Q.1), using the underframe of ex-Manchester & Milford composite No 149 provided with a new 43ft 6in by 8ft 0¾in low-roof body. Its accommodation included two saloons (at each end), a lavatory and a guard's compartment. This was latterly the Gloucester saloon and is now on the Dart Valley Railway.

In 1948, purpose-built engineer's saloons were constructed, as described on page 114.

At the time of Grouping, most Divisions were allocated small, four-wheeled ex-Bristol & Exeter Railway vehicles, built in 1875 as six-wheeled composites. The centre pair of wheels was removed in the late 1880s, but conversion for engineers' use did not take place until the 1900s. These box-like vehicles had verandahs at each end. The last to survive was the Wolverhampton saloon, condemned by 1955 and then still carrying its livery of the 1920s. Two conversions of third-class GWR saloons on Diagram G.20 later took place, No 9315 (Lot 750) becoming engineer's saloon No 80975 in March 1939, and No 9340 (Lot 774) to No 80943 in 1936. Both were replaced by purpose-built vehicles in 1948.

From the 1930s, several bogie clerestory saloons, previously family or special vehicles, were appropriated for service use. One notable example was the former Paddington-based 'special saloon' No 9044, built in 1881. This was converted for service use in August 1936, displacing a B & ER vehicle, and by nationalisation was at Oswestry as No 80973. It moved to Shrewsbury in the 1960s, was withdrawn in 1964 and preserved.

Family saloon No 247 (Lot 628), later No 9043, built 1892, was converted to become the Worcester saloon as No 80970, but was seemingly displaced by the 1948 vehicle of that number.

The GWR directors' saloon No 249 (Lot 745, built 1894), latterly No 9045, was converted to become the Plymouth saloon in October 1940 (replacing a B & ER vehicle) and was numbered 80978. It was displaced by a new conversion in 1963, and was subsequently preserved.

The number 80971 was taken by family brake saloon No 231 (Lot 804, built 1896), latterly No 9035, which was converted in November 1941 and based at Bristol. Withdrawn from Newport, this was the last ex-GWR clerestory inspection saloon in BR stock by 1966, and was also acquired for preservation.

The remaining family saloons in capital stock were withdrawn by the late 1940s, but a late survivor was No 9029 (Lot 950), used as the Paddington summer peak control office in the late 1940s, permanently requisitioned for office accommodation in April 1951 and scrapped c1957.

Conversions to Auto-trailers

CONVERSION OF RAIL-MOTORS TO TRAILERS: 1915–1936

Conversion Lot No.	Trailer Diagram	Length	Rail-Motor Nos	Seating after Conversion	New trailer Nos	Date
—	Z	59′ 6″	*3–8	58	*99–104	1915
—	A6	57′ 0¾″	†1/2	54	†105/106	1917
—	A7	59′ 6″	*9–14	58	*107–112	1916–9
—	A9	59′ 6″	*17–28	62	*113–124	1919/20
—	A10	59′ 6″	†29/32/1/3–6	60/67	†125/8–33	1920–3
—	A13	70′ 0″	†59	78	C*126	1920
—	A14	70′ 0″	†60	74	C*127	1920
—	A15	70′ 0″	*46/47	80	*136/7	1923
—	A17	70′ 0″	*43	76A	C*134	1923
—	A18	70′ 0″	*44	78B	C*135	1923
—	A19	70′ 0″	*50–52	80	*138–40	1923
1511/	A23	70′ 0″	†38–40	76	†146/97/8	1927–33
—	A24	59′ 6″	*41	66	*147	1927
—	A25	70′ 0″	*45	82	C*148	1927
—	A26	70′ 0″	†57	77	*149	1927
—	,,		†85/7/9/90	(3 saloons) ,,	*154–7	1927
—	,,		†99	,,	*158	1927
1432/	,,		†54/6/84/95/4/62	,,	C*181–6	1930
1511/	,,		†53/8/86	,,	*199/200/6	1933
1542/	,,		†91/3/6/7/8	,,	*210/2–5	1934/35
—	A29	70′ 0″	†61/3/7/8	,,	†150–3	1927
1511/	,,		†69	,,	†201	1933
1545/	,,		†64/6/72	79	†216–8	1935
1511/	A31	59′ 6″	†73/4/82/3	81	†202–5	1933
1521/			†75/8/9	,,	†207–9	1934
1542/			†81	79	†211	1934
1545/			†76	,,	†219	1935

Rail-motors: Nos 15/6 (Kerr Stuart) sold out of service in 1920 and 1927.
Nos 30/7/55/65/70/1/7/80/8/92 withdrawn as rail-motors in 1935.
No 42 sold out of service to Port of London Authority in 1920.
Nos 48/9 destroyed by fire in 1916/20, respectively.

NB: Auto-trailers Nos 141 (ex-Cambrian Rlys), 142–5 (ex-Cardiff Rlys).

Notes: *Suburban type. †Branch-type. Columns 3/5.
A – altered with gangway at driver's end. Column 4.
B – altered with gangway inner end. Column 4.
C – fitted with electric lighting when converted. Column 5.

A rail-motor conversion to an auto-trailer – W124, formerly rail motor No 28, having been converted on Diagram A.9 in 1920. At Caerphilly Works, May 1952.

Auto-trailer No W197W was originally rail-motor No 39, converted in 1934 to an auto-trailer, and running on 7ft wheelbase bogies. Diagram A23. At Gloucester, March 1956.

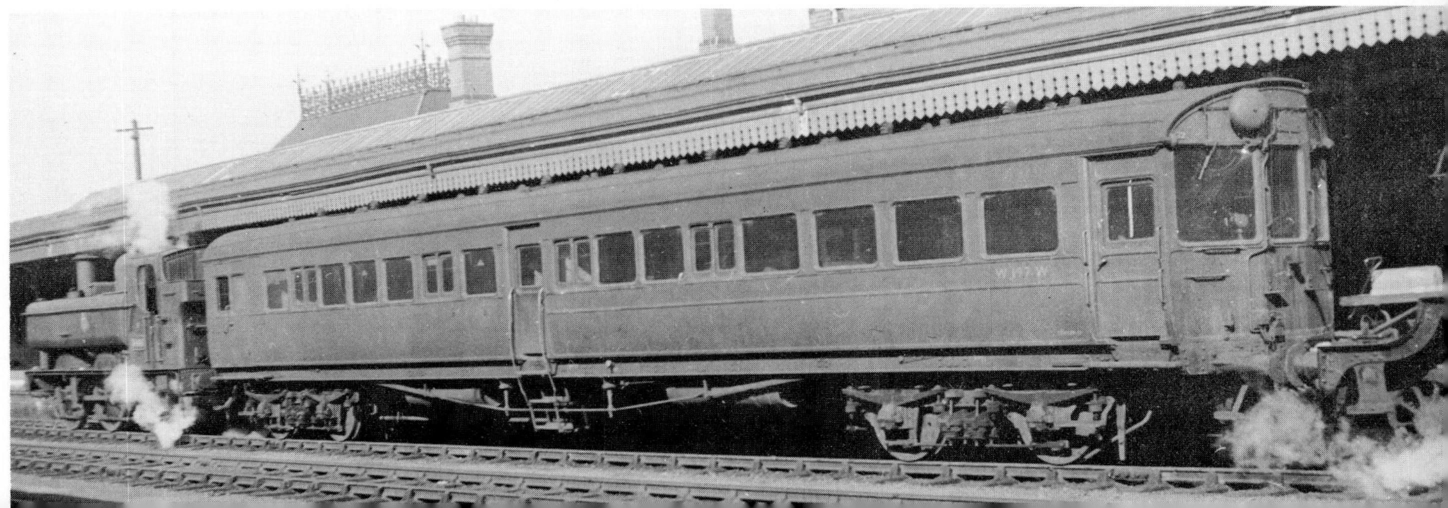

CONVERSION OF CLERESTORY THIRDS TO AUTO-TRAILERS

Orig Diagram	Diagram as converted	Lot No	Original Running Nos	Running Nos as converted
C8	G	692	2833	14
C8	G1	692	2841	15
C8	H	692	2839	16
C8	H	692	2842	17
C17	M	905	3148	18
C17	M1	905	3152	35

Vehicles converted July–September 1905.
No 18 was a composite, converted to all-third in 1917.

CONVERSION OF THIRDS FOR AUTO-WORKING FROM 1953 Diagrams A41, A42 (Nos 455/8 only)

Diagram	Lot No	Running Nos
C66	1492	5473/81
	1506	5461/6
	1524	4282
	1551	4030/43
C75	1569	1415/7
	1598	1678/90/2/5/9/1707/9
	1631	455/8

Vehicles converted 1953/54. Fitted with through auto control gear for use as intermediate coaches on auto-trains. Existing running numbers retained.

CONVERSION OF BRAKE THIRDS TO AUTO-TRAILERS FROM 1955 Diagram A44 (see page 91)

New Nos	Original Nos	Lot Nos	Converted
245	5491	1493	4/55
246	5495	1493	4/55
247	4015	1552	6/55
248	4016	1552	6/55
249	4005	1552	6/55
250	4019	1552	8/55
251	4343	1525	9/55
252	5871	1507	8/55
253	4358	1525	8/55
254	5875	1507	10/55
255	4351	1525	10/55
256	4345	1525	10/55

57ft–70ft Corridor Stock Damaged by Enemy Action or Fire and Rebuilt: 1942–1951

One of the more intriguing categories of GWR coaches were these hybrids produced by building new bodies for vehicles damaged during the war, tailored to fit the original underframe and to follow the original internal layout. In most cases the result was a coach which, from the compartment side, resembled a 1933–35 standard corridor coach, although its original identity was revealed by the running number and bogies. The interior, too, of the coaches rebuilt during the war followed 1938 standard practice or, for those damaged by fire in 1949, the Hawksworth style of décor. Of previous rebuilds, there had been the case of the 1911 paintshop fire at Swindon where mostly new vehicles had been destroyed and so the Lots were re-ordered. There was also the instance of 'Dreadnought' brake third No 3476 which had been burnt in 1926 and given a new contemporary body of all-steel construction.

According to information from Swindon, it was considered practicable to renew one damaged side

Auto-trailer No W251W, one of the 1955 conversions. This was originally brake third No 4343 on Diagram D.117, but is non-standard as the body was rebuilt probably during the war to the later, low-waisted pattern.

57ft–70ft CORRIDOR STOCK DAMAGED BY ENEMY ACTION OR FIRE AND REBUILT: 1942–1951

Type	Running No	Original body (length x width)	Replacement body (length x width)	Weight (tons)	Original Building Date	Rebuilding Date	Remarks
56ft/57ft 'Toplight' stock							
Composite	6942	56ft 11¼in x 8ft 11¼in	56ft 6in x 8ft 11in	29	1914	1942	
	7573	57ft x 9ft	56ft 6in x 8ft 11in	30	1912	1943	
	7728	56ft x 9ft	55ft 6in x 8ft 11in	30	1908	1943	
Third	2431	56ft x 9ft	56ft 6in x 8ft 11in	29	1910	1943	Frame lengthened 1ft (see text)
	2445	57ft x 9ft	56ft 6in x 8ft 11in	29	1911	1942	
	2452	57ft x 9ft	56ft 6in x 8ft 11in	29	1922*	1942	
	4524	57ft x 9ft	57ft x 9ft†	29	1923*	1942/49	†Turn-under ends. Burnt 1949 and rebuilt again
	4541	57ft x 9ft	56ft 6in x 8ft 11in	29	1924*	1943	*Ex-ambulance coaches repurchased after 1918
Brake third	2359	56ft x 9ft	55ft 6in x 8ft 11in	29	1911	1943	*Ex-ambulance
	3509	57ft x 9ft	57ft x 9ft†	28	1922*	1942	coach repurchased
	3537	57ft x 9ft	56ft 6in x 8ft 11in	28	1909	1942	after 1918
	3573	57ft x 9ft	56ft 6in x 8ft 11in	28	1912	1942	†Turn-under ends
70ft 'Toplight' stock							
Restaurant car	9534	70ft x 9ft	70ft x 9ft	47	1907	1944	
First	8191	70ft x 9ft	69ft 6in x 8ft 11in	33	1910	1943	
Brake third	3576	70ft x 9ft	69ft 6in x 8ft 11in	35	1912	1942	
	3578	70ft x 9ft	69ft 6in x 8ft 11in	35	1912	1942	
57ft 1923–9 standard stock (58ft 4½in bow-ends)							
Composite	6078	57ft 4½in x 9ft	)	30	1928	1943	
	6522	58ft 4½in x 9ft	) same as original	30	1925	1943	
	7622	57ft x 9ft	)	30	1923	1943	
Brake composite	7980	57ft x 9ft	same as original	30	1923	1942	
Third	4785	58ft 4½in x 9ft	)	31	1926	1942	Original eight corridor side doors retained
	4857	58ft 4½in x 9ft	) same as original	31	1926	1942	Four doors on
	4859	58ft 4½in x 9ft	)	31	1926	1942	corridor side
	4863	58ft 4½in x 9ft	)	31	1926	1949	Fire damage. Four doors on corridor side
Third	5015	58ft 4½in x 9ft	same as original	31	1928	1949	Fire damage. Four doors on corridor side
Brake third	4935	58ft 4½in x 9ft	) same as original	29	1927	1942	Original number of
	5103	58ft 4½in x 9ft	)	30	1928	1943	doors on corridor side
60ft 1929–33 standard stock							
Third	5397	61ft 4½in x 9ft 3in	same as original	31	1932	1942	Retained eight doors on corridor side
Third	5428	61ft 4½in x 9ft 3in	same as original	31	1932	1951	Fire damage 1949. Four doors on corridor.
57ft 1933–35 standard stock							
Third	5837	57ft x 9ft	) same as original	30½	1935	1942	
	5937	57ft x 9ft	)	30½	1935	1951	Fire damage Poole 11/51
Nos 5813/5901/72 rebuilt identical to original design 1941/1941/1951							
60ft 1936/7 standard stock							
Composite	6859	60ft 11¼in x 9ft	) same as original	32	1936	1942	5 corridor side doors
Third	4319	60ft 11¼in x 9ft	)	31½	1936	1942	4 corridor side doors
60ft 1937–40 standard stock							
Third	1133	60ft 11¼in x 8ft 11¼in	) Frames only) used for	—	1938	1945	Saloon No 9006 1133 condemned 7/42
Brake third	1598	60ft 11¼in x 9ft	) VIP saloons	—	1937	1945	No 9007 1598 condemned 1945

A case of changed identity. W4863W seen here was a standard bow-ended corridor third (Lot 1372 – Diagram C.54), but after fire damage in 1949 it received a new body with a low waistline and only four doors on the corridor side. The compartment side is illustrated. Ahead of 4863 is a Diagram K.41 passenger brake van.

of a coach with new steel-panelling, while leaving the undamaged side framing almost as it was. However, there are no known cases of an 'unbalanced' coach such as this, and generally the other side would also be patched up. It should also be mentioned that a number of coaches were modernised, following more superficial damage, with new steel panelling and new interiors, but sufficient details are not available. Incidentally, a number of wood-panelled coaches were given partial face-lifts in the post-war period with steel panels covering up wooden mouldings and toplights: the 'Dreadnoughts' were particularly susceptible to this treatment.

Former 56ft 11¼in/57ft-body 'Toplights'
Twelve of these coaches were given new bodies at Swindon in 1942–43 although, no doubt, damaged at different times. The replacement bodies followed contemporary standard practice in the roof outline and construction, ends, gangways and interior, but those fitted to brake third No 3509 and third No 4524 had turn-under-ends. These last two bodies were 57ft over the ends but the others were given flat-ended bodies of 55ft 6in or 56ft 6in length and generally 8ft 11in width, to fit the frames. All were low-waisted, like some Lots of the 1936 standard corridor stock, with the droplights extending to the position of where the bottom of toplights might have been. Third No 2431, a 56ft-body coach built in 1910, was the subject of an interesting mistake. The Swindon Works staff were under the impression that the coach was No 2451, a *57ft* example, and the replacement body was built accordingly. When the error was realised, the frame of No 2431 was lengthened by a foot to take the new 56ft 6in body so that a further part of its identity was changed! It retained its equalised 9ft bogies and was probably the last wartime rebuild in service, lasting as it did until October 1961. The remainder had been withdrawn from 1955 onwards.

Incidentally, No 4524, rebuilt in 1942, was unlucky enough to be damaged by fire in 1949 and its bodywork was restored to the same appearance as the wartime rebuilding.

Former 70ft-body 'Toplights'
Only four coaches, including restaurant car No 9534, were damaged badly enough to have wartime replacement bodies, of 69ft 6in length and, except in the case of No 9534, 8ft 11in width. Nos 3576 and 8191 had the corridor sides renewed with the large windows to the same depth as the 1951 rebuilds of 1933–35 standard stock. All were withdrawn in 1959.

Former Bow-ended 1923–33
Standard Corridor Stock
In the same way as mentioned for the damaged 'Toplight' stock, some bow-ended 58ft 4½in standard coaches received low-waist 'modernised' bodies, whether following wartime destruction, or post-war fire damage. In most cases the corridor side as renewed had four doors only in place of the original eight, and with the same window arrangement as the 1933–35 57ft standard corridor coaches. It is interesting that the original C-design commode handles were retained in some of the rebuilds. Nearly all these renewed vehicles were withdrawn before the rest of the batch to which they belonged, but one of the brake thirds, No 4935, survived in departmental use at Cheltenham Malvern Road up to 1964.

Only two 60ft-plus bow-ended coaches come under notice. Third, No 5428, had been damaged by fire in 1949 and was rebuilt with a low-waist and four doors per corridor-side body in 1951. All these rebuilds were withdrawn between 1959 and 1962.

Former 57ft 1933–35
Standard Corridor Stock
It has been mentioned that the compartment-side of the rebuilt coaches of 'Toplight' and bow-ended types resembled the 1933–35 corridor stock. Two 1933–35 stock thirds, Nos 5837 and 5937, were damaged during the war, and by fire in 1951, respectively. On rebuilding, they were given low-waist bodies, but otherwise the same in layout as their originals. The interior of No 5937 was modernised with cream Holoplast panelling and fitments to the same style as the Hawksworth corridor stock. Both Nos 5837 and 5937 were withdrawn in 1962.

Other Renewed Corridor Stock
Although one or two 1936–40 corridor coaches were destroyed by enemy action and the complete vehicle written off, only two had bodywork dam-

aged enough to warrant substantial rebuilding. A 1936 composite had the corridor-side altered with five doors, previously having end doors only, and a 1936 third had the corridor-side renewed to the 1938 arrangement with four doors. Two 1938 standard corridors had their bodywork completely destroyed and the frames were used for the VIP saloons Nos 9006/7 of 1945 (see page 103).

Accident casualties

The GWR and WR's excellent safety record meant that there were few instances of coaches totally destroyed in accidents involving trains. Certainly, the accidents at Shrivenham in 1936 and at Norton Fitzwarren resulted in vehicles being written off: in the first case, 70ft 'Toplight' No 4000, and Ocean Mails van No 1203 were involved, in the latter case the unique Diagram C.55 third No 4377. The most destructive recent accident in terms of rolling stock, and one in which 11 passengers lost their lives, occurred at Milton, west of Didcot, on 20 November 1955 when a Treherbert–Paddington excursion train derailed and the three leading coaches with the locomotive went down the embankment. Four vehicles were demolished, or heavily damaged; bow-ended thirds, Nos 4866 and 5221; 57ft third No 5907 and Hawksworth third No 919. All were written-off:

Additional Notes on Restaurant Cars

Ten cars were included in a programme during 1936 in which the exteriors were repanelled above the waists – the saloon section only – and large bodyside windows with sliding (Airstream) ventilators fitted. Settees (bench-type seats) replaced individual chairs. The cars concerned were Nos 9527/37/8/41–44/51–3. Between 1936–38, the series Nos 9522–8/30–55 was modified, although not all seemed to have received new windows. From 1939–41, Nos 9505/7/8–15 were renovated and equipped with new windows with Airstream ventilators. Nos 9556–61 were reconditioned in 1938–42. Airstream or fixed vane ventilators were fitted from 1936–47 to vehicles Nos 9562–94/6–610/21/4/6/9/31–42, which were also modernised in this period.

From the 1936 period onwards, a number of restaurant cars were fitted with six-wheeled bogies to improve riding. The official dates of conversion are:

> 1936: 9556; 1938: 9533/43; 12/38: 9526, 9648/50; 1/39: 9527; 2/39: 9651; 3/39: 9572/3; 4/39: 9532/74; 6/39: 9647; 8/39: 9505; 10/39: 9596; 6/40: 9511; 8/40: 9508; 9/40: 9515/29; 10/41: 9507; 6/46: 9530/1/8; 8/46: 9534; 9/46: 9537; 6/47: 9528/97; 10/47: 9525. Nos 9522–24 fitted with 12-wheel bogies in 1938–47 period.

Incidentally, sleeping cars fitted with six-wheeled bogies, formerly eight-wheel vehicles, were No 9090 (converted 5/39), 9091 (converted 9/39).

In 1945, the GWR announced that a programme for renovating the interiors of restaurant cars was to be undertaken, and that the consultant designer and supplier of materials would be Hampton & Sons. The majority of catering vehicles were stored at some time during the Second World War, and for the modernisation programme the restaurant cars were stripped internally at Swindon Works before reconditioning by Hampton & Sons. The original specification was much more thorough and adventurous than the modified versions generally adopted in practice. The first four vehicles were refurbished by the end of 1945, and the *Great Western Railway Magazine* (by then nationalised!) of January 1948 reported the programme as involving 90 catering vehicles, of which 44 'are now completed'. Hampton was also responsible for the redecoration of sleeping cars: No 9065/6 (circa 1947), 9079 (1948) and 9087 (1949).

The list of Hampton & Sons' programme is not recorded, but Swindon records and the late R. P.

There is a double purpose in including this photograph. This was restaurant car No 9527, modernised in the late 1930s and given six-wheel bogies in January 1939. It is seen at Swindon stock shed c1964, in internal use and redesignated 079128.

Camping coach No W9906W in WR chocolate and cream livery at Luxulyan, July 1960. This was formerly corridor composite No 7472, Lot 987 – Diagram E.72.

Walford's notes give the following: 1945: 9671/2 (see page 102); 12/45: 9674/5; 1/46: 9605/6; 2/46: 9603/4; 3/46: 9571/2; 4/46: 9573/4; 5/46: 9576/7; 8/46: 9570/5; 10/46: 9601/2; 11/46: 9568/9; 12/46: 9561; 1/47: 9559/60; 2/47: 9557/8; 3/47: 9585/91; –/47: 9556. What R. P. Walford termed the 'Mk 2' Hampton scheme (see page 97) was, he recorded, applied to Nos 9635–8/40/2 and most other cars, and the 'Mk 3' type to Nos 9611–30. This was done at Swindon from 1948–52. Hampton also dealt with Nos 9553/63/4/6/7, 9607–10/43/4/73 and possibly others.

For the June 1956 summer timetable, chocolate and cream livery, in what is referred to in this book as the WR variety, was introduced on some Western Region named trains. The sets were made up of BR Mk I stock, with former GWR catering vehicles and, where relevant, slip coaches. The first ex-GWR coaches involved were restaurant cars Nos 9574/6 (for the 'Torbay Express' – both sets), 'pairs' Nos 9618/9/23/5 (for both sets used on the 'Cornish Riviera Limited' which regained its former name) and buffet car No 9677 for the 'Bristolian'. Three slip coaches (Lot 1597) were repainted for use on the 'Cornish Riviera Limited'. Until c1959, further catering vehicles were repainted and the full list is thought to have covered Nos 9524/50/3/7/60/3/71/4/5/6/86/7, 9614/5/7/8/9/21/2/3/4/5/7/63/67/72/3/7/8. In addition, there were the slip coaches Nos 7374–6, 'Super Saloons' (all at some time), 1940-built Saloons Nos 9001/2 and various specialised vehicles not in revenue earning traffic.

Service vehicles

The term 'service vehicle' covers all rolling stock provided for the maintenance of the railway and its associated works. Such vehicles are not in revenue earning stock and are usually numbered in a series of their own. Former carriage and passenger van stock have been used for these purposes almost since railways began and the tasks they fulfil rank from the most exalted to the lowliest. However, there have been cases of coaching stock being built new for some purposes – the Divisional Engineer's inspection saloons on Lot 1701 being one example already quoted – while in 1961 a buffet car (No 9580, Diag H.33, Lot 1349) was converted for the same purpose but was the sole example. Even the last Western Region dynamometer car, DW 150192 built in 1961 to replace the famous No 7, was a converted Diagram C.82 Hawksworth corridor coach although its predecessor had been built new for the purpose.

Certain types of vehicle tended to be employed more often than others, the favourite being those with a guard's compartment, thereby having a hand-brake already fitted. However, this was by no means universal and a large number of former GWR thirds and composites found their way into the 'permanent' service lists to perform a variety of tasks, usually receiving a hand-brake. Some of these were completely stripped internally, others remained almost complete. The scale of internal alterations depended upon their intended use, of course, but compartments were normally only left intact for use as bedrooms or drying-rooms.

The lifespan of a coach converted for service use was usually about ten years, but there have been cases where vehicles have been retained for longer than this. There has been one example which lasted for no less than 47 years – 17 years longer than its time in capital stock! At the other end of the scale, some vehicles were practically unaltered after being taken from traffic and lasted only a matter of months, usually branded 'For temporary use of the . . . Department'. This was usually because the job for which they were appropriated was for a limited period, or they were due to be replaced by a 'purpose-built' conversion. Even here, the rule could be broken as one of these temporary users became the oldest ex-Great Western coach on BR when it was finally condemned (and then preserved) after 23 years' 'temporary' use! This was composite No 7545 (Lot 1138), 'borrowed' by the S & T Dept in Cornwall in 1957 as No 079076 and finally offered for sale at Carmarthen in 1980. Another remarkable example was 57ft 'Toplight' brake third No W2368W (Lot 1195) which in GWR post-war chocolate and cream livery was 'temporarily' appropriated by the Engineer's Department at some time in the 1950s and was reported at Wellington, on the Settle & Carlisle, and at Northwood, Middlesex, in the 1959/60 period.

Retention for service use has meant that types of vehicle extinct in normal stock have attracted interest from enthusiasts, and it has been possible for many to be preserved because of their extended lives. Open vehicles such as diners or auto-trailers have made excellent offices, and a number were converted for this purpose. Saloons were also used, but tended to go to depots as mess rooms, possibly because most were condemned at the time depots were being rebuilt. Passenger full brakes were very popular at one time and have been employed as stores vans, tunnel inspection units and, even in one case, as a diesel generator van. Those condemned since nationalisation saw little service use, apart from odd examples mostly taken direct from traffic. A couple of TPO vehicles were unusually retained as Enparts vans by Swindon in the early 1970s, and one of these, No 814, has been preserved.

The final diagrams of passenger brake vans have been a little luckier as no less than six are in use at the time of writing although three are temporary users. For some reason, none of the excursion stock built from 1935 was used, which is surprising as its open layout was well-suited for service purposes. An unexpected vehicle to be appropriated for a short time was one of the 'Centenary' composite brakes on Lot 1539. This acted as a crane riding van at Laira during late 1963 until the crane was required at a location where the Red Triangle restriction coach was forbidden!

The example of the 'Centenary' brake composite is a good illustration as to why the longer and wider types of GWR coaches saw little favour for service purposes, with certain exceptions. They were ideal for static use and ten 'Dreadnought' and 'Concertina' thirds were converted as sleeping accommodation at three sites during 1950. Only two 70ft coaches are known to have been used for 'mobile' purposes, one being with the Taunton Engineering Department as a temporary user for five years (No 4609, Lot 1321) and the other surprisingly converted at Swindon and put into permanent stock as an S & T staff and tool van in the London area. This also lasted for about the same time, but one wonders whether its conversion was intended.

The GWR numbered its locomotive department mobile service stock in the Chief Mechanical Engineer's list, but vehicles in use by the permanent way and signals and telegraph departments appeared in the wagon list for no apparent reason, usually in specified blocks of numbers. Like all things Great Western, there were exceptions to this rule!

After nationalisation, the system remained in use with new conversions often taking their predecessors' numbers, this being a time-honoured practice on the GWR. In 1950, a new series was started for temporary user stock which had received little or no conversion work. These were allotted numbers from 079000 upwards as part of a national scheme for these vehicles. Five years later, a new service list was started, commencing at the top of the GWR wagon list at 150000. This continued in use until 1968, the Hawksworth brakes DW150390–407 being the last, and then all service vehicle conversions were numbered as part of the BR series from DB 975000 upwards. This included both mobile and static stock, irrespective of purpose. A few former GWR vehicles were included in this series. In 1983, it was expected that the remaining ex-GWR vehicles in service use would be renumbered in the higher ranges of the DB975xxx series.

Westinghouse-Fitted 'Alive' Train for SHAEF
The GWR adapted several vehicles from 1942 onwards to serve as a mobile headquarters in Britain for the use of Winston Churchill, Generals Eisenhower and Montgomery and their staffs. After the landings in France, the train was fitted with Westinghouse brakes and the formation implemented to serve the Supreme Headquarters Allied Expeditionary Force. Two sleepers were re-fitted internally to provide larger than normal first-class sleeping compartments, with additional features such as shower-baths. Of the vehicles given in the 1945 formation below, the exact formation cannot be verified. Despite researches at the Imperial War Museum and elsewhere, no photographs depicting full-views of the train or individual coaches can be traced, and no doubt restrictions on such views were part of security measures.

c.1945 Formation

'Monster' vans Nos 483/5. Returned to ordinary traffic 7/46.

Generator van No 2†.

Brake third No 601 or 1647, Diagram D.127, both to 'Alive' train 1944. 1647 to ordinary traffic 5/46.

Armour-plated third No 574, Diagram C.77. Returned to ordinary traffic 6/46.

Restaurant car No 9673, Diagram H.57, to ordinary traffic 11/46.

*Conference saloon No 9364, 1901/21 design.

Sleeping-car No 9079, 1929/35 design. Returned from 'Alive' train 9/47.

Sleeping-car No 9093, 1921 design. Returned from 'Alive' train 3/47.

Brake third No 1647 or 601. See above.

Third (32 sleeping-berths) No 4329, see above. Diagram C70. To 'Alive' train 4/45. To ordinary traffic 5/46.

'Monster' vans Nos 585/8/90/2–4.

*Returned to traffic in 1946, recorded as to office accommodation April 1951.
†Possibly passenger brake van No 121.

Telegraphic code descriptions of GWR coaches

These were employed in railway telegraphic messages for transmission between GWR stations only, and were in use during the mid-1930s and before. The codes given are for eight-wheeled vehicles only.

Type	Code
Composite slip, eight-wheel, double ended, 70ft long	Gnat
Eight-wheel slip coach	Gnat A
Eight-wheel double-ended slip coach	Gnat B
Eight-wheel third-class coach	Termite A
Third eight-wheel, with corridor, clerestory roof, 8ft 6in wide	Termite C
Third eight-wheel, with corridor, ten compartments, 9ft wide	Termite D
Third eight-wheel, with corridor, eight compartments, not more than 9ft 3in wide	Termite E
Third eight-wheel, with corridor, 9ft 6in wide	Termite F
Third eight-wheel, non-corridor, ten compartments	Termite G
Third eight-wheel, with corridor, 9ft 5¾in wide (over body), 9ft 7in (over handles)	Termite H
Third eight-wheel, with centre corridor and vestibule ends	Termite J
Eight-wheel brake third coach	Emmett A
Eight-wheel van end, third	Melon
Brake third, eight-wheel, with corridor, not more than 9ft 3in wide	Melon B
Brake third, eight-wheel, with corridor, 9ft 6in wide	Melon C
Brake third, eight wheel, with corridor, 8ft 6in wide, clerestory roof	Melon D
Brake third, eight wheel, with corridor, 9ft 5¾in wide (over body), 9ft 7in (over handles)	Melon E
Brake third, eight-wheel, with centre corridor and vestibule ends	Melon F
Eight-wheel passenger brake van	Snake B
Eight-wheel gangwayed passenger brake van with side corridor	Snake C
Eight-wheel gangwayed open passenger brake van without side corridor	Snake D
Family carriage	Chintz
Invalid carriage	Chafer
Eight-wheel third-class or nondescript saloon	Chub A
Eight-wheel third-class or nondescript brake saloon	Chub B
Eight-wheel first-class coach	First A
Composite, eight-wheel	Cricket
Composite, eight-wheel, with luggage body	Cricket A
Composite, eight-wheel, coach with brake	Cricket B
Composite, eight-wheel corridor	Cricket C
Composite, eight-wheel corridor with brake	Cricket D

COMPARISON OF AGES OF PASSENGER STOCK: 1914 AND 1925

Eight and twelve-wheel stock:

	At 31/12/14	At 31/12/25	Notes to 1925 totals:
50 years & over	—	1	
45 ,, ,, ,,	—	88	
40 ,, ,, ,,	—	161	
35 ,, ,, ,,	55	339	
30 ,, ,, ,,	123	544	Stock built 1890–1895
25 ,, ,, ,,	206	853	1895–1900 'boom'
20 ,, ,, ,,	602	665	
15 ,, ,, ,,	737	557	First Churchward designs
10 ,, ,, ,,	614	471	
5 ,, ,, ,,	635	148	
Under 5 years	516	597 + 60 in hand	
Total and percentage of total stock	3448 (59.9%)	4425+60 (65.4%)	

Four and six-wheel stock:

	At 31/12/14	At 31/12/25
50 years & over	—	165
45 ,, ,, ,,	—	309
40 ,, ,, ,,	323	583
35 ,, ,, ,,	396	371
30 ,, ,, ,,	553	512
25 ,, ,, ,,	364	264
20 ,, ,, ,,	284	87
15 ,, ,, ,,	292	28
10 ,, ,, ,,	99	3
5 ,, ,, ,,	—	32
Not dated	22*	19
Total and percentage of total stock	2332 (40.1%)	2373 (34.6%)

The above totals include the stock of railways absorbed by the GWR.
*These were Port Talbot Railway and Rhondda & Swansea Bay Railway coaches.

It is impossible to give a full and useful list of preserved GWR vehicles, for so many remain unrestored, or in converted form, and so are of limited interest. Instead, this edition concludes its photographic coverage with some of the best examples of restoration, and all credit to those who have worked hard to bring them to this state.

Above:
A Dart Valley Railway train behind 14xx 0-4-2T No 1420 in April 1977. Leading the rake is the former GWR directors' saloon No 249, latterly with BR as Plymouth engineer's saloon No 80978.

Right:
A former articulated diner, in post-1934 livery as No 9653 (rebuilt 1936 on Diagram H.52) and latterly allocated to a WR control train. Bewdley 1982.

Below:
Excellently recreated GWR atmosphere on the Severn Valley Railway: 5101 2-6-2T No 5164 approaches Hampton Loade in March 1980, with its crew about to give up the single-line token. The leading vehicle is brake composite No 6913 (Lot 1508 – Diagram E.148), with 1938–41 period stock behind.

Beautifully restored Hawksworth period corridor third No 829 (Lot 1691 – Diagram C.82) after shopping, at Bewdley, December 1979. This vehicle went to Rainhill 150 the following year with No 6913 (illustrated earlier).

Valete: Will the Great Western Society's Vintage Train reappear on British Rail main line metals? Here it is at Paddington before a diesel-hauled run to Paignton in July 1978. Nearest is Hawksworth period corridor brake composite No 7372 (Lot 1690 – Diagram E.164) with two 'Super Saloons' ahead of it.

APPENDIX
LOT LIST OF GWR PASSENGER COACHES AND VANS

The Lot List appendix shows all GWR passenger coaches and vans by the Lot numbers under which they were ordered. The following notes explain the classifications – in order of the columns – abbreviations and symbols used.

(a) *Lot Numbers*
This table is based on the progression of Carriage Department Lot numbers from No. 532 to No. 1777. Missing numbers indicate that the lot covered horse-boxes, milk trucks, 'Siphon series' vans, carriage trucks, gas tanks, fish trucks and other such vehicles. Also, up to Lot 682 of late 1892, the Carriage Department series covered goods vehicles which from that date onwards had their own series. One or two other vehicles are included, however, such as the 1901 dynamometer car which was ordered on a goods lot.

Other blanks in the Lot series are explained by the fact that the Lot was not issued or transferred to another number.

The final GWR-ordered passenger coach Lot was No. 1732 of November 1947, and the last GWR series Lot number for a passenger-carrying design was No 1777, issued early in 1951. The very last in the series was No. 1780, covering a batch of 'Fruit D' vans, completed in 1955.

(b) *Completion Date*
The completion dates given are from the Carriage Department Lot books and indicate the date at which the final vehicle of the Lot was accepted for service.

(c) *Types of Roof, Type Description*
In the table, the various forms of roof contour are indicated by the abbreviations shown below. Modern elliptical roofs are not marked and entries having no indication of roof shape are of this type.

Arc	–	where the contour of the roof is that of an arc of a single circle.
3–Centre	–	where the contour of the roof is that of three circles each having a different centre.
Cler. (1)	–	a clerestory roof with the tops of both decks in the form of an arc of a circle.
Cler. (2)	–	a clerestory roof where the upper deck top is in the form of an arc and the lower has the three-centre shape.
Cler. (3)	–	a clerestory roof with both decks of the three-centre shape.
Royal Cler.	–	a form of clerestory roof where the ends of the upper deck slope down to meet the lower deck.

Other explanations: lavatory composite – non-corridor coach with lavatory provision; luggage composite – luggage (non-brake) compartment in coach; G – identifies gangwayed stock when following type description.

(d) *Carriage Diagram Designation*
In the Swindon drawing office, and for general identification on carriage references, vehicle types were identified by a diagram letter, with successive new designs receiving a numerical designation from 1 upwards. Letters A–M apply largely to eight or twelve-wheeled vehicles (G being a notable exception) and were introduced during Churchward's time as Chief Mechanical Engineer. About a decade later, letters R–W were applied to four and six-wheeled vehicles. The series encompassed 'brown' vehicles and associated passenger-rated vehicles. A further refinement appearing in some Swindon drawing office references took the form of a small numeral interposed between the letter and main diagram number (eg $D_2 15$) to identify types of roof, dimensions (length and width) and whether the vehicle type was corridor or not. This is not referred to in these lists to avoid complication.

A	First-class
B	(Second-class)
C	Third-class
D	Brake third
E	Composite *and* composite brake
F	Slip
G	Saloon
H	Catering vehicle
J	Sleeping car
K	Passenger brake van
L	Mail van
*M	Parcels (and similar) van
*N	Horse box
*O	Milk van
*P	Carriage truck
Q	Inspection vehicle/saloon
R	First-class
S	Third-class (and ex-second)
T	Brake third (and ex-brake second)
U	Composite and composite brake
V	Passenger brake van

W Parcels and miscellaneous van
*Not dealt with in this book

Diagram numbers (eg C.31) generally referred to a design of vehicle, to which successive batches might be built on separate Lot Numbers, although there might be detail differences as between the individual Lots, or variations within the Lots or diagrams, particularly as to the bogies fitted.

Auto-trailers carried a different designation, starting with A (Lot 1055), continuing to Z, and then from A1 upwards to A44. A *separate* series A–T overall covered the steam rail motors. Diesel railcar designs also had their own diagram series from U to Z, then A1–A4.

(e) *Dimensions*
The measurements given are length and width over the body, including the mouldings and bow-ends where appropriate, but disregarding the handles. Four, six and twelve-wheel coaches are noted as they occur, only if this applies to the whole Lot. Where no indication is shown, the Lot is eight-wheeled. Subsequent conversions are noted in the text only.

(f) *Running Numbers*
Before 1907, the GWR numbered all its vehicles in series from 1 upwards in each class: i.e. there were firsts, seconds and thirds all bearing the same serial number. In that year, however, there was a complete re-numbering, as shown below:

Third-class	retained their existing numbers
Second-class	had 5000 added to their numbers
Composites	had 6000 added to their numbers
First-class	had 8000 added to their numbers
Saloons	were re-numbered in the 90xx, 91xx, 92xx and 93xx series
Sleepers	re-numbered in the 90xx series
Diners	re-numbered in the 95xx series

Later series used were 96xx for diners etc., 98xx and 100xx for articulated stock, and 99xx for camp coaches – these were numbered downwards from 9999 so the later conversions were in the higher reaches of the 98xx. Various numbers in the 809xx, 14xxx, 40xxx and 23xxx were used for vehicles converted from departmental use.

Steam rail-motors, saloon auto-trailers and diesel railcars each had a separate series, starting from 1.

Separate series, each starting at 1, were also used for non-passenger-carrying vehicles built on passenger carriage Lots:

(1) Passenger brake vans, parcel vans, mail vans, fruit vans and milk vans.
(2) Horse-boxes and cattle vans.
(3) Carriage trucks and vans.

Throughout the table, the post-1907 form is used, but to differentiate the stock built before this date the added 5, 6, or 8 thousand is written in brackets,

e.g. Composite 1078 is shown as (7)078

Broad-gauge numbers carried by 'convertible' stock are shown alongside the final narrow-gauge series in the tables. *Serial numbers so marked were afterwards altered and the new numbers can be found in the list following these notes.

From 1953/4, some 'Toplight' vehicles in the 37/38xx series were renumbered to 33/34xx to avoid confusion with BR standard stock being built for the Western Region.

(g) *Notes*
The most usual name applied to non-standard stock is used to draw attention to these lots:

NG/BG convertible – vehicle with narrow-gauge body built for broad-gauge but easily converted.

Replacement – vehicle built to replace earlier coach of same number which had been destroyed.

Ex-ambulance – see page 67 – for further details.

BE – steel-panelled bow-ended vehicle of 1923–33 period. 'Toplight', 'Bars 1', 'Bars 2', 'Multibar' – see page 71 – for explanation.

Coach Weights
This summary shows the approximate minimum and maximum weights of standard designs and important types. Generally, brake vehicles were about one ton lighter than full third, first and composite coaches. The firsts were usually heavier than the thirds or composites.

The pre-1939 and post-1945 renovation schemes increased the weight of older restaurant-cars which were, in many cases, fitted with new six-wheel bogies. Such increased weights are marked by an asterisk.

Type	Ordinary Corridor Stock	Non-corridor Stock	Restaurant Cars
Non-corridor Clerestory Stock 1890–1905	—	19–25 tons	—
Four–wheel stock 1890–1902	—	9½–11 tons	—
Standard Clerestory Stock 1896–1904	22½–26 tons	—	27–28 tons
Rail Motors 1903–1908	—	56–59ft 6ins: 34–40 tons 70ft: 40–44 tons	— —
Rail Motors 1904–1913	—	59ft 6ins: 22–25 tons 70ft: 28–30½ tons	— —
'Dreaunought' stock	30–32½ tons	—	35–38 tons 36–45 tons*
56–57ft 'Toplight' stock	25½–28 tons	26½–28 tons	31 tons
70ft 'Toplight' stock (wooden panels) including 'Concertina' stock	31–34 tons	—	35–38 tons 39–45 tons*

Type	Ordinary Corridor Stock	Non-corridor Stock	Restaurant Cars
70ft 'Toplight' stock (steel panels)	34–36 tons	34–34½ tons	39–42 tons 41–45 tons*
57–58ft Bow-ended stock 1923–9	28½–31 tons	28½–30 tons	30–33½ tons
60–61ft Bow–ended stock 1929–33	31½–34 tons	30½–32 tons	very varied
57ft Stock 1933–36	29½–30½ tons	28½–30 tons	—
Excursion Stock 1935–40	29½–31½ tons	—	—
'Centenary' Stock 1935	31½–33 tons	—	32t, 40t(42t)*
1936–40 Standard Stock	30–32 tons	27–30 tons	—
Hawksworth Stock	30–32 tons	29–31½ tons	—
40ft Dean passenger brake vans	13½–19½ tons	—	—
'Toplight' passenger brake vans	24½–29½ tons	—	—
Post-1925 passenger brake vans	28½–30 tons	—	—

TABLE OF RE-NUMBERED COACHES

This table gives all the details, as far as they are known, of final re-numberings of coaches, largely as a result of the 1907 re-numbering scheme and the abolition of second-class. The altered number is the one carried by the coach open withdrawal. An asterisk indicates a change of class.

Lot No.	Original No.	New No.	Lot No.	Original No.	New No.	Lot No.	Original No.	New No.
543	8011	9004	843	(8)235	9504	1022	(5)226/7	3718/9*
552	(5)253	3731*	846	(6)955–64	1053–62*	1023	(7)626/7	3706/7*
598	2080	838	867	(6)945–54	3708–17*	1027	(8)221/2	9025/6
628	(8)247	9043	888	2545–54	9351–60	1035	(5)221–5	3546–50*
632	2501–6	9307–12	905	3162	3691*	1045	(8)323/4	9050/1
633	(8)518–21	9076–9	912	3163–73	3692–3702*	1046	(8)219/20	9023/4
643	(8)512–7	9070–5	923	3305	3733*	1051	(8)217/8	9021/2
669	(7)600	3173*	924	(8)227–30	9031–4	1052	2593/4	9361/2
672	(7)599	3152*	929	(8)236/7†	9516/7†	1056	(7)575	9515
694	(5)249–52	3723–6*	937	(5)242	3690*	1060	(7)572–4	9512–4
696	(5)247/8	3727/8*	940	(7)601–10	3162–71*	1076	(7)569–71	9509–11
723	2813/4	2396/7	941	(8)295–8	2329/8/31/27	1086	(7)567/8	9507/8
735	2083	839	950	(8)223–6	9027–30	1093	(7)565/6	9505/6
740	2507–18	9313–24	966	(5)241	3689*	1114	(8)401–4	9522–5
745	(8)249	9045	970	(5)260–74	1351/3–5/9	1115	(8)405/6	9526/7
747	(7)595/6	3148/72*			1361–4/6–9,	1118	(8)407–12	9528–33
764	2519–24	9325–30			1371/3	1123	(8)237–40	9082–5
772	2959/60	2398/9	971	(5)231–40	1331/3/6–9,	1251	(7)596/	9092/3
774	2525–34	9331–40			1341–3/9		(7)600	
787	(8)241–3	9037–9	980	(8)300–3	9046–9	1269	3879–85	3379–85††
790	(5)243/4	3729–30*	981	(5)275–9	1375/6/9/82/3	1278	3793–3804	3393–3404††
797	(5)245/6	3734/2*	984	2595–2600	9363–8	1279	3805–10	3405–10††
801	(8)250–2†	9501–3	1002	(5)228–30	3720–2*	1283	3811–8	3411–8††
804	(8)231/2	9035/6	1003	(7)623–5	3703–5*	1304	3819–23	3419–23††
811	(8)253	2330*	1006	(5)282	2340*	§1357		
824	2535–44	9341–50	1010	(7)580/1	9518/9	–64		
840	(8)233/4	9002/3	1011	(7)578/9	9520/1	1395	5141	9079*

Notes: †No. 9517 re-numbered 9097 before 1920. Nos. 237/51 composites (7)576/7 in 1903.
††1953–5 re-numbering.
§For re-numbering see page 80.

APPENDIX: LOT LIST OF GWR PASSENGER COACHES AND VANS

Lot	Completed	Type	Diag. No.	Dimensions ft in ft in	Running Numbers	Notes
532	5/ 7/90	Brake Van 3-centre	K.4	40. 0¾ x 8. 0¾	923–7	Convertible NG/BG, orig. Nos. 206–10
543	9/ 8/90	First Saloon Cler (2)	G.17	27. 0¾ x 8. 0¾ 4-wheel	(80)11*	
544	27/ 9/90	Lavatory Composite Cler (2)	E.27	46. 6¾ x 8. 0¾	(70)50–5 BG Nos. 581–6	NG/BG convertible
			E.28	48. 6¾ x 8. 0¾	(70)56–8 BG Nos. 613–5	NG/BG convertible
545	27/12/90	Brake Third Cler (2)	C.5 D.4	48. 6¾ x 8. 0¾	2171–6 2177–2200 BG Nos. 659–684	NG/BG convertible

Lot	Completed	Type	Diag. No.	Dimensions ft in ft in	Running Numbers	Notes
550	1/ 8/91	Brake Van 3-centre	K.4	40. 0¾ x 8. 0¾	1001–50	
551	8/11/90	First Cler (3) G	A.1	50. 0¾ x 8. 6¾	(8)254	First corridor train
552	8/11/90	Second Cler (3) G	C.6	50. 0¾ x 8. 6¾	(5)253*	First corridor train
553	8/11/90	Third Cler (3) G	C.7	50. 0¾ x 8. 6¾	255	First corridor train
554	1/ 8/91	Lavatory Tri-composite Cler (2)	E.31	46. 6¾ x 8. 0¾	(7)341–60	
555	28/ 2/91	Third Cler (2)	C.3	46. 6¾ x 8. 0¾	1839–58	
557	28/ 3/91	Luggage First/Second composite Cler (2)	E.32	46. 6¾ x 8. 0¾	(7)381–400	
558	9/ 1/92	Third Cler (2)	C.3	46. 6¾ x 8. 0¾	1859–1938	
572	28/ 2/91	Third Cler (2)	C.3	46. 6¾ x 8. 0¾	2201–10 BG Nos. 689–698	NG/BG convertible
579	20/ 2/92	P.O. Stowage Cler (3)	L.8	46. 6¾ x 8. 6¾	859	TPO vehicle
580	8/ 8/91	Lav brake Third Cler (3) G	D.5	50. 0¾ x 8. 6¾	220	First corridor train
582	4/ 7/91	Brake Third 3-centre	T.?	31. 0¾ x 8. 0¾ 4-wheel	400/10/1/3/4/6/9/ 20/2/7/9/42/4 453/61–4/75/6	
586	4/ 7/91	First/second composite 3-centre	U.4	26. 10 x 8. 0¾ 4-wheel	(6)132/6/71; (6)291; (6)397/482/4/96/9/731	6496 to Third 701, 1932, 6499 to Third 722, 1933
587	4/ 7/91	Third 3-centre	S.9	28. 0¾ x 8. 0¾ 4-wheel	305/20/35/86/478/ 80/1/2/3/90	
589	4/ 7/91	Brake Third 3-centre	T.32	31. 0¾ x 8. 0¾ 4-wheel	330; 905/11/2/3/8/ 9/35/46/97	
591	23/ 1/92	Lavatory First/second composite Cler (3)	E.33	48. 6¾ x 8. 0¾	(7)361–80	
596	5/12/91	Composite Mail Cler (2)	D.6	48. 6¾ x 8. 0¾	2081/2	TPO vehicles
597	5/12/91	Sorting & Luggage Van Cler (3)	V.6	28. 0¾ x 8. 0¾ 4-wheel	499/500	TPO vehicles
598	27/ 2/92	P.O. Sorting Van Cler (2)	L.3	48. 6¾ x 8. 6¾	2080*	TPO vehicle
599	16/ 4/92	Brake Van 3-centre	V.5	28. 0¾ x 8. 0¾ 4-wheel	1401–10	
601	28/11/91	Double Tri-compo Slip Cler (2)	F.5	50. 0¾ x 8. 0¾	(70)65–70	
604	5/12/91	P.O. Sorting & Bag Tender Cler (3)	L.9	46. 6¾ x 8. 6¾	860/1	TPO vehicles
607	30/ 4/92	Foreign Mail Van Cler (3)	L.10	40. 0¾ x 8. 6¾	862–5	TPO vehicles
610	5/12/91	Lavatory First/second composite Cler (3)	E.33	48. 6¾ x 8. 0¾	(7)401–4	
611	27/ 2/92	Brake Third Cler (3)	D.7	48. 6¾ x 8. 0¾	2231–40	
612	5/ 3/92	Third Cler (3)	C.3	46. 6¾ x 8. 0¾	2211–30	
613	9/ 4/92	Brake Third Cler (3)	D.8	48. 6¾ x 8. 0¾	2241–50	
614	23/ 1/92	Lavatory First/third composite Cler (3)	E.34	48. 6¾ x 8. 0¾	(7)059–64	
628	21/ 5/92	Tri-compo saloon Cler (3)	G.30	38. 6¾ x 8. 0¾	(8)247*	
630	10/ 9/92	Brake Composite Cler (3)	E.35 E.?	54. 0¾ x 8. 6¼ 56. 0¾ x 8. 6¼	(7)289 (7)290	
631	13/ 8/92	Third Cler (3)	C.3	46. 6¾ x 8. 0¾	2251–64	
632	21/ 5/92	Third Saloon 3-centre	G.19	31. 0¾ x 8. 0¾ 6-wheel	2501–6*	
633	23/ 7/92	First Saloon Cler (3)	G.15	31. 0¾ x 8. 0¾ 6-wheel	(8)518–21*	
634	2/ 7/92	Lavatory Tri-composite Cler (3)	E.37	46. 6¾ x 8. 0¾	(7)279–88	

Lot	Com-pleted	Type	Diag. No.	Dimensions ft in ft in	Running Numbers	Notes
643	30/ 7/92	First Saloon Cler (3)	G.37	33. 0¾ x 8. 0¾ 6-wheel	(8)512–7*	
644	16/ 6/94	Composite 3-centre	U.4	26. 10 x 8. 0¾ 4-wheel	(6)611–20	
645	20/ 8/92	Brake van 3-centre G	K.5	40. 0¾ x 8. 0¾	1051	
646	13/ 8/92	Sorting & Luggage Van Cler (3)	V.6	28. 0¾ x 8. 0¾ 4-wheel	490/1	TPO vehicles
649	27/ 8/92	Brake Van 3-centre	V.5	28. 0¾ x 8. 0¾ 4-wheel	1411–20	
655	21/ 1/93	Bullion Van	W.	26. 8½ x 7. 11	799	
658	12/11/92	Lavatory Tri-composite Cler (3)	E.37	46. 6¾ x 8. 0¾	(7)269–78	
659	17/12/92	Third Cler (3)	C.3	46. 6¾ x 8. 0¾	2265–84	
660	3/12/92	Brake Van 3-centre	K.6	48. 6¾ x 8. 0¾	1052–7	
669	10/ 9/92	Sleeper Composite Cler (3)	J.4	50. 0¾ x 8. 6¾	(7)600*	
671	28/ 1/93	Third Cler (3)	C.3	46. 6¾ x 8. 0¾	2285–92	
672	5/11/92	Sleeper Composite Cler (3)	J.4	50. 0¾ x 8. 6¾	(7)599*	
673	18/ 2/93	Brake Third Cler (3)	D.8	48. 6¾ x 8. 0¾	2801–4	
674	4/ 2/92	Brake Third Cler (3)	D.9	48. 6¾ x 8. 0¾	2805–8	
675	18/ 2/93	Brake Third Cler (3)	D.7	48. 6¾ x 8. 0¾	2809–12	
683	1/ 4/93	Brake Van 3-centre	K.4	40. 0¾ x 8. 0¾	1058–61	
684	4/11/93	Brake Third 3-centre	T.17	28. 0¾ x 8. 6¾ 4-wheel	301	
685	4/11/93	Third 3-centre	S.18	26. 0¾ x 8. 6¾ 4-wheel	302	
686	4/11/93	First 3-centre	R.5	26. 0¾ x 8. 6¾ 4-wheel	(8)028–30	To Thirds Nos 709/10/3, 1933
687	4/11/93	Second 3-centre	S.18	26. 0¾ x8. 6¾ 4-wheel	(50)41–3	
688	4/11/93	Brake Second 3-centre	T.17	28. 0¾ x 8. 6¾ 4-wheel	(50)44	
691	14/10/93	Brake Third Cler (3) G	D.10	56. 0¾ x 8. 6¾	2823–32	'Cornishman' series stock
692	21/10/93	Third Cler (3) G	C.8	52. 0¾ x 8. 6¾	2833–42	'Cornishman' series stock
693	14/10/93	First Cler (3) G	A.2	50. 0¾ x 8. 6¾	(8)255–8	'Cornishman' series stock
694	14/10/93	Second Cler (3) G	C.9	50. 0¾ x 8. 6¾	(5)249–52*	'Cornishman' series stock
695	3/ 6/93	Lavatory First/Third composite Cler (3) G	E.38	56. 0¾ x 8. 6¾	(7)597–8	'Cornishman' series stock
696	3/ 6/93	Luggage Second Cler (3) G	D.12	56. 0¾ x 8. 6¾	(5)247/8*	'Cornishman' series stock
697	30/ 6/94	Lavatory Tri-Composite Cler (3)	E.39	56. 0¾ x 8. 6¾	(7)254–68	'Falmouth coupé' type
699	17/ 2/94	Second 3-centre	S.18	26. 0¾ x 8. 6¾ 4-wheel	(50)45–53/75/6/7	For Middle Circle trains
700	16/ 6/94	Brake Third 3-centre	T.49	31. 0¾ x 8. 6¾ 4-wheel	2601–5	
701	18/ 8/94	Brake Third 3-centre	T.32	31. 0¾ x 8. 0¾ 4-wheel	2606–20	
702	6/10/94	Composite 3-centre	U.4	26. 10 x 8. 0¾ 4-wheel	(7)801–10	7806 to Third No. 739, 1937
703	1/ 9/94	Third 3-centre	S.9	28. 0¾ x 8. 0¾ 4-wheel	2701–10	
704	30/12/93	Brake Third 3-centre	T.59	31. 0¾ x 8. 6¾ 4-wheel	2621–6	To form Hammersmith & City trains with Lots 708/9 (Lots 704–707)
705	30/12/93	Third 3-centre	S.17	25. 0¾ x 8. 6¾ 4-wheel	2711–28	
706	30/12/93	First/third composite 3-centre	U.6	28. 0¾ x 8. 6¾ 4-wheel	(7)811–6	
707	30/12/93	First 3-centre	R.3	25. 0¾ x 8. 6¾ 4-wheel	(8)118–23	

Lot	Com-pleted	Type	Diag. No.	Dimensions ft in ft in	Running Numbers	Notes
708	30/12/93	Second 3-centre	S.17	25. 0¾ x 8. 6¾ 4-wheel	(50)45–65	To form Hammersmith & City trains with Lots 704–7
709	30/12/93	Brake Second 3-centre	T.59	31. 0¾ x 8. 6¾ 4-wheel	(50)66–71	
711	3/ 2/94	Brake Third 3-centre	T.59	31. 0¾ x 8. 6¾ 4-wheel	2627	
712	3/ 2/94	Third 3-centre	S.17	25. 0¾ x 8. 6¾ 4-wheel	2729–31	To form Hammersmith & City trains
713	3/ 2/94	First/Third composite 3-centre	U.6	28. 0¾ x 8. 6¾ 4-wheel	(7)817	
714	3/ 2/94	First 3-centre	R.3	25. 0¾ x 8. 6¾ 4-wheel	(8)117	
715	3/ 2/94	Second 3-centre	S.17	25. 0¾ x 8. 6¾ 4-wheel	(50)73/4	
716	3/ 2/94	Brake Second 3-centre	T.59	31. 0¾ x 8. 6¾ 4-wheel	(50)72	
717	3/ 2/94	Brake Third 3-centre	T.8	26. 0¾ x 8. 6¾ 4-wheel	2628	
718	3/ 2/94	Third 3-centre	S.18	26. 0¾ x 8. 6¾ 4-wheel	2732–4	
719	3/ 2/94	First 3-centre	R.5	26. 0¾ x 8. 6¾ 4-wheel	(8)115/6	
720	3/ 2/94	Second 3-centre	S.18	26. 0¾ x 8. 6¾ 4-wheel	(50)78/9	
721	3/ 2/94	Brake Second 3-centre	T.8	26. 0¾ x 8. 6¾ 4-wheel	(50)80	
722	5/ 5/94	Brake Third Cler (3)	D.13	50. 0¾ x 8. 0¾	2818–22	
723	5/ 5/94	Brake Third Cler (3)	D.14	50. 0¾ x 8. 0¾	2813–7*	
724	21/ 7/94	Third Cler (3)	C.10	46. 6¾ x 8. 0¾	2843–62	
726A 726B	1/ 9/94	Third 3-centre	S.13	31. 0¾ x 8. 0¾ 6-wheel	2043–7	2 at 30ft 0¾in (Lot 726B–Diag S.12)
727	1/ 9/94	Brake Third 3-centre	T.22	30. 0¾ x 8. 0¾ 4-wheel	2629/30	
728	1/ 9/94	Composite 3-centre	U.5	27. 6¾ x 8. 0¾ 4-wheel	(6)621/2	
729	2/ 2/95	Brake Tri-Composite 3-centre	E.40	50. 0¾ x 8. 0¾	(7)248–53	
730	1/ 6/95	Brake Third 3-centre	D15	38. 6¾ x 8. 0¾	2863–82	
731	10/11/94	Brake Third 3-centre	T.34	31. 0¾ x 8. 0¾ 4-wheel	2631–50	
732	10/11/94	Third 3-centre	S.9	28. 0¾ x 8. 0¾ 4-wheel	2735–44	
733	29/ 6/95	Composite 3-centre	U.4	26. 10 x 8. 0¾ 4-wheel	(7)818–37	Several to Thirds, 699–748, series, 1933–36
735	8/ 9/94	P.O. Sorting Composite Cler (3)	L.12	48. 6¾ x 8. 0¾	2083*	TPO vehicle, Replace-ment
736	1/12/94	Double Slip Cler (3)	F.5	50. 0¾ x 8. 0¾	(7)075–8	
737	29/ 6/95	Third 3-centre	S.11	30. 0¾ x 8. 0¾ 4-wheel	2745–54	
738	29/ 6/95	Brake Third 3-centre	T.34	31. 0¾ x 8. 0¾ 4-wheel	2651–70	
739	6/ 4/95	Tri-composite 3-centre	U.25	31. 0¾ x 8. 0¾ 4-wheel	(7)838–47	7846/7 to Thirds 737/9, 1937
740	12/12/94	Third Saloon 3-centre	G.20	31. 0¾ x 8. 0¾ 6-wheel	2507–18*	
742	28/12/95	Brake Composite Cler (3)	E.41	56. 0¾ x 8. 6¾	(7)228–37	(7)238–47 cancelled
743	1/ 6/95	Brake Third Cler (3)	D.14	50. 0¾ x 8. 0¾	2883–2907	
744	14/12/95	Third Cler (3)	C.10	46. 6¾ x 8. 0¾	2908–32	
745	27/10/94	Director's Saloon Royal Cler G	G.3	56. 0¾ x 8. 6¾	(8)249*	Later reclass as first-class
746	3/11/94	Parcels Sorting Cler (3)	L.9	46. 6¾ x 8. 6¾	846	TPO vehicle
747	9/ 2/95	Sleeper Composite Cler (3)	J.4	50. 0¾ x 8. 6¾	(7)595/6*	

Lot	Completed	Type	Diag. No.	Dimensions ft in ft in	Running Numbers	Notes
748	16/ 3/95	Luggage Tri-composite Cler (3)	E.42	52. 0¾ x 8. 6¾	(6)715	
749	16/ 3/95	Brake Tri-composite Cler (3)	E.43	56. 0¾ x 8. 6¾	(6)716	
750	20/ 7/95	First/Second Composite 3-centre	U.4	26. 10 x 8. 0¾ 4-wheel	(7)848–57	7851/3 to Thirds 721/50, 1936
751	31/ 8/95	Brake Third 3-centre	D.16	48. 6¾ x 8. 0¾	2068–73	
752	31/ 8/95	Brake Third 3-centre	D.17	52. 0¾ x 8. 0¾	2074–9	
753	31/ 8/95	Brake Third 3-centre	T.17	28. 0¾ x 8. 6¾ 4-wheel	322	
754	31/ 8/95	Third 3-centre	S.18	26. 0¾ x 8. 6¾ 4-wheel	323	
755	31/ 8/95	First 3-centre	R.5	26. 0¾ x 8. 6¾ 4-wheel	(80)31–3	Main Line & City Train No. 8
756	31/ 8/95	Second 3-centre	S.18	26. 0¾ x 8. 6¾ 4-wheel	(50)82–4	
757	31/ 8/95	Brake Second 3-centre	T.17	28. 0¾ x 8. 6¾ 4-wheel	(50)81	
759	26/10/95	Brake Composite Cler (3)	E.44	56. 0¾ x 8. 6¾	(7)592–4	
760	9/11/95	Third 3-centre	S.9	28. 0¾ x 8. 0¾ 4-wheel	2757–76	Second hand underframes – ten only
761	16/11/95	Brake Third 3-centre	T.34	31. 0¾ x 8. 0¾ 4-wheel	2673–92	Second hand underframes – ten only
762	31/ 8/95	Parcels Van 3-centre	W.4	31. 0¾ x 8. 0¾ 6-wheel	505/6	
763	21/12/95	Composite 3-centre	U.4	26.10 x 8. 0¾ 4-wheel	(7)858–77	Some to Thirds 706/8/28/36, 1934–6
764	14/12/95	Third Saloon 3-centre	G.20	31. 0¾ x 8. 0¾ 6-wheel	2519–24*	
765	13/ 6/96	Brake Composite Cler (3)	E.45	58. 0¾ x 8. 6¾	(7)238–47	Nine with steam heating
766	1/ 8/96	Brake Third 3-centre	D.15	38. 6¾ x 8. 0¾	2058–67	Secondhand underframes/bogies
767	18/ 1/96	Brake Tri-Composite 3-centre	U.25	31. 0¾ x 8. 0¾ 4-wheel	(6)485–90	
769	14/12/95	Brake Third Cler (3)	D.8	48. 6¾ x 8. 0¾	2245	Replacement, secondhand underframe/bogies
771	23/ 5/96	Brake Third Cler (3)	D.14	50. 0¾ x 8. 0¾	2973–82	Six with steam heating
772	9/ 5/96	Brake Third Cler (3)	D.14	50. 0¾ x 8. 0¾	2953–72*	Steam heating
773	17/10/96	Third Cler (3)	C.10	46. 6¾ x 8. 0¾	2933–52	
774	2/ 5/96	Third Saloon 3-centre	G.20	31. 0¾ x 8. 0¾ 6-wheel	2525–34*	Steam heating. 2534 (9340) to Engineer's Dept as 80943, 1936
775	25/ 1/96	Passenger Brake Van 3-centre	V.11	30. 0¾ x 8. 0¾ 4-wheel	1/2/8/9	Originally 20 to be built Secondhand underframes
776	19/ 9/96	Third Cler (3)	C.10	46. 6¾ x 8. 0¾	1944–53	
777	22/ 2/96	Brake Third 3-centre	T.59	31. 0¾ x 8. 6¾ 4-wheel	2693/4	
778	22/ 2/96	Third 3-centre	S.17	25. 0¾ x 8. 6¾ 4-wheel	2777–82	
779	22/ 2/96	First/Third Composite 3-centre	U.6	28. 0¾ x 8. 6¾ 4-wheel	(7)878/9	Middle Circle Trains. 7879 to Third 745, 1937
780	22/ 2/96	First 3-centre	R.3	25. 0¾ x 8. 6¾ 4-wheel	(800)9/10	
781	22/ 2/96	Second 3-centre	S.17	25. 0¾ x 8. 6¾ 4-wheel	(50)85–8	
782	22/ 2/96	Brake Second 3-centre	T.59	31. 0¾ x 8. 6¾ 4-wheel	(50)89/90	
783	15/ 2/96	Brake Third 3-centre	T.34	31. 0¾ x 8. 0¾ 4-wheel	3401–4	3405–20 cancelled
784	8/ 2/96	Third 3-centre	S.9	28. 0¾ x 8. 0¾ 4-wheel	3601/2	3603–20 cancelled
785	8/ 2/96	First/Second Composite 3-centre	U.4	26.10 x 8. 0¾ 4-wheel	(7)880/1	7882–99 cancelled
787	13/ 2/97	First Sleeper Cler (3) G	J.5	56. 0¾ x 8. 6¾	(8)241–3*	One ordinary compt

Lot	Completed	Type	Diag. No.	Dimensions ft in ft in	Running Numbers	Notes
789	12/ 9/96	First Cler (3) G	A.3	50. 0¾ x 8. 6¾	(8)259–62	'Ocean Special' sets
790	22/ 8/96	Second Cler (3) G	C.12	50. 0¾ x 8. 6¾	(5)243/4*	
791	22/ 8/96	Third Cler (3) G	C.13	54. 0¾ x 8. 6¾	2989–92	
792	12/ 9/96	First/Second Composite Cler (3) G	E.46	55. 0¾ x 8. 6¾	(7)405/6	
793	22/ 8/96	Luggage & Kitchen Cler (3) G	K.9	48. 0¾ x 8. 6¾	1062–5	
794	11/ 7/96	Brake Third Cler (3) G	D.18	56. 0¾ x 8. 6¾	2983/4	'South Wales Corridor' sets
795	11/ 7/96	Third Cler (3) G	C.13	54. 0¾ x 8. 6¾	2985–8	
796	11/ 7/96	First/Second Composite Cler (3) G	E.47	52. 0¾ x 8. 6¾	(7)590/1	
797	11/ 7/96	Brake Second Cler (3) G	D.113	56. 0¾ x 8. 6¾	(5)245/6*	
798	11/ 7/96	Tri-Composite Cler (3) G	E.48	56. 0¾ x 8. 6¾	(7)220–7	
801	18/ 7/96	First Diner Cler (3) G	H.2	56. 0¾ x 8. 6¾	(8)250–2*	(8)250/1 58. 6¾ over ends
802	5/ 9/96	Brake Tri-Composite 3-centre	E.49	54. 0¾ x 8. 0¾	(6)712/3	
803	5/ 9/96	Brake Tri-Composite 3-centre	E.50	54. 0¾ x 8. 0¾	(6)717/8	
804	17/10/96	First Saloon Cler (3)	G.31	45. 6¾ x 8. 6¾	(8)231/2*	
805	10/10/96	Brake Third 3-centre	T.59	31. 0¾ x 8. 6¾ 4-wheel	2695/6	Middle Circle trains. 7883 to Third 697, 1933
806	10/10/96	Third 3-centre	S.17	25. 0¾ x 8. 6¾ 4-wheel	2783–8	
807	10/10/96	First/Third Composite 3-centre	U.6	28. 0¾ x 8. 6¾ 4-wheel	(7)882/3	
808	10/10/96	First 3-centre	R.3	25. 0¾ x 8. 6¾ 4-wheel	(80)50/1	
809	10/10/96	Second 3-centre	S.17	25. 0¾ x 8. 6¾ 4-wheel	(50)93/4/5/6	
810	10/10/96	Brake Second 3-centre	T.59	31. 0¾ x 8. 6¾	(50)91/2	
811	6/ 3/97	First Brake Diner Cler (3) G	D.19	56. 0¾ x 8. 6¾	(8)253*	
812	19/ 9/96	Passenger Brake Van 3-centre	K.11	40. 0¾ x 8. 0¾	1066–8	
813	31/10/96	Brake Tri-Composite 3-centre	E.51	56. 0¾ x 8. 6¾	(7)214–9	For branch line working
814	28/11/96	Brake First/Third Composite Cler (3)	E.44	56. 0¾ x 8. 6¾	(7)584–9	Three with Westinghouse brakes
815	21/11/96	Third Cler (3)	C.10	46. 6¾ x 8. 0¾	2993–3012	
816	12/ 6/97	Brake Third 3-centre	T.59	31. 0¾ x 8. 6¾ 4-wheel	2697/8	
817	12/ 6/97	Third 3-centre	S.17	25. 0¾ x 8. 6¾ 4-wheel	2789–94	
818	12/ 6/97	First/Third Composite 3-centre	U.6	28. 0¾ x 8. 6¾ 4-wheel	(7)884/5	
819	12/ 6/97	First 3-centre	R.3	25. 0¾ x 8. 6¾ 4-wheel	(80)52/3	8053 to Third 718, 1933
820	12/ 6/97	Second 3-centre	S.17	25. 0¾ x 8. 6¾ 4-wheel	(50)97–100	
821	12/ 6/97	Brake Second 3-centre	T.59	31. 0¾ x 8. 6¾ 4-wheel	(5)101/2	
823	26/12/96	Third Cler (3)	C.10	46. 6¾ x 8. 0¾	3013–32	
824	12/12/96	Third Saloon 3-centre	G.20	31. 0¾ x 8. 0¾ 6-wheel	2535–44*	
826	10/ 4/97	First Cler (3)	A.4	50. 0¾ x 8. 6¾	(8)263–82	8264/6/7/9/75/6/9/80/2 to Thirds 325–33, 1941–3
827	20/ 2/97	Third Cler (3)	C.10	46. 6¾ x 8. 0¾	3033–52	
829	3/ 4/97	Third Cler (3)	C.10	46. 6¾ x 8. 0¾	3053–82	

Lot	Completed	Type	Diag. No.	Dimensions ft in ft in	Running Numbers	Notes
830	31/ 7/97	Brake Third Cler (3) G	D.20	56. 0¾ x 8. 6¾	2052–7	
831	2/ 5/97	First/Third Composite Cler (3) G	E.53	55. 0¾ x 8. 6¾	(7)407–16	
832	3/ 7/97	Lavatory Tri-Composite Cler (3)	E.55	54. 6¾ x 8. 6¾	(7)204–13	
833	9/10/97	Brake Third Cler (3)	D.21	50. 0¾ x 8. 6¾	3391–3400	
836	12/ 6/97	Brake Third 3-centre	D.22	51. 0¾ x 8. 6¾	1962–7	Pembroke & Tenby line (Lots 836–837)
837	12/ 6/97	Tri-Composite 3-centre	E.56	51. 0¾ x 8. 6¾	(6)733–5	
838	22/ 5/97	Brake Van Royal Cler G	K.12	56. 0¾ x 8. 6¾	1069/70	For Royal Train (Lots 838–840)
839	22/ 5/97	First Royal Cler G	A.5	56. 0¾ x 8. 6¾	(8)283	
840	22/ 5/97	First Saloon Royal Cler G	G.4	58. 0¾ x 8. 6¾	(8)233/4*	
841	31/ 7/97	Double Slip Tri-Composite Cler (3)	F.9	56. 0¾ x 8. 6¾	(7)079–84	
842	30/10/97	Bullion Van 3-centre	W.9	26. 6 x 8. 0	797/8	
843	11/ 9/97	First Diner Cler (3)	H.2	56. 0¾ x 8. 6¾	(8)235*	
844	26/ 6/97	Double Slip Tri-Composite Cler (3) G	F.10	58. 0¾ x 8. 6¾	(7)085–8	For Folkestone service
846	18/ 9/97	Lavatory Second/Third Composite Cler (3)	C.14	56. 0¾ x 8. 6¾	(6)955–64*	
847	6/11/97	Third Cler (3)	C.10	46. 6¾ x 8. 0¾	3083–3112	
850	18/12/97	Lavatory Tri-Composite Cler (3)	E.57	58. 0¾ x 8. 6¾	(7)189–203	
851	19/ 3/98	Third Cler (3)	C.10	46. 6¾ x 8. 0¾	3113–32	
852	5/ 2/98	Brake Third Cler (3)	D.24	50. 0¾ x 8. 6¾	3381–90	
853	18/12/97	Brake Third Cler (3)	D.24	50. 0¾ x 8. 6¾	3341–50	
854	25/12/97	Third Cler (3)	C.10	46. 6¾ x 8. 0¾	3183–92	
858	15/ 1/98	Brake Third 3-centre	T.59	31. 0¾ x 8. 6¾ 4-wheel	313/2699–2700	City trains. 7886/7 to Thirds 733/4, 1936 (Lots 858–863)
859	15/ 1/98	Third 3-centre	S.17	25. 0¾ x 8. 6¾ 4-wheel	303/4/11/2795–800	
860	15/ 1/98	First/Third Composite 3-centre	U.6	28. 0¾ x 8. 6¾ 4-wheel	(7)886–8	
861	15/ 1/98	First 3-centre	R.3	25. 0¾ x 8. 6¾ 4-wheel	(8)133/8/9	
862	15/ 1/98	Second 3-centre	S.17	25. 0¾ x 8. 6¾ 4-wheel	(5)106–111	
863	15/ 1/98	Brake Second 3-centre	T.59	31. 0¾ x 8. 6¾ 4-wheel	(5)103–5	
865	5/ 3/98	Passenger Brake Van 3-centre	K.14	40. 0¾ x 8. 0¾	1071–90	
866	26/ 3/98	Bullion Van 3-centre	W.9	26. 6 x 8. 0	795/6	
867	9/ 4/98	Second/Third Composite Cler (3) G	C.15	56. 0¾ x 8. 6¾	(6)945–54*	
870	14/ 5/98	Brake Third Cler (3) G	D.25	56. 0¾ x 8. 6¾	3371–80	
871	4/ 6/98	Third Cler (3) G	C.17	54. 0¾ x 8. 6¾	3133–42	
872	25/ 6/98	Brake Third 3-centre	D.27	51. 0¾ x 8. 0¾	3331–40	Lots 872/3 for Tondu and Bridgend area
873	25/ 6/98	Tri-Composite 3-centre	E.58	50. 0¾ x 8. 0¾	(7)169–72	
874	30/ 7/98	Brake Third 3-centre	T.59	31. 0¾ x 8. 6¾ 4-wheel	312/7	To form two City trains. with Lots 877–9 7888 to Third 740, 1937. 8141 to Third 707, 1936 (Lots 874–876)
875	30/ 7/98	Third 3-centre	S.17	25. 0¾ x 8. 6¾ 4-wheel	319/21/5/7/8/33	
876	30/ 7/98	First/Third Composite 3-centre	U.6	28. 0¾ x 8. 6¾ 4-wheel	(7)889/90	

Lot	Com-pleted	Type	Diag. No.	Dimensions ft in ft in	Running Numbers	Notes
877	30/ 7/98	First 3-centre	R.3	25. 0¾ x 8. 6¾ 4-wheel	(8)140/1	To form two City trains 7888 to Third 740, 1937. 8141 to Third 707, 1936 to form two City trains with Lots 874–6
878	30/ 7/98	Second 3-centre	S.17	25. 0¾ x 8. 6¾ 4-wheel	(5)112–5	
879	30/ 7/98	Brake Second 3-centre	T.59	31. 0¾ x 8. 6¾ 4-wheel	(5)116/7	
882	25/ 6/98	Tri-Composite 3-centre	E.59	51. 0¾ x 8. 0¾	(7)173	
883	20/ 8/98	Passenger Brake Van 3-centre	K.14	40. 0¾ x 8. 0¾	639/40/928–35	
884	18/ 6/98	Brake Tri-Composite Cler (3)	E.60	58. 0¾ x 8. 6¾	(7)165/6	For Bournemouth service
885	18/ 6/98	Brake Tri-Composite Cler (3)	E.61	58. 0¾ x 8. 6¾	(7)167/8	
886	30/ 4/98	Single Slip Tri-Composite Cler (3)	F.11	38. 6¾ x 8. 6¾	(70)89/90	For Liverpool Cen. – Folkestone service
888	13/ 8/98	Third Saloon 3-centre	G.20	31. 0¾ x 8. 0¾ 6-wheel	2545–54*	
889	10/ 9/98	Lavatory Tri-Composite Cler (3)	E.62	53. 0¾ x 8. 6¾	(7)174–88	
890	25/ 6/98	Single Slip Tri-Composite Cler (3)	F.12	38. 6¾ x 8. 6¾	(70)91/2	For Liverpool Cen. – Folkestone service
895	8/10/98	Passenger Brake Van 3-centre	K.14	40. 0¾ x 8. 0¾	631/2/936/7–43	
896	22/10/98	Third Cler (3)	C.10	46. 6¾ x 8. 0¾	1954–9/69/71/2/3	
897	26/11/98	Brake Third 3-centre	T.59	31. 0¾ x 8. 6¾ 4-wheel	334/7	For City trains
898	26/11/98	Third 3-centre	S.17	25. 0¾ x 8. 6¾ 4-wheel	340/1/3/4/5/7	
899	26/11/98	First/Third Composite 3-centre	U.6	28. 0¾ x 8. 6¾	(7)891/2	
900	26/11/98	First 3-centre	R.3	25. 0¾ x 8. 6¾ 4-wheel	(8)142/3	
901	26/11/98	Second 3-centre	S.17	25. 0¾ x 8. 6¾ 4-wheel	(5)120–3	
902	26/11/98	Brake Second 3-centre	T.59	31. 0¾ x 8. 6¾ 4-wheel	(5)118/9	
903	12/11/98	Lavatory First/Second Composite Cler (3)	E.63	51. 0¾ x 8. 6¾	(7)417–20	For 4.45 pm ex-Paddington
904	19/11/98	Brake Third Cler (3)	D.28	56. 0¾ x 8. 6½	2048–51	
905	1/ 4/99	Third Cler (3) G	C.17	54. 0¾ x 8. 6¾	3143–62*	
906	24/12/98	Lavatory Tri-Composite Cler (2)	E.62	53. 0¾ x 8. 6¾	(7)150–2	Original order for 15
907	6/ 5/99	Lavatory Tri-Composite Cler (3)	E.57	58. 0¾ x 8. 6¾	(7)153–64	
909	5/11/98	Brake Third 3-centre	T.59	31. 0¾ x 8. 6¾ 4-wheel	2695	Replacement body. See Lot 805
910	22/ 4/99	First/Second Composite Cler (3) G	E.64	55. 0¾ x 8. 6¾	(7)421–35	
911	11/ 3/99	Passenger Brake Van 3-centre	K.15	40. 0¾ x 8. 0¾	1091–1100	
912	16/ 9/99	Third Cler (3)	C.17	54. 0¾ x 8. 6¾	3163–82*	
915	26/ 8/99	Third Cler (3)	C.10	46. 6¾ x 8. 0¾	3193–3202	
916	27/ 5/99	Brake Third Cler (3) G	D.29	56. 0¾ x 8. 6¾	3361–70	
917	1/ 7/99	Brake Third Cler (3) G	D.29	56. 0¾ x 8. 6¾	3351–60	
918	9/ 9/99	First/Second Composite Cler (3) G	E.64	55. 0¾ x 8. 6¾	(7)436–45	
919	1/ 7/99	Passenger Brake Van 3-centre	K.16	40. 0¾ x 8. 0¾	1101–10	
921	30/ 9/99	Lavatory Tri-Composite Cler (3)	E.57	58. 0¾ x 8. 6¾	(7)145–9	
923	7/10/99	Brake Third Cler (3) G	D.29	56. 0¾ x 8. 6¾	3301–10*	
924	18/11/99	First Saloon Cler (3)	G.32	45. 6¾ x 8. 6¾	(8)227–30*	

Lot	Completed	Type	Diag. No.	Dimensions ft in ft in	Running Numbers	Notes
925	4/11/99	Brake Third Cler (3)	D.24	50. 0¾ x 8. 6¾	3321–30	
926	2/12/99	Brake Third Cler (3)	D.24	50. 0¾ x 8. 6¾	3311–20	
927	3/ 2/00	Third Cler (3) G	C.17	54. 0¾ x 8. 6¾	3218–27	
928	13/ 1/00	First/Second Composite Cler (3) G	E.68	55. 0¾ x 8. 6¾	(7)446–55	
929	24/ 3/00	First Diner Cler (3) G	H.2	56. 0¾ x 8. 6¾	(8)236/7*	
931	10/ 3/00	Brake Third Cler (3) G	D.30	56. 0¾ x 8. 6¾	2059/60/4/82–6/ 2813/5	
932	3/ 3/00	First Cler (3)	A.4	50. 0¾ x 8. 6¾	(8)284–93	8284/5/6/8/91–3 to Thirds 334–40, 1941/2
933	21/ 4/00	Third Cler (3) G	C.17	54. 0¾ x 8. 6¾	3228–37	
935	5/ 5/00	Brake Third Cler (3) G	D.32	56. 0¾ x 8. 6¾	3411/2	Milford Boat set
936	5/ 5/00	Third Cler (3) G	C.18	54. 0¾ x 8. 6¾	2834	Milford Boat set
937	5/ 5/00	Buffet Second Cler (3) G	H.5	58. 0¾ x 8. 6¾	(5)242*	Milford Boat set
938	5/ 5/00	First Cler (3) G	A.6	52. 0¾ x 8. 6¾	(8)294	Milford Boat set
939	12/ 5/00	Brake Third Cler (3)	D.24	50. 0¾ x 8. 6¾	3401–10	
940	28/ 7/00	Lavatory Second/Third Composite Cler (3) G	C.15	56. 0¾ x 8. 6¾	(7)601–10*	
293	16/ 3/01	Dynamometer Car Royal Cler	—	45. 0¾ x 8. 6¾	790	Ordered on wagon Lot 293
941	23/ 6/00	Brake First Kitchen Cler (3) G	D.33	56. 0¾ x 8. 6¾	(8)295–8*	
944	30/ 6/00	First/Second Composite 3-centre	U.4	26.10¾ x 8. 0¾ 4-wheel	(600)3/8/9/49/59/ 128/9/62/70/2/4	To form Ruabon–Dolgelley local sets. 6008 to Third 747, 1938. 6049 to Third 715, 1933. 6174 to Third 724, 1933 (Lots 944–947)
945	30/ 6/00	Third 3-centre	S.9	28. 0¾ x 8. 0¾ 4-wheel	902/17/30–4/6/7/8/9	
946	30/ 6/00	Brake Third 3-centre	T.47	31. 0¾ x 8. 0¾ 4-wheel	940/1/3/4/5/7/8	
947	30/ 6/00	Passenger Brake Van 3-centre	V.5	28. 0¾ x 8. 0¾ 4-wheel	7/12/5/6/7/8/20	
949	8/ 9/00	Third Cler (3)	C.10	46. 6¾ x 8. 0¾	3203–17	
950	20/10/00	First Saloon Cler (3) G	G.33	47. 6¾ x 8. 6¾	(8)223–6*	
953	3/11/00	Brake Third Cler (3) G	D.31	56. 0¾ x 8. 6¾	3413–22	
955	22/11/00	Brake Third Cler (3) G	D.30	56. 0¾ x 8. 6¾	3423–32	
(956)		First Saloon	—	—	482–7	Lot cancelled
957	3/11/00	Third Cler (3)	C.10	46. 6¾ x 8. 0¾	1252–61	
958	24/11/00	Third Cler (3)	C.10	46. 6¾ x 8. 0¾	1246–50/62/4/6/7/8	
959	22/11/00	Brake Third Cler (3)	D.24	50. 0¾ x 8. 6¾	2301–6/2864/81/ 2959/60	
960	10/11/00	Newspaper Van 3-centre G	M.7	46. 6¾ x 8. 0¾	868/9	
962	2/ 2/01	Third Cler (3)	C.10	46. 6¾ x 8. 0¾	1230–3/1939–43/60	
963	9/ 3/01	Third Cler (3)	C.10	46. 6¾ x 8. 0¾	1222–5/7–9/69/70/ 1968	
964	27/ 4/01	Brake Third Cler (3) G	D.36	56. 0¾ x 8. 6¾	3433/4	Milford Boat set
965	27/ 4/01	Third Cler (3) G	C.18	54. 0¾ x 8. 6¾	2840	Milford Boat set
966	27/ 4/01	Buffet Second Cler (3) G	H.6	58. 0¾ x 8. 6¾	(5)241*	Milford Boat set
967	27/ 4/01	First Cler (3) G	A.6	52. 0¾ x 8. 6¾	(8)299	Milford Boat set
970	8/ 6/01	Second Cler (3)	C.19	50. 0¾ x 8. 6¾	(5)260–74*	
971	22/ 6/01	Second Cler (3)	C.19	50. 0¾ x 8. 6¾	(5)231–40*	

Lot	Completed	Type	Diag. No.	Dimensions ft in ft in	Running Numbers	Notes
972	29/ 6/01	Brake Third Cler (3)	D.24 D.37	50. 0¾ x 8. 6¾	2307–11 2312–6	Four compartments Five compartments
974	31/ 8/01	Brake Third Cler (3)	D.38	50. 0¾ x 8. 6¾	3435–44	
975	13/ 7/01	Double Slip Tri-Composite Cler (3)	F.10	58. 0¾ x 8. 6¾	(70)93/4	
977	22/ 3/02	Third Cler (3)	C.10	46. 6¾ x 8. 0¾	1188–92/4/9/ 1202/3/5/8/9–11 1214–7/9/20	
978	2/11/01	Brake Third 3-centre	T.36	31. 0¾ x 8. 0¾ 4-wheel	942/9–57	
980	17/ 8/01	First Saloon Cler (3) G	G.6	52. 0¾ x 8. 6¾	(8)300–3*	
981	14/ 9/01	Second Cler (3)	C.19	50. 0¾ x 8. 6¾	(5)275–9*	
982	5/ 4/02	First/Second Composite Cler (3) G	E.70	55. 0¾ x 8. 6¾	(7)456–61	
983	1/ 2/02	Lavatory Tri-Composite Cler (3)	E.72	58. 0¾ x 8. 6¾	(7)125–44	
984	14/12/01	Third Saloon Cler (3)	G.18	46. 6¾ x 8. 6¾	2595–2600*	Fitted with Westinghouse brake
985	29/ 3/02	First Cler (3)	A.4	50. 0¾ x 8. 6¾	(8)304–13	8304/5/7/8–10/2/3 to Thirds 1981–8, 1938/9
986	26/ 4/02	Composite Cler (3) G	E.70	55. 0¾ x 8. 6¾	(7)462–71	
987	21/ 6/02	First/Second Composite Cler (3) G	E.73	55. 0¾ x 8. 6¾	(7)472–81	
988	24/ 5/02	Lavatory Tri-Composite Cler (3)	E.72	58. 0¾ x 8. 6¾	(7)115–24	
989	21/ 6/02	Brake Third Cler (3)	D.24	50. 0¾ x 8. 6¾	2317–26	
990	16/ 8/02	First/Second Composite 3-centre	U.4	26.10 x 8. 0¾ 4-wheel	(6)190/230/47/90/ 2/3/6/9/300/1/2/ 4/6–8	For Bristol local sets. 6300/1/2/4/6, 6247 to Thirds 716/49/31/42/ 35/39, from 1936
991	16/ 8/02	Brake Third 3-centre	T.47	31. 0¾ x 8. 0¾ 4-wheel	958–72	
992	16/ 8/02	Third 3-centre	S.9	28. 0¾ x 8. 0¾ 4-wheel	973–6/8/80/81/2/ 4–90	
994	6/ 9/02	First/Second Composite Cler (3) G	E.73	55. 0¾ x 8. 6¾	(7)482–5	
995	30/ 8/02	Newspaper Van 3-centre	M.7	46. 6¾ x 8. 0¾	870–3	
996	11/ 4/03	Bullion Van	M.16	36. 0 x 8. 0	791/2	
998	1/11/02	Brake Third Cler (3) G	D.29	56. 0¾ x 8. 6¾	3445–8	
999	8/11/02	Third Cler (3) G	C.17	54. 0¾ x 8. 6¾	3238–41	
1000	18/10/02	Brake Van 3-centre	K.15	40. 0¾ x 8. 0¾	1111–4	
1001	22/11/02	First Cler (3) G	A.7	58. 0¾ x 8. 6¾	(8)314/5	
1002	20/12/02	Second Cler (3) G	C.20	51. 0¾ x 8. 6¾	(5)228–30*	
1003	29/11/02	Composite Cler (3) G	C.21	56. 0¾ x 8. 6¾	(7)623–5*	
1004	25/10/02	Third Cler (3)	C.10	46. 6¾ x 8. 0¾	1172/3/9/80/1/2/4–7	
1005	15/11/02	Brake Third Cler (3) G	D.39	68. 0¾ x 8. 6¾	2400	Experimental
1006	10/ 1/03	Brake Second Cler (3) G	D.40	56. 0¾ x 8. 6¾	(5)282*	
1007	10/ 1/03	First Cler (3) G	A.7	58. 0¾ x 8. 6¾	(8)319–22	
1008	10/ 1/03	First/Second Composite Cler (3) G	E.73	55. 0¾ x 8. 6¾	(7)486	
1009	10/ 1/03	Brake Third Cler (3) G	D.29	56. 0¾ x 8. 6¾	3305	
1010	24/ 1/03	Composite Diner Cler (3) G	H.7	56. 0¾ x 8. 6¾	(7)580/1*	
1011	24/ 1/03	Composite Diner Cler (3) G	H.7	56. 0¾ x 8. 6¾	(7)578/9*	
1012	13/12/02	First/Second Composite 3-centre	U.4	26.10 x 8. 0¾ 4-wheel	(6)311/4/5/7/8	6317 to Third 713, 1933

Lot	Com-pleted	Type		Diag. No.	Dimensions ft in ft in	Running Numbers	Notes
1013	13/12/02	Brake Third 3-centre		T.47	31. 0¾ x 8. 0¾ 4-wheel	314/53/7/8/60	
1014	13/12/02	Third 3-centre		S.9	28. 0¾ x 8. 0¾ 4-wheel	977/92/3/4/6	
1015	7/ 2/03	Third Cler (3)		C.22	46. 6¾ x 8. 6¾	1156/9/60/1/2/4/5/ 7/70/7	
1017	14/ 2/03	Passenger Brake Van 3-centre		K.16	40. 0¾ x 8. 0¾	201–10	
1018	28/ 2/03	Third Cler (3)		C.22	46. 6¾ x 8. 6¾	1302–6/11/6/9/20/2	
1019	16/ 5/03	Brake Third Cler (3)	G	D.29	56. 0¾ x 8. 6¾	3449–54	
1020	16/ 5/03	Third Cler (3)	G	C.17	54. 0¾ x 8. 6¾	3242–7	
1021	16/ 5/03	First Cler (3)	G	A.8	58. 0¾ x 8. 6¾	(8)316–8	
1022	16/ 5/03	Second Cler (3)	G	C.20	51. 0¾ x 8. 6¾	(5)226/7*	
1023	4/ 4/03	Second/Third Composite Cler (3)	G	C.21	56. 0¾ x 8. 6¾	(7)626/7*	
1024	4/ 4/03	Passenger Brake Van 3-centre		K.15	40. 0¾ x 8. 0¾	1115–20	
1027	25/ 4/03	Invalid Saloon Cler (3)		G.33	47. 6¾ x 8. 6¾	(8)221/2*	Westinghouse brake fitted
1028	20/ 6/03	Lavatory Tri-Composite Cler (3)		E.74	58. 0¾ x 8. 6¾	(6)601–10	Luggage compt
1029	1/ 8/03	Brake Third Cler (3)		D.24	50. 0¾ x 8. 6¾	3455–66	
1030	26/ 9/03	First/Second Composite Cler (3)	G	E.73	55. 0¾ x 8. 6¾	(7)487–92	
1031	15/ 8/03	Lavatory Tri-Composite Cler (3)		E.75	58. 0¾ x 8. 6¾	(7)628–33	Luggage compt
1032	11/ 7/03	Double Slip Tri-Composite Cler (3)		F.10	58. 0¾ x 8. 6¾	(70)95–100	
1033	1/ 8/03	Passenger Brake Van 3-centre		K.16	40. 0¾ x 8. 0¾	211–20	
1035	19/ 9/03	Brake Second Cler (3)	G	D.40	56. 0¾ x 8. 6¾	(5)221–5*	
1036	5/ 9/03	Brake Third Cler (3)	G	D.29	56. 0¾ x 8. 6¾	2332–6	
1037	17/10/03	Steam Rail Motor		A/A.1	57. 0¾ x 8. 6¾	1/2	
1038	3/10/03	Third Cler (3)		C.22	46. 6¾ x 8. 6¾	1330/2/5/40/4/6/ 52/6/7/60	
1040	12/12/03	First/Second Composite Cler (3)	G	E.73	55. 0¾ x 8. 6¾	(7)493–504	
1041	6/ 2/04	Third Cler (3)		C.23	58. 0¾ x 8. 6¾	3248–72	
1042	7/ 5/04	Lavatory Tri-Composite Cler (3)	G	E.75	58. 0¾ x 8. 6¾	(7)634–8	Luggage compt
1043	26/12/03	Postal Brake Cler (3)	G	K.17	54. 0¾ x 8. 6¾	1125–8	For TPO use. 1121–4 cancelled
1045	27/ 2/04	First Saloon Cler (3)	G	G.6	52. 0¾ x 8. 6¾	(8)323/4*	
1046	30/ 1/04	Invalid Saloon Cler (3)	G	G.33	47. 6¾ x 8. 6¾	(8)219/20*	
1048	13/ 1/04	Passenger Brake Van 3-centre	G	K.15	40. 0¾ x 8. 0¾	1121–4	
1049	26/ 3/04	First/Second Composite Cler (3)	G	E.73	55. 0¾ x 8. 6¾	(7)505–9	
1050	12/ 3/04	Third Brake Cler (3)	G	D.29	56. 0¾ x 8. 6¾	2337–41	
1051	27/ 2/04	Invalid Saloon Cler (3)	G	G.33	47. 6¾ x 8. 6¾	(8)217/8*	Gangway each end
1052	2/ 4/04	Third Saloon Cler (3)	G	G.18	46. 6¾ x 8. 6¾	2593/4*	Alloc Bristol
1053	7/ 5/04	Third Cler (3)		C.22	46. 6¾ x 8. 6¾	1345/7/50/8/72/5/ 7/8/80/1	
1054	23/ 7/04	Steam Rail Motor		B/C/D	59. 6¾ x 8. 6	3–14	
1055	17/12/04	Auto Trailer		A	59. 6 x 8. 6	1	
				B	70. 0¾ x 8. 6¾	2	
1056	28/ 5/04	Composite Diner	G	H.8	68. 0¾ x 9. 6¾	(7)575*	'Dreadnought' stock
1057	28/ 5/04	Third Cler (3)		C.23	58. 0¾ x 8. 6¾	1001–5	

Lot	Com-pleted	Type	Diag. No.	Dimensions ft in ft in	Running Numbers	Notes
1058	2/ 7/04	Lavatory Tri-Composite Cler (3)	E.76	58. 0¾ x 8. 6¾	(7)110–4	
1059	30/ 4/04	Passenger Brake Van 3-centre G	K.15	40. 0¾ x 8. 0¾	221–5	
1060	13/ 8/04	Composite Diner G	H.8	68. 0¾ x 9. 6¾	(7)572–4*	'Dreadnought' stock
1061	14/ 1/05	P.O. Sorting Slip G	M.8	68. 0 x 9. 6	837	TPO vehicle. non-corr, 1935
1062	17/ 9/04	P.O. Stowage G	M.8	68. 0 x 9. 6	821–4	TPO vehicles 821, non-corr, 1935
1063	24/ 9/04	Steam Rail Motor	F/G/G1	59. 6 x 8. 6	17–28	
1066	8/ 7/05	Brake Third G	D.42	70. 0 x 9. 6	3467–72	'Dreadnought' stock
(1067)	—	Second G	—	68. 0 x 9. 6	395/6	Lot cancelled
1068	8/ 7/05	First/Third Composite G	E.77	68. 0 x 9. 6	(7)639–44	'Dreadnought' stock. Lot originally to be first class Nos 325/6
1069	5/ 8/05	Third G	C.24	69. 0 x 9. 6	2295–2300	'Dreadnought' stock. Originally to be 68ft Nos 3273–6
1070	29/10/04	Third Cler (3)	C.23	58. 0¾ x 8. 6¾	1009–28	
1075	12/11/04	Brake Van 3-centre G	K.15	40. 0¾ x 8. 0¾	226–9/31–6	
1076	21/ 1/05	Composite Diner G	H.8	68. 0¾ x 9. 6¾	(7)569–71*	'Dreadnought' stock
1077	14/ 1/05	Third	C.25	58. 0¾ x 8. 6¾	1029–32/4–9	NB: elliptical roofs
1078	1/ 4/05	Steam Rail Motor	H/J/J1 K/K1	59. 6 x 9. 0 70. 0 x 9. 0	29–36 37–40	
1079	8/ 4/05	Steam Rail Motor	L M/M1/N	59. 6 x 9. 0 70. 0 x 9. 0	41/2 43–52	
1080	11/ 2/05	Third	C.25	58. 0¾ x 8. 6¾	1040/1/2/4/5/6/ 7/50/1/2	NB: elliptical roofs
1081	1/ 4/05	Auto Trailer	B	70. 0 x 9. 0	3–6	
1084	5/ 8/05	Third G	C.24	69. 0 x 9. 6	3277–90	'Dreadnought' stock 3291–3300 cancelled
1085	2/ 9/05	Brake Third G	D.42	70. 0 x 9. 6	3473–8	'Dreadnought' stock
1086	1/ 7/05	Composite Diner G	H.11	70. 0 x 9. 6¾	(7)567/8*	'Dreadnought' stock
1087	19/ 8/05	Auto Trailer	C	59. 6 x 9. 0	7/8	For Lambourn Valley
1088	7/10/05	Steam Rail Motor	O	70. 0 x 9. 0	53–8	
1089	4/11/05	Steam Rail Motor	P	70. 0 x 9. 0	59/60	
1090	4/11/05	Auto Trailer G	D	70. 0 x 9. 0	9/10	
1091	11/11/05	Parcels Van G	M11	70. 0 x 8. 6¾	825–9	
1092	14/10/05	Brake Tri-Composite G	E.78	69. 0 x 8. 6¾	(7)645–54	
1093	26/ 8/05	Composite Diner G	H.11	70. 0 x 9. 6¾	(7)565/6*	'Dreadnought' stock
1094	11/11/05	P.O. Sorting G	L.13	70. 0 x 8. 6¾	834–6	TPO vehicles
1095	28/10/05	P.O. Sorting G	L.14	70. 0 x 8. 6¾	830–2	TPO vehicles
1097	2/12/05	Auto Trailer	E/F G/G1/H	70. 0 x 9. 0 52. 0¾ x 8. 6¾ Cler (3)	11–13 14–17	Conversion from Lot 692
1098	30/ 9/05	Third G	C.24	69. 0 x 9. 6	3291–3300	'Dreadnought' stock Built B'ham RCW
1099	11/11/05	Steam Rail Motor	E	56. 3¾ x 9. 0	15/16	Built Kerr, Stuart
1100	7/ 7/06	Steam Rail Motor	O	70. 0 x 9. 0	61–72	
1101	23/ 6/06	Steam Rail Motor	Q	59. 6 x 9. 0	73–80	Built Gloster RCW
1102	24/ 3/06	Auto Trailer	J/J1	59. 6 x 9. 0	19–24	Built Bristol CW
1103	23/12/05	Auto Trailer	K/K1	70. 0 x 9. 0	25–8	
1107	14/ 4/06	Third G	C.27	70. 0 x 9. 0	2401–9/11–21	'Concertina' type
1108	27/ 1/06	Auto Trailer	L M/M1	70. 0 x 9. 0 54. 0¾ x 8. 6¾ Cler (3)	29–34 18/35	Conversions from Lot 905
1110	23/ 6/06	Third G	C.27	70. 0 x 9. 0	3601–16	'Concertina' type
1111	28/ 4/06	First/Second Composite G	E.79	70. 0 x 9. 0	(7)512–7	'Concertina' type
1112	29/ 9/06	Brake Third G	D.43	70. 0 x 9. 0	3479–92	'Concertina' type
1113	7/ 7/06	Brake Tri-Composite G	E.80	70. 0 x 9. 0	(7)658–67	'Concertina' type
1114	21/ 7/06	First Diner G	H.13	70. 0 x 9. 0	(8)401–4*	'Concertina' type
1115	23/ 6/06	First Diner G	H.14	70. 0 x 9. 0	(8)405/6*	'Concertina' type
1116	22/12/06	Passenger Brake Van 3-centre G	K.15	40. 0¾ x 8. 0¾	237–46	
1117	25/ 8/06	Double Slip Tri-Composite	F.13	70. 0 x 9. 0	(7)685–99	'Concertina' type
1118	8/ 9/06	First Diner G	H.13	70. 0 x 9. 0	(8)407–12*	'Concertina' type
1119	22/12/06	First/Third Composite G	E.81	70. 0 x 9. 0	(7)675–84	'Concertina' type
1120	26/ 1/07	Brake Third G	D.43	70. 0 x 9. 0	3493–3502	'Concertina' type
1121	6/ 4/07	Brake Tri-Composite G	E.80	70. 0 x 9. 0	(7)655–7/68–74	'Concertina' type

Lot	Completed	Type	Diag. No.	Dimensions ft in ft in	Running Numbers	Notes
1122	27/ 4/07	Third G	C.27	70. 0 x 9. 0	3617–28	'Concertina' type
1123	4/ 5/07	First Sleeper G	J.6	70. 0 x 9. 0	(8)237–40*	12-wheel
1126	16/ 2/07	Auto Trailer	N	59. 6 x 9. 0	36–41	
1127	22/12/06	Auto Trailer	L	70. 0 x 9. 0	42–7	
1128	30/ 3/07	Auto Trailer	O	70. 0 x 9. 0	48	Experimental
1129	4/ 5/07	Steam Rail Motor	Q1	59. 6 x 9. 0	81–3	
1130	4/ 5/07	Auto Trailer	P	70. 0 x 9. 0	49–52	
1131	31/ 8/07	Diner G	H.15	70. 0 x 9. 0	9534–45	
1135	11/ 1/08	Brake Third G	D.44	57. 0 x 9. 0	3503–17	Bars 1 'Toplight'
1136	28/ 3/08	Third G	C.28	57. 0 x 9. 0	3629–58	Bars 1 'Toplight'
1137	9/11/07	First/Third Composite G	E.82	56. 0 x 9. 0	7518–32	Bars 1 'Toplight'
1138	14/12/07	Brake Tri-Composite G	E.83	57. 0 x 9. 0	7533–47	Bars 1 'Toplight'
1139	8/ 2/08	Bullion Van	M.17	36. 0 x 8. 0	819/20	
1140	11/ 1/08	Steam Rail Motor	R	70. 0 x 9. 0	84–90	
1141	4/ 1/08	Auto Trailer	L	70. 0 x 9. 0	53–8	
1142	29/ 2/08	Steam Rail Motor	R	70. 0 x 9. 0	91–9	
1143	29/ 2/08	Auto Trailer	L	70. 0 x 9. 0	59–70	
1144	4/ 4/08	Stowage Van G	M.12	70. 0 x 9. 0	874/5	Fishguard Ocean Mails
1145	11/ 4/08	First/Second Composite G	E.84	70. 0 x 9. 0	7548–53	Bars 1 'Toplight'
1146	26/ 6/09	Brake Third G	D.45	57. 0 x 9. 0	3518–33	Bars 1 'Toplight'
1147	24/ 7/09	First/Third Composite G	E.85	56. 0 x 9. 0	7712–27	Bars 1 'Toplight'
1148	1/ 8/08	Brake Composite G	E.82	56. 0 x 9. 0	7700–11	Bars 1 'Toplight' (First/Third)
1149	1/ 8/08	Diner G	H.16	57. 0 x 9. 0	9546–51	
1150	19/ 9/08	Single Slip Composite G	F.14	57. 0 x 9. 0	7101/2	Bars 1 'Toplight'
1151	26/ 9/08	Composite G	E.85	56. 0 x 9. 0	7728–9	Bars 1 'Toplight'
1152	3/10/08	Brake Third G	D.45	57. 0 x 9. 0	3534/5	Bars 1 'Toplight'
1153	30/ 1/09	Third G	C.28	57. 0 x 9. 0	3659–68	Bars 1 'Toplight'
1154	1/ 5/09	Third G	C.29	70. 0 x 9. 0	3669–88	Bars 1 'Toplight'
1155	7/11/08	Brake Composite G	E.86	57. 0 x 9. 0	7730/1	Bars 1 'Toplight'
1156	22/ 5/09	Brake Third G	D.45	57. 0 x 9. 0	3536–45	Bars 1 'Toplight'
1157	19/12/08	First	A.9	60. 0 x 9. 0	8197–8216	Bars 1 'Toplight'
1160	15/ 5/09	Auto Trailer G	Q	70. 0 x 9. 0	71/2 }	Alloc Plymouth
1161	15/ 5/09	Auto Trailer G	R	70. 0 x 9. 0	73/4 }	
1165	10/10/08	Parcels Van	M.13	70. 0 x 8. 11¼	833	
1166	20/11/09	Double Slip Composite	F.15	57. 0 x 9. 0	7103–9/7994–8000	Bars 1 'Toplight'
1167	19/ 2/10	Third G	C.30	56. 0 x 9. 0	2422–35	Bars 1 'Toplight'
1168	2/ 4/10	Brake Third G	D.46	56. 0 x 9. 0	2342–5	Bars 1 'Toplight'
1169	12/ 2/10	Brake Composite G	E.87	56. 0 x 9. 0	7732–7	Bars 1 'Toplight'
1170	13/ 8/10	Inspection Saloon	Q.1	43. 6 x 8. 0¾	6479	Rebuild, on old underframe
1171	4/ 2/11	Composite G	E.88	57. 0 x 9. 0	7738–47	Bars 1 'Toplight'
1172	20/ 2/11	Third G	C.31	57. 0 x 9. 0	2436–55	Bars 1 'Toplight'
1173	4/ 3/11	Brake Third G	D.47	57. 0 x 9. 0	2346–55	Bars 1 'Toplight'
1174	4/ 3/11	Brake Third G	D.46	56. 0 x 9. 0	2356–65	Bars 1 'Toplight'
(1175)	—	Brake Third G	—	70. 0 x —	2366–9	Lot cancelled, replaced by Lots 1181/2
1176	3/10/10	First G	A.10	70. 0 x 9. 0	8181–96	Fishguard Boat stock
1177	4/ 2/11	Diner G	H.19	70. 0 x 9. 0	9552–5	Fishguard Boat stock
1178	29/10/10	Parcels Van G	M.14	70. 0 x 9. 0 12-wheel	876/7	Fishguard Boat stock
1179	26/ 8/11	Third G	C.31	57. 0 x 9. 0	2466–91	Bars 1 'Toplight'
1180	5/ 8/11	Brake Third G	D.47	57. 0 x 9. 0	2370–3	Bars 1 'Toplight'
1181	3/12/10	Brake Third G	D.48	70. 0 x 9. 0	2366 }	Fishguard Boat stock
1182	24/ 9/10	Brake First G	A.11	70. 0 x 9. 0	8178–80 }	
1185	29/10/10	Stowage Van G	M.15	70. 0 x 9. 0 12-wheel	1201–6 }	1203–6 'Ocean Mails' vans
1187	13/ 5/11	Composite	E.89	57. 0 x 9. 0	6596–8/6604/62–5	Bars 2 'Toplight' Alloc Birmingham Suburban trains
1188	13/ 5/11	Brake Third	D.49	57. 0 x 9. 0	2388–95	Bars 2 'Toplight' Alloc Birmingham Suburban trains
1189	18/ 3/11	Kitchen First Brake G	H.20	70. 0 x 9. 0	8303	Plymouth Boat Trains
1190	3/ 6/11	Auto Trailer G	T	70. 0 x 9. 0	75–80	
1193	10/ 2/12	Composite G	E.88	57. 0 x 9. 0	7554–73	Bars 2 'Toplight'
1194	18/ 1/13	Third G	C.31	57. 0 x 9. 0	2456–64/92–2532	Bars 2 'Toplight'
1195	26/10/12	Brake Third G	D.47	57. 0 x 9. 0	2367–9/74–81/ 3551-9	Bars 2 'Toplight' four-compt,
		G	D.52		3560–9	three-compt

Lot	Completed	Type	Diag. No.	Dimensions ft in ft in	Running Numbers	Notes
1196	10/ 6/11	First Sleeper G	J.7	56. 0¾ x 9. 0	9086–9	Ex-LSWR 9086/7 destroyed by fire
1198	7/ 9/12	Auto Trailer G	U	70. 0 x 9. 0	81–92	
1199	16/11/12	First	A.12	57. 0 x 9. 0	8263	Bars 2 'Toplight'
1200	2/11/12	Brake Composite G	E.94	57. 0 x 9. 0	7581–3	Bars 2 'Toplight'
1201	24/ 8/12	Composite G	E.88	57. 0 x 9. 0	7748–51	Bars 2 'Toplight'
1202	28/ 9/12	Third G	C.31	57. 0 x 9. 0	2533–8	Bars 2 'Toplight'
1203	28/ 9/12	Brake Third G	D.52	57. 0 x 9. 0	3570–4	Bars 2 'Toplight'
1204	14/12/12	Passenger Brake Van G	K.18	57. 0 x 9. 0	247–9	'Toplight'
1207	31/ 8/12	Brake Third G	D.51	70. 0 x 9. 0	3575–84	Bars 2 'Toplight'
1208	31/ 8/12	Third G	C.29	70. 0 x 9. 0	2539–48	Bars 2 'Toplight'
1209	30/11/12	First Saloon G	G.43	57. 0 x 9. 0	9055	
1210	31/ 8/12	Composite G	E.93	70. 0 x 9. 0	7752–61	Bars 2 'Toplight'
—	7/ 8/12	Official Saloon	Q	54. 0 x 9. 0	9100	Using underframe of Royal saloon No 9001
1212	15/ 5/13	Brake Composite G	E.95	57. 0 x 9. 0	6945–64	Bars 2 'Toplight' 6962–4 single-ended composite slips as built
1213	3/ 5/12	Composite G	E.93	70. 0 x 9. 0	7762–4	Bars 2 'Toplight'
1214	21/ 6/13	Third G	C.29	70. 0 x 9. 0	2549–68	Bars 2 'Toplight'
1215	21/ 6/13	Brake Third G	D.51	70. 0 x 9. 0	3585–92	Bars 2 'Toplight'
1218	30/ 5/14	First Sleeper G	J.8	56.11¼ x 8.11¾	9090/1	'Toplight'
1219	12/ 7/13	Diner G	H.22	70. 0 x 9. 0 12-wheel	9556	
1220	22/11/13	Bullion Van	M.17	36. 0 x 8. 0	878	
1224	11/10/13	Auto Trailer G	Q	70. 0 x 9. 0	93–5	
1225	11/10/13	Auto Trailer G	R	70. 0 x 9. 0	96–8	
1226	29/11/13	Composite	E.97	69.11¼ x 8.11¼	6863–70	
1227	29/11/13	Brake Third	D.55	69.11¼ x 8.11¼	1070–7	Multibar 'Toplight'
1228	18/10/13	Composite	E.96	56.11¼ x 8.11¼	6500–11	Multibar 'Toplight'
1229	18/10/13	Brake Third	D.53	56.11¼ x 8.11¼	3735–46	Multibar 'Toplight' Alloc London Suburban trains
(1230)	—	Composite	—	—	(7901–12)	Lot cancelled 4/15
(1231)	—	Third	—	—	(3901–12)	Lot cancelled 4/15
(1232)	—	Brake Third	—	—	(3747–58)	Lot cancelled 4/15
1233	31/ 1/14	Composite G	E.98	56.11¼ x 8.11¼	6938/9/41/2/3/4	Multibar 'Toplight'
1234	21/ 2/14	Third G	C.32	56.11¼ x 8.11¼	2569–80	Multibar 'Toplight'
1235	31/ 1/14	Brake Third G	D.56	56.11¼ x 8.11¼	3593–8	Multibar 'Toplight'
1236	11/ 4/14	Third G	C.33	69.11¼ x 8.11¼	2581–2600	Multibar 'Toplight'
1237	28/ 3/14	Brake Third G	D.57	69.11¼ x 8.11¼	3759–62	Multibar 'Toplight'
1239	4/ 7/14	First G	A.13	69.11¼ x 8.11¼	8323–37	Multibar 'Toplight'
1240	11/ 7/14	Brake Composite G	E.99	69.11¼ x 8.11¼	7766–75	Multibar 'Toplight'
1241	22/ 8/14	Passenger Brake Van G	K.19	56.11¼ x 8.11¼	250–4	'Toplight'
1246	29/ 5/15	Third G	C.32	56.11¼ x 8.11¼	3913–47	Multibar 'Toplight'
1247	2/ 8/19	Brake Third G	D.56	56.11¼ x 8.11¼	3763–77	Multibar 'Toplight'
1248	2/10/21	Third G	C.39	57. 0 x 9. 0	3948	Experimental, all-steel
1249	4/ 6/22	Diner G	H.24	69.11¾ x 8.11¼	9557–61	
1250	11/ 3/23	Nondescript Saloon G	G.56	56.11¼ x 8.11¼	9369–71	9369 alloc Bristol; 9370 Padd; 9371 Cardiff
1251	27/11/21	Sleeper Composite G	J.9	57. 0 x 8.11⅜	7596/7600*	Multibar 'Toplight'
1252	28/10/16	Double Slip Composite	F.21	69.11¼ x 8.11¼	7990–3	Multibar 'Toplight'
1253	24/ 4/15	Passenger Brake Van G	K.22	56.11¼ x 8.11¼	255/6	'Toplight'
1256	29/11/19	Third G	C.35	56.11¼ x 8.11¼	3949–81	Multibar 'Toplight'
1257	22/11/19	Brake Third G	D.56	56.11¼ x 8.11¼	3778–86	Multibar 'Toplight'
(1260)	—	Brake First Saloon	—	—	(9098/9)	Lot cancelled Ordered 21/ 4/15
1261	22/ 2/20	Composite	E.101	48. 0 x 8. 5¼	7901/2	Main Line & City
1262	22/ 2/20	Third	C.37	48. 0 x 8. 5¼	3901/2	Main Line & City
1263	22/ 2/20	Brake Third	D.62	48. 0 x 8. 5¼	3747/8	Main Line & City
1269	15/ 8/20	Third G	C.32	56.11¼ x 8.11¼	3879–3900*	Multibar 'Toplight'
1270	17/ 1/20	Brake Third G	D.56	56.11¼ x 8.11¼	3787–92	Multibar 'Toplight'
1273	19/ 6/21	Composite	E.101	48. 0 x 8. 5¼	7903–12	Main Line & City
1274	19/ 6/21	Third	C.37	48. 0 x 8. 5¼	3903–12	Main Line & City
1275	19/ 6/21	Brake Third	D.62	48. 0 x 8. 5¼	3749–58	Main Line & City
1276	12/ 6/21	Composite G	E.102	69.11¼ x 8.11¼	7776–87	Multibar 'Toplight'
1277	12/ 6/21	Third G	C.38	69.11¼ x 8.11¼	3988/90–4000	Multibar 'Toplight'
1278	12/ 6/21	Brake Third G	D.69	69.11¼ x 8.11¼	3793–3804*	Multibar 'Toplight'
1279	28/11/20	Brake Third G	D.56	56.11¼ x 8.11¼	3805–10*	Ex-Ambulance, Multibar

Lot	Com-pleted	Type		Diag. No.	Dimensions ft in ft in	Running Numbers	Notes
1280	9/ 7/22	Brake Composite	G	E.104	60.11¼ x 8.11¼	7788–97	Multibar 'Toplight'
1281	9/ 4/22	Passenger Brake Van	G	K.22	56.11¼ x 8.11¼	257–66	'Toplight'
1282	19/ 3/22	Composite		E.103	56.11¼ x 8.11¼	7913–20	Multibar 'Toplight'
1283	19/ 3/22	Brake Third		D.67	56.11¼ x 8.11¼	3811–8*	Multibar 'Toplight'
1284	20/ 2/21	Third Saloon	G	G.54	46. 6¾ x 8. 6¾	9364/6	Ex-Ambulance (ex-Cler)
1285	9/ 1/21	Brake Third	G	D.68	57. 0 x 9. 0	3526	Ex-Ambulance Bars 1
1286	15/ 5/21	Third	G	C.31	57. 0 x 9. 0	3629/30/2–5	Ex-Ambulance Bars 1
			G	C.32	56.11¼ x 9. 0	3631	Ex-Ambulance Bars 1
1287	15/ 5/21	Brake Third	G	D.68	57. 0 x 9. 0	3504	Ex-Ambulance Bars 1
1288	18/ 6/22	Passenger Brake Van	G	K.22	56.11¼ x 8.11¼	267	Ex-Ambulance
1289	25/12/21	Third	G	C.31	57. 0 x 9. 0	3636–44	Ex-Ambulance Bars 1
1290	25/12/21	Third	G	C.35	56.11¼ x 8.11¼	3645–52	Ex-Ambulance Multibar
1291	15/ 5/21	Brake Third	G	D.56	56.11¼ x 8.11¼	3503	Ex-Ambulance Multibar
1292	25/ 9/21	Third	G	C.31	57. 0 x 9. 0	3653–9	Ex-Ambulance Bars 1
1293	25/12/21	Brake Third	G	D.56	56.11¼ x 8.11¼	3505/6	Ex-Ambulance Multibar
1294	9/10/21	Third	G	C.31	57. 0 x 9. 0	3660/1	Ex-Ambulance Bars 1
1295	16/10/21	Third	G	C.35	57. 0 x 8.11¼	3662–7	Ex-Ambulance Multibar
1296	23/10/21	Brake Third	G	D.52	57. 0 x 9. 0	3573	Ex-Ambulance Bars 2
1297	23/10/21	Third	G	C.31	57. 0 x 9. 0	2524	Ex-Ambulance Multibar
1298	30/10/21	Third Saloon	G	G.54	46. 6¾ x 8. 6¾	9365	Ex-Ambulance (ex-Cler)
(1300)	—	PO Van		—	—	(851)	Lot cancelled. To be in replacement of original No 851, destroyed
1301	9/ 7/22	Passenger Brake Van	G	K.22	56.11¼ x 8.11¼	1129–53	'Toplight'
1302	24/12/22	First		A.15	56.11¼ x 8.11¼	8072–89	Multibar 'Toplight' First with steel roofs
1303	5/ 2/22	Composite		E.103	56.11¼ x 8.11¼	7921–8	Multibar 'Toplight' London area
1304	5/ 2/22	Brake Third		D.67	56.11¼ x 8.11¼	3819–26*	Multibar 'Toplight' London area
1305	25/12/21	Nondescript Saloon	G	G.55	57. 0 x 8.11¼	9372–4	Multibar 'Toplight' – Ex-Ambulance. 9372/3 alloc Padd, 9374 B'ham
1308	—/ 4/23	Third	G	C.44/5	70. 8¼ x 9. 0	2472–5	One bow-end
1309	—/ 5/23	Brake Third	G	D.82/3	70. 8¼ x 9. 0	3518/9	One bow-end
					70. 0 x 9. 0	3516/7	
1310	—/ 4/23	Composite	G	E.109	71. 4½ x 9. 0	7601/4	BE
			G	E.110	71. 4½ x 9. 0	7602/3	BE
1311	—/12/22	Third	G	C.31	57. 0 x 9. 0	2452/5–62	Ex-Ambulance Bars 1
1312	—/10/22	Third	G	C.31/2	57. 0 x 9. 0	2463/4/6–71/6	Ex-Ambulance Bars 1
1313	—/10/22	Third	G	C.35	57. 0 x 9. 0	3668	Ex-Ambulance Multibar
1314	—/11/22	Brake Third	G	D.52/80	57. 0 x 9. 0	3507/8/10	Ex-Ambulance Multibar Bars 1/2, 3 compts
			G	D.47/68		3509/11/2/3	Ex-Ambulance Bars 2, 4 compts
1315	—/11/22	Brake Third	G	D.56A	56.11¼ x 8.11¼	3515	Ex-Ambulance Bars 2
1317	—/ 2/24	Third		C.43	57. 0 x 9. 0	4379–98	
1318	—/ 4/24	Brake Third		D.85	57. 0 x 9. 0	4399–4408	
1319	—/ 7/24	Composite	G	E.109	71. 4½ x 9. 0	7943/5	BE
				E.110	71. 4½ x 9. 0	7929/30/44/6/7/8	BE
				E.111	70. 0 x 9. 0	7932/6–42	
				E.112	70. 0 x 9. 0	7931/3–5	
1320	—/ 7/24	Third	G	C.44	70. 8¼ x 9. 0	4501/2	One bow-end
				C.46	70. 0 x 9. 0	4503–14	
				C.50	71. 4½ x 9. 0	4515–20	BE
1321	—/ 7/24	Brake Third	G	D.83/4	70. 0 x 9. 0	4601–12	
				D.82	70. 8¼ x 9. 0	4613/5/7/9	One bow-end
				D.90	70. 8¼ x 9. 0	4614/6/8/20	One bow-end
1322	—/ 7/23	Brake Composite	G	E.113	57. 0 x 8. 6	7949–64	7949–57 Westinghouse fitted
1323	—/ 9/23	Brake Composite	G	E.114	57. 0 x 9. 0	7965–89	7965–73 Westinghouse fitted
1324	—/12/23	Composite	G	E.115	57. 0 x 9. 0	7605–7/11/3/5/7/9/21/3	
				E.118		7608–10/2/4/6/8/20/2/4	
1325	—/12/23	Third	G	C.49	57. 0 x 9. 0	4521–40	Ex-Ambulance Bars 1

Lot	Completed	Type		Diag. No.	Dimensions ft in ft in	Running Numbers	Notes
1326	—/12/23	Brake Third	G	D.87 D.88	57. 0 x 9. 0	4621/3/5/7/9/ 31/3/5/7/9 4622/4/6/8/30/ 2/4/6/8/40	Ex-Ambulance Bars 1
1327	2/ 8/24	Brake Composite		E.116	57. 0 x 9. 0	7169/70, 7171/2, 7510/1, 7574/5, 7576/7, 7578/9 and 7625/6	Formed as 'B' sets, pairs as shown.
1328	2/ 8/24	Third		C.43	57. 0 x 9. 0	4409–33	
1329	2/ 8/24	Brake Third		D.85	57. 0 x 9. 0	4434–43	
1330	9/ 2/24	Composite Diner	G	H.25	57. 0 x 8. 0	9562–7	
1331	8/ 7/23	Composite Diner	G	H.26 H.27 H.28	71. 4½ x 9. 0 70. 0 x 9. 0 70. 0 x 9. 0	9568–71 9572 9573	BE
1332	—/10/23	Brake Third	G	D.87 D.88	57. 0 x 9. 0 57. 0 x 9. 0	4641/3/5/7 4642/4/6/8	Ex-Ambulance Bars 1
1333	—/ 8/23	Open Third		C.48	32. 0 x 6. 0	4997–5000	Vale of Rheidol stock – 1ft 11⅝in gauge
1334	—/ 7/24	Composite Diner	G	H.29	71. 4½ x 9. 0	9574–7	BE
1335	4/ 4/25	Brake Third		D.86 D.91	58. 2 x 9. 0 58. 2 x 9. 0	4652–77 4658–4705	BE BE To form set trains, London, Birmingham, Plymouth and Exeter Districts
1336	4/ 4/25	Composite		E.124 E.125	58. 2 x 9. 0 58. 2 x 9. 0	6666–91 6692–6702/14/9/ 20/1/37/42/6871 6872/7/6905/26/ 33–7/66	BE BE
1337	—/ 4/25	Third	G	C.46	70. 0 x 9. 0	4706–50	
1338	—/12/24	Brake Third	G	D.80	57. 0 x 9. 0	4225–32/41	Ex-Ambulance Bars 1
1339	—/12/24	Brake Third	G	D.56A D.68	56.11¼ x 8.11¼ 57. 0 x 9. 0	4243 4233/5/7/9	Ex-Ambulance Bars 1
1340	15/ 8/25	Composite		E.126 E.133	48. 0 x 8. 6	9809/10/5/6 9803/4	Formed as three Main Line & City Articulated six-coach sets
1341	15/ 8/25	Third		C.53	48. 0 x 8. 6	9802/5/8/11/4/7	
1342	15/ 8/25	Brake Third		D.93	48. 0 x 8. 6	9801/6/7/12/3/8	
1343	—/12/24	Third	G	C.31	57. 0 x 9. 0	4541–4	Ex-Ambulance Bars 1
1344	—/ 2/25	Passenger Brake	G	K.34 K.35 K.36	57. 0 x 9. 0 57. 0 x 9. 0 57. 0 x 9. 0	1156/64 1154/5 1157–63	Ex-Ambulance
1345	—/ 2/25	Passenger Brake	G	K.34 K.37	57. 0 x 9. 0 56.11¼ x 8.11¼	1166–8 1165	Ex-Ambulance
1346	—/10/26	Passenger Brake	G	K.38	58. 4½ x 9. 0	1169–74	BE Ocean Mails vans
1349	15/ 8/25	Composite Diner	G	H.33	58. 4½ x 9. 0	9578–81	BE
1350	—/ 1/26	Brake Composite	G	E.128	58. 4½ x 9. 0	6475–81/3/91– 5/7/8/6512–8	BE
1351	—/12/25	Composite	G	E.127	58. 4½ x 9. 0	6519–22/5–8/30/ 1/2/6	BE To form six sets each two brake thirds, two thirds and two composites
1352	—/12/25	Third	G	C.54	58. 4½ x 9. 0	4545–56	BE
1353	—/12/25	Brake Third	G	D.94	58. 4½ x 9. 0	4751–62	BE
1354	—/12/25	Brake Third	G	D.94	58. 4½ x 9. 0	4763–9	BE
1355	6/ 2/26	Brake Composite		E.129	58. 2 x 9. 0	6545/7, 6551/3, 6556/60, 6561/3, 6565/6	BE Formed as 'B' sets pairs as shown, Bristol Division
1357	—/10/25	First Diner	G	H.30	50. 6¾ x 9. 0	10002/10/8/26/ 34/42*	BE Articulated Corridor Stock to form six eight-car trains. Lots 1363/4, pairs; Lots 1357/8/9, triplets Lots 1360/1/2, triplets
1358	—/10/25	Kitchen Car	G	H.31	46. 3 x 9. 0	10003/11/9/27/35/ 43*	BE
1359	—/10/25	Third Diner	G	H.32	50. 6¾ x 9. 0	10004/12/20/8/36/ 44*	BE
1360	—/10/25	Brake Third	G	D.92	50. 6¾ x 9. 0	10007/15/23/31/9/ 47*	BE
1361	—/10/25	Third	G	C.51	52. 3 x 9. 0	10006/14/22/30/8/ 46*	BE
1362	—/10/25	Third	G	C.52	52. 3 x 9. 0	10005/13/21/9/37/ 45*	BE
1363	—/10/25	First	G	A.16	48. 0¾ x 9. 0	10001/9/17/25/33/ 41*	BE
1364	—/10/25	Brake First	G	A.17	50. 6¾ x 9. 0	10000/8/16/24/32/ 40*	BE
1365	6/ 2/26	Third	G	C.54	58. 4½ x 9. 0	4557–62	BE
1366	—/ 1/26	Third	G	C.55	57. 0 x 9. 0	4377	Ex-Ambulance. New body on old underframe
1369	—/ 9/26	Third	G	C.54	58. 4½ x 9. 0	4776–4854	BE

Lot	Completed	Type		Diag. No.	Dimensions ft in ft in	Running Numbers	Notes
1371	—/ 8/26	Third	G	C.54	58. 4½ x 9. 0	4855/6	BE First with slam locks
1372	—/ 1/27	Third	G	C.54	58, 4½ x 9. 0	4857–80	BE
1373	21/ 5/27	Composite	G	E.127	58. 4½ x 9. 0	6024/6/9/30/4/47/ 50/68/99 6105/35/7/8/45/6/ 9/50/5/6/8/60/7 6181/7/92/4/8/ 6201/3/9/11	BE
1374	21/ 5/27	Third	G	C.54	58. 4½ x 9. 0	4881–4912	BE
1375	21/ 5/27	Brake Third	G	D.95	58. 4½ x 9. 0	4913–44	BE
1376	1/10/27	Composite		E.131	58. 2 x 9. 0	6231/3/5/6/7/42/ 8/9/50/2/5/6/8/9 6260/4/72/6329/ 31/44/5/6/9/ 50/4/7 6360/2/4/9/70/6/ 87/8/90 6416/35/58/68/9	BE Lots 1376/7 To form 20 four-coach trains, two brake thirds and two composites
1377	1/10/27	Brake Third		D.98	58. 2 x 9. 0	4945-84	BE
1382	4/ 8/28	Composite	G	E.132	57. 4½ x 9. 0	6011–6/8–23/5/7 31/2/5/8–45/7 6051/4/5/65/6/ 7/70/2–4/6–83/5 6089–94/6	BE
1383	30/ 6/28	Third	G	C.54	58. 4½ x 9. 0	5001–86	BE
1384	30/ 6/28	Brake Third	G	D.95	58. 4½ x 9. 0	5087–5132	BE
1388	23/ 2/29	Composite		E.131	58. 2 x 9. 0	6624–39	BE } To form eight trains for Chester and B'ham areas
1389	23/ 2/29	Brake Third		D.98	58. 2 x 9. 0	5501–16	BE }
1390	8/12/28	Composite		E.134	58. 2 x 9. 0	6567–78	BE } To form 12 trains for Cardiff/ Newport valleys
1391	8/12/28	Third		C.56	56. 8 x 9. 0	5541–64	BE }
1392	8/12/28	Brake Third		D.101	58. 2 x 9. 0	5517–40	BE }
1393	30/ 3/29	Brake Composite		E.135	58. 2 x 8.10¼	6640/1, 2/3	BE Formed as 'B' sets Bristol Division
1394	5/ 1/29	Auto Trailer		A.27	59. 6 x 9. 0	159–170	BE
1395	5/ 5/29	Third	G	C.54	58. 4½ x 9. 0	5143–54/6–80	BE
		Sleeper/Third	G	J.10	58. 4½ x 9. 0	5140–2*	
		Third	G	C.57	58. 4½ x 9. 0	5155	
1398	27/ 4/29	Composite	G	E.136	57. 4½ x 8.10¼	6101–4	BE } To form two six-coach trains with Nos 5177–80 (Lot 1395), two of each type of vehicle
1399	4/ 5/29	Brake Third	G	D.104	58. 4½ x 9. 0	5133–9	BE }
1400	4/ 5/29	Third Saloon	G	G.58	58. 4½ x 9. 0	9101–10	BE
1402	14/ 2/31	Composite		E.142	61. 2 x 9. 3	6644–9	BE } To form nine five-coach sets in South Wales, two brakes, two thirds and a composite
1403	14/ 2/31	Third		C.61	61. 2 x 9. 3	5565–76	BE }
1404	14/ 2/31	Brake Third		D.110	61. 2 x 9. 3	5577–88	BE }
1405	1/11/30	Composite		E.141	61. 2 x 9. 3	6431–4/6–43	BE } To form six four-coach trains for Birmingham area
1406	1/11/30	Brake Third		D.109	61. 2 x 9. 3	5589–5600	BE }
1407	5/ 4/30	Brake Composite		E.140	61. 2 x 9. 3	6445/6, 6447/8, 6449/50, 6451/2, 6453/4, 6455/6, 6457/9, 6460/1, 6462/3, 6464/5	BE Formed as 'B' sets, pairs as shown. Bristol area
1410	29/ 3/30	Auto Trailer		A.28	62. 8 x 9. 0	171–80	BE
1411	14/ 9/29	Third	G	C.58	58. 4½ x 8.10¼	5181–5230	BE
1412	24/ 8/29	Brake Third	G	D.104	58. 4½ x 8.10¼	5231–42	BE
1413	8/ 3/30	Passenger Brake	G	K.40	61. 4½ x 9. 0	1175–84	BE
1418	20/ 9/30	First Sleeper	G	J.12	61. 4½ x 9. 7	9080/1/6–8	BE Six-wheel bogies
1419	4/ 5/29	Third Sleeper	G	J.11	61. 4½ x 9. 7	9094–6	BE
1420	8/ 2/30	Kitchen Car	G	H.35	61. 4½ x 9. 7	9594–9600	BE } 'Cornish Riviera'/ 'Torbay Ltd' stock To form six three-coach sets, one spare kitchen car
1421	21/12/29	Composite Diner	G	H.36	61. 4½ x 9. 7	9582–7	BE }
1422	21/12/29	Third Diner	G	H.37	61. 4½ x 9. 7	9588–93	BE }
1423	25/ 1/30	Third	G	C.60	61. 4½ x 9. 0	5243–57	BE
1424	21/12/29	Composite	G	E.137	61. 4½ x 9. 5¾	6017/28/33/46/ 8/52/8/60/3/4/ 9/71/86	BE 'Cornish Riviera'/ 'Torbay Ltd' stock

Lot	Com-pleted	Type		Diag. No.	Dimensions ft in ft in	Running Numbers	Notes
1425	21/12/29	Brake Composite	G	E.138	61. 4½ x 9. 5¾	6087/8/95/7/8/ 6100/7/8/18/ 20/1/4 6134/47/8/51/2/3	BE 'Cornish Riviera'/ 'Torbay Ltd' stock
1426	21/12/29	Third	G	C.59	60. 4½ x 9. 5¾	5258–80	BE 'Cornish Riviera'/ 'Torbay Ltd' stock
1427	21/12/29	Brake Third	G	D.105	61. 4½ x 9. 5¾	5281–92	BE 'Cornish Riviera/ 'Torbay Ltd' stock
1428	21/12/29	Brake Third	G	D.106	61. 4½ x 9. 5¾	5293–8	BE 'Cornish Riviera'/ 'Torbay Ltd' stock
1429	21/12/29	Double Slip		F.23	61. 4½ x 9. 5¾	7898/9/7900	BE 'Cornish Riviera' stock
1430	14/12/29	P.O. Sorting	G	L.18	57. 0 x 8. 6	806–8	TPO vans
1431	7/ 6/30	First Saloon	G	G.59	61. 4½ x 9. 0	9004/5	BE
1432	21/ 6/30	Auto Trailer		A.26 A.29	70. 0 x 9. 0	181–5 186	Ex-Rail motors
1433	5/ 7/30	Composite	G	E.137	61. 4½ x 9. 5¾	6163–6	BE
1434	5/ 7/30	Third	G	C.59	61. 4½ x 9. 5¾	5355/6	BE
1435	5/ 7/30	Brake Third	G	D.108	61. 4½ x 9. 5¾	5299–5302	BE
1436	28/ 6/30	Third	G	C.60	61. 4½ x 9. 0	5315–54	BE
1437	7/ 6/30	Brake Third	G	D.107	61. 4½ x 9. 0	5303–14	BE
1438	31/ 5/30	Composite	G	E.139	61. 4½ x 9. 0	6176–9/82–5	BE
1439	21/ 2/31	First Sleeper	G	J.12	61. 4½ x 9. 7	9065–8	BE
1440	10/10/30	Third Sleeper	G	J.11	61. 4½ x 9. 7	9069–74	BE
1442	30/ 5/31	Composite Sleeper	G	J.13	61. 4½ x 9. 7	9075	BE
1445	13/ 9/30	Brake Composite		E.140	61. 2 x 9. 3	6381/2, 6409/10, 6411/2, 6413/4, 6470/1, 6523/4, 6534/5, 6537/8, 6541/2, 6548/9, 6554/5, 6557/8, 6589/90, 6703/4, 6722/3, 6894/5, 6979/80, 6986/7, 6995/6, 6999/7000	BE Formed as 'B' sets, pairs as shown
1446	27/12/30	Composite	G	E.143	61. 4½ x 9. 3	6205–8/10/2–4	BE
1447	27/12/30	Third	G	C.62	61. 4½ x 9. 3	5357–60	BE
1448	27/12/30	Brake Third	G	D.111	61. 4½ x 9. 3	5361–8	BE
1449	29/11/30	Composite		E.141	61. 2 x 9. 3	6336/7/9/40/1–3/ 7/53/8	BE
1450	29/11/30	Brake Third		D.109	61. 2 x 9. 3	5601–10	BE
1451	13/ 6/30	Composite Diner	G	H.38	61. 4½ x 9. 0	9601–10	BE
1452	28/ 3/31	Composite	G	E.143	61. 4½ x 9. 3	6113/5/7/9/33/41/ 54/7	BE
1453	28/ 3/31	Third	G	C.62	61. 4½ x 9. 3	5369–72	BE
1454	28/ 3/31	Brake Third	G	D.111	61. 4½ x 9. 3	5373–80	BE
1455	2/ 5/31	Brake Composite		E.140	61. 2 x 9. 3	6240/1, 6261/2, 6365/6, 6371/2, 6374/5, 6656/7, 6968/9, 6975/6, 6977/8, 6983/4, 6989/90	BE Formed as 'B' sets, pairs as shown, for Bristol Division
1456	15/ 5/31	Composite		E.141	61. 2 x 9. 3	6724/31/4/44/7/ 50/2/4/8/61/ 6/8 6775/80/95/6802/ 4/86/92/6929	BE To form London area sets
1457	15/ 8/31	Brake Third		D.109	61. 2 x 9. 3	5611–30	BE
1458	27/ 2/32	Composite		E.142	61. 2 x 9. 3	6970/2/4	BE To form three five-coach sets for South Wales
1459	27/ 2/32	Third		C.61	61. 2 x 9. 3	5667–72	BE
1460	27/ 2/32	Brake Third		D.110	61. 2 x 9. 3	5631–6	BE
1462	21/11/31	Passenger Brake	G	K.40	61. 4½ x 9. 0	3/4/5/6/9/11/3/ 9/27/8/31–7/ 9/41/3/51/3/5–7	BE
1464	26/12/31	Brake Third		D.112	61. 2 x 9. 0	5637–66	BE
1465	30/ 1/32	Third		C.63	61. 2 x 9. 0	5673–88	BE
1466	31/10/31	Third	G	C.60	61. 4½ x 9. 0	5689–5708	BE
1468	25/ 6/32	First Diner	G	H.39	61. 4½ x 9. 3	9611–20	BE Formed as pairs
1469	25/ 6/32	Third Diner	G	H.40	61. 4½ x 9. 3	9621–30	BE
1471	7/ 5/32	First Saloon	G G	G.60 G.61	61. 4½ x 9. 7	9111/2 9113–8	BE 'Super Saloons'
1474	13/ 8/32	Composite	G	E.14	61. 4½ x 9. 3	6377/80/3/6/9/98/ 6415/44	BE To form four five-coach sets with Lot 1476
1475	13/ 8/32	Third	G	C.62	61. 4½ x 9. 3	5381–4	BE

Lot	Completed	Type	Diag. No.	Dimensions ft in ft in	Running Numbers	Notes
1476	13/ 8/32	Brake Third G	D.115	61. 4 x 9. 3½	5385–92	BE See Lots 1474/5
1477	9/ 7/32	Third G	C.62	61. 4½ x 9. 3	5393–5446	BE
1478	1/10/32	Brake Third G	D.115	61. 4½ x 9. 3	5447–60	BE
1479	11/ 2/33	Brake Composite	E.145	61. 2 x 9. 3	6061/75/6122/3/59/61/8/75/6180/6/8/91/3/9/6200/2/4/6215–7/9–22/4/5/8/9/32/6234/8/9/46/51/3/4/7/6263/8/97/6316/35/8/48/59/6361/3/7/8/73	BE Formed as 'B' sets where required
1480	1/ 4/33	Auto Trailer	A.30	62. 8 x 9. 0	187–96	BE
1481	21/ 1/33	Passenger Brake G	K.40	61. 4½ x 9. 0	71–85	BE
1484	1/10/32	P.O. Sorting G	L.19	57. 0 x 9. 0	848/9	TPO vans
1487	25/ 4/32	Café-Car Cler (3) G	H.3	58. 0¾ x 8. 6¾	9502/16	Conversions from Lot 801/929
1489	2/ 9/33	Third G	C.64 C.65	61. 4½ x 9. 3 60. 0 x 9. 3	5709–43 5744–78	BE (flat-ended)
1490	7/10/33	Brake Third G	D.116	57. 0 x 9. 0	5779–97	
1491	14/11/33	Brake Composite G	E.146	57. 0 x 9. 0	6579–88	
1492	3/ 2/34	Third	C.66	55. 3½ x 9. 0	5471–90	
1493	24/ 2/34	Brake Third	D.117	57. 0 x 9. 0	5491–5500	
1494	16/12/33	Brake Composite	E.147	57. 0 x 9. 0	6762/3, 6764/5, 6769/70, 6771/2, 6773/4, 6776/7, 6778/9, 6781/2, 6783/4, 6785/6, 6787/8, 6789/90, 6791/2, 6793/4, 6796/7, 6800/1	Formed as 'B' sets, pairs as shown, for Newport Division
1495	24/ 2/34	Passenger Brake G	K.41	57. 0 x 9. 0	101–10	
1499	4/11/33	P.O. Collector Van G	L.21	57. 0 x 8. 6	793–5	TPO vans
1500	14/10/33	P.O. Sorting G	L.20	57. 0 x 8. 6	796	TPO vans
1501	23/12/33	P.O. Delivery G	L.22	50. 0 x 8. 6	797–800	TPO vans
1502	3/ 2/34	P.O. Sorting G	L.22	50. 0 x 8. 6	801–3	TPO vans
1503	23/12/33	P.O. Stowage G	L.23	50. 0 x 8. 6	812–4	TPO vans
1504	30/12/33	P.O. Stowage G	L.24	46. 6 x 8. 6	815–7	TPO vans
1505	—/10/34	Brake Composite	E.147	57. 0 x 9. 0	6873–6/8–85/7–91/3/6–9/6900–4/6906–8	Formed as 'B' sets
1506	13/10/34	Third	C.66	55. 3½ x 9. 0	5461–70	
1507	10/11/34	Brake Third	D.117	57. 0 x 9. 0	5868–77	
1508	14/ 7/34	Brake Composite G	E.148	57. 0 x 9. 0	6909–24/7/8/30/1	
1509	28/ 2/35	Third G	C.67	57. 0 x 9. 0	5808–67	
1510	11/ 8/34	Brake Third G	D.118	57. 0 x 9. 0	5798–5807	
1511	27/ 1/34	Auto Trailer	A.23 A.26 A.29 A.31	70. 0 x 9. 0 70. 0 x 9. 0 70. 0 x 9. 0 59. 6 x 9. 0	197/8 199/200/6 201 202–5	Ex-Rail-motors
1512	29/ 9/34	Passenger Brake G	K.41	57. 0 x 9. 0	111-20	
1513	12/ 5/34	Third G	C.67	57. 0 x 9. 0	5888–5927	
1514	2/ 6/34	Brake Third G	D.118	57. 0 x 9. 0	5878–87	
1516	5/ 2/34	Diesel Railcar	U	60. 0 x 9. 0	1	†AEC/Park Royal built
1518	7/ 7/34	Buffet Car G	H.41	57. 0 x 9. 0	9631/2	
1519	10/11/34	Third Sleeper G	J.14	57. 0 x 9. 0	9076–8	
1521	—/—/35	Auto Trailer	A.31	59. 6 x 9. 0	207–9	Ex-Rail-motors
1522	26/ 9/34 8/ 7/35	Diesel Railcar Diesel Railcar	V W	60. 0 x 9. 0 60. 0 x 9. 0	2–4 5–7	†AEC/Park Royal built †AEC/Gloucester RC&W built
1523	16/11/35	Brake Composite	E.147	57. 0 x 9. 0	6803/5–17/9/21	Formed as 'B' sets for Newport Division
1524	26/10/35	Third	C.66	55. 3½ x 9. 0	4244–91	
1525	7/ 9/35	Brake Third	D.117	57. 0 x 9. 0	4342–67	
1526	11/ 5/35	Brake Composite G	E.148	57. 0 x 9. 0	6824–6/8/32–6/40/2–9/51/2	
1527	17/ 8/35	Third G	C.67	57. 0 x 9. 0	5928–82	
1528	17/ 8/35	Brake Third G	D.118	57. 0 x 9. 0	5983–95	
1529	13/ 4/35	Kitchen Car G	H.42	60. 0 x 9. 0	9633/4	Excursion stock
1530	20/ 4/35	Open Third G	C.68	60. 0 x 9. 0	4563–70	Excursion stock
1531	20/ 4/35	Open Brake Third G	D.119	60. 0 x 9. 0	4571–4	Excursion stock
1532	21/12/35	First Diner G	H.47	60. 0 x 9. 0	9641/2	

†Not described in text.

Lot	Completed	Type	Diag. No.	Dimensions ft in ft in	Running Numbers	Notes
1533	21/12/35	Third Diner G	H.48	60. 0 x 9. 0	9639/40	
1535	7/12/35	Passenger Brake G	K.41	57. 0 x 9. 0	181–200	
1536	27/ 7/35	Brake Third G	D.120	61. 4½ x 9. 7	4575–80	'Centenary' stock
1537	27/ 7/35	Third G	C.69	61. 4½ x 9. 7	4581–6	'Centenary' stock
1538	27/ 7/35	Composite G	E.149	61. 4½ x 9. 7	6658–61	'Centenary' stock
1539	27/ 7/35	Brake Composite G	E.150	61. 4½ x 9. 7	6650–5	'Centenary' stock
1540	27/ 7/35	First Diner G	H.43	61. 4½ x 9. 7	9635/6	'Centenary' stock Formed as pairs (1540–1541)
1541	27/ 7/35	Third Diner G	H.44	61. 4½ x 9. 7	9637/8	
1542	22/ 2/36	Auto Trailer	A.26	70. 0 x 9. 0	210/2–5	Ex-Rail-motors
			A.31	59. 6 x 9. 0	211	
1545	18/ 1/36	Auto Trailer	A.29	70. 0 x 9. 0	216–8	Ex-Rail-motors
			A.31	59. 6 x 9. 0	219	
1546	17/ 4/36	Diesel Railcar	W	60. 0 x 9. 0	9/13–6	†AEC/Gloucester RC&W built
1547	17/ 2/36	Diesel Railcar	X	60. 0 x 9. 0	10–12	†AEC/Gloucester RC&W built
	27/ 4/36	Diesel Parcels Railcar	Y		17	
1550	3/10/36	Brake Composite	E.147	57. 0 x 9. 0	6707/8–10, 6711/5/25/6/7/9/30/2/6/8/9/40/6741/3/5/6/8/9/51/3/5/6/7/9/60/7/6798/9/6818/20/22/3/7	Majority formed as 'B' sets, except 6707–10, 6822/3/7/37/8/50 with long buffers, 6818/20 auto-trailers
1551	12/ 9/36	Third	C.66	55. 3½ x 9. 0	4026–65	
1552	10/10/36	Brake Third	D.117	57. 0 x 9. 0	4001–20	
1553	14/ 3/36	Composite G	E.151	58. 7½ x 9. 0	6853–8	
1554	15/ 2/36	Third G	C.70	60.11¼ x 9. 0	4304–31	
1555	30/ 5/36	Brake Third G	D.121	60.11¼ x 9. 0	4066–9/73–4102/4–25	
1556	27/ 6/36	Buffet/Third G	H.53	60. 0 x 9. 0	9643/4	
1557	27/ 6/36	Brake Composite G	E.152	60.11¼ x 9. 0	6859–62/6925/32/40/65/7/71/3/6981/2/5/8/91–4/7	
1558	9/ 5/36	Open Third G	C.71	60. 0 x 9. 0	4158–67	Excursion stock
1559	11/ 4/36	Third G	C.70	60.11¼ x 9. 0	4444–83	
1560	11/ 4/36	Composite G	E.151	58. 7 x 9. 0	6606/7/11/2/4/7/8/20/2/3	
1562	25/ 4/36	Passenger Brake G	K.41	57. 0 x 9. 0	138–57	
1564	4/ 4/37	Diesel Railcar	Z	60. 0 x 9. 0	18	†AEC/Gloucester RC&W built
1566	31/ 7/37	First	A.21	57. 2¼ x 8.11	8033–42	
1567	7/ 8/37	Composite	E.156	59. 3½ x 8.11	6591–4	
1568	4/ 9/37	Brake Composite	E.157	57. 0 x 8.11	6218/23/6/7/30/43/4/5/65/96/6300/3/5/7/9/12/3/4/7/8	
1569	16/10/37	Third	C.75	55. 3½ x 8.11	1384–1418	
1570	20/11/37	Brake Third	D.125	57. 0 x 8.11	1419–35/7–9	
1571	28/11/36	Composite G	E.154	58. 7 x 9. 0	6001/2/4–7/10/36	
1572	14/11/36	Brake Composite G	E.153	60.11¼ x 9. 0	6378/9/84/5/97/6400/6/7/66/7/6472/3/4/84/6/9/90/6/9/6529	
1573	22/ 5/37	Third G	C.73	60.11¼ x 9. 0	1442–1516	
1574	10/ 7/37	Brake Third G	D.124	60.11¼ x 9. 0	1583–1603/5–26	
1575	17/ 4/37	Third Open G	C.74	60. 0 x 9. 0	1271–97	Excursion stock
1576	20/ 2/37	Open Brake Third G	D.123	60. 0 x 9. 0	1298–1301	Excursion stock
1579	27/ 3/37	Kitchen Car G	H.54	60. 0 x 9. 0	9663–8	Excursion stock
1581	13/ 3/37	First G	A.20	60. 1¼ x 9. 0	8043–52	
1582	29/ 5/37	Composite G	E.155	59.10 x 9. 0	6049/53/6/7/9/62/84/6106/9–12/6114/6/28/32/6/40	
1586	12/11/38	First G	A.22	60. 1¼ x 8.11	8092–8111	
1587	21/ 5/38	Composite G	E.158	59.10 x 8.11	7001–56	
1588	1/10/38	Composite G	E.160	58. 7 x 8.11	6142–4/62/9–74/96/6266/74/5/91 6302/6/11/51/2	
1589	15/10/38	Brake Composite G	E.159	60.11¼ x 8.11	6355/6/6408/21/85/7/6533/9/40/6543/4/6/50/2/9/62/4/95/9/6600/3/5/8/9/10/9/6705/6/13/6829	

†Not described in text.

Lot	Completed	Type		Diag. No.	Dimensions ft in ft in	Running Numbers	Notes
1590	22/10/38	Brake Composite	G	E.159	60.11¼ x 8.11	7060–4	
1591	29/ 1/38	Open Third	G	C.76	60.11¼ x 8.11	1530–9	Excursion stock
1592	15/ 1/38	Open Brake Third	G	D.126	60.11¼ x 8.11	1541/2	Excursion stock
1593	1/10/38	Third	G	C.77	60.11¼ x 8.11	1080–9/91/3–8/ 1100–16/8–28/ 30–4/1136–55	
1594	18/ 6/38	Brake Third	G	D.127	60.11¼ x 8.11	1627–47/9–54	
1595	30/ 4/38	Brake Third	G	D.127	60.11¼ x 8.11	1655–7	
1596	17/12/38	Composite		E.156	59. 3½ x 8.11	7091–8	
1597	24/12/38	Double Slip Composite		F.24	60.11¼ x 8.11	7069–74	
1598	1/ 4/39	Third		C.75	55. 3½ x 8.11	1673–84/6/8–90/ 2–1712	
1599	24/12/38	Brake Third		D.125	57. 0 x 8.11	1660–6	
1600	22/ 4/39	Auto Brake Third		A.34	57. 0 x 8.11	1668–71	
1601	3/12/38	Composite Diner	G	H.57	60.11¼ x 8.11 12-wheel	9671–5	
1602	25/ 6/38	Buffet Car	G	H.55	60.11¼ x 8.11 12-wheel	9676–80	
1603	9/ 7/38	Kitchen Car	G	H.56	60.11¼ x 8.11 12-wheel	9669/70	
1604	4/12/37	Passenger Brake	G	K.42	57. 0 x 8.11	158–67	
1608	4/ 2/39	Brake Composite		E.161	57. 0 x 8.11	6830/1	Highworth branch stock
1609	4/ 2/39	Third		C.75	55. 3½ x 8.11	1237/8	Highworth branch stock
1610	4/ 2/39	Brake Third		D.125	57. 0 x 8.11	1239/40	Highworth branch stock
1611	4/ 3/39	Brake Third		D.129	57. 0 x 8. 8	1323–8	BPGV line stock
1612	25/ 3/39	Third		C.80	55. 3½ x 8. 8	1329	BPGV line stock
1615	—/ 6/38	Closed Third		C.78	32. 0 x 6. 0	4143–8/4994	Vale of Rheidol stock – 1ft 11⅝in gauge *Four wheel
1616	—/ 6/38	Brake Third		D.128	32. 0 x 6. 0	4995/6	
1617	—/ 6/38	Passenger Brake		K.43	13. 8 x 6. 5	137–9*	
1618	—/ 6/38	Open Third		C.48	32. 0 x 6. 0	4149–51	
1621	10/ 2/40	Composite	G	E.158	59.10 x 8.11	7301–40	
1622	22/ 4/39	Brake Composite	G	E.159	60.11¼ x 8.11	7341–6	
1623	11/ 5/40	Third	G	C.77	60.11¼ x 8.11	501–95	
1624	23/ 3/40	Brake Third	G	D.127	60.11¼ x 8.11	601–25	
1625	18/ 3/39	Open Third	G	C.76	60.11¼ x 8.11	626–37	Excursion stock
1626	27/ 7/40	First Saloon	G	G.62	60.11¼ x 8.11	9001/2	
(1627)	—	Composite Sleeper	G	—	—	(9082)	Lots cancelled. Ordered 5/4/38
(1628)	—	Third Sleeper	G	—	—	(9083)	
1629	8/ 6/40	Brake Composite		E.161	57. 0 x 8.11	7347–52	
1630	22/ 6/40	Composite		E.156	59. 3½ x 8.11	7110–5	
1631	17/ 8/40	Third		C.75	55. 3½ x 8.11	451–75	
1632	31/ 8/40	Brake Third		D.125	57. 0 x 8.11	476–81	
(1633)	—	Double Slip		—	—	(7085–7)	Lot cancelled. Ordered 7/4/38
1635	3/ 3/41	Diesel Railcar		A.1	62. 0 x 9. 0	19–33	†AEC/Swindon built
1636	15/ 9/41	Diesel Parcels Railcar		A.2	62. 0 x 9. 0	34	†AEC/Swindon built
1637	28/ 2/42	Diesel Railcar		A.3 A.4	62. 0 x 9. 0	36/8 35/7	†AEC/Swindon built
(1638)	—	First	G	—	—	(8001–4)	Lot cancelled. Ordered 1/5/39
1639	14/ 6/41	Composite	G	E162	59.10 x 8.11	7271–90	Some completed as Lot 1667
1640	11/ 1/41	Brake Composite	G	E.159	60.11¼ x 8.11	7357–71	
1641	13/ 9/41	Third	G	C.81	60.11¼ x 8.11	751–80	781–845 cancelled
1642	25/ 1/41	Brake Third	G	D.127	60.11¼ x 8.11	652–75	
1643	6/ 4/40	Open Third	G	C.76	60.11¼ x 8.11	644–9	Excursion stock
1644	20/ 4/40	Open Brake Third	G	D.130	60.11¼ x 8.11	650/1	Excursion stock
(1645)	—	Composite		—	—	(7118–21)	Lots cancelled. Ordered 1/5/39
(1646)	—	Brake Composite		—	—	(7353–6)	
(1647)	—	Third		—	—	(490–7)	
(1648)	—	Brake Third		—	—	(482–9)	
1652	1/ 6/40	Passenger Brake	G	K.42	57. 0 x 8.11	121–30	
(1655)	—	Composite	G	—	—	(7261–70)	Lots cancelled. Ordered 15/4/40
(1656)	—	Brake Composite	G	—	—	(7372–81)	
(1657)	—	Third	G	—	—	(846–85)	
(1658)	—	Brake Third	G	—	—	(886–905)	
(1659)	—	Composite		—	—	(7122–31)	
(1660)	—	Brake Composite		—	—	(7136–55)	
(1661)	—	Third		—	—	(383–417)	
(1662)	—	Brake Third		—	—	(418–42)	
1665	26/ 5/45	Passenger Brake	G	K.42	57. 0 x 8.11	91–100/268–77	268–77 built 1943
1666	—/—/40	P.O. Sorting Van	G	L.23	50. 0 x 8. 6	814	Replacement TPO vehicle

†Not described in text.

Lot	Completed	Type		Diag. No.	Dimensions ft in ft in	Running Numbers	Notes
1667	2/ 8/41	Passenger Brake	G	K.44	59.10 x 8.11	61–70	In place of some deferred composites on Lot 1639
1673	29/12/45	Special Saloon	G	G.64 G.65	60.11¼ x 8.11	9006 9007	Secondhand underframes
1685	29/ 4/50	Third	G	C.85	64. 0 x 8.11	2239	Experimental
1688	19/11/49	First	G	A.23	64. 0 x 8.11	8001–3	
1689	23/10/48	Composite	G	E.163	64. 0 x 8.11	7252–62	
1690	25/12/48	Brake Composite	G	E.164	64. 0 x 8.11	7372–85	
1691	12/ 6/48	Third	G	C.82	64. 0 x 8.11	781–832	
1692	27/12/47	Brake Third	G	D.131	64. 0 x 8.11	833–54	
1693	13/11/48	Third		C.83	63. 0¾ x 8.11	374–413	
1694	9/10/48	Brake Third		D.132	63. 0¾ x 8.11	414–38	
1701	—/—/48	Inspection Saloon		Q.13	52. 0 x 8.11	80943/69/70/2/4/–6	
1702	17/ 2/51	First Sleeper	G	J.18	64. 0 x 8.11 12-wheel	9082–5	
1703	28/ 1/50	First	G	A.23	64. 0 x 8.11	8053–64	
1704	5/11/49	Composite	G	E.165	64. 0 x 8.11	7798–7816	7817–22 cancelled
1705	30/ 7/48	Brake Composite	G	E.164	64. 0 x 8.11	7838–47	7848–67 cancelled, see Lot 1738
1706	16/ 4/49	Third	G	C.84	64. 0 x 8.11	1713–37	1738–62 cancelled
1707	2/ 7/49	Brake Third	G	D.133	64. 0 x 8.11	1772–86	Built B'ham RCW 1787–96 cancelled
(1708)	—	Third	G	—	—	(1797–1806)	Lots cancelled. Ordered 24/5/46
(1709)	—	Brake Third	G	—	—	(1807–10)	
(1710)	—	Composite		—	—	(7416–25)	
(1711)	—	Brake Composite		—	—	(7386–7405)	
1712	20/ 8/49	Third		C.83	63. 0¾ x 8.11	2002–16	2017–51 cancelled, see Lot 1739
1713	29/ 4/50	Brake Third		D.132	63. 0¾ x 8.11	2087–2106	
1714	27/11/48	Third	G	C.82	64. 0 x 8.11	855–924	Built Gloster RCW
1719	—/ 1/47	P.O. Sorting Van	G	L.25	63. 0¾ x 8.11	843–7	TPO vehicles
1720	30/ 4/49	Third	G	C.82	64. 0 x 8.11	2107–36	Built Gloster RCW
1722	3/12/49	Passenger Brake	G	K.45	64. 0 x 8.11	290–99	
1726	9/ 9/50	Third		C.83	63. 0¾ x 8.11	1840–59	Built B'ham RCW
(1730)	—	Passenger Brake	G	—	—	(335–9)	Lot cancelled. Ordered 25/10/48
1732	4/11/50	Brake Third	G	D.133	64. 0 x 8.11	2137–85/7–2223/5–38	Last Lot ordered by GWR. Built B'ham RCW
1734	1/ 7/50	First	G	A.23	64. 0 x 8.11	8112–25	
1735	22/ 4/50	Third	G	C.84	64. 0 x 8.11	2264–92	
1736	25/ 8/51	Auto Trailer		A.38 A.39 A.40	64. 0 x 8.11 64. 0 x 8.11 64. 0 x 8.11	222–34 220 221	
1737	9/ 9/50	Composite	G	E.165	64. 0 x 8.11	7817–22	
1738	30/12/50	Brake Composite	G	E.164	64. 0 x 8.11	7848–67	
1739	12/ 8/50	Third		C.83	63. 0¾ x 8.11	2017–26	
1740	25/11/50	Passenger Brake	G	K.45	64. 0 x 8.11	300–24	
1744	20/ 1/51	Brake Third	G	D.133	64. 0 x 8.11	2240–59	Built Metro-Cammell
1745	16/ 6/51	Third		C.83	63. 0¾ x 8.11	2601–90/2700–20	Built B'ham RCW
1746	26/ 7/52	Brake Third		D.132	63. 0¾ x 8.11	2721–65/76–90	Built Gloster RCW
(1747)	—	First	G	—	64. 6 x 9. 3	(8338–)	First BR Standard stock built at Swindon.††
1748	17/11/51	Third		C.83	63. 0¾ x 8.11	2797–2832	
1749	24/ 1/53	Composite		E.156	59. 3½ x 8.11	M16797–16841 (LMS series Nos)	To pre-war diagram Built for LMR Alloted Nos 7116–60
1750	18/10/52	Brake Composite		E.167	63. 0¾ x 8.11	7081–90	
1752	7/ 7/51	Passenger Brake	G	K.46	64. 0 x 8.11	325–34	
1762	19/ 4/52	Composite		E.166	63. 0¾ x 8.11	7173–82	
1764	—/—/53	Brake Third		D.132	63. 0¾ x 8.11	4126–31/3/4/6/7/9/40–2/52	Built R. Y. Pickering
1766	25/ 9/54	Auto Trailer		A.43	64. 0 x 8.11	235–44	
1767	—/ 8/53	Composite		E.166	63. 0¾ x 8.11	7183–7208	
1772	26/12/53	Composite		E.156	59. 3½ x 8.11	M16842–76 (LMS series Nos)	To pre-war diagram Built for LMR Alloted Nos 7209–22/4–44
1775	—/—/53	Brake Composite		E.167	63. 0¾ x 8.11	7386–97	
1777	—/10/54	Brake Composite		E.167	63. 0¾ x 8.11	6276–85	Plymouth area Sets 1–5, formed as pairs 6276/7 etc. Last GWR series Lot for passenger-carrying stock.

††Transferred to BR Lot 30019, running Nos 13000–32/6–59

ACKNOWLEDGEMENTS

Archives and Unpublished Material

I would like to thank the following authorities for permission to quote from records and papers in their possession which I have freely used:

The Archivist, British Transport Historical Records for general assistance. Material made use of included:

Report on Dining-Cars (GWR General Manager's Dept.). July 1891.

Report on Cleaning of Passenger Carriages (GWR General Manager's Dept.). Nov. 1902.

Report on the Abolition of Second-class Accommodation (GWR General Manager's Dept.). April 1909.

Various other papers were also referred to.

Mechanical Engineer (Design), BRB Swindon Works.

Material obtained from GWR Passenger Stock Lot Lists 1890–1954, GWR Passenger Stock diagram books and other papers.

To the Librarian, the National Railway Museum for records now held at York.

Acknowledgement to the successors of the GWR Junior Engineering Society and GWR (London) Debating Society for several references to printed copies of their proceedings held in the BRB Archives and Swindon Public Library.

GWR General Appendices to the Book of Rules dated October 1920 and August 1936 (with subsequent amendments) were also consulted.

In the course of research, I referred to copies of unpublished copyright records of the Historical Model Railway Society covering GWR coach diagrams, and I would like to thank the Committee of that Society for permission to examine these records.

The Postmaster-General for information concerning TPO vehicles and their operation.

The Imperial War Museum.

Notes compiled by the late R. P. Walford, in the possession of J. B. Hollingsworth, Esq., were also referred to.

Journals

Copies of the following journals covering the period under review provided a considerable amount of material:

The Engineer
The GWR Magazine
The Locomotive Magazine
Model Railway News
The Railway Engineer (ceased publication 1935 and incorporated in *The Railway Gazette)*
The Railway Gazette
The Railway Magazine
The Railway Observer
Railway World
Trains Illustrated and subsequently *Modern Railways*

Books

The following were of use, in varying degrees:

Express Trains English & Foreign: Foxwell & Farrer.
War Record of the GWR: Pratt (Selwyn & Blount) 1922.
History of the Great Western Railway, Vol. II: E. T. MacDermott (1927), revised by C. R. Clinker, published in new edition 1982 (Ian Allan).
The Cheltenham Flyer: W. G. Chapman (GWR) 1934.
Nineteenth Century Railway Carriages: C. Hamilton Ellis (Modern Transport) 1949.
Locomotives of the Great Western Railway: Part Eleven (RCTS) 1952.
The Great Western Railway in the Nineteenth Century: O. S. Nock (Ian Allan) 1962.
The Great Western Railway in the Twentieth Century: O. S. Nock (Ian Allan) 1963.
Gone With Regret: George Behrend (Lambard Press) 1963.
Next Station: Christian Barman (GWR/George Allen & Unwin) 1947. New edition as *The Great Western Railway's Last Look Forward*: (David & Charles) 1972.
A Pictorial Record of Great Western Coaches: Parts 1/2: J. H. Russell (Oxford Publishing Co) 1972, 1973.
T.P.O. A History of the TPOs of Great Britain: Parts 1/2: (The Railway Philatelic Group) 1975, revised 1979.
Auto-Trains and the Steam Rail Motors of the Great Western: Colin Veal and the Rev John Goodman (Great Western Society) 1981.
The Great Western at Swindon Works: Alan S. Peck (Oxford Publishing Co) 1983.

Of the many people who have given assistance in several ways I should like particularly to thank the following:

George Behrend, John Booth, Michael Burbidge, J. E. Cull, D. A. Digby, A. H. Hastie, J. B. Hollingsworth, Colin Jenkins, David Loveday, P. Radford, R. C. Riley, David Rouse, Colin Stevens, Bob Timmins, V. R. Webster, and Peter Winding.

Photographs

With the exception of those detailed below, all the photographs in this book were supplied by the Public Relations and Publicity Officer, British Rail, Western Region, to whom acknowledgement and thanks are credited.

Acknowledgement and gratitude for assistance where appropriate are also owing to the following whose photographs are reproduced:

J. H. Aston, page 82, Hugh Ballantyne, page 105 (foot), Colin Boocock, page 83 (lower), H. W. Burman (courtesy C. C. Green), page 10 (upper);

page 14, H. C. Casserley, page 59 (top); page 72 (lower); page 77 (upper); page 105 (centre); page 114 (upper), R. M. Casserley, page 69; page 123 (lower), Dr J. A. Coiley, page 25 (upper), C. R. L. Coles, opposite title page (lower), J. E. Cull, page 98, the late M. W. Earley, page 37, Great Western (SVR) Association, page 131 (centre); page 132 (upper), Great Western Society, for the BR photograph reproduced on page 20, M. R. Henney, page 114 (lower), Lens of Sutton (courtesy of Brian Stephenson), page 59 (foot); page 91, Locomotive & General Railway Photographs Collection, copyright David & Charles: page 9 (upper); page 10 (lower); page 11 (lower); page 12 (top); page 45 (lower); page 58 (lower); page 77 (lower); page 79; page 82 (upper); page 93, C. J. Marsden, page 70, Brian Morrison, page 119, R. C. Riley, page 45 (upper); page 46; page 64 (lower); page 74 (lower); page 92 (upper); page 101 (upper); page 113; page 123 (upper); page 128, David Rouse, page 64 (upper); page 76 (lower); page 111 (upper), John Titlow, page 131 (top); page 132 (foot), Graham Wighall, page 131 (foot), and the late T. E. Williams, page 12 (centre).

The line drawings appearing on the following pages were prepared by Colin Stevens: page 80; page 84; page 90; page 94; page 99.

CHRONOLOGY

1892 7 March: First corridor train put into service, first GWR train with through steam heating.

1896 May: First restaurant car goes into traffic. General introduction of steam heating.

1897 5 May: New Royal Train complete, first train with electric lighting.

1900 Milford Boat set first general service stock with electric lighting.

1902 1 June: Dean succeeded by Churchward as Chief Mechanical Engineer.

1903 January: First restaurant cars with accommodation for all three classes. October: First steam rail-motor.

1904 May: First 'Dreadnought' into traffic. Last clerestory stock built.

1905 July: 'Dreadnought' stock inaugurates new 'Cornish Riviera'. Incandescent gas lighting introduced.

1907 First of standard 57ft 'Toplight' stock into traffic.

1908 Two-colour livery scheme discontinued.

1910 Final withdrawal of second class from GWR services.

1911 Last gas-lit coaches – except rail-motors and trailers – completed.

1912 First steel-panelled stock into traffic.

1920 F. W. Marillier, Carriage Manager, retires.

1921 First all-steel coach built.

1922 1 January: Collett succeeds Churchward as CME. July: Chocolate and cream livery reintroduced.

1925 Last 70ft stock of any type built. Articulated express and suburban sets. Introduction of 7ft wheelbase bogie.

1929 New stock for 'Cornish Riviera' and general introduction of 60ft-plus coaches.

1931 'Super Saloons'.

1935 April: First 'open' excursion sets. July: 'Centenary' stock for 'Cornish Riviera'. December: First fully air-conditioned restaurant cars.

1936 First batches of end-door corridor coaches – 'Sunshine' stock.

1937 Autumn: Yellow disc cross-country dimensions standardised for all new stock.

1941 Last ordinary passenger coaches to pre-war orders completed. Hawksworth succeeds Collett as CME.

1942 New wartime livery.

1945 Newly renovated restaurant cars reintroduce services on 31 December.

1946 First post-war design coaches into traffic, including fluorescent lighting prototype.

1950 First lots of BR standard corridor coaches under construction. Last GWR corridor coaches completed.

1953 Last ordinary clerestory coaches withdrawn from general traffic.

1954 September: Last passenger coaches to GWR designs completed at Swindon and by outside contractors.

1956 First Swindon designed 'Inter-City' diesel units put into service.

1960 September: Last slip coach working discontinued.

1961 Coaches with B4 bogies enter service for first time. New dynamometer car.

1963 1 January: Control of Works passes from Western Region to Central Workshops authority. (In effect, from February.) Prototype integral-construction coach into traffic. Final 'Inter-City' units completed. November: Last passenger coach to be built at Swindon.

1964 July: General termination of major overhauls of passenger coaches. Final stages of running-down carriage and wagon workshops.

1967 31 December: Withdrawal of GWR-design passenger coaches in general service (other than sleeping cars).

INDEX